Fiscal Policy In the Smaller Industrial Countries, 1972–82

by Gísli Blöndal

INTERNATIONAL MONETARY FUND
Washington, D.C.
1986

ISBN 0-939934-36-1 (cloth)
ISBN 0-939934-53-1 (paper)

Contents

Page

Preface vii

Part I: A Comparative Analysis

1 *The Smaller Industrial Countries* 3

Some Economic Characteristics 3
Role of Central Government 5
Main Objectives of Fiscal Policy 9

2 *Growth of the Government Sector* 12

Expenditure 13
Revenue 23
Fiscal Balance, Financing, and Debt Accumulation 35

3 *Fiscal Policy, 1972–82, An Overview* 41

Economic Setting and Fiscal Stance in the Early 1970s 41
Policy Response to First Oil Crisis 43
Shift in Fiscal Stance after the Mid-1970s and Changes in
    Policy Approach 45
Policy Response to Second Oil Crisis 48
Fiscal Policy and Prospects in the Early 1980s 48

4 *Obstacles to Fiscal Improvement* 51

Recession and the Working of Automatic Fiscal Stabilizers . . 51
Narrowed Scope for Fiscal Policy Action 53
Role of Medium-Term Planning and Budgetary Forecasting . 54
Fiscal Politics 56

5 *Implications of Past Fiscal Developments and Policies* 59

Enlarged Public Sector 59
Increased Tax Burdens 62
Fiscal Deficits and Debt Accumulation 64

Page

Employment Policies 69

Social Security Schemes 72

Incomes Policies 76

6   *Summary and Conclusions*............................... 80

Tables in the Text

1.1.   Smaller Industrial Countries: Selected Basic Statistics...   4

2.1.   Total Expenditure as a Percentage of GDP   14

2.2.   Expenditure on Goods and Services   15

2.3.   Interest Payments   19

2.4.   Subsidies and Other Current Transfers   21

2.5.   Capital Expenditure and Net Lending   24

2.6.   Total Revenue as a Percentage of GDP   25

2.7.   Income Taxes   29

2.8.   Social Security Contributions   31

2.9.   Taxes on Goods and Services   33

2.10. Other Tax and Nontax Revenue and Grants...........   34

2.11. Deficit/Surplus as a Percentage of GDP   36

2.12. Central Government Outstanding Debt   37

6.1.   Smaller Industrial Countries: Selected Fiscal Indicators .   84

Charts

1. Size of General Government Sector: Expenditure as a
   Ratio to GDP..   7

2. Consolidated Central Government Expenditure...........   16

3. Consolidated Central Government Revenue   26

4. Smaller Industrial Countries: Fiscal Balances   38

Part II: Developments in Individual Countries

Introduction...   89

1. Australia   91

2. Austria..   102

3. Belgium...   112

4. Denmark..   122

5. Finland...   134

Page
6. Iceland 144
7. Ireland 155
8. Luxembourg 166
9. Netherlands 175
10. New Zealand 187
11. Norway 198
12. Spain 209
13. Sweden 219

Tables in the Text

Australia: Selected Economic Indicators, 1972–82 93
Australia: Consolidated Central Government Finances,
    1972–82 94
Austria: Selected Economic Indicators, 1972–82 103
Austria: Consolidated Central Government Finances,
    1972–82 104
Belgium: Selected Economic Indicators, 1972–82 113
Belgium: Consolidated Central Government Finances,
    1972–82 114
Denmark: Selected Economic Indicators, 1972–82 123
Denmark: Consolidated Central Government Finances,
    1972–82 124
Finland: Selected Economic Indicators, 1972–82 135
Finland: Consolidated Central Government Finances,
    1972–82 136
Iceland: Selected Economic Indicators, 1972–82 145
Iceland: Consolidated Central Government Finances,
    1972–82 146
Ireland: Selected Economic Indicators, 1972–82 157
Ireland: Consolidated Central Government Finances,
    1972–82 158
Luxembourg: Selected Economic Indicators, 1972–82 167
Luxembourg: Consolidated Central Government Finances,
    1972–82 168
Netherlands: Selected Economic Indicators, 1972–82 177
Netherlands: Consolidated Central Government Finances,
    1973–82 178
New Zealand: Selected Economic Indicators, 1972–82 189

Page

New Zealand: Consolidated Central Government
Finances, 1972–82 190
Norway: Selected Economic Indicators, 1972–82 199
Norway: Consolidated Central Government Finances,
1972–82 200
Spain: Selected Economic Indicators, 1972–82 211
Spain: Consolidated Central Government Finances, 1972–82 . . 212
Sweden: Selected Economic Indicators, 1972–82 221
Sweden: Consolidated Central Government Finances,
1972–82 222

References 231

Preface

This study was undertaken to provide information and analyses of developments in the public finances of the smaller industrial countries over the decade 1972–82. It also reflects an evolving pattern in the Fiscal Affairs Department of the International Monetary Fund of following fiscal developments in groups of member countries. At the same time, the study is intended to partially meet recent requests of the Executive Board for international comparison and analysis of various aspects of fiscal developments and policies. The choice of countries was made on the basis of two criteria: first, the availability of statistical and other sources suitable for comparative purposes; and second, the considerable gap in the literature on comparative fiscal policies in these countries, much more so than in the major industrial countries—the only other homogeneous group of member countries that meets the first criterion.

Owing to lack of comparable statistical data, the study does not go beyond 1982, and in one instance, not beyond 1981—the last years for which such data were available when the study was completed. Although inclusion of a more recent period would have been desirable, its omission has little effect on this study, as it focuses on institutional arrangements and fiscal developments over a longer period of time for the purpose of revealing features that might enhance knowledge and understanding of various aspects of public finances and fiscal policy. Moreover, the study covers the most turbulent years of the postwar period for the world economy: a period that posed an exceptionally strong challenge to fiscal policy. In considering the likely path of fiscal policy in the future, limited account is taken of the events that occurred in 1983 and 1984. It is clear, however, that in this period the orientation of fiscal policy underwent changes in some of these countries. There-fore, to avoid giving an inaccurate impression of the current situation, footnotes at the end of the relevant country sections briefly indicate the general direction of such changes.

Various Fund documents and Organization for Economic Coopera-tion and Development (OECD) country surveys are the basic sources used in the analysis. Other sources are quoted separately as appropriate. Statistical data on consolidated central government finances are derived from the 1983 and 1984 *Government Finance Statistics (GFS) Yearbooks*, which provide statistics that are consistent over time and comparable across countries. *GFS* data may differ from those conventionally used by national authorities, owing to different conceptual interpretation. According to the *GFS* definition, consolidated central government includes social security funds and may cover other entities that in some countries are not usually attributed to central government. Also, net lending is grouped with expenditure in *GFS*. Ratios of revenue and expenditure to gross domestic product (GDP), for example, may for these reasons tend to be larger than those derived from national sources, and measurements of fiscal balances may also differ. The source for GDP statistics is the 1984 *International Financial Statistics (IFS)* Yearbook and subsequent updates. For countries whose fiscal years do not coincide with calendar years, the GDP data have been adjusted to fiscal years. Data on selected economic indicators presented at the end of each country section are taken from *OECD Economic Outlook*, December 1984, and national sources as indicated.

The study is divided into two parts. Part I is a comparative analysis, and Part II deals with institutional arrangements and fiscal developments in individual countries. Part I is organized as follows. Chapter 1 sets forth some major economic characteristics of this group of countries, their implications for the pursuit of fiscal policy, and the role played in that respect by the central government. The chapter concludes by reviewing the main aims of fiscal policy over the period. Chapter 2 accounts for the growth of expenditure and revenue and the implications for the fiscal balance and debt accumulation. Chapter 3 provides a broad account of fiscal policies pursued by these countries over the period and examines how changes in economic circumstances, like the impact of the two oil crises, affected the policy stance. Chapter 4 considers major obstacles encountered by most countries in the group in their endeavors to bring about targeted fiscal adjustments; and Chapter 5 goes on to analyze implications of past fiscal developments and policies for overall economic performance. Chapter 6 summarizes the main findings and draws some conclusions. The structure of the study of developments in individual countries is accounted for in the introduction to Part II.

For assistance in writing this book, the author is indebted to many colleagues at the International Monetary Fund. Particular thanks are due to Vito Tanzi, Director of the IMF Fiscal Affairs Department, for constructive comments and encouragement throughout; to Klaus-Walter Riechel for helpful comments on the comparative part of the book; and to his colleagues in the IMF's European Department who commented in detail on individual country sections. Ms. Ziba Farhadian provided valuable research assistance. Mrs. Juanita Roushdy edited the first draft, and Ms. Sara Kane edited the final draft of the book and saw it through the various stages of publication. Miss Mary Riegel typed most of the first draft, and Mrs. Sonia A. Piccinini typed the final draft and prepared it for printing. Mr. Hördur Karlsson of the Graphics Section of the IMF designed the cover, and Mr. Alva Madairy and his associates provided the book design and composition.

The views expressed here are those of the author and should not be ascribed to the International Monetary Fund.

PART I

A COMPARATIVE ANALYSIS

1

The Smaller Industrial Countries

SOME ECONOMIC CHARACTERISTICS

A revised classification of countries was adopted by the Fund in December 1979 for the purpose of statistical presentation and economic analysis and was first used in the March 1980 issue of *International Financial Statistics* (*IFS*). Subsequently, this classification was used in other Fund documents such as the *Annual Report* and the *World Economic Outlook*. The countries included in the present study belong to the subgroup of industrial countries identified as the smaller industrial countries, or other industrial countries, as distinct from the seven major industrial countries. They include Australia, Austria, Belgium, Denmark, Finland, Iceland, Ireland, Luxembourg, the Netherlands, New Zealand, Norway, Spain, and Sweden. Switzerland, which also belongs to this group of countries, is not a member of the Fund and, owing to a lack of satisfactory background information, was not included.

The smaller industrial countries share certain economic features, and some of these have an important bearing on the conduct of fiscal policy. Although they are small in population size and economic weight compared with the major industrial countries, their stage of industrial development is advanced by any standard according to which the word "industrial" is taken to imply "the predominance of relatively sophisticated technology throughout the country's economy," as defined in the relevant Fund document. In other respects the countries differ substantially among themselves. Spain, for example, has a population of 38 million; Australia and the Netherlands follow with 15 million and 14 million; Iceland and Luxembourg have the smallest populations of 231,000 and 366,000, respectively (Table 1.1). Population density also differs markedly. The Netherlands, with 346 inhabitants per square

3

Table 1.1. Smaller Industrial Countries: Selected Basic Statistics

| | Population (thousands)[1] | Inhabitants Per Sq. Km.[1] | GDP Per Capita (U.S. dollars)[2] | Foreign Trade as a Percentage of GDP[3] | |
				Exports of goods	Imports of goods
Australia	14,293	2	10,763	14.0	15.3
Austria	7,508	89	8,842	23.6	29.1
Belgium	9,852	323	9,651	60.6[4]	66.9[4]
Denmark	5,122	119	11,350	27.2	29.9
Finland	4,800	14	10,328	26.9	27.6
Iceland	231	2	12,791	26.3	36.5
Ireland	3,443	49	4,855	46.2	55.3
Luxembourg	366	141	10,566	—	—
Netherlands	14,247	346	9,861	48.3	45.6
New Zealand	3,176	12	7,957	23.3[5]	23.5[5]
Norway	4,100	13	13,937	31.3	27.6
Spain	37,654	75	4,938	11.5	17.7
Sweden	8,324	19	13,505	27.3	28.2

Source: Organization for Economic Cooperation and Development, *Economic Surveys.*
[1] Mid-1981.
[2] 1981 at current prices and exchange rates.
[3] 1982.
[4] Including Luxembourg.
[5] 1980.

kilometer, ranks among the most densely populated countries in the world; while Australia and Iceland, with only 2 inhabitants per square kilometer, are among the most sparsely populated countries. It might be argued that a priori this last feature implies special fiscal burdens because of the cost of providing adequate infrastructure and other services in conditions of limited economies of scale. However, the rather scanty studies available on this subject are inconclusive, and the statistical evidence does not seem to support this argument, except perhaps in the case of national defense.[1] Moreover, in the two countries concerned, evidence does not seem to support the argument either, as their expenditure/gross domestic product (GDP) ratios are among the lowest in the group and their infrastructure and public services are adequate. Perhaps the relatively high per capita income of these two countries explains part of this phenomenon.

---

[1] See, for example, E.A.G. Robinson, ed., *Economic Consequences of the Size of Nations* (London: Macmillan & Co., Ltd., 1960), pp. xxi–xxii.

A corollary of an advanced stage of industrial development is a high standard of living of the population. Per capita GDP figures indicate that by and large the smaller industrial countries rank high on this scale and exhibit per capita income in the neighborhood of or exceeding US$10,000, based on 1981 statistics. Only in Ireland and Spain is per capita income substantially lower, around US$5,000 in each country.

For this study, the most significant economic characteristic of these countries is the openness of their economies. Measured by the commodity export and import ratios to GDP, the Benelux countries and Ireland have the largest foreign trade sectors of nearly 50 percent or over. In most other countries in the group, foreign trade amounts to more than 25 percent of GDP, and only in Australia and Spain is this ratio considerably lower, some 15 percent on average in each country. For some countries, the criterion of openness is substantially enlarged when services are included. This applies, in particular, to Austria and Spain, for tourism; Iceland, for air transport; Luxembourg, for international banking; and Norway, for shipping. This economic openness made the smaller industrial countries especially vulnerable to external impulses caused by the oil crises of 1973–74 and 1979–80 and the ensuing world recession. Another implication of large external sectors is that the effects of measures designed to stimulate activity and employment tended to be weakened by leakages into imports. The small values of fiscal multipliers thus restricted the effectiveness of fiscal measures and frequently aggravated the balance of payments problems most of the countries had to cope with over the period. These issues are considered further in Chapter 3.

ROLE OF CENTRAL GOVERNMENT

An analysis of fiscal policy should ideally encompass the public sector as a whole, as significant activities are carried out by local governments and in some countries by other public entities. But lack of statistical data prevents any detailed examination of the public sector, so the analysis is confined mostly to the central government. This approach should not be too misleading, because the nature and national character of the central government's activities and the sheer size of its operations within the public sector allow it to dominate fiscal policy. This would appear to be particularly relevant in the context of stabilization policy, an aspect of fiscal policy that assumed a heightened role in most countries during this turbulent period. However, because the role of local authorities and other public entities in the pursuit of fiscal policy cannot be totally disregarded, this section considers some of the relevant relationships.

The size of the public sector in relation to total economic activity, and especially the relative size of the central government sector, determines in large measure the framework for using the public finances as a tool of economic management. The higher the ratio of government expenditure to GDP, the greater the leverage of fiscal policy. Chart 1 demonstrates these relationships in each country in 1982 except where otherwise indicated. Sweden has the highest general government expenditure/GDP ratio (71 percent), and Spain, the lowest (35 percent). But when the relative size of the central government is taken into account, the Netherlands has the highest ratio (59 percent), and Australia, the lowest (28 percent).

The chart shows that the relative size of the local government sector differs substantially among these countries. The Nordic countries—with the exception of Iceland—and Austria have the largest local governments in terms of expenditure/GDP ratios, while Spain's local government sector, by comparison, is the smallest. Although there is not, in principle, a causal link between relative size and the financial autonomy of local governments, experience in these countries nonetheless indicates a certain degree of correlation. Where local governments are largest, the degree of financial autonomy tends to be highest. For example, in Denmark, Finland, and Sweden, local governments enjoy a high degree of autonomy, as their ability to raise revenue from major sources such as local income or property taxes demonstrates. The economic significance of the local government sector in these countries has made it necessary to develop procedures that would coordinate fiscal policy with high priority objectives, such as the maintenance of employment, containment of public expenditure growth, and limitation of revenue raising measures that would affect the price level. Such coordination ordinarily takes place through negotiations between central and local authorities. In Denmark these procedures have led to the presentation of an annual public sector budget. Similar arrangements were established in Austria in the early 1970s when local authorities undertook to pursue a restrictive expenditure policy and to refrain from raising fees and charges. Also in Austria, local government shares in federal taxes were temporarily frozen as special deposits in the central bank to be used for countercyclical purposes. In Australia, where the local government sector is relatively large, five-year agreements are

Chart 1. Size of General Government Sector:
Expenditure as a Ratio to GDP
(1982 unless otherwise indicated)

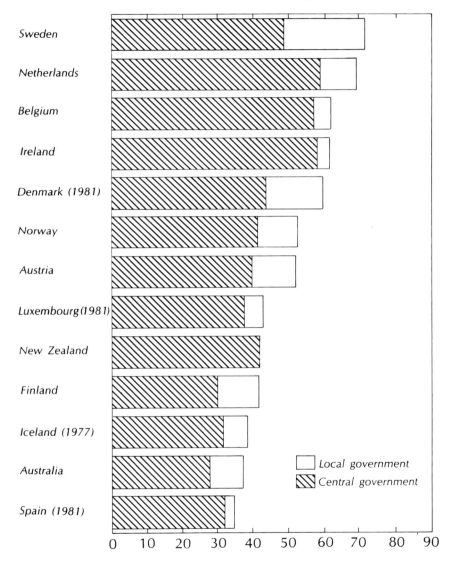

Note: Transfers to local governments are counted at the central level. Data on general
government for the Netherlands are based on national sources and may not be fully
comparable with those for other countries. Data on general government for New
Zealand are not available.

made about commonwealth government financial assistance to the states. However, even in countries with large local government sectors, the central government can usually influence their activity through transfers from the budget and control of some of their revenues.

In countries with the smallest local government sectors, the financial autonomy of local authorities tends to be the most restricted. In Iceland, Luxembourg, and Spain, for example, the central government dominates public sector activity and exerts influence on local authorities through cost or revenue sharing arrangements. Local authorities in these countries also have very limited revenue raising and borrowing authority; their dependence on central government transfers and other commitments made each year in the budget is significant. It is also common for the central government in these countries, and indeed in others with larger local government sectors, to command the most productive and elastic revenue sources.

In some countries in the group, local governments are required, in principle, to observe budgetary balance as an operational rule, at least as far as current revenue and expenditure are concerned. Borrowing for investment is frequently controlled or supervised by the central government or by commissions or boards where central government representation is marked as in, for example, Australia, the Netherlands, New Zealand, Norway, and Spain. A balanced local government budget is, however, not a rule without exceptions. In Australia and Belgium, for example, deficits in local government finances have been substantial in recent years. In Belgium the authorities have responded by imposing balanced budgets on the local authorities by law from 1988.

In addition to exerting varying degrees of influence on local government activity, the central government in some countries in the group uses other public entities in the pursuit of fiscal objectives. In Austria, for example, the central government has relied on the nationalized industries to promote the high-priority aim of sustaining employment during recessions; in Norway the state banks play a significant role in financing projects that are specifically conceived as an instrument of employment support, and part of their lending is financed by direct government loans; in Ireland the Government has encouraged capital expenditure by semipublic bodies to sustain employment; and in Spain funds obtained from the banking sector through captive arrangements are channeled to official credit institutions through the budget to finance priority investments in line with official policy. Similar arrangements outside ordinary budgetary channels have been made in some other countries in the group, although perhaps not to the same degree.

MAIN OBJECTIVES OF FISCAL POLICY

This section provides an overview of major objectives of fiscal policy. These objectives may be taken as fairly representative for the group as a whole over the period covered, although there are differences in degree in individual cases. Measures to attain these objectives and the implications of these measures are dealt with in Chapters 3 and 5.

While in all countries in the group the maintenance of a high level of employment was declared a special aim of economic policy, some placed this objective at the very top of the priority list and kept it there throughout the period. Cases in point are Austria, Luxembourg, New Zealand, and the five Nordic countries. In most instances, fiscal policy played an instrumental role although approaches differed among countries. A notable exception to fiscal policy involvement is Iceland, where other policy approaches sustained a high level of employment.

Inflation remained a cause for concern in most of the countries, and this problem, on occasion, called for action on the fiscal front. Ordinarily such action took the form of a shift in the fiscal stance in a restrictive direction to affect the price level through demand management. However, a number of countries preferred measures that sought to attack inflation through the cost side and, for this purpose, adopted various incomes policy approaches. Countries where the central government has been closely involved in incomes policy include Austria, the Netherlands, and the five Nordic countries. In other countries in the group, attempts at moderating wage settlements through fiscal means were less marked, and in one case, Ireland, the failure of one such attempt led to the abandonment of the approach.

In all countries in the group, the promotion of social welfare schemes was a high-priority objective of fiscal policy. A special impetus emanated from the recession in the mid-1970s when stimulatory measures relied heavily on increases in social expenditure as a means of mitigating the adverse impact on living standards. In some countries, special efforts were made to preserve or improve already high living standards by increasing benefits in real terms and extending their coverage. However, the extent of this policy response differed significantly among the countries. The automatic impact of the recession on budgetary expenditure was accentuated in some countries by schemes that had been laid down in the more prosperous 1960s, or earlier, when expectations of continuing high rates of economic growth enhanced the generosity of the schemes. In countries where governments were closely involved in incomes policy, fiscal measures designed to dampen wage demands frequently took the form of increased social security benefits.

The social security measures, whether taken independently or in the context of incomes policy, had as an underlying aim the redistribution of income in favor of lower income groups. The objective of income redistribution was given an especially high priority in Spain in the post-1976 period when comprehensive reviews of the tax and social security systems were announced and partially implemented, specifically to favor lower income groups. Other countries took tax measures for the same purpose, often as a fiscal contribution to incomes policy and usually in the form of reductions in personal income tax rates and indexation of tax scales.

The policy response to the first oil crisis and the ensuing world recession was generally to shift the fiscal stance in a highly expansionary direction. This posture was commonly intended to be temporary because the recession was expected to be short lived. However, as the recession persisted, both internal and external imbalances emerged and became a growing cause for concern to the authorities. A fairly general response by the authorities was to give aid in various forms to industries facing structural adjustment problems and grant incentives for transferring resources to sectors exposed to foreign competition. In some cases, aid of this kind was attached to the government's employment policy, in that assistance was made contingent upon the preservation of employment in the industries concerned.

As the period progressed, fiscal imbalances assumed increased proportions, and fiscal policy was increasingly directed at containing these imbalances. This new emphasis implied a restrictive policy posture that attempted to contain or reduce the large-scale absorption of resources by the public sector, which was seen as having an adverse long-term impact on economic performance. This attitude is in vivid contrast to the prevailing view in the early 1970s when public sector expansion was not generally perceived as detrimental to the growth of the economy. On the contrary, in at least two countries in the group, Australia and Luxembourg, the governments declared it a special objective of fiscal policy to enlarge the role of the public sector in the economy. An increasing number of countries in the group have adopted the approach of setting specific targets to contain or reduce the ratio of certain fiscal aggregates to GDP over a given period of time. Most usual are targets relating to the deficit/GDP ratio, but similar targets for total revenue or expenditure, or a combination of two or all three, have been officially announced in some countries.

As will be demonstrated in the following chapter, the growing efforts to reduce fiscal imbalances met with only limited success. The various potential reasons for this failure will be considered in Chapter 4.

2

Growth of the Government Sector

The sharp increase in the proportion of community output appropriated by the state is among the most outstanding changes in industrial economies during this century. Studies of this phenomenon have revealed a certain historical pattern in which periods of social upheavals, such as two world wars and the depression of the 1930s, were associated with abrupt upward shifts in the public expenditure/GDP ratio. Although the expenditure level generally subsided after the upheavals, it came to rest at a level appreciably above the one prevailing before the disturbance. This pattern has been explained in terms of a displacement effect hypothesis advanced in a study of long-term public expenditure growth in the United Kingdom.[1] In essence, the hypothesis emphasizes the role of social disturbances in changing taxpayers' perceptions of tolerable tax burdens. Relaxation of these financial stringencies enables governments that are under constant pressure for increased public spending to maintain expenditure after the disturbance at a level substantially above the earlier level. The Peacock-Wiseman study was followed by a number of similar studies in other countries that appeared to lend support to this hypothesis.

Although the severity of the two oil crises in the 1970s and the associated worldwide recession hardly matches that of the social upheavals earlier in the century, the explosive growth of expenditure/GDP ratios in some of the smaller industrial countries during the 1970s and early 1980s falls into a pattern that might conform to the displacement effect hypothesis. However, the role of tax burden perception as a check on expenditure growth evidently lost much of its perceived

---

[1] Alan T. Peacock and Jack Wiseman, *The Growth of Public Expenditure in the United Kingdom* (Princeton: Princeton University Press, 1961), pp. 24–30.

previous strength, with the result that deficits of an unprecedented magnitude and persistence are now a fairly common fiscal feature. While this line of analysis could prove interesting, it will not be pursued any further, as the focus here is rather on the economic implications of the expansion of the government sector. To set the stage, this chapter accounts for major changes in fiscal aggregates during 1972–82, with emphasis on total change over the period. The time pattern of change in each country is demonstrated in Charts 2, 3, and 4 in this chapter and is discussed in some detail in Part II.

EXPENDITURE

Total expenditure of the consolidated central government rose as a proportion of GDP in all countries in the group over the period covered (Table 2.1 and Chart 2). However, the expansion differed markedly among individual countries. From 1972 to 1982, two countries, Ireland and Belgium, experienced the sharpest increase in this ratio, 21 and 17 percentage points, respectively. Sweden and Denmark followed with over a 13 percentage point rise each, and the Netherlands (1973–82) and Spain (1972–81), with increases of 13 and 12 percentage points, respectively. Countries whose expenditure/GDP ratios expanded between 5 and 11 percentage points over this period are New Zealand, Austria, Iceland, and Finland; Luxembourg's and Australia's shares rose moderately by less than 4 percentage points. The smallest expansion of the government sector took place in Norway, 2½ percentage points over the ten-year period.

Expenditure on goods and services, chiefly wages and salaries, absorbed a declining proportion of budgetary resources over the period in all countries in the group except Iceland where its proportion of total expenditure, as well as its share in GDP, rose substantially[2] (Table 2.2). The ratio of expenditure on goods and services to total expenditure is highest in Spain, at 36 percent, and lowest in the Netherlands and Sweden, at 14 percent.

A comparison of individual categories of expenditure with total expenditure and changes in ratios over time is of limited explanatory value, however, as it essentially reflects different relative sizes of the government sector in the various countries and changes in other expenditure categories in each country. A sounder basis for comparison

---

[2]The increase resulted in part from a change in definition.

Table 2.1. Total Expenditure as a Percentage of GDP

	1972	1973	1974	1975	1976	1977	1978	1979	1980	1981	1982
Australia	24.6	24.3	24.5	29.4	30.7	29.6	30.4	28.9	28.1	28.1	28.3
Austria	30.1	31.9	32.3	35.5	36.1	35.9	38.8	38.7	38.6	39.7	39.9
Belgium	39.8	39.9	39.6	44.8	46.0	47.7	49.5	50.5	51.3	56.2	56.9
Denmark	32.0	31.0	34.4	35.0	35.2	36.0	37.0	38.1	40.6	43.7	45.2
Finland	25.5	24.5	25.5	30.1	31.1	32.0	30.5	30.0	29.5	29.6	30.6
Iceland	30.5	32.3	33.8	35.9	30.8	31.9	31.6	32.4	30.9	31.9	35.9
Ireland	36.7	37.9	43.9	44.3	45.4	43.7	45.2	47.1	52.0	55.0	57.8
Luxembourg	32.1	29.8	29.0	36.7	36.8	39.4	37.8	38.2	39.3	37.9	35.8
Netherlands	...	46.0	47.3	52.4	52.1	50.3	51.3	52.6	54.3	56.7	58.8
New Zealand	31.0	31.3	35.0	40.2	34.7	38.5	40.8	37.7	38.5	40.5	42.2
Norway	39.4	39.3	39.1	40.7	44.6	45.4	45.6	45.2	43.1	41.0	41.8
Spain	20.5	20.4	21.1	22.7	21.6	24.9	26.0	27.8	29.0	32.3	...
Sweden	35.4	34.2	36.1	36.4	38.7	41.3	44.8	45.7	46.5	48.3	48.9

Source: International Monetary Fund, *Government Finance Statistics Yearbook*, 1983 and 1984.

Table 2.2. Expenditure on Goods and Services

	1972	1973	1974	1975	1976	1977	1978	1979	1980	1981	1982
Ratio to GDP											
Australia	6.2	5.9	5.7	6.1	6.0	6.0	6.1	5.8	5.8	5.9	6.1
Austria	9.1	8.2	8.5	9.6	9.8	9.7	10.1	10.0	9.9	10.2	10.3
Belgium	9.9	9.8	9.8	11.1	11.0	11.2	11.5	11.4	11.4	12.0	11.7
Denmark	10.4	8.9	9.7	9.8	9.1	8.8	8.6	8.4	8.7	9.0	9.0
Finland	5.8	5.5	5.4	6.1	6.1	6.0	6.1	5.9	6.0	6.0	6.3
Iceland	9.3	9.5	10.2	10.2	10.0	10.2	11.0	11.1	11.2	11.4	12.0
Ireland	7.4	7.4	8.0	8.7	8.5	8.0	7.9	8.4	9.0	9.6	9.6
Luxembourg	7.3	6.9	6.9	8.3	8.0	8.3	8.2	8.3	8.7	7.4	8.1
Netherlands	..	8.0	8.0	8.7	8.5	8.3	8.1	8.4	8.4	8.5	8.5
New Zealand	9.5	9.3	9.2	9.4	8.9	9.4	9.9	9.5	10.4	10.7	10.9
Norway	7.6	7.4	7.3	7.6	7.7	7.6	7.5	7.2	6.9	7.4	7.4
Spain	8.9	9.1	9.1	9.5	9.9	10.5	11.2	10.3	12.2	11.6	..
Sweden	7.3	7.3	7.3	7.2	7.0	7.1	7.3	7.4	7.4	7.2	6.8
Share in Total Expenditure											
Australia	25.1	24.1	23.4	20.6	19.5	20.1	20.1	20.0	20.4	21.0	21.7
Austria	30.4	25.8	26.2	27.1	27.1	27.0	26.0	25.8	25.6	25.7	25.9
Belgium	24.9	24.6	24.8	24.7	24.0	23.4	23.2	22.6	22.2	21.4	20.5
Denmark	32.5	28.8	28.1	28.1	25.7	24.4	23.3	22.2	21.3	20.7	20.0
Finland	22.7	22.4	21.2	20.2	19.7	18.9	19.9	19.7	20.5	20.2	20.4
Iceland	30.7	29.3	30.2	28.3	32.4	32.0	34.8	34.1	36.3	35.8	33.4
Ireland	20.1	19.5	18.2	19.6	18.7	18.2	17.5	17.8	17.3	17.5	16.6
Luxembourg	22.7	23.7	23.7	22.7	21.7	21.1	21.8	21.7	22.1	19.6	22.6
Netherlands	..	17.4	16.9	16.7	16.3	16.4	15.9	15.9	15.4	14.9	14.5
New Zealand	30.8	29.8	26.2	23.3	25.5	24.5	24.2	25.2	27.1	26.5	25.8
Norway	19.2	18.8	18.8	18.7	17.3	16.8	16.5	16.0	16.0	18.0	17.6
Spain	43.3	44.8	43.0	42.0	45.6	42.1	42.8	37.2	42.1	35.9	..
Sweden	20.8	21.2	20.1	19.8	18.2	17.2	16.3	16.2	15.8	14.9	14.0

Source: International Monetary Fund, *Government Finance Statistics Yearbook*, 1983 and 1984.

Chart 2. Consolidated Central Government Expenditure
(As a percentage of GDP)

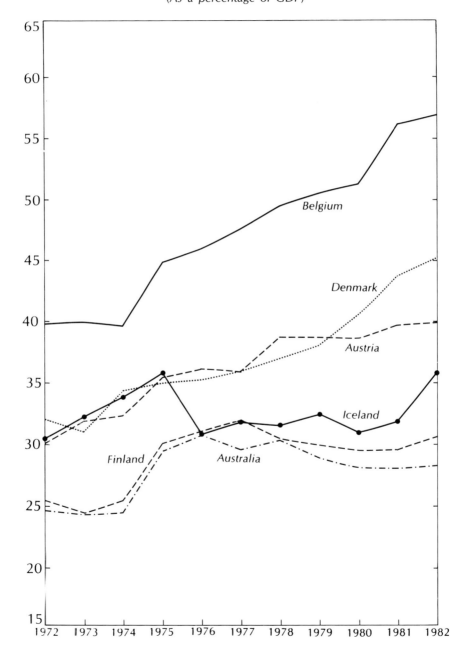

Chart 2 (*continued*). Consolidated Central Government Expenditure
(*As a percentage of GDP*)

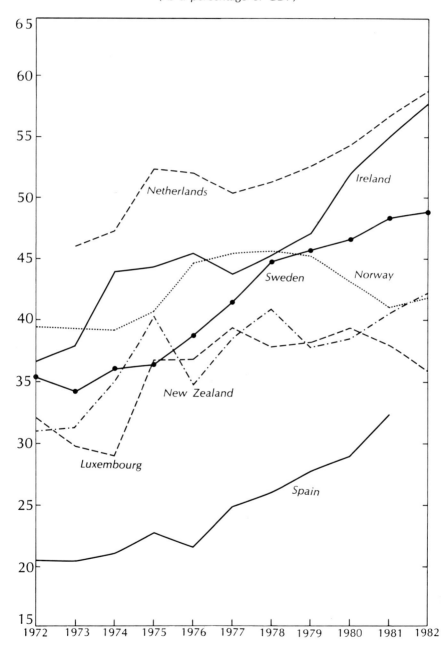

is GDP, which is also shown in Table 2.2. This criterion reveals greater similarity and a more stable pattern of change. Spain, Belgium, and Iceland have the highest ratios at about 12 percent, while Australia and Finland exhibit the lowest ratios at around 6 percent. In all countries except Denmark and, to a lesser extent, Norway, Australia, and Sweden, the ratio of expenditure on goods and services to GDP increased over the period; the largest increases were registered in Spain, Ireland, and Iceland, with between 2 and 3 percentage points each. To a certain extent these percentages show an increased government absorption of labor in line with official employment policies, although not in every case. Measures to stimulate employment frequently took other forms, such as increased capital expenditure and lending operations; or, they were carried out in the same form, but by other public entities, such as local governments, as in Denmark and Sweden; in Austria, the nationalized industries received increased central government transfers to compensate for higher costs of creating additional employment.

Interest payments on government debt rose as a proportion of both total expenditure and GDP in all countries (Table 2.3) except Luxembourg, where the government finances registered surpluses for most of the period, and Spain, where continuous surpluses in the 1960s partially absorbed persistent fiscal deficits over the period covered, as did an erosion of outstanding debt brought about by inflation. In five countries—Belgium, Denmark, Ireland, New Zealand, and Sweden—interest payments absorbed a substantial proportion of budgetary resources— between 10 percent and 16 percent of total government expenditure based on 1982 figures; evidence shows that these ratios will increase markedly in the next few years. Interest payments rose abruptly over the period in these countries, although in 1972 the ratios were already quite high in Ireland and New Zealand, at 9½ percent and 7½ percent, respectively. The interest payment ratios are the highest for Belgium and Ireland, at 7½–9 percent of GDP; in the middle range are Denmark, New Zealand, and Sweden, with ratios in the 4–5 percent range. At the lower end are Finland, Luxembourg, and Spain, with ratios of less than 1 percent.

The mounting budgetary burden of interest payments in most countries in the group was mainly caused by large and widening fiscal deficits. Rising interest rates over the period also contributed, and other factors tended to increase the debt-servicing burden. Among these was the growing size of the external component of government debt, which was protected against the erosion of domestic inflation in the long run

Table 2.3. Interest Payments

	1972	1973	1974	1975	1976	1977	1978	1979	1980	1981	1982
Ratio to GDP											
Australia	1.6	1.6	1.4	1.4	1.3	1.7	1.8	1.9	1.9	1.9	1.9
Austria	0.6	0.6	0.6	0.8	1.1	1.3	1.6	1.7	1.8	2.0	2.2
Belgium	2.6	2.6	2.7	2.7	2.9	3.2	3.6	4.1	5.0	6.7	7.7
Denmark	0.4	0.5	0.5	0.5	0.7	1.1	1.3	2.3	2.7	3.8	4.6
Finland	0.5	0.4	0.3	0.3	0.2	0.3	0.4	0.6	0.6	0.7	0.9
Iceland	0.8	1.0	1.1	2.0	1.6	1.7	2.2	2.4	1.8	2.0	2.4
Ireland	3.5	3.6	3.7	4.3	5.0	5.2	5.7	6.1	6.5	7.5	9.1
Luxembourg	1.0	0.8	0.7	0.7	0.7	0.7	0.8	0.8	0.7	0.7	0.7
Netherlands	...	1.3	1.3	1.3	1.5	1.5	1.6	1.7	2.0	2.5	3.2
New Zealand	2.3	2.2	2.2	2.3	2.6	3.0	3.4	3.6	3.6	4.1	4.6
Norway	1.0	1.0	1.1	0.9	1.6	1.9	2.2	2.6	2.7	2.6	2.4
Spain	0.5	0.5	0.4	0.4	0.3	0.4	0.5	0.5	0.5	0.6	...
Sweden	1.0	1.1	1.1	1.3	1.3	1.5	1.8	2.0	2.9	4.3	4.6
Share in Total Expenditure											
Australia	6.6	6.4	5.6	4.9	4.3	5.7	6.0	6.7	6.8	6.9	6.8
Austria	2.1	1.9	1.9	2.2	3.1	3.6	4.1	4.3	4.6	4.9	5.6
Belgium	6.6	6.6	6.9	6.1	6.2	6.7	7.2	8.1	9.8	11.9	13.5
Denmark	1.3	1.5	1.4	1.5	1.9	3.1	3.4	6.1	6.6	8.6	10.1
Finland	1.9	1.7	1.1	0.8	0.8	1.1	1.4	1.9	2.1	2.4	2.9
Iceland	2.6	3.1	3.2	5.6	5.0	5.2	6.9	7.4	5.7	6.2	6.6
Ireland	9.5	9.4	8.5	9.7	11.0	12.0	12.6	12.9	12.6	13.6	15.7
Luxembourg	3.1	2.8	2.4	1.9	1.8	1.9	2.1	2.0	1.9	1.9	2.0
Netherlands	...	2.8	2.7	2.5	2.8	2.9	3.1	3.2	3.7	4.4	5.4
New Zealand	7.6	7.0	6.2	5.7	7.5	7.8	8.3	9.5	9.5	10.1	10.9
Norway	2.5	2.5	2.8	2.3	3.6	4.1	4.8	5.7	6.4	6.3	5.8
Spain	2.3	2.7	2.0	1.7	1.6	1.6	1.7	1.8	1.9	1.7	...
Sweden	2.9	3.1	3.1	3.7	3.3	3.7	4.0	4.4	6.3	9.0	9.5

Source: International Monetary Fund, *Government Finance Statistics Yearbook*, 1983 and 1984.

and could have added to the budgetary burden in high inflation countries like Iceland, Ireland, and New Zealand where fiscal deficits were increasingly financed by external sources. Also, in a number of countries, interest rates were determined, for balance of payments reasons, with regard to international rates rather than to domestic market conditions, which tended to put upward pressure on interest rates over the period. However, where financial markets were not well developed and inflation was only partially reflected in interest rates, inflation eroded the stock of outstanding debt in real terms and lessened the budgetary burden of interest payments. Indexation of financial assets, as practiced in Finland in the early part of the period and in Iceland over the whole period, reduced this erosion—but only partially, as not all financial assets were indexed.

Subsidies and other current transfers form the largest expenditure category in all countries in the group. The category includes such items as social security benefits and aid to ailing industries—both of which played a major role in efforts to cushion the recessionary impact—and transfers to other levels of government and to public enterprises. By the end of the period, this category accounted for one half to two thirds of total expenditure in all countries except Spain and Iceland where the ratios were 42 percent and 37 percent, respectively (Table 2.4). Generally, this category increased faster than total expenditure, thus implying a still faster growth in its ratio to GDP. The largest increases in this ratio occurred in Sweden, Ireland, the Netherlands, Denmark, and Belgium; the smallest increases took place in Iceland, Norway, Luxembourg, and Finland. Not unexpectedly, this significant expenditure category was a major determinant of the total expansion of the government sector. A comparison of the relative increases in total expenditure and in subsidies and other current transfers in relation to GDP reveals that in five countries, between 70 percent and 90 percent of the total expansion is accounted for by this category; and in four countries—Australia, Finland, Luxembourg, and Sweden—the category accounts for more than the total expansion, implying that the share of other expenditure categories taken as a whole shrank over the period.

As discussed further in the following two chapters, the abrupt relative increase in subsidies and other current transfers in most countries in the group stems in part from endeavors to mitigate the adverse impact of the recession on living standards and on employment and activity in the sectors hardest hit. The types of expenditure involved are mainly social security benefits, industrial assistance, and, in some cases, transfers to other levels of government and to public enterprises.

Table 2.4. Subsidies and Other Current Transfers

	1972	1973	1974	1975	1976	1977	1978	1979	1980	1981	1982
Ratio to GDP											
Australia	11.7	12.1	12.3	14.5	17.3	17.4	18.5	18.2	17.8	17.8	17.9
Austria	16.8	17.9	18.8	20.8	21.2	21.4	23.3	23.1	22.8	23.3	23.5
Belgium	22.3	23.1	23.0	26.8	27.7	28.8	29.6	30.4	29.6	31.9	31.6
Denmark	18.7	19.3	21.7	22.0	22.6	23.8	24.9	25.4	27.0	28.4	28.9
Finland	13.9	13.5	14.7	17.4	18.4	19.0	18.9	19.0	18.1	18.7	19.5
Iceland	12.1	11.2	12.8	13.0	10.2	10.2	11.0	12.3	11.5	11.7	13.2
Ireland	18.8	19.0	21.3	24.1	24.4	23.4	24.3	25.0	27.4	28.5	30.6
Luxembourg	18.9	17.1	16.7	22.6	22.8	24.8	23.8	23.8	24.7	24.6	22.8
Netherlands	...	30.4	32.9	36.4	36.9	36.1	37.4	37.9	38.2	39.2	41.1
New Zealand	13.4	14.2	15.5	18.1	16.0	18.5	20.5	19.4	19.6	20.8	22.3
Norway	24.4	24.4	24.3	25.0	26.6	27.2	28.5	28.0	26.0	25.6	26.5
Spain	7.2	7.4	7.7	8.3	8.0	9.4	11.2	13.3	12.3	13.6	...
Sweden	17.8	18.2	20.1	20.9	23.3	25.8	28.5	30.1	30.0	31.2	32.3
Share in Total Expenditure											
Australia	47.6	49.8	50.2	49.1	56.2	58.7	61.0	62.8	63.4	63.2	63.2
Austria	55.7	56.2	58.0	58.6	58.6	59.6	60.0	59.7	59.1	58.7	58.9
Belgium	56.0	58.0	57.9	59.9	60.1	60.5	59.7	60.1	57.7	56.7	55.6
Denmark	58.3	62.2	63.1	62.9	64.2	66.3	67.3	66.7	66.5	64.9	64.0
Finland	54.6	55.1	57.8	57.7	59.3	59.5	62.2	63.5	61.5	63.1	63.8
Iceland	39.7	34.6	37.7	36.1	33.2	32.1	34.8	37.9	37.1	36.6	36.9
Ireland	51.2	50.1	48.4	54.3	53.7	53.5	53.6	53.2	52.8	51.8	52.9
Luxembourg	58.9	57.5	57.6	61.4	61.9	63.1	63.0	62.4	62.8	64.8	63.7
Netherlands	...	66.1	69.5	69.5	70.9	71.7	72.9	72.0	70.4	69.1	69.9
New Zealand	43.2	45.3	44.2	44.9	46.0	48.1	50.3	51.5	51.0	51.3	52.9
Norway	61.9	62.2	62.2	61.4	59.6	59.8	62.4	61.9	60.4	62.4	63.4
Spain	35.3	36.3	36.3	36.4	37.0	37.6	42.9	47.8	42.6	41.9	...
Sweden	50.2	53.2	55.6	57.5	60.1	62.4	63.7	65.8	64.5	64.6	66.0

Source: International Monetary Fund, *Government Finance Statistics Yearbook*, 1983 and 1984.

As far as social security expenditure is concerned, measures commonly taken over the period include adjustments for inflation or wage increases, often through automatic mechanisms, increases in real benefits and extension of their coverage, and, in some instances, relaxation of qualifying criteria, such as a reduction of the retirement age in Belgium, Denmark, Luxembourg, and Sweden; the introduction of a flexible retirement option in Sweden; and more generous disability schemes in the Netherlands. Demographic factors also contributed to the increase in social security outlays in some countries; the most notable cases are the aging structure of the population, for example, in Belgium, the Netherlands, and Sweden; a rising female participation rate in Denmark and New Zealand; and a reversal of net emigration patterns in Ireland and of migratory flows of the labor force in Spain. A reverse migratory pattern took place in a host country like Luxembourg. Unemployment compensations rose markedly in most countries, and the recessionary conditions also reduced social security contributions from both employers and employees, which in some countries necessitated increased central government grants. In countries with close government involvement in income determination, increases in various social security benefits were often decided in the context of incomes policy.

Most countries in the group engaged in some form of industrial support to aid industries hardest hit by the recession and by structural changes brought about by changed relative prices, cost structures, and demand patterns. In Norway the rapid development of the oil sector accentuated the need for structural adjustment. Generally, the measures taken were selective, depending on the particular circumstances in each case, and were directed at such objectives as the transfer of resources to the export- or import-competing sectors (Denmark, New Zealand, and Sweden) and the preservation of regional balance in terms of employment opportunities (Austria, Finland, and Norway). Only a part of this assistance is reflected in this expenditure category, however, as other measures such as tax incentives and loan finance were frequently involved.

In some countries, a prominent item under this category is transfers to other levels of government and to public enterprises. Increased transfers to other levels of government sometimes stemmed from obligations assumed by the authorities in carrying out tasks in line with official employment policies, as was the case in Denmark and Sweden; in other countries, such as Australia and Spain, growing transfers reflected official policy to enhance the role of local governments. Similarly, increased transfers to public enterprises in countries such as Austria and Spain were partly the result of the role imposed on the enterprises in pursuing employment and anti-inflation policies, respectively.

Capital expenditure and net lending, taken together, are the expenditure categories most directly involved in policies to stimulate employment and activity; at the same time, they were the type of expenditure most easily reduced when the stance of fiscal policy shifted toward a restrictive direction. For this reason and also because of the nature of expenditure involved, the time pattern of change over the period was rather irregular. By the end of the period, Iceland, Spain, Ireland, Norway, and Finland had devoted relatively the largest portion of budgetary resources to capital expenditure and net lending, ranging from 13 percent in Finland to 23 percent in Iceland (Table 2.5). Ireland and Iceland had the highest ratios to GDP, about 8½ percent each. By contrast, Denmark and Australia had the lowest ratios to total expenditure (6 percent and 8½ percent, respectively), and also the lowest ratios to GDP (2½ percent each). The highest ratios reflect heavy central government involvement in the provision of infrastructure (Luxembourg, Ireland), or a large role played by the government in financial intermediation (Iceland, Norway, Spain). In most countries the ratio of capital expenditure and net lending to GDP declined over the period or remained approximately constant. In three countries, however, this ratio expanded: by 1 percentage point in Belgium, by 1½ percentage points in Ireland, and by almost 3½ percentage points in Spain. As already indicated, this comparison between end-years conceals significant changes within the period, as may be seen in Table 2.5.

REVENUE

Total revenue and grants, expressed as a ratio to GDP, increased in all countries in the group over the period (Table 2.6 and Chart 3). While the rate of increase differed markedly among individual countries, it was much more evenly spread than the rate of growth of expenditure. The largest increases were experienced in Belgium and Ireland, at 9½ and 11½ percentage points, respectively, followed by Sweden and New Zealand, at about 7 percentage points each. The lowest rate of growth occurred in Luxembourg, at just over 1 percentage point; Finland and Denmark were the next lowest, each with about 2 percentage points. A

Table 2.5. Capital Expenditure and Net Lending

	1972	1973	1974	1975	1976	1977	1978	1979	1980	1981	1982
Ratio to GDP											
Australia	5.1	4.8	5.1	7.5	6.1	4.6	3.9	3.0	2.6	2.5	2.3
Austria	3.6	5.1	4.5	4.3	4.0	3.5	3.8	4.0	4.1	4.2	3.8
Belgium	5.0	4.3	4.1	4.2	4.4	4.5	4.9	4.6	5.2	5.6	5.9
Denmark	2.5	2.4	2.5	2.6	2.9	2.2	2.2	1.9	2.1	2.5	2.7
Finland	5.3	5.1	5.1	6.4	6.3	6.6	5.0	4.4	4.7	4.2	4.4
Iceland	8.2	10.6	9.8	10.8	9.0	9.8	7.4	6.7	6.5	6.8	8.3
Ireland	7.0	8.0	10.9	7.3	7.6	7.1	7.4	7.6	9.0	9.4	8.5
Luxembourg	4.9	4.9	4.8	5.1	5.3	5.5	5.0	5.3	5.9	5.7	4.5
Netherlands	..	6.3	5.1	5.9	5.2	4.5	4.2	4.7	5.7	6.6	6.0
New Zealand	5.7	5.6	8.2	10.5	7.3	7.5	7.1	5.2	4.8	4.9	4.4
Norway	6.5	6.5	6.4	7.1	8.7	8.8	7.4	7.4	7.4	5.5	5.2
Spain	3.8	3.4	4.0	4.8	3.4	5.3	4.4	4.4	4.8	7.1	..
Sweden	9.2	7.7	7.6	6.9	7.1	6.9	7.2	6.2	6.2	5.6	5.2
Share in Total Expenditure											
Australia	20.7	19.7	20.8	25.5	20.0	15.4	12.9	10.6	9.3	8.8	8.3
Austria	11.8	16.1	13.8	12.1	11.2	9.9	9.9	10.2	10.7	10.6	9.6
Belgium	12.6	10.9	10.4	9.4	9.6	9.3	9.9	9.2	10.2	10.0	10.4
Denmark	7.9	7.6	7.4	7.5	8.1	6.2	6.0	5.1	5.3	5.7	5.9
Finland	20.8	20.8	19.9	21.3	20.3	20.6	16.5	14.8	16.0	14.3	13.0
Iceland	27.0	33.0	28.9	30.1	29.3	30.7	23.5	20.5	20.9	21.4	23.1
Ireland	19.1	21.0	24.8	16.4	16.6	16.3	16.3	16.1	17.3	17.1	14.7
Luxembourg	15.4	16.6	16.4	13.9	14.5	13.9	13.2	13.9	14.9	15.1	12.7
Netherlands	..	13.7	10.8	11.3	9.9	8.9	8.2	8.9	10.5	11.6	10.2
New Zealand	18.5	17.9	23.4	26.0	21.0	19.6	17.3	13.8	12.4	12.1	10.5
Norway	16.4	16.5	16.3	17.6	19.5	19.3	16.3	16.4	17.3	13.3	13.2
Spain	18.4	16.6	18.8	21.0	15.7	21.2	16.8	15.7	16.5	22.0	..
Sweden	26.1	22.5	21.2	19.0	18.4	16.8	16.1	13.6	13.3	11.5	10.6

Source: International Monetary Fund, *Government Finance Statistics Yearbook*, 1983 and 1984.

Table 2.6. Total Revenue as a Percentage of GDP

	1972	1973	1974	1975	1976	1977	1978	1979	1980	1981	1982
Australia	24.3	22.6	24.0	25.4	25.7	26.3	26.7	25.6	26.3	27.3	28.0
Austria	29.9	30.3	30.8	31.5	31.5	32.2	34.7	35.0	35.3	36.8	35.5
Belgium	35.4	36.5	37.4	40.1	40.4	41.7	42.7	42.9	43.6	43.9	44.7
Denmark	34.6	34.5	35.0	33.0	34.9	34.7	36.7	37.4	37.8	37.5	36.9
Finland	26.7	27.3	26.3	27.9	31.0	30.5	28.6	27.4	27.5	28.6	28.6
Iceland	27.9	29.2	29.2	29.7	28.3	27.4	29.0	30.2	29.6	31.1	32.9
Ireland	31.1	31.1	32.0	31.9	35.3	34.3	33.8	35.0	38.6	40.0	42.6
Luxembourg	33.5	32.3	32.9	37.7	37.1	39.9	40.6	38.0	40.0	37.6	34.7
Netherlands	. . .	46.0	47.3	49.6	49.8	48.4	48.4	48.6	49.9	50.5	51.3
New Zealand	27.2	28.8	30.9	30.0	30.4	33.4	32.3	32.4	32.2	33.3	34.8
Norway	37.9	38.4	37.8	37.5	38.7	38.6	38.8	38.9	41.3	43.1	42.6
Spain	20.0	20.2	19.9	21.0	20.7	22.7	23.7	24.3	24.7	25.3	. . .
Sweden	34.1	32.8	32.8	33.7	38.3	39.6	39.5	38.1	37.8	38.9	39.0

Source: International Monetary Fund, *Government Finance Statistics Yearbook*, 1983 and 1984.

Chart 3. Consolidated Central Government Revenue
(As a percentage of GDP)

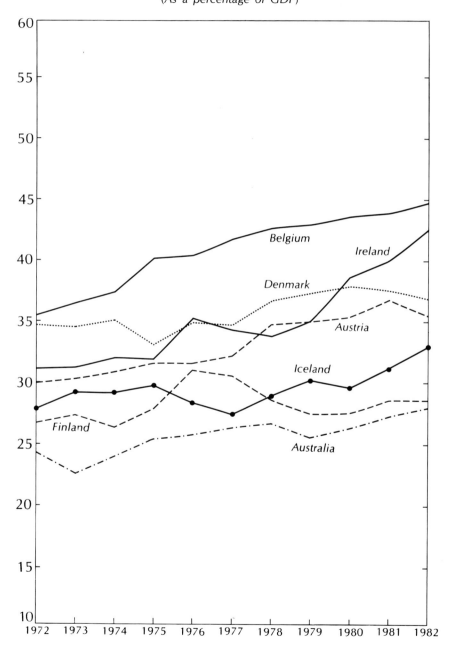

Chart 3 (*continued*). Consolidated Central Government Revenue
(As a percentage of GDP)

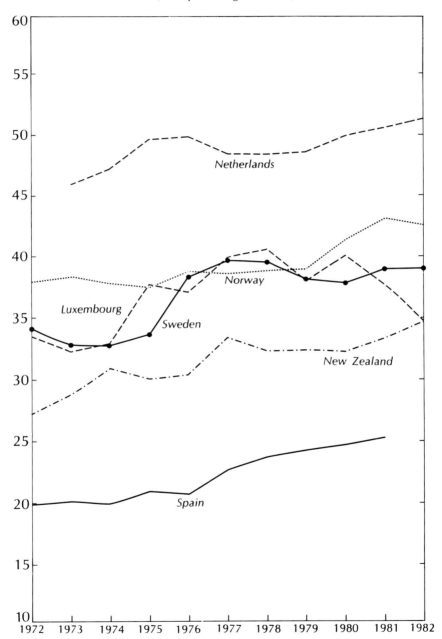

comparison of rates of growth of revenue and expenditure reveals that in all countries except Norway expenditure grew faster and, in a few cases, substantially faster than revenue. In Norway revenue grew faster than expenditure between 1972 and 1982 because of rapidly growing oil revenue. Here again, it should be noted that a comparison of end-year ratios in some instances conceals important changes within the period; these are discussed in some detail in Part II of the study. Countries that experienced the greatest disparity in revenue and expenditure growth were Denmark, Ireland, Belgium, the Netherlands, and Sweden, where the difference in terms of ratios to GDP ranged between 6½ and 11 percentage points. This disparity implies a sharp deterioration in the fiscal position in these countries—an aspect that is examined further in the following section.

Income taxes at the central level differ significantly in relative importance among individual countries. Their weight in total revenue is largest in New Zealand and Australia, at 66½ percent and 63½ percent, respectively (Table 2.7). This tax is also highest in relation to GDP in these countries—23 percent in New Zealand and 18 percent in Australia. The high ratios are explained in part by the absence of social security contributions in both countries and the consequent financing of social security expenditure by general taxation. Income tax at the central level is lowest in Iceland and Sweden—11 percent and 15½ percent, respectively, of total revenue and 3½ percent and 6 percent, respectively, of GDP.[3] On the whole, personal income tax is the main source of revenue in this category, except in Norway, where, because of the oil industry, the corporate income tax is the most important. In 9 out of the 13 countries revenue from the income tax grew faster than GDP; the highest rates of growth, as a ratio to GDP, were in New Zealand and Belgium, at 6½ percentage points; and in Ireland and Norway, between 4 and 4½ percentage points. This increase occurred despite a series of reductions over the period as the progressivity of rates secured a still faster growth of revenue yield. However, tax cuts reduced tax elasticities with respect to income to such an extent in Sweden, Iceland, Denmark, and the Netherlands that the ratio fell to a range of 3.1–0.9 percentage points.

Most countries in the group introduced measures over the period to reduce the personal income tax, although the extent of cuts varied

---

[3] In both countries, and especially in Sweden, the income tax is a major revenue source at the local government level.

Table 2.7. Income Taxes

	1972	1973	1974	1975	1976	1977	1978	1979	1980	1981	1982
Ratio to GDP											
Australia	14.1	13.3	14.6	16.4	16.3	16.8	17.0	15.5	16.0	16.9	17.8
Austria	6.1	6.0	6.6	6.4	6.2	6.4	7.4	7.3	7.3	7.5	7.1
Belgium	11.0	12.0	12.9	14.8	14.5	15.6	16.5	17.0	16.7	16.5	17.6
Denmark	13.6	14.4	15.9	13.4	13.0	12.2	12.7	12.5	12.7	12.7	12.4
Finland	7.9	8.4	8.8	9.1	11.0	9.8	7.7	7.0	7.7	8.6	8.1
Iceland	4.8	5.0	3.6	2.6	2.6	2.2	2.8	3.7	3.2	3.3	3.6
Ireland	8.7	9.0	9.3	9.5	10.6	10.7	10.7	11.2	12.7	13.2	13.2
Luxembourg	11.4	11.9	13.5	14.0	13.6	15.8	16.7	14.6	14.3	13.1	12.1
Netherlands	...	14.9	15.3	15.9	15.5	15.0	14.7	14.7	14.8	14.2	14.0
New Zealand	16.7	18.6	21.1	19.7	20.1	22.6	20.9	21.2	21.7	22.2	23.1
Norway	8.2	6.1	6.5	6.2	6.7	6.8	7.0	8.0	11.2	12.3	11.6
Spain	3.2	3.3	3.4	3.8	4.2	4.3	4.9	5.3	5.9	5.2	...
Sweden	9.1	7.4	7.1	7.2	9.6	9.3	7.4	7.0	6.8	6.2	6.0
Share in Total Revenue and Grants											
Australia	57.9	58.6	61.1	64.5	63.1	63.6	63.6	60.6	60.8	62.0	63.5
Austria	20.4	19.8	21.4	20.4	19.6	19.8	21.2	20.7	20.6	20.5	20.0
Belgium	31.2	33.0	34.6	36.8	35.8	37.3	38.8	39.6	38.2	37.6	39.4
Denmark	39.3	41.6	45.4	40.6	37.2	35.2	34.6	33.4	33.5	33.7	33.8
Finland	29.4	30.9	33.4	32.7	35.4	32.1	27.0	25.5	28.0	30.0	28.5
Iceland	17.3	17.2	12.2	8.8	9.3	8.0	9.8	12.3	10.7	10.6	11.1
Ireland	28.1	29.0	29.1	29.7	30.1	31.1	31.6	32.1	32.8	32.9	31.0
Luxembourg	33.9	36.7	40.8	37.2	36.6	39.5	41.1	38.5	35.7	34.9	34.9
Netherlands	...	32.3	32.3	32.1	31.1	31.0	30.3	30.3	29.7	28.2	27.4
New Zealand	61.2	64.5	68.4	65.6	66.0	67.6	64.7	65.4	67.3	66.8	66.5
Norway	21.7	16.0	17.2	16.5	17.3	17.6	18.0	20.6	27.2	28.5	27.1
Spain	15.8	16.4	17.3	18.1	20.1	18.8	20.8	21.9	23.9	20.5	...
Sweden	26.8	22.7	21.6	21.4	25.1	23.5	18.7	18.3	18.1	15.9	15.5

Source: International Monetary Fund, *Government Finance Statistics Yearbook*, 1983 and 1984.

according to, inter alia, the rate of inflation. The stated objectives included a reduction or elimination of fiscal drag, which, although in some cases had begun on an ad hoc basis, tended to turn into regular adjustments and, for most countries in the group, ended up as an automatic or a semi-automatic indexation mechanism. In some countries, such as Austria, Denmark, Finland, the Netherlands, Norway, and Sweden, reduction of the tax burden was a stated policy aim, either to reduce disincentives, stimulate private sector demand, or, in certain instances, redistribute income in favor of lower income groups (Spain, Norway). As indicated earlier, a number of countries in the group reduced the personal income tax with the aim of moderating wage settlements.

The corporate income tax was also reduced in several countries to stimulate investment, employment, and activity in the private sector. The measures commonly took the form of rate reductions and increased or accelerated depreciation allowances; and at least in two countries (Denmark and Iceland) depreciation allowances and other deductions were price indexed for corporate income tax purposes.

Social security contributions range from 0 to 47 percent of total revenue in the smaller industrial countries (Table 2.8). These contributions were highest in Spain, at 47 percent, and nonexistent in Australia and New Zealand. In four other countries, the Netherlands, Austria, Sweden, and Belgium, social security contributions range between 30 percent and 40 percent of total revenue, while in Denmark and Iceland they account for only about 3½ percent and 2½ percent of the total; Iceland has no such taxes on employees. In relation to GDP, social security contributions are highest in the Netherlands, at almost 20 percent, followed by Sweden, Belgium, and Austria, at about 13 percent each. The fastest increase in relation to GDP over the 1972–82 period took place in Sweden—some 6 percentage points—followed by Austria—about 3½ percentage points—while Iceland was the only country in which this ratio fell appreciably, by ½ of 1 percentage point, over the period.

In countries where the relevant social security schemes were self-financing in nature, the rapid growth of expenditure pulled up contribution rates and, in some instances, necessitated special transfers to the social security system from the central budget. As the period progressed, however, and higher rates imposed a mounting burden on labor costs, an increasing number of countries implemented a series of reductions in contribution rates. The declared objectives were to

Table 2.8. Social Security Contributions

	1972	1973	1974	1975	1976	1977	1978	1979	1980	1981	1982
Ratio to GDP											
Australia	—	—	—	—	—	—	—	—	—	—	—
Austria	9.0	9.2	9.5	10.3	10.4	10.8	12.2	12.2	12.5	12.9	12.6
Belgium	11.4	11.7	11.9	13.0	13.0	13.2	13.1	13.1	13.2	13.5	13.4
Denmark	1.7	0.6	0.6	0.5	0.5	0.6	0.6	0.7	0.8	1.0	1.3
Finland	2.1	2.4	2.2	2.6	3.0	2.9	2.5	2.7	2.6	2.7	2.8
Iceland	1.3	1.0	1.0	1.2	0.8	1.1	1.2	1.4	1.3	0.8	0.8
Ireland	2.8	3.0	3.7	4.4	4.7	4.5	4.4	4.5	4.9	5.1	5.7
Luxembourg	9.3	8.6	8.8	10.9	11.2	11.6	11.1	10.6	10.4	9.7	8.7
Netherlands	· · ·	16.8	17.9	18.4	17.9	17.0	17.3	17.8	18.2	18.8	19.9
New Zealand	—	—	—	—	—	—	—	—	—	—	—
Norway	7.5	10.4	10.2	10.2	9.9	9.9	10.0	9.9	9.1	9.4	9.5
Spain	7.7	8.0	8.2	9.3	8.9	10.7	11.3	11.7	11.6	11.9	· · ·
Sweden	7.3	7.2	7.7	9.0	10.2	11.0	12.2	12.3	12.4	13.5	13.2
Share in Total Revenue and Grants											
Australia	—	—	—	—	—	—	—	—	—	—	—
Austria	29.9	30.4	30.9	32.7	33.0	33.7	35.1	34.8	35.2	35.0	35.4
Belgium	32.2	32.1	31.8	32.3	32.2	31.5	30.6	30.6	30.4	30.7	29.9
Denmark	5.0	1.6	1.6	1.7	1.6	1.7	1.6	1.8	2.2	2.6	3.4
Finland	7.7	8.7	8.5	9.4	9.6	9.4	8.9	9.8	9.6	9.5	9.6
Iceland	4.8	3.5	3.5	4.0	3.0	3.8	4.3	4.5	4.2	2.7	2.3
Ireland	8.9	9.6	11.5	13.6	13.2	13.2	12.9	12.9	12.8	12.7	13.3
Luxembourg	27.7	26.6	26.8	29.0	30.3	29.2	27.5	28.0	26.0	25.8	25.2
Netherlands	· · ·	36.5	37.8	37.1	36.0	35.2	35.8	36.7	36.4	37.3	38.7
New Zealand	—	—	—	—	—	—	—	—	—	—	—
Norway	19.8	27.2	26.9	27.2	25.5	25.6	25.7	25.5	22.1	21.8	22.3
Spain	38.8	39.7	41.2	44.5	43.0	47.4	47.9	48.2	47.0	47.2	· · ·
Sweden	21.5	22.1	23.8	26.7	26.6	27.8	30.9	32.3	32.8	34.7	33.7

Source: International Monetary Fund, *Government Finance Statistics Yearbook*, 1983 and 1984.

stimulate activity and employment in the private sector, and in countries like Norway rates were differentiated by regions to promote regional employment policy. In Finland and Norway cuts in contribution rates were at times associated with incomes policy, and in Spain—a country with a serious unemployment problem—the Government committed itself toward the end of the period to reversing the trend of a constantly increasing burden of social security contributions on labor costs. In Sweden where these contributions have grown fastest and are among the highest in terms of ratios to GDP, an increasing proportion has been borne by employers, with the result that the overall ratio of contributions to the total payroll was about 35 percent at the end of the period.

Taxes on goods and services are for a large part value-added or sales taxes and various excise duties and levies. They range between 18 and 48 percent of total revenue and grants, with Spain having the lowest ratio and Finland and Iceland the highest (Table 2.9). In most countries this ratio declined over the period, although it increased in Australia, Denmark, Finland, and Iceland. In Australia the rise was due to a levy on domestic crude oil that was gradually equated with import prices. In the other three countries, value-added or sales taxes were raised to curb private sector demand and to compensate for revenue losses resulting from cuts in the income tax. In terms of GDP ratios, this tax category rose or remained constant in most countries in the group; the largest increases were in Iceland (6 percent) and Denmark (2 percent). In two countries, the ratio declined over the period; in Norway, by 1½ percentage points, and in the Netherlands, by less than 1 percentage point.

Other tax and nontax revenue and grants include payroll taxes, property taxes, taxes on international trade, other taxes, and nontax revenue and grants. This heterogeneous category accounts for 7–39 percent of total revenue and grants (Table 2.10). It is lowest in Belgium and highest in Iceland, where taxes on foreign trade are a significant, albeit declining, revenue source. Expressed as a ratio to GDP, the category ranges between 3 percent in Belgium and 13 percent in Iceland. On the whole, this ratio rose slightly or remained constant for most countries over the period; the most notable exception was the Netherlands, where because of vastly increased revenue from the sale of natural gas, it increased by almost 4 percentage points. Because of their membership in or agreements with the European Communities (EC) or the European Free Trade Association (EFTA), most countries in the group experienced a relative decline in taxes on international trade in relation to GDP over

Table 2.9. Taxes on Goods and Services

	1972	1973	1974	1975	1976	1977	1978	1979	1980	1981	1982
Ratio to GDP											
Australia	5.3	5.0	5.2	4.8	5.3	5.1	5.2	5.7	6.2	6.3	6.1
Austria	8.3	8.9	8.6	8.5	8.7	8.7	8.9	9.0	8.8	9.1	8.9
Belgium	10.2	10.0	9.9	9.8	10.3	10.3	10.4	9.9	10.7	10.7	10.7
Denmark	14.3	14.3	13.4	13.2	14.3	15.3	16.3	16.9	16.7	16.6	16.1
Finland	12.5	12.1	11.1	11.4	11.9	12.8	13.4	13.4	13.3	13.5	13.6
Iceland	9.6	9.4	11.8	13.8	13.6	13.1	13.0	13.1	13.9	14.8	15.5
Ireland	10.1	10.3	9.9	9.5	10.6	10.3	10.1	9.3	9.6	9.5	10.9
Luxembourg	7.0	6.6	5.8	7.5	6.9	6.9	6.9	6.5	7.6	7.3	7.1
Netherlands	...	10.2	9.6	10.0	10.1	10.3	10.4	9.9	10.0	9.6	9.4
New Zealand	5.4	5.2	5.1	5.9	5.5	5.8	6.1	5.9	5.8	6.2	6.7
Norway	17.5	16.8	15.9	16.3	17.1	17.8	17.2	16.3	16.2	16.3	16.1
Spain	4.7	4.7	3.8	3.7	3.3	3.0	3.3	3.3	4.1	4.6	...
Sweden	11.5	11.3	10.8	10.1	10.5	10.9	11.4	11.3	11.0	11.5	11.5
Share in Total Revenue and Grants											
Australia	21.7	21.9	21.5	19.1	20.5	19.5	19.5	22.3	23.4	23.0	22.0
Austria	27.9	29.5	28.1	27.0	27.7	26.9	25.6	25.7	25.0	24.8	25.0
Belgium	28.7	27.5	26.5	24.4	25.4	24.6	24.5	23.2	24.5	24.4	23.9
Denmark	41.4	41.5	38.2	40.0	41.1	44.2	44.3	45.4	44.2	44.3	43.6
Finland	46.8	44.4	42.3	40.8	38.3	42.1	46.7	48.9	48.2	47.2	47.6
Iceland	34.3	32.0	40.3	46.4	48.1	47.9	44.8	43.2	46.9	47.5	47.1
Ireland	32.5	33.0	31.1	29.9	30.1	30.0	29.8	26.6	24.8	23.9	25.6
Luxembourg	21.0	20.4	17.5	19.8	18.6	17.3	17.1	17.2	18.9	19.5	20.3
Netherlands	...	22.2	20.4	20.1	20.4	21.3	21.5	20.5	20.1	19.0	18.3
New Zealand	19.9	18.2	16.6	19.5	18.1	17.4	18.8	18.1	18.0	18.5	19.2
Norway	46.1	43.8	42.1	43.5	44.2	46.1	44.3	41.9	39.3	37.9	37.7
Spain	23.3	23.5	19.3	17.8	15.8	13.3	13.8	13.4	16.7	18.1	...
Sweden	33.8	34.5	32.8	29.9	27.5	27.5	28.8	29.8	29.0	29.6	29.4

Source: International Monetary Fund, *Government Finance Statistics Yearbook*, 1983 and 1984.

Table 2.10. Other Tax and Nontax Revenue and Grants

	1972	1973	1974	1975	1976	1977	1978	1979	1980	1981	1982
Ratio to GDP											
Australia	4.9	4.4	4.2	4.2	4.2	4.4	4.5	4.4	4.2	4.1	4.1
Austria	6.5	6.2	6.1	6.3	6.2	6.3	6.3	6.6	6.8	7.2	7.0
Belgium	2.8	2.7	2.7	2.6	2.7	2.7	2.6	2.9	3.0	3.2	3.0
Denmark	4.9	5.3	5.2	5.9	7.0	6.6	7.2	7.3	7.6	7.3	7.1
Finland	4.3	4.4	4.2	4.7	5.2	5.0	5.0	4.3	3.9	3.8	4.1
Iceland	12.2	13.8	12.8	12.1	11.2	11.1	11.9	12.1	11.3	12.2	13.0
Ireland	9.5	8.8	9.1	8.5	9.3	8.8	8.7	9.9	11.4	12.2	12.8
Luxembourg	5.8	5.3	4.9	5.3	5.3	5.6	5.8	6.2	7.8	7.5	6.8
Netherlands	...	4.1	4.5	5.3	6.3	6.1	6.0	6.1	6.9	7.8	8.0
New Zealand	5.1	5.0	4.6	4.5	4.8	5.0	5.3	5.3	4.8	4.9	5.0
Norway	4.7	5.0	5.2	4.8	5.1	4.1	4.7	4.7	4.7	5.1	5.5
Spain	4.4	4.1	4.4	4.1	4.4	4.7	4.1	4.0	3.1	3.6	...
Sweden	6.1	6.8	7.2	7.4	8.0	8.4	8.5	7.5	7.6	7.7	8.4
Share in Total Revenue and Grants											
Australia	20.3	19.4	17.4	16.4	16.3	16.9	17.0	17.0	15.8	15.0	14.6
Austria	21.9	20.3	19.7	19.9	19.7	19.5	18.1	18.9	19.1	19.7	19.7
Belgium	7.9	7.5	7.2	6.5	6.6	6.6	6.1	6.6	7.0	7.4	6.8
Denmark	14.3	15.3	14.9	17.8	20.1	18.9	19.5	19.5	20.1	19.4	19.2
Finland	16.1	16.0	15.8	17.0	16.7	16.5	17.4	15.8	14.3	13.4	14.3
Iceland	43.6	47.3	44.0	40.7	39.7	40.3	41.1	40.0	38.1	39.2	39.5
Ireland	30.5	28.4	28.3	26.7	26.5	25.6	25.7	28.4	29.6	30.5	30.0
Luxembourg	17.4	16.3	14.9	14.1	14.4	14.0	14.3	16.3	19.5	19.8	19.5
Netherlands	...	9.0	9.5	10.7	12.6	12.6	12.5	12.5	13.8	15.5	15.7
New Zealand	18.8	17.3	15.0	14.9	15.9	15.0	16.5	16.5	14.8	14.7	14.3
Norway	12.4	13.0	13.8	12.8	13.0	10.7	12.0	12.0	11.5	11.9	12.9
Spain	22.1	20.4	22.2	19.6	21.1	20.6	17.5	16.5	12.4	14.2	...
Sweden	17.9	20.7	21.9	22.0	20.8	21.2	21.6	19.6	20.1	19.8	21.4

Source: International Monetary Fund, *Government Finance Statistics Yearbook*, 1983 and 1984.

the period. Only in Australia and New Zealand, which are not members of either organization, did this ratio remain roughly constant.

FISCAL BALANCE, FINANCING, AND DEBT ACCUMULATION

The period covered witnessed persistent and in most instances widening fiscal deficits (Table 2.11). Of the 13 countries, 8 incurred a deficit in every year of the period; another 3 experienced a deficit in every year after 1974; one country, Norway, realized its only surpluses in 1981 and 1982; only in Luxembourg was there a positive balance in central government finances over the period as a whole—surpluses in 1972–78 and in 1980 and 1982 but deficits in 1979 and 1981. The time pattern of the fiscal balance is demonstrated in Chart 4, which reveals a sharp deterioration in fiscal positions in the period 1974–75 as a result of an expansionary policy response to the recession in the wake of the first oil price shock. A partial recovery followed in 1976 and 1977, when growing internal and external imbalances, especially accelerating rates of inflation and widening current external deficits, induced governments to shift the stance of fiscal policy in a restrictive direction. Belgium and, to a lesser extent, Norway, where deficits continued to widen, are notable exceptions. After 1977, the results were mixed, but in 1979 and 1980, the years of the second oil crisis,. most countries experienced a renewed increase in deficits that in some cases continued over the rest of the period. However, in two countries, Australia and Norway, the 1980–82 period witnessed an improvement in fiscal positions, especially in Norway where oil revenue soared.

The countries that experienced the sharpest deterioration in their government finances relied increasingly on foreign financing of the deficits; a number of these countries had recourse, in growing measure, to domestic monetary financing to meet the borrowing requirement. These developments are discussed in some detail under individual country sections in Part II.

As a consequence of mounting fiscal deficits, government indebtedness increased in most of the smaller industrial countries over the period (Table 2.12). Expressed as a ratio to GDP, government debt in 1982 was the highest in Ireland, at 109 percent. Other countries recording high government debt were Belgium (74 percent), and Denmark and New Zealand (almost 60 percent each). There is evidence that these ratios have since expanded. By contrast, Finland's government debt was a moderate 12½ percent of GDP in 1982, and in Luxembourg, it was negligible. The rate of debt accumulation by the central government was

Table 2.11. Deficit/Surplus as a Percentage of GDP

	1972	1973	1974	1975	1976	1977	1978	1979	1980	1981	1982
Australia	-0.3	-1.7	-0.5	-4.0	-5.0	-3.3	-3.7	-3.3	-1.8	-0.8	-0.3
Austria	-0.2	-1.6	-1.5	-4.0	-4.6	-3.7	-4.0	-3.7	-3.2	-2.9	-4.4
Belgium	-4.3	-3.5	-2.2	-4.7	-5.6	-5.9	-6.9	-7.6	-7.7	-12.3	-12.2
Denmark	2.6	3.5	0.7	-1.9	-0.4	-1.3	-0.3	-0.7	-2.7	-6.2	-8.3
Finland	1.2	2.9	0.8	-2.3	—	-1.5	-1.9	-2.6	-2.0	-1.0	-2.0
Iceland	-2.6	-3.1	-4.6	-6.2	-2.5	-4.4	-2.6	-2.2	-1.4	-0.8	-2.9
Ireland	-5.6	-6.8	-11.9	-12.4	-10.2	-9.5	-11.5	-12.1	-13.3	-15.0	-15.2
Luxembourg	1.4	2.5	3.9	1.0	0.3	0.6	2.7	-0.2	1.0	-1.6	0.5
Netherlands	...	—	—	-3.0	-2.6	-3.0	-3.1	-4.6	-4.6	-6.5	-7.6
New Zealand	-3.8	-2.5	-4.1	-10.2	-4.4	-5.1	-8.6	-5.3	-6.3	-7.2	-7.4
Norway	-1.5	-0.9	-1.4	-3.2	-5.9	-6.9	-6.8	-6.3	-1.8	2.1	0.8
Spain	-0.5	-0.3	-1.2	-1.8	-0.9	-2.2	-2.4	-3.5	-4.3	-7.1	...
Sweden	-1.3	-1.5	-3.3	-2.7	-0.4	-1.7	-5.2	-7.6	-8.7	-9.4	-9.9

Source: International Monetary Fund, *Government Finance Statistics Yearbook*, 1983 and 1984.

Table 2.12. Central Government Outstanding Debt

	1972	1973	1974	1975	1976	1977	1978	1979	1980	1981	1982
Ratio to GDP											
Australia	...	34.8	29.8	28.8	27.9	28.0	29.8	30.4	28.6	24.9	22.7
Austria	10.5	10.4	10.0	15.3	18.5	20.8	23.6	25.2	26.3	28.0	30.0
Belgium	45.0	42.5	39.0	40.0	40.3	43.2	46.2	49.7	54.8	65.2	73.9
Denmark	−1.6	−3.6	−1.7	4.5	8.4	13.2	18.2	24.7	33.7	45.9	59.2
Finland	6.6	4.5	3.0	3.5	3.9	5.2	8.5	9.1	9.3	10.1	12.3
Iceland	15.8	12.5	13.4	18.1	18.9	20.7	22.4	23.9	26.4	23.6	31.4
Ireland	52.3	59.7	65.0	73.4	79.2	77.9	82.1	89.5	91.4	99.3	108.7
Luxembourg	...	...	8.9	8.5	7.6	7.3	6.7	5.7	5.1	5.0	4.7
Netherlands	...	22.1	21.0	22.1	22.4	22.5	23.8	25.7	29.1	33.5	39.4
New Zealand	44.6	41.2	41.8	47.8	44.7	48.7	50.5	49.2	47.6	49.2	58.2
Norway	28.1	26.8	24.8	25.7	27.8	33.1	38.4	42.1	37.0	32.1	26.5
Spain	15.6	13.2	11.8	12.1	13.0	15.3	14.3	15.4	17.2	19.4	...
Sweden	16.6	16.7	18.3	18.9	17.0	18.3	21.3	25.7	32.3	38.8	45.4
Foreign Debt as a Percentage of Total Debt											
Australia	...	8.6	6.7	6.7	6.5	8.0	13.5	16.9	16.5	14.2	15.9
Austria	20.4	16.0	22.0	31.9	26.1	28.7	30.1	27.5	27.8	32.0	31.7
Belgium	1.7	1.1	0.8	0.8	0.6	0.5	1.4	3.9	8.1	15.8	20.9
Denmark											
Finland	39.5	43.7	42.4	44.3	48.6	54.8	60.2	58.9	57.5	60.3	62.2
Iceland	66.6	65.4	70.2	61.9	61.3	64.6	69.1	62.7	58.1	54.7	65.7
Ireland	8.9	10.3	15.9	20.7	28.8	24.6	20.6	23.6	28.0	37.2	41.2
Luxembourg	...	0.1	0.1								
Netherlands											
New Zealand	16.0	12.4	20.4	26.2	29.0	32.6	33.0	34.4	36.4	38.5	41.4
Norway	5.9	4.3	3.7	14.6	20.5	26.3	34.1	32.0	28.4	25.0	22.5
Spain	5.4	4.8	5.1	4.7	7.3	14.3	8.9	7.1	4.6	4.9	...
Sweden	—	—	0.1	0.2	0.3	7.8	13.4	13.3	20.1	21.9	22.9

Sources: International Monetary Fund, *Government Finance Statistics Yearbook*, 1983 and 1984; national sources; and Fund staff estimates.

Chart 4. Smaller Industrial Countries: Fiscal Balances
(As a percentage of GDP)

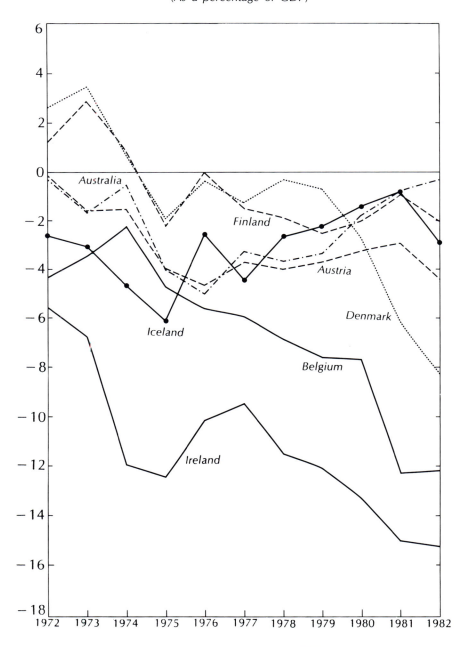

Chart 4 (*continued*). Smaller Industrial Countries: Fiscal Balances
(*As a percentage of GDP*)

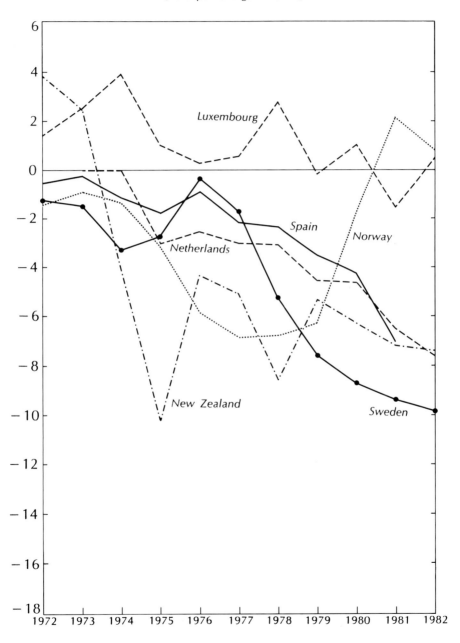

most rapid in Denmark and Ireland, at 61 and 56 percentage points, respectively; the rate of expansion in Belgium and Sweden was also high, at approximately 30 percentage points each. In Australia, on the other hand, the ratio of government debt to GDP declined by 12 percentage points from 1973 to 1982. As already indicated, the external component of government debt grew over the period in most countries in the group. The fastest relative increase occurred in the same countries that had experienced the fastest expansion of total debt, with the addition of New Zealand and Finland whose external component grew at an unusually fast rate toward the end of the period. The external component was relatively largest in Finland and Iceland, at 62 percent and 66 percent, respectively, of total government debt, followed by New Zealand and Ireland, at 40 percent each; in contrast, the Netherlands and Luxembourg had no or negligible foreign debt at the central government level.

3

Fiscal Policy, 1972–82,
An Overview

This chapter contains a broad account of the pursuit of fiscal policy over a decade that witnessed the largest economic imbalances experienced on a global basis in the postwar period. While the sheer magnitude of the external shocks emanating from the two oil crises and the ensuing world recession had a broadly similar impact on the smaller industrial countries, differences in individual circumstances caused deviations from the more general policy reactions. As this part of the study emphasizes the general aspects of fiscal policy, events peculiar to individual countries are given very limited coverage. Therefore, certain policy actions, although significant in a narrower context, may be neglected in this chapter. Some of these are contained in Part II, which deals with individual countries in some detail.

ECONOMIC SETTING AND
FISCAL STANCE IN THE EARLY 1970s

The first two years of the period under review witnessed a continuation of the strong growth performance that most countries in the group had achieved during the l960s. Expansion of economic activity in the latter half of 1972 and the first half of 1973, in particular, was accompanied by a marked acceleration of inflation rates that had been on the rise in most industrial countries since the mid-1960s. Concern over the inflation problem induced governments in a number of countries to tighten financial restraint policies. Partly as a result of the stricter stance of fiscal and monetary policies, signs of a slowdown of output expansion began surfacing even before the abrupt oil price increases late in l973. Although levels of unemployment differed

41

substantially among the countries—Ireland suffered the highest rate of about 6 percent—the employment situation was not a problem, and most countries in the group actually experienced a fall in the unemployment rate in 1973. Similarly, in these years the current external balances were not a matter of great concern generally, although there were exceptions, such as Denmark, which experienced persistent balance of payments problems. In fact, 7 of the 13 countries had current account surpluses in both 1972 and 1973; that is, Australia, Belgium, Luxembourg, the Netherlands, New Zealand, Spain, and Sweden.

As indicated, inflation was a growing problem in the early years of the period, even before the first oil price explosion. All countries in the group experienced accelerated price increases in 1973, and in some countries inflation was regarded as the dominant economic policy problem. The rates of inflation differed markedly among the countries, however, with Iceland experiencing the highest rates (10 percent in 1972 and 20 percent in 1973), and Luxembourg the lowest (5 percent in 1972 and 6 percent in 1973). The policy response on the fiscal front in most countries was to tighten the stance, usually as part of a more general approach to overall demand management. About half the countries in the group succeeded in improving their fiscal positions from 1972 to 1973 (Table 2.11 and Chart 4), and in a few additional countries, the balance remained approximately constant. Only in four countries— Australia, Austria, Iceland, and Ireland—was there a marked increase in the fiscal deficit in 1973. In Australia, the increase was the result of a conscious policy of fiscal expansion; in Austria and Ireland, a higher priority was assigned to stimulating activity through increased public spending; and in Iceland, incomes policy-oriented tax and expenditure measures led to fiscal deterioration.

Although most countries in the group incurred fiscal deficits in 1972 and 1973 (Table 2.11), except Denmark, Finland, and Luxembourg, which realized surpluses in both years, the size of the deficits was generally small compared with subsequent developments, and deficit financing did not pose problems at this time. External financing was nonexistent in most countries, the only exceptions being Iceland and Ireland, which financed part of their public investment by foreign borrowing. Similarly, domestic monetary financing was in most instances not resorted to in any significant measure. On the contrary, a number of countries pursued active open market operations in support of monetary policy. Thus, in 1972 and 1973, in Australia, Belgium, the Netherlands, and Spain, more was borrowed from the nonbank private sector than was needed to finance the deficit, in order to reduce liquidity in the economy, much of which stemmed from capital inflows. The proceeds were used to reduce external debt or to repay short-term domestic debt.

Fiscal policy achieved a fair amount of success in the early 1970s; moreover, improvements in fiscal positions contributed to the anti-inflationary efforts of general demand management. There are several explanations, both economic and political, for this success. An important one may be the relatively flexible fiscal systems that made possible the pursuit of flexible policies in these years. In the early 1970s, expenditure levels and tax burdens were substantially lower than they are now; automaticity in significant expenditure categories was much less pronounced, as were inflation-adjustment mechanisms on the revenue side. Public finances were generally more balanced than they later became, and interest payments did not constitute an overly heavy claim on budgetary resources in most instances. Moreover, tax reforms had been recently, or were being, undertaken at the beginning of the period in a number of countries; notably, the introduction of value-added taxes in countries connected with the EC. It was a widely held view at this time that these tax reforms would substantially improve the fiscal armory for both allocation and stabilization purposes.

Not all measures taken around this time were conducive to flexibility in fiscal policy, however. Foundations previously laid for generous social entitlement programs were being strengthened, and in a number of countries social security expenditure had been increasing rapidly since the 1960s. This development would prove a major element in the subsequent difficulties policymakers encountered in their attempts to control public expenditure growth.

POLICY RESPONSE TO FIRST OIL CRISIS

The abrupt increase in energy prices late in 1973 and in 1974, as well as the ensuing world recession, affected the smaller industrial countries profoundly: their economies were generally highly open and susceptible to external impulses, and most of them were not endowed with rich domestic energy sources. In a number of these countries, fiscal policy was the major instrument of economic stabilization, and the policy response was generally to shift the fiscal stance in a highly expansionary direction. This policy was broadly viewed as a proper reaction to the recession, which was believed to be short lived. Growth, it was argued, would soon pick up globally and a more normal stance of policy could then be resumed.

The strength of the policy reaction to the recession naturally differed among individual countries, depending on their perception of the economic threat and domestic policies already in place. As indicated above, output expansion had started to slow down in some countries before the oil price explosion; for this reason, several of them had already introduced expansionary fiscal policies to counteract emerging slack in labor market conditions. Among these were energy-rich countries such as Australia, the Netherlands, and Norway, which might be expected to have been less severely affected by the oil crisis than other countries in the group. Similarly, domestic policies in Australia and, to a lesser extent, in Spain—the two countries in the group with the smallest foreign trade sectors—were actively directed at an expansion of social benefits and, in Australia, at a general expansion of public sector absorption of resources in line with the Government's policy at the time. A policy aimed at enlarging the role of the public sector in the economy was also being pursued in Luxembourg during 1974–75.

When the recession deepened and it became clear after the mid-1970s that the adverse impact of the oil crisis would extend to output and employment as well as to prices, the expansionary stance of fiscal policy was strengthened in almost all countries in the group. With the sharp deterioration in employment in 1975, the highest priority was shifted from controlling inflation, which had been considered the main problem in the preceding years, to maintaining employment. Although the type of expansionary measures differed in individual countries, they frequently included both expenditure increases and tax reductions and entailed a very sharp deterioration in the fiscal positions of all the countries except Sweden, which managed to contain its deficit until 1978.

A typical expenditure measure in these years was increased employment-oriented outlays, such as public investment, in some cases, through increased advances to states and local governments and subsidies to enterprises. Some countries, including Denmark, Luxembourg, the Netherlands, and Sweden, introduced special employment policies that were implemented through schemes either to increase public employment or to compensate private sector enterprises for increasing or maintaining the number of their employees. Also, a special boost was given to the objective of maintaining living standards through improvements in social benefits. Countries that pursued this policy with special vigor were Australia, Belgium, the Netherlands, Spain, and most of the Nordic countries. Examples of more specific measures in 1974 and 1975 include activation of contingency budgets and release of frozen funds of local governments in Austria; relaxation of ceilings on local government investment and subsidization of interest costs on loans for residential construction in Denmark; and the setting up of special credit facilities for enterprises in the Netherlands.

In addition to expenditure measures, a number of countries implemented tax reductions to stimulate the economy. These often took the form of reductions in personal income tax rates or tax incentives for private sector investment, such as rate reductions and, more often, special depreciation allowances. In Austria, the Netherlands, and Denmark, the high tax burden motivated a reduction in income taxes. In Denmark especially, considerable political opposition in 1975 over the high marginal rates of the income tax led to a substantial reduction in personal income tax. Also in Denmark, revenue measures to stimulate demand included a large reduction in 1975 in the value-added tax; similarly in Ireland, items were exempted from the value-added tax. Several countries introduced special tax incentives, originally on a temporary basis, to encourage transfer of resources to the export sector. The fiscal measures thus usually aimed at the stimulation of both investment and private consumption. Norway is the one notable exception. As investment levels were already high in Norway, the authorities decided instead to stimulate private consumption, with improvements in social security benefits and income tax reductions playing a significant role.

SHIFT IN FISCAL STANCE AFTER MID-1970s
AND CHANGES IN POLICY APPROACH

Shortly after the mid-1970s it was becoming widely recognized that the strength and duration of the recession had been underestimated. While economic activity had picked up in most countries in the group in 1976 and the unemployment situation had stabilized in a few countries, these did not prove to be lasting improvements. Although two years of highly expansionary fiscal policies had contributed to the temporary improvement, it was nonetheless clear that these policies had at the same time fueled accelerating rates of inflation and widening current external deficits. These developments were of grave concern to governments in the smaller industrial countries; they generally responded by endeavoring to redirect the stance of fiscal policy in a restrictive direction.

The economic imbalances, which in a number of countries had reached unprecedented proportions in the postwar period and were assuming an increasingly structural character, brought about a shift in policy approaches in many countries. There was growing recognition that the imbalances could not be eliminated in the short term, and a few countries, including Finland, Ireland, and Spain, adopted medium-term overall economic policies to address the problem. To reinforce their political resolution to restore fiscal balance, a growing number of countries publicly announced specific medium-term fiscal targets for the containment or reduction of fiscal deficits, tax burdens, or public expenditure/GDP ratios, or all of these. Another, and perhaps more fundamental, change in approach emanated from a growing doubt as to the appropriateness of traditional demand management policies in dealing with economic imbalances of this magnitude. Such policies were seen as liable to cause still higher rates of unemployment. Views of this kind were expressed at different times, for example, in Australia, Ireland, the Netherlands, and New Zealand. Preference was expressed for measures that would be directed at the cost side by attacking the wage-price spiral or measures that directed resources into the export sector. Of course, certain countries in the group already had long experience with measures of this kind, notably incomes policy measures, but selective measures tended to assume an enhanced role in the following years.

While there was growing awareness of the need to improve fiscal positions, most governments nonetheless remained committed to the objective of stimulating employment and economic activity and to preserving living standards. This set of objectives posed an acute dilemma for fiscal policy and frequently led to inconsistencies in the pursuit of policy, as discussed in the following section. A number of countries addressed the problem by adopting strategies that sought to maintain a restrictive overall stance of fiscal policy while at the same time introducing selective measures of stimulus that would not impart undue pressure on prices and the current external position. This approach was perhaps most clearly spelled out in the so-called dual strategy followed in Austria.

The results of these changes in approach were mixed, however, as fiscal deficits did not generally decline in subsequent years, although in many instances they tended to stabilize. But with a few exceptions, levels of expenditure continued to rise in relation to GDP, as did tax burdens. The commitment of governments to cushioning the adverse impact of the recession on the economy and living standards meant the maintenance and, in several cases, intensification of measures from the preceding period of fiscal expansion and even the introduction of new ones.

The selective measures taken at this time and in subsequent years included various public investment programs, special employment promoting schemes, personal income tax reductions, and selective tax incentives for investment, including tax credit for special types of investment. Social benefits remained in many countries the underlying force of expenditure growth because of demographic factors, rate increases, extension of coverage, and the automatic effects of the depressed state of economic activity on unemployment compensations. Indexation mechanisms relating to personal income taxation as well as significant expenditure categories proliferated over the period. In some countries, fiscal measures to support incomes policies were pursued vigorously, commonly entailing both increased spending and revenue loss. As the decade progressed and structural problems became more pronounced, selective measures increasingly took the form of industrial support, including transfer of resources to the export sector, interest cost subsidies, assumption of loan obligations, and the granting of loan guarantees.

To counteract an undue expansionary impact of these selective measures, a common response was to increase indirect taxes, such as the value-added tax and, in some cases, taxes on energy use. Indirect tax increases were especially pronounced in Austria, Denmark, Iceland, Ireland, and the Netherlands. Also, in certain countries, including Austria, Belgium, the Netherlands, and especially Spain and Sweden, social security contributions rose rapidly, sometimes with adverse repercussions on business activity and employment. Australia, the Netherlands, and Norway benefited from a large increase in revenue from oil and natural gas in the later years of the period. However, the protracted recessionary conditions generally retarded revenue growth. Most countries tried to contain overall expenditure growth from 1976 onward, but with little success.

Although some countries were initially able to improve their fiscal positions, it soon became clear that notwithstanding public policy announcements of fiscal restraint, several obstacles blocked restoration of fiscal balance; the record shows that for the rest of the period, most countries had severe fiscal difficulties.

POLICY RESPONSE TO SECOND OIL CRISIS

The second oil price explosion in 1979 contributed to a renewed slowdown in economic activity, an upsurge in prices, and widening current external deficits. These events proved to be a major obstacle to fiscal improvement. Mindful of the disappointing experience with expansionary fiscal policies in the wake of the first oil crisis, governments generally reacted cautiously, and initially the battle against inflation was assigned priority. In contrast to the policy stance during 1974–75, fiscal policy remained tight for a time, as far as discretionary action was concerned. Apart from the need for fiscal adjustment, which had grown continuously in preceding years, the tight fiscal stance was required to support the efforts to prevent the impact of the oil price increase from causing a domestic wage-price spiral.

As already mentioned, the practice of stating policy objectives in quantitative terms had become more common, and by this time more than half the countries in the group had announced specific fiscal targets for restoring balance over a specified period. The second oil crisis upset basic assumptions underlying such plans, with the result that countries found it necessary to phase reduction of the deficit over a longer period of time. Improvements in external conditions also tended to be viewed as a prerequisite for fiscal adjustment, while additional factors further contributed to the slippages in the tight fiscal stance that soon emerged in a number of countries. Thus, as a result of deteriorating employment, some governments intensified employment-supporting measures, including wage-cost subsidies. In other instances, social security expenditure and support to industries facing difficult structural adjustment problems were increased. In addition to slippages in the policy stance, fiscal adjustment after the second oil crisis was further complicated by the responses of the automatic stabilizers to the recessionary conditions and by a markedly reduced scope for fiscal action on account of growing rigidities in fiscal systems. These issues are considered in the following chapter.

FISCAL POLICY AND PROSPECTS IN THE EARLY 1980s

The plans for fiscal adjustment that have been announced in many of the smaller industrial countries and expressed as specific medium-term fiscal targets are in some cases supplemented with programs in specific areas. Some of these programs have already been formulated with a considerable degree of precision and are even in varying stages of implementation; others are still under consideration. In still other instances, there is general awareness of an urgent need to undertake a fundamental restructuring of the public finances, but political controversies have hampered progress. This section concludes with a brief look at some of these programs.

In Austria, Belgium, and Spain reforms or reviews of the social security system are being undertaken. In Austria a contemplated review would pay particular attention to the pension system. In Belgium, where the financial position of the social security system has deteriorated rapidly, measures have been taken to limit the increase in benefits, and a comprehensive review is being worked out that would improve efficiency with respect to income redistribution and work effort. Also under consideration is a new means of financing the system that would cease to distort the cost of labor relative to other domestic factor costs. In Spain, although the economic program aimed at improving the social security system was initiated in 1977, progress has been slow. Renewed efforts are being made, however, to reduce anomalies in the present system, with special emphasis on its negative impact on labor costs. In Denmark and Iceland measures have been taken to reduce automaticity in expenditure decisions by suspending indexation mechanisms. How permanent this arrangement will be, however, remains to be seen. And, on the expenditure side, although not intended as a fiscal adjustment, Luxembourg's substantial new and temporary budgetary outlays to restructure the steel industry were largely financed by increased taxation, probably of a more permanent nature; and in Sweden there has been a growing tendency in recent years to make industrial support conditional upon restructuring.

Programs relating to the revenue side are more equity and efficiency oriented, although revenue-raising objectives are also involved. In New Zealand a tax reform was initiated in 1982, with the aim of reducing progressivity in the income tax to reduce its adverse impact on work effort and initiative, tax compliance, and resource allocation. Extension of the sales tax or the introduction of a value-added tax is under consideration. In Norway progression of personal income taxes at the lower income levels and heavier taxation of higher incomes is being considered, as well as an enlarged share of indirect taxes. And in Sweden, where marginal income tax rates are among the highest in industrial countries, the adverse impact on work incentives, in particular, induced the authorities to prepare a reform of the personal income tax system for implementation in 1985; under the reform, the marginal rates would be reduced substantially and the revenue loss met, inter alia, by a reduction in the indexation of tax brackets and a ceiling on interest deductibility. Finally, several countries have in recent years implemented a series of reductions of social security contributions to lessen the cost of labor.

4

Obstacles to Fiscal Improvement

Apart from the external shocks discussed in the preceding section, obstacles to fiscal improvement encountered by most of the smaller industrial countries since the mid-1970s are diverse and include elements of both an economic and political nature. This chapter deals with those issues that relate to the working of automatic stabilizers in recessionary conditions, growing rigidities in fiscal systems that restricted the scope for fiscal policy action, and the ineffectiveness of multiyear budgeting, combined with a potential upward pressure on public spending generated by certain forecasting practices. Moreover, although political considerations usually pose complicated and controversial problems, an applied study of fiscal policy would suffer seriously from a total omission of this important issue. Therefore, on the basis of experience over this period, certain aspects of fiscal politics are considered.

RECESSION AND THE WORKING OF
AUTOMATIC FISCAL STABILIZERS

The protracted recessionary conditions strained government finances through both sides of the budget. Sluggish economic growth slowed down the growth of revenue, and on the expenditure side social security schemes in particular triggered increased spending. Experience indicates that automatic stabilizers steadily weakened fiscal positions over the period and constituted an especially strong obstacle to fiscal improvement in the wake of the second oil crisis when governments endeavored to maintain a tight fiscal stance.

On the revenue side the practice of reducing personal income taxes was already common in a few countries at the beginning of the period. To counteract fiscal drag caused by accelerating inflation, adjustments of tax brackets and standard deductions to price indexes were widely used. While these practices had usually been initiated on an ad hoc basis, a growing tendency arose to adopt indexation mechanisms that automatically adjusted rates and deductions for inflation. Also, a growing number of countries reduced real rates in order to stimulate private sector demand and to lower the tax burden, especially on low- and middle-income groups. In countries where government interference in income formation was customary, income tax reductions were frequently determined in the context of incomes policy. Although a number of countries granted tax relief of various kinds to the enterprise sector to stimulate investment and activity, the personal income tax reductions were generally most instrumental in affecting automatic stabilizers on the revenue side, because they eroded the impact of the progressive rate structure. It should be noted, however, that this was not a uniform experience in all countries in the group. In Belgium, for example, the tax system remained highly elastic with respect to GDP, because for most of the period the progressive income taxes were only partially adjusted for the impact of inflation. Also, in New Zealand, the highly progressive personal income tax rates continued to produce sharply increased revenue yields in the inflationary conditions, despite a series of tax reductions.

An outstanding feature of fiscal developments over the period was an explosive growth of social security expenditure. In the present context, it is significant that underlying this development are various schemes that provide for automatic compensations when specified criteria are met, including certain age limits, employment status, degree of disability, and, in some cases, family size and income level. In most countries in the group these criteria underwent a series of changes over the period that normally implied improvement in benefits—both increases in real benefits and extension of their coverage; it became a widespread practice to incorporate indexation mechanisms in the various schemes. A number of countries, including Belgium, Denmark, Ireland, Luxembourg, and Sweden, introduced early retirement schemes, usually in connection with employment policies, with the aim of withdrawing wage earners from the labor force. The impact of these measures was felt with growing force in budgets as was the impact of increasingly generous benefits of other types, including relaxed qualification criteria for unemployment and disability compensations.

The budgetary burden of the various social security schemes was aggravated by demographic factors, which over the period broadened the basis on which automatic stabilizers work. The most important of such factors is the aging structure of the population whose impact on pensions and health care costs was especially strong in Belgium, Finland, the Netherlands, and Sweden. The rising ratio of pension receivers to members of the work force who contribute entailed growing budgetary transfers to pension funds. Increased female participation rates enlarged the size of the labor force and implied higher unemployment compensation costs, most notably in Denmark and New Zealand. A similar impact emanated from migratory flows of the labor force from abroad and from agriculture in Ireland and Spain.

NARROWED SCOPE FOR FISCAL POLICY ACTION

A fairly widespread development in these countries over the past decade is a growing tendency to determine expenditure by specific legislation rather than in the annual budget, thus providing for present and future expenditure commitments. The budgetary burden of such commitments is frequently aggravated by the practice of linking the relevant expenditure categories to a price index. As noted in the preceding section, various social security schemes are typical of such commitments, but other expenditure categories are also based on specific legislation or contracts with similar long-term implications. While legislation and contracts can be amended, such action is subject to cumbersome parliamentary processes or lengthy renegotiations that impart an element of inflexibility to fiscal policy. Rigidities in fiscal systems have increasingly restricted the scope for implementing needed fiscal adjustment in several countries in the group.

Persistent fiscal deficits in most of the smaller industrial countries have led to a mounting debt-servicing burden. For example, by the end of the period five countries in the group had to devote 8½ percent to 13 percent of total expenditure to interest payments on the government debt. The debt-servicing burden of several countries in the group could well increase sharply over the next several years, thus absorbing an increasing proportion of budgetary resources. For some countries in the group, this likely development is the major cause of the growing inflexibility being built into future fiscal policy.

A precise measure of rigidities in fiscal systems is not available for most countries in the group, but a look at the systems in three of the countries may throw some light on the issue, even if the data are not comparable across countries. In Denmark, major expenditure categories, notably transfers to persons and to local governments, are based on law; at the central level, such categories accounted for approximately 50 percent of total government expenditure at the beginning of the period.[1] In Iceland, it has been estimated that about 70 percent of total expenditure is "'uncontrollable,' in that this portion of central government expenditure cannot be affected except by amending laws or contracts."[2] And in Sweden an estimated 80 percent of central government spending is determined automatically, owing to indexation and previous spending commitments, and about 50 percent of expenditure is automatically indexed.[3] As indicated, the percentages quoted above refer to different years within the period and have most likely risen since the calculations were made.

As already noted, a widely used device to cushion the adverse impact of external impulses and the recessionary conditions on economic activity and living standards was to reduce income taxes. As fiscal positions deteriorated, an increasing number of countries sought to compensate for the revenue loss by raising indirect taxes, such as value-added or sales taxes, excise duties, and energy taxes. However, this policy soon encountered difficulties, as increases in indirect taxes were reflected in the price level and further price increases tended to be generated through indexation mechanisms or indirectly through higher wage claims. In several countries, governments thus found themselves severely restricted by the inflationary implications of their efforts to improve the fiscal positions by raising indirect taxes.

ROLE OF MEDIUM-TERM PLANNING
AND BUDGETARY FORECASTING

Most countries in the group have a tradition of multiyear planning or budgeting. The forms and procedures differ considerably from one country to another with respect to coverage, relation between the plans and annual budgeting, and degree of sophistication in forecasting techniques. Only two countries, Austria and Iceland, have relied entirely on annual budgeting. The arrangements and procedures in individual countries are further considered in Part II.

---

[1] Denmark, Ministry of Economic Affairs and the Budget, *The Danish Budgetary System* (Copenhagen, 1972), p. 5.

[2] Gísli Blöndal, "Balancing the Budget: Budgeting Practices and Fiscal Policy Issues in Iceland," *Public Budgeting and Finance*, Vol. 3 (Summer 1983), p. 58.

[3] Björn Eriksson, "Sweden's Budget System in a Changing World," *Public Budgeting and Finance*, Vol. 3 (Autumn 1983), p. 70.

Multiyear budgeting serves to enhance rational choice by viewing the implications of past and present decisions in a longer-term perspective. In principle, the emphasis is on improving resource allocation and on ensuring a sustainable long-term balance between expenditure and the availability of financial resources. With rising future expenditure commitments and a growing need for efficient financial management, the case for medium-term budgeting might have been expected to strengthen. However, in view of publicly announced commitments to curb expenditure growth and to contain or reduce fiscal deficits, it is surprising to find that multiyear budgeting was so ineffective in pursuing these official policy objectives.

It is inherently difficult to appraise the actual policy relevance of long-term budgeting and other forecasting techniques, because political decision making in budgetary matters rarely emerges in a tangible form. However, it is important to note that multiyear budgets in these countries do not constitute future commitments on the part of governments; rather, they are viewed as an aid to fiscal decision making. The noncommittal nature of multiyear budgeting is generally intended to preserve flexibility in fiscal policy and to prevent undue future growth in expenditure. During the period under review, it would appear, however, that lack of commitment presented in a systematic and legal form contributed to the failure of this approach to act as a brake on political pressures for increased spending and weakened governments' resolve to observe self-imposed spending limits.

The limited effectiveness of medium-term budgeting may also be explained by the disturbing impact of external developments on the small and open economies, which tended to grossly upset basic assumptions of medium-term forecasts and resulted in a loss of confidence in such exercises. Toward the end of the period, countries such as Norway and the Netherlands, both of which have a long history of sophisticated budgeting techniques, moved away from the longer-term approach. Norway ceased to prepare the traditional medium-term programs, while the Netherlands abandoned the structural approach to fiscal policy as growing imbalances in the economy obscured the distinction between cyclical and structural factors and external uncertainties complicated the projection of medium-term trends in the economy. In Denmark long-term planning and public discussion did not prevent an explosive growth of public expenditure and a sharp deterioration in the fiscal position.

Tendencies to make unrealistic assumptions about the growth potential of the economy are known to have led to the setting of overambitious fiscal policy goals, with adverse implications for the budgetary position. Such tendencies were pronounced in Dutch budgetary forecasting, notably in the latter half of the period. Ireland had a similar experience in the 1978 national economic planning exercise that was subsequently abandoned because of the disturbing effects of the second oil crisis. In the Netherlands, the impact on expenditure growth was strengthened as, contrary to intentions, multiyear expenditure estimates were in fact widely regarded as minimum commitments on the part of the Government. Overoptimistic assumptions in medium-term budgeting thus introduced upward pressure on government spending; and although the experiences of only two countries in the group are quoted here, the phenomenon is probably more widespread.

It may be noted that, somewhat ironically, the two countries in the group—Austria and Iceland—that did not resort to multiyear budgeting over the period in question appear to have fared relatively well in overall fiscal performance. Thus, Austria managed to contain expenditure growth and increases in the fiscal deficit below the average for all the countries in the group; and Iceland experienced one of the smallest relative increases in expenditure over the period.

FISCAL POLITICS

A major problem in public finance derives from the interdependence of the general aims of fiscal policy. Improvement of resource allocation to strengthen the basis for long-term growth of the economy, change in the distribution of income, and promotion of economic stability are objectives ordinarily sought implicitly or explicitly in each year's budget, but measures designed to obtain one objective are liable to affect one or more of the others. As the effects tend to be mutually adverse, an efficient fiscal policy would have to take this interdependence into account. This in turn implies a requirement on the part of governments to establish a clear order of priorities among the different objectives and to follow a reasonably steady and resolute course of policy implementation.

The failure of policymakers to set priorities within a context of interdependent but conflicting objectives contributed to inconsistent policy actions over the period, as ample evidence has proven. Conflict of objectives can arise not only between the general aims of fiscal policy but also within the same broad objective. In this period of pronounced economic imbalances, stabilization measures in different areas provide the clearest evidence of such inconsistencies. As already noted, major stabilization measures were designed to stimulate employment and economic activity, combat inflation, and improve the current external position. While the latter two objectives would generally be sought through a tightening of the fiscal stance, the first would be served by expansionary measures. So far, this analysis has shown that on several occasions during the period all these measures tended to be introduced at the same time or in rapid succession, without reference to a clear ordering of priorities. The impact of restrictive measures to counteract rising prices and widening deficits on the external current account was frequently reduced or more than outweighed by measures to promote employment, economic growth, and social welfare. Attempts to solve this dilemma by selective stimulative measures that would not impart undue pressure on prices and the external current account position appear not to have been very successful.

The frequent changes in the stance of fiscal policy in several countries over the period are not necessarily a sign of inconsistency, as they may in part reflect a response to changes in underlying economic conditions. However, the evidence strongly suggests that such changes also resulted from political considerations that took limited notice of economic circumstances or attempted to achieve short-term gains that often were at the expense of the longer-term performance of the economy.

The problem of inconsistent policies may in part be explained by the political structure of the countries. The smaller industrial countries all have a system of political democracy, often characterized by a number of relatively small political parties and, of necessity, coalition governments. In some of the countries, minority governments are not uncommon. As a result, the formation of strong governments with consistent and clearly defined objectives is rare and changes of government tend to be frequent. The political environment thus is not generally conducive to the formulation of consistent long-term policies, and the frequent changes of government, in particular, are liable to weaken effective resistance to pressures for increased public spending. Priorities among governments may differ, and new governments will tend to initiate new expenditures without making offsetting reductions in existing areas; or, different and changing political ideologies can frustrate any planned long-term expenditure goals. A case in point is

Australia where the government in office during 1972–75 pursued the policy of increasing the public sector's absorption of resources, so as to change the social fabric over a short period of time. The government that took office at the end of 1975, by contrast, regarded the sharply enlarged role and relative size of the public sector as a major cause of depressed private sector activity and, for most of the remaining years of the period, managed to reduce the ratio of government expenditure to GDP.

The significance of the political element in the formulation of fiscal policy in these countries is thus fairly obvious. It is also clear that imperfections in the political system, from an economic viewpoint, have contributed to difficulties in achieving desired fiscal adjustments. The precise manner in which political decision making influences the formulation of fiscal and economic policy is beyond the scope of this study. However, the above observations would appear to lend support to the assertion advanced in theories of political behavior that a major objective of government is self-preservation. In the present context, it would appear plausible that "governments may be more interested in stabilizing votes in the short run than the economy in a somewhat longer perspective."[4]

---

[4] Assar Lindbeck, "Stabilization Policy in Open Economies with Endogenous Politicians," *The American Economic Review*, Vol. 66 (May 1976), p. 17.

5

Implications of Past Fiscal Developments and Policies

In this chapter, a desirable method of analysis would have been to link movements in the fiscal data presented in Chapter 2 to indicators of economic performance; however, such an approach was not possible for a number of reasons. First, the period for which comparable data were available was too short to permit meaningful conclusions to be drawn. Second, the available statistics were not detailed enough to enable identification of expenditures that match the separate schemes dealt with below, such as unemployment compensations, pensions, employment support, and incomes policy-oriented schemes. Third, the issue of causation referred to below would in any case have rendered such an analysis inconclusive. The following analysis is, therefore, based largely on separate studies as quoted, while reference is made to the statistical data in particular contexts.

ENLARGED PUBLIC SECTOR

The growing size of the public sector, combined with poor economic performance over the past several years, has lent support to the opinion that an inverse relationship exists between the two. The sharp increase in public expenditure relative to GDP and a concomitant increase in tax burdens and fiscal deficits are seen as a major cause of the difficulties many countries are facing in terms of sluggish economic growth, high rates of unemployment, and rapid price increases. Implicit in this hypothesis is the view that an effective way to cure the economic malaise is to reduce the relative size of the public sector and government interference in the market mechanism. While public sector size is commonly interpreted as total public expenditure in relation to GDP, the argument against large government somewhat confusingly concentrates more on the financing of expenditure by stressing the adverse impact of heavy tax burdens and deficit financing on economic performance. A similar impact is seen as emanating from separate expenditure schemes rather than from expenditure at the aggregate level. Although these items are obviously closely interdependent, it is useful to consider them separately, beginning with aggregate expenditure.

The contention that large and growing government adversely affects economic performance appears to rest on assumptions that reflect a mixture of economic criteria and ideological persuasion. Among the former is the doctrine that as the public sector grows beyond some unspecified limit, resources are diverted from more productive use in the private sector, and economic growth suffers. Moreover, the theory that increased expenditure in conditions of less than full capacity utilization has a beneficial impact on growth, in line with traditional Keynesian multiplier analysis, has come under growing critical scrutiny, because it disregards the financial stringencies of taxation and deficit financing. Also, public sector growth is allegedly associated with growing government interference in the market mechanism, which distorts optimum resource allocation, with adverse repercussions on the long-term growth performance of the economy. Regarding price performance, the size and rate of growth of the public sector may, depending on the degree of capacity utilization, affect the rate of inflation through the traditional Keynesian aggregate demand influences. A causal relationship between public sector size and unemployment may be expected to be largely indirect, however, through the impact of slower economic growth. Unemployment is, indeed, more likely to expand the public sector in terms of increased outlays both to compensate the unemployed and to stimulate employment through discretionary action.

The argument against large government has been challenged on the ground that it rests on assumptions that indirectly imply certain ideological and political value judgments rather than economic logic. It is argued that critics of large government assume the efficacy of the invisible hand and the superiority of freely functioning markets. According to the proponents of large government, the case for the alleged harmful consequences of large government, such as lower productivity than in the private sector, inherent inefficiency, and diminished freedom, rests on such doctrines, rather than on verifiable evidence. The central role attached to the market mechanism is further challenged by sympathizers of large government on the ground that such a view largely disregards egalitarian values, which, of course, removes the issue from the realm of economic analysis.[1]

Whatever the attitude toward the size of the public sector, it is generally recognized that public expenditure generates economic and social benefits. The question is whether there is a point beyond which expenditure growth begins to exert a harmful impact on economic performance. Considering the prominence of this issue in public debate in recent years, it is surprising that the subject has been given only limited coverage in the literature. However, a recent Organization for Economic Cooperation and Development (OECD) study addressed this issue and reviewed available empirical evidence on the economic consequences of the size and growth of public sector activity. It was found that previous research had not succeeded in establishing strong relationships between economic performance indicators and public sector size and growth at the aggregate level. The study reaches the unsurprising conclusion that "it is extremely difficult, if not inherently impossible, to arrive at an objective assessment of the economic consequences of the broad range of public sector activities. Not only do the outcomes of many activities defy quantification, but there are additional problems associated with any attempt to aggregate across programmes."[2]

Analyzing the economic consequences of the size and growth of the public sector immediately focuses attention on the composition of expenditure, since it is generally accepted that separate expenditure categories affect the economy differently. But the usefulness of analyzing expenditure at the aggregate level then becomes questionable, not least if the emphasis is on comparison over time or across countries. If the composition of expenditure has changed sharply over time or if it is substantially different in individual countries, the economic impact may be markedly different, even though the relative size of the public sector remained unchanged over time. The issue of causation raises an additional problem, as factors outside the realm of public finance can influence economic performance, and their impact is not separable from that of fiscal factors. These are serious limitations from an analytical point of view, and underscore the need for caution when the implica-

---

[1] For a thorough examination of these issues, see David Heald, *Public Expenditure: Its Defence and Reform*, Oxford: Martin Robertson, 1983.

[2] Peter Saunders and Friedrich Klau, "The Role of the Public Sector: Causes and Consequences of the Growth of Government," *OECD Economic Studies* (Paris), No. 4 (Spring 1985), p. 21.

tions of expenditure are being interpreted at the aggregate level, or when the relationship between the size and growth of the public sector and economic performance is being examined. The analytical ground is firmer with respect to separate taxes and expenditure schemes, and these aspects, together with fiscal deficits, are considered in the remainder of this chapter.

INCREASED TAX BURDENS

Generally, the ratio of total revenue and grants to GDP rose during the period, although the rate of expansion differed markedly among individual countries in the group, as noted in Chapter 2. While few would support the argument that tax burdens had not risen enough, expenditure growth was in most cases substantially faster. This disparity in growth rates therefore entailed large and, in most cases, widening fiscal deficits, with adverse economic implications as considered in the following section.

Most countries in the group have a progressive tax structure and an otherwise responsive tax system, although these features differ from one country to another. Despite the prolonged recession, high rates of inflation were widely experienced, so that even in the absence of discretionary revenue-raising measures, rising nominal incomes and turnover might have been expected to produce revenue yields that were more in line with expenditure growth. Also, three energy-rich countries in the group—Australia, the Netherlands, and Norway—benefited from an upsurge in revenue from oil and natural gas. However, policy objectives to cushion the adverse impact of external impulses on the economy and to preserve living standards resulted in a series of tax reductions over the period, which contributed significantly to the slowdown of revenue growth. The ways in which tax cuts were intended to counteract the recessionary impulses were manifold and included reduction of disincentive effects of high marginal income tax rates; containment of tax burdens; redistribution of income in favor of lower income groups; stimulation of private sector demand, investment, and employment; and moderation of wage settlements.

The general economic impact of high tax burdens is not easily determined and, as is the case with expenditure at the aggregate level, much depends on the composition of the various types of taxes and other revenue sources. Attempts have been made to establish specific limits beyond which the tax burden begins to exert an adverse impact on the economy. The best known is probably Clark's celebrated thesis, first published in 1945, that the safe limit of taxation is 25 percent of net national income, and as soon as total taxation exceeds that limit inflation pressures are generated.[3] Although this proposition has been refuted by the empirical evidence, it is easily conceded that there are some limits beyond which taxation at the aggregate level becomes excessive. However, due to the complexity of this issue, including its interdependence with the relative size and composition of expenditure, the implications of high taxation are more easily dealt with in terms of individual taxes.

The tax reductions mentioned above related largely, though not exclusively, to direct taxation, notably personal and corporate income taxes and social security contributions. However, in certain countries the progressiveness of personal income tax rates and the self-financing nature of the social security system caused a substantial increase in these two types of tax, which in many countries are the principal revenue sources at the central level. The increased burden of these particular taxes had detrimental economic implications; examples from selected countries are provided below.

In Belgium, the progressive income tax rates were for most of the period only partially adjusted for inflation. As a result, the tax burden rose markedly over the period, raising concerns about potential encouragement to the underground economy and tax evasion. In New Zealand, the significance of the personal income tax is a striking feature of the tax system; over the period it accounted for the entire relative increase in revenue—7 percentage points of GDP. It is a commonly held view that the steep progressivity of the personal income tax rates has adversely affected work effort and initiative, encouraged tax avoidance and evasion, and contributed to wage-push pressures and distortions in resource allocation. In Norway, income tax progression is quite steep, with marginal rates ranging between 30 percent and 70 percent; and about one third of taxpayers face a marginal tax of 50 percent or more. The adverse impact on work effort, savings, and income distribution is considered to be especially marked. In Sweden, despite a series of reductions, the personal income tax rates are still among the highest in industrial countries, with the highest marginal rate reaching 85 percent.

---

[3]Colin Clark, "Public Finance and Changes in the Value of Money," *Economic Journal*, Vol. 55 (December 1945), pp. 371–89. For a restatement of this proposition see his article, "The Scope for, and Limits of, Taxation" in *The State of Taxation*, by A.R. Prest, and others (London: Institute of Economic Affairs, 1977), pp. 19–34.

Not least among the various problems this high rate has occasioned is the detrimental impact on the work effort.[4]

Turning to social security contributions, the importance of this tax is especially marked in the Netherlands where it is equivalent to 19 percent of GDP and is the most important single revenue source of the central government. Employers bear about one half of this tax, which has grown over the period in relation to both total revenue and GDP and has seriously aggravated the cost position of a depressed enterprise sector. In Spain, social security contributions are by far the largest revenue source, accounting for almost one half of total central government revenue and grants. About 80 percent of this tax, which has grown sharply along with a concomitant increase in wage costs, is borne by employers. By 1980 these contributions were about 25 percent of the total wage bill, having risen from 16 percent in 1973. As a result, factor costs are distorted against labor, which is especially detrimental in a country like Spain that faces a serious unemployment problem. In Sweden, revenue developments over the period were characterized by a rapid increase in social security contributions. These have been borne increasingly by employers and amounted in recent years to some 35 percent of the total payroll, compared with 14 percent in 1970. This burden has intensified the strains on private sector activity.

Finally, although the revenue loss resulting from cuts in direct taxes was partially offset in some countries by increases in indirect taxes, most countries encountered difficulty in taking this course of action. For one thing, the shift toward indirect taxation was complicated by the significance of specific rather than ad valorem taxes and duties. An even greater obstacle was the concern over the impact on costs and prices. Despite cuts in direct taxes and widening fiscal deficits, the authorities were thus generally reluctant to raise indirect taxes because of the inflationary implications of such a move.

FISCAL DEFICITS AND DEBT ACCUMULATION

The implications of sustained fiscal deficits for economic performance have received a great deal of attention and aroused controversy

---

[4]The relationship between personal income tax structures and economic growth in six major industrial countries is analyzed in Vito Tanzi, *The Individual Income Tax and Economic Growth: An International Comparison* (Baltimore: The Johns Hopkins Press, 1969). The study concludes that there is a significant negative relationship; that is, the growth rates are lower for countries that rely most heavily on the individual income tax as a source of revenue.

over the past several years. The subject is well known and will not be reviewed here at any length. However, a brief overview of the main issues will serve as a useful background against which to view experiences in individual countries in the group.

The most obvious implication of large and sustained fiscal deficits is the associated debt accumulation and the resulting claims on present and future budgetary resources. As was seen in Chapter 2, the debt burden rose in most of the smaller industrial countries over the period and, in certain instances, quite substantially. For some countries in the group, a continuation of this trend is foreseen over the next several years unless drastic counteractive measures are introduced. This is true, in particular, where the fiscal deficit has assumed a structural character and would persist even if cyclical conditions returned to normal. Those countries that experienced the largest debt accumulations over the period, such as Ireland, Belgium, Denmark, New Zealand, and Sweden, will thus be facing difficult fiscal adjustment problems over the next several years. Sustained deficits have pre-empted a growing proportion of budgetary resources, imposed burdens on future generations, and, from the point of view of economic management, implied growing inflexibility in fiscal systems and restrictions on the scope for pursuing fiscal policy in an efficient manner. Although in certain instances, like Iceland, Ireland, and New Zealand, the debt-servicing burden was somewhat lessened as inflation eroded the stock of outstanding debt, this development is likely to have had undesirable consequences from the point of view of equity.

Another implication of fiscal deficits is their effect on the price level and balance of payments. Fiscal deficits may, depending on the method of financing, add to inflationary pressures via direct cost and demand impact and through the monetary repercussions, thus exerting pressure on the current account of the balance of payments. Such influences characterized fiscal developments in most countries in the group, and the problems tended to intensify as the period progressed, not only because large deficits persisted and in several cases widened, but also because the deficit tended increasingly to be financed by external borrowing or by domestic monetary sources. Although most countries in the group had to struggle with this problem, it was a particular cause for concern in a country like Australia, where inflation was already the major economic problem. It was aggravated by the monetary implications of a persistent large public sector deficit and the inflationary expectations it generated. The liquidity impact of the deficits has also severely complicated the task of monetary management in a number of countries, including Finland, Iceland, Ireland, New Zealand, Norway, Spain, and Sweden. In Spain the problem assumed an added significance, as monetary policy is the major instrument of short-term demand management.

While fiscal deficits added to inflationary pressures in a number of countries, inflation in turn affected the budgetary outcome in different ways; it may be of interest to note the experiences of three countries in the group for which information on the subject is available. In Belgium in the mid-1970s, inflation itself rendered expenditure restraint difficult, not only because of indexation of significant expenditure components, but also because the responsive tax system made it easier to finance new expenditures. In Denmark expenditure was more affected by inflation than revenue. Because of the indexation of expenditure components, the importance of specific excise and other taxes, and the indexation of tax scales and deductions, the fiscal position thus tended to deteriorate as a result of inflation. In Iceland, by contrast, inflation automatically influenced revenue more than expenditure in the early part of the period, owing to a responsive tax system that relied on ad valorem indirect taxes. However, a proliferation of indexation mechanisms has since eroded this stabilizing feature of the fiscal system.

It is relevant here to consider the effectiveness of a deficit-creating fiscal stimulus, which over the period was a typical policy response to increasing slack in economic activity. The impact of such measures is reduced through counteracting leakages into imports or increases in private savings. In the former case, much of the fiscal stimulus to the domestic economy will be neutralized, since part of the added demand will be directed at imports. It has been estimated that for a typical European country, taking such action in isolation results in about 40 percent of the potential output-generating effect being absorbed by imports.[5] The smaller industrial countries are characterized by relatively large external sectors, and because of the low value of the domestic multipliers, fiscal stimulus is presumably still more restricted than in a typical European case. Private savings might increase as a result of a fiscal stimulus, leading to or increasing deficits, if private households equate government spending with their own consumption. Then private consumption would be cut accordingly and savings increased.

---

[5] Robert W.R. Price and Jean-Claude Chouraqui, "Public Sector Deficits: Problems and Policy Implications," OECD *Occasional Studies* (Paris) (June 1983), p. 27.

Considerations of future needs for increased taxation necessitated by sustained fiscal deficits might also induce increased personal household savings. It must be said, however, that these propositions do not rest on very firm foundations, and the impact of fiscal stimulus on private savings is fairly indeterminate.

The impact of fiscal deficits on economic activity is commonly analyzed in terms of crowding-out effects, of which there are two kinds—real and financial.[6] Real crowding out may occur when government action pre-empts real resources, such as manpower and materials, but this need not necessarily be associated with deficit financing. Financial crowding out is widely believed to be a major cause for limited effectiveness of fiscal policy in stimulating economic activity. The argument relies essentially on the perceived effect of noninflationary deficit financing on interest rates and the curtailing repercussions on private sector investment. Although fiscal stimulus may under certain conditions lead to higher overall domestic demand, private borrowers may nonetheless be "crowded out" of the capital market through higher costs of borrowing. Under conditions of high capital mobility and floating exchange rates, the higher rate of return to investors is also likely to have an adverse impact on the international competitiveness of the economy, as capital inflows would tend to have an appreciatory impact on the exchange rate. As a consequence, activity in the export- and import-competing sectors would contract. If increased government spending were financed by money creation, it has been argued that this would lead to an upward revision of inflationary expectations, as households attempted to maintain their real money balances. This would result in an upward pressure on interest rates, with a detrimental impact on private sector investment.

Several other mechanisms exist through which crowding out might be expected to take place, in addition to those described above. The results these mechanisms might produce depend in large measure on the specifications assumed with regard to private financial savings behavior and the institutional setup and functioning of financial markets.[7] There is also considerable uncertainty about the relative strength of financial crowding-out effects, on the one hand, and the

---

[6]The counteracting impact of leakages into imports and increases in private savings discussed above is sometimes defined as a crowding-out effect. See Price and Chouraqui, pp. 27–28.

[7]For a further discussion of this issue, for example, see Price and Chouraqui, pp. 28–31.

stimulating effects of increased public spending, on the other. The significance of institutional factors and economic characteristics such as external sector size suggests a need for caution in making generalizations in this regard. Examining individual countries would probably be a more rewarding approach. However, since available evidence does not permit such an ambitious undertaking here, this study will limit itself to a brief discussion of some major aspects of crowding out, based on individual country experience.

Financial markets in the smaller industrial countries are in different stages of development and are subject to different exposure to international capital markets. Those differences appear to have significant implications for crowding-out mechanisms. In countries such as Australia, Belgium, the Netherlands, and Sweden, where the capital markets are highly developed, some financial crowding out has resulted from the application of the mechanisms described above. In Belgium and the Netherlands, both of whose public sector borrowing requirements have been growing, nonmonetary financing of the deficit by the sale of bonds has put upward pressure on long-term interest rates and has had an adverse impact on business investment. In Sweden a sharp increase in the government borrowing requirement exerted upward pressure on interest rates, and industrial investment suffered. The authorities endeavored to avoid the crowding out of industry from the capital market by limiting government borrowing outside the banks, but this led to growing monetary financing of the fiscal deficit, as well as excessive monetary expansion.

The crowding-out effect of the mechanisms is not so clear-cut where domestic market forces are less effective in determining interest rates. In Austria and Denmark, for example, the impact of fiscal deficits on interest rates is limited, as the latter are determined by external rather than domestic considerations. Exchange rate considerations in Austria have helped keep the deficits from crowding out private investment, although the depressed state of economic activity and limited private sector demand for credit may have also contributed. In Denmark monetary policy was preoccupied with preserving the foreign reserve position, which implied high interest rates to induce capital inflows needed to adequately finance the external deficit. Although crowding-out effects may have been felt, their connection with the fiscal deficit was not immediately obvious. In other countries, such as Norway and Spain, funds are acquired by the public sector to a certain extent through captive arrangements; and in others, interest rates are administered by the authorities and do not reflect market forces. This practice is known to have resulted in the existence of negative real interest rates over an extended period.

EMPLOYMENT POLICIES

Government policies supporting employment have assumed an enhanced role in the postwar period, and fiscal measures have been an important ingredient in the overall strategy. While previously, policies of unemployment insurance, employment exchange, and public relief work were pursued in many countries, the 1960s witnessed a spread of strategies that involved training and retraining and similar devices to increase labor mobility. In the 1970s and early 1980s, with rising unemployment and growing structural adjustment problems, the emphasis shifted to job maintenance and job creation in private industry, and a number of countries adopted the policy of relieving unemployment through increased public sector absorption of labor. At the same time, employment policies became more permanent and there was a growing tendency to introduce selective employment-supporting measures to favor certain kinds of industry and labor or to maintain regional balance.[8] Government support to industry has in many countries been closely connected with employment policies.

Since the early 1970s most of the smaller industrial countries have pursued active employment policies of a protective or preventive nature, with an emphasis on protecting the workers involved. The extent of employment support by the government has varied, however, with Australia perhaps placing most emphasis on the role of market forces and thereby minimizing direct government involvement. The countries have had mixed results on this front. Whereas a few managed to prevent the rate of unemployment from exceeding 4 percent of the total labor force for the major part of the period covered (Austria, Iceland, Luxembourg, New Zealand, Norway, and Sweden), other countries suffered unemployment rates in excess of 8 percent over an extended period (Denmark, Ireland, and Spain). As the employment situation at any given time is determined by the general economic environment, which in turn is influenced by a multiplicity of external and internal factors, it is inherently difficult to assess the effectiveness of

---

[8]For a historical overview of employment policy strategies, see Robert B. McKersie and Werner Sengenberger, *Job Losses in Major Industries: Manpower Strategy Responses*, Chapt. IV (Paris: Organization for Economic Cooperation and Development, 1983).

fiscal measures in this regard. However, the following examples provide an illustration of some of the major government schemes for sustaining employment since the early 1970s; subsequently, certain implications of these policies for economic performance will be considered.

Increased public sector employment. Several countries pursued a policy of increasing public sector employment to ameliorate the unemployment problem, for example, Belgium, Spain, Denmark, and Sweden; the last two emphasized local government employment in this regard with the support of special grants from the central budget. Public sector absorption of labor was especially pronounced in Sweden over this period: the share of the government services sector in total employment rose from 20½ percent to 29 percent between 1970 and 1978, compared with a rise from 12 percent to 14½ percent on the average in industrial countries for which data are available.[9] It is also relevant that Austria has traditionally followed a policy of having the nationalized industries absorb labor in times of depression.

Direct budgetary outlays to create or sustain employment. This is probably the most common employment-supporting device adopted by this group of countries. Direct budgetary outlays for this purpose took various forms, most frequently, capital expenditure for public works projects, relief works or building programs, or specific employment-creating schemes (Ireland, New Zealand, Sweden). Some countries (Australia, Finland, the Netherlands) emphasized employment at the regional level by increasing advances for local or state government investment.

Retraining. Central government grants for training and retraining in the local government and private sectors served the objective of facilitating labor mobility in an environment of structural change in the derived demand for labor. In some instances, special emphasis was put on training disabled persons and the long-term unemployed. Although many countries in the group adopted this approach at different times within the period covered, it was most pronounced in Denmark, Finland, the Netherlands, Norway, and Sweden.

Compensating for shorter working hours. Belgium set up a program to support firms that had agreed to cut working hours in the form of credit to finance additional hiring; and Luxembourg granted subsidies to firms to partially compensate employees that had been put on short-term work. The purpose of these schemes was essentially to avoid the

---

[9] Organization for Economic Cooperation and Development, *Economic Surveys: Sweden* (April 1980), p. 42.

cost of dismissal and rehiring and to enable employers to keep experienced workers, while at the same time reducing the earnings loss of employees during short-time work.

General incentives for job creation. Such incentives took various forms and affected both sides of the budget. Several measures of this kind that had the broader objectives of general economic stimulus have already been discussed in previous sections; the stimulating objective of the examples mentioned here was more confined to employment. Incentives for capital expenditures that would sustain employment in particular were granted in Ireland. In Luxembourg, wage costs were subsidized (20 percent of these costs) to mitigate the effect of structural change on the employment situation, especially in the declining steel industry. In Austria interest costs were subsidized; and in Denmark interest costs on loans for residential housing were reduced. Also in Austria, tax credits were granted for certain types of employment-creating investments, and in Finland and Spain, employers' social security contribution rates were reduced as a means of reducing factor cost distortions against labor. Norway sought to sustain employment in separate parts of the country by differentiating employers' social security contributions by region.

Conditional employment-supporting measures. Schemes that required a minimum level of employment to be maintained by firms receiving grants were practiced in the Netherlands, Norway, and Sweden. In the Netherlands, grants were made available to the clothing industry provided that employment was kept at a specified minimum level. In Norway, a special stock financing scheme was operated whereby firms received subsidies to cover a certain proportion of the increase in stocks on condition employment was not reduced. And in Sweden, a temporary stock support scheme whereby enterprises received grants amounting to 20 percent of the volume increase in their inventories was conditional upon the maintenance of employment levels by the enterprises over the grant period. An additional measure under this category practiced in Luxembourg to encourage labor mobility was the payment of a bonus for workers who voluntarily transferred to new industries.

Grants to encourage recruitment of special kinds of labor. In order to directly alleviate the unemployment problem, Finland, Ireland, and the Netherlands paid special grants to employers who hired from the unemployment register. The Netherlands also granted subsidies to enterprises that employed teenagers.

Retirement schemes. The introduction of early retirement schemes or flexible retirement options in countries like Belgium, Denmark, Luxembourg, and Sweden, besides serving a broader social objective, also was presented in an employment policy context that aimed at alleviating unemployment through the removal of older workers from the unemployment register.

Evidence suggests that some of these schemes had a fair amount of success, such as mobility schemes and training programs. The same holds true for certain short-term job creation or preservation schemes, especially when combined with training programs, e.g., the Swedish scheme that covered a quarter of a million people in 1978 and obliged employers to provide training for the subsidized workers.[10] Job creation, along with many other employment-sustaining programs, was originally intended to be temporary to help firms and industries over cyclical downturns in the level of economic activity and thereby minimize the social cost of employment dislocation. As mentioned, these schemes tended to assume a more permanent character, with adverse repercussions on overall long-run economic performance. This experience was fairly general among the smaller industrial countries, although it was most marked in countries that had a combination of high employment policies and large structural change, like Austria, Norway, and Sweden. Policies to absorb labor in the public sector to alleviate unemployment and selective measures to support ailing industries exposed to foreign competition and to preserve regional balance contributed to a slowdown in labor mobility; this potential inefficient allocation of resources tended to retard the adjustment process, which otherwise might have taken fuller advantage of the production potential of the countries concerned. Of course, these adverse long-run repercussions on economic performance have to be weighed against any social benefits these policies may have produced.

SOCIAL SECURITY SCHEMES

In almost all countries in the group, subsidies and other current transfers have been the most dynamic element in public expenditure growth as discussed in Chapter 2. Unfortunately, the basic statistical source used, *Government Finance Statistics* (*GFS*), does not permit a disaggregation of this expenditure category, so the following analysis

---

[10]Organization for Economic Cooperation and Development, *The Challenge of Unemployment* (Paris, 1982), p. 109.

has to rely on less comprehensive data. It is clear, however, that within this category expenditure on social security is the major component and old age and disability pensions have the heaviest weight. Unemployment compensations form another subcategory and although this type of expenditure is a relatively small part of total government spending, it increased rapidly over the period. The generosity of entitlement programs has in some instances reached a level that has caused concern over their potentially adverse repercussions on the economy. A few examples of exceptionally generous schemes are provided here, and the main economic implications of the expansion of social security entitlements are considered, with emphasis on old age pensions and unemployment compensations.

In the Netherlands the general social security system includes a guaranteed minimum income equivalent to US$750 a month. Also, taking account of the hidden unemployment element in this scheme, the estimated proportion to the potentially active population that is not working is as high as 20 percent. In neighboring Belgium, where social benefits, notably unemployment compensation, have become more generous than in most other countries, it is estimated that over 80 percent of households receive support from the system and that one quarter of all households are entirely dependent on it financially. In Sweden, traditionally a country with intensive social insurance, the effect of a supplementary pension scheme, which became fully effective in 1979 after a 20-year phasing-in period, increased the pension to 65 percent of the individual's income over the best five years, with an upper limit amounting to the equivalent of about US$17,500 a year. All new pensioners from 1979 qualify. The generosity of unemployment compensations has also reached unusual proportions in Denmark; benefits amount to 90 percent of earnings up to the equivalent of approximately US$33 a day payable from the first day of unemployment for six days a week.[11]

Social security schemes may exert an impact on the economy in various ways. The most frequently studied are the effects of pension schemes on employment and household savings and of unemployment compensations on work incentives. Studies of the impact of pension schemes on labor supply and retirement decisions are not conclusive. While some maintain that there is an inverse relationship between the

---

[11] United States, Department of Health and Human Services, *Social Security Programs Throughout the World, 1983* (Washington: Government Printing Office, 1984).

two, that is, improved pension schemes reduce labor supply and increase incentives to retire, the impact is considered relatively modest.[12] Others have come to the opposite conclusion. Thus, an OECD cross-country study found little evidence of a systematic relationship between participation rates, on the one hand, and eligibility and transfer ratios, on the other.[13] The same inconclusiveness is attached to the impact of pension schemes on household savings. Whereas earlier studies purported to have found a significant negative relationship between old age pension schemes and private savings, later empirical work failed to consolidate such findings. As the OECD study just quoted concluded, ". . . it would appear that the effects of social security provision on savings remain ambiguous on the basis of both theoretical reasoning and empirical investigation."[14]

It would appear, however, that the empirical evidence is not always easily reconciled with these inconclusive findings. Thus, the aging structure of the population, which is a fairly general characteristic of demographic developments over the period, did not entail a concomitant increase in the participation rate of older people in the labor force as might have been expected. On the contrary, this proportion declined over the period. This decline has been attributed to a general increase in the wealth of older people, some of which has surely been generated by increased real pensions. Another contributing factor is the adoption of early retirement schemes in a number of countries in the group, as already discussed. Such increases in generosity would appear to support the presumption that improved pension schemes reduced the participation rate of older workers in the labor force in the 1970s. However, it is unlikely that during this period of severe slack in economic activity in most of the countries, such a withdrawal adversely affected the performance of the economies, even if it imposed additional strains on government budgets.

Elsewhere in this study references have been made to an adverse economic impact of high unemployment compensations on employment. As the generosity of unemployment benefits increases, the "moral hazards" inherent in income maintenance schemes become greater for employable people. The other side of the coin is that

---

[12]Sheldon Danziger, Robert Haveman, and Robert Plotnick, "How Income Transfer Programs Affect Work, Savings and the Income Distribution: A Critical Review," *Journal of Economic Literature*, Vol. 19 (September 1981), pp. 975–1028.

[13]Saunders and Klau, pp. 141–142.

[14]Saunders and Klau, p. 146.

generous benefits induce increased female participation in the labor force, which, under the adverse economic conditions prevailing for a large part of the period, added to registered unemployment. The Netherlands, Belgium, Denmark, and Sweden have already been mentioned as typical examples of countries with generous social security programs. In all these countries concern over the potentially adverse impact of high unemployment benefits on work incentives and economic growth has been growing. In addition, in New Zealand, unemployment benefits have been a growing incentive to register as unemployed, which has had a strong impact on the female participation rate, accounting for the entire increase in employment between 1976 and 1981. A similar, if less pronounced, increase in the female participation rate took place in Denmark and is considered to have arisen from generous unemployment compensations.

Since social security outlays contributed significantly to the explosive growth of government expenditure in most countries in the group, the impact of large and sometimes widening fiscal deficits on the economies is an important corollary. The economic implications of fiscal deficits were discussed earlier in this chapter, but to conclude this section a few additional reflections on factors that may have driven the generosity of some programs further than intended seem in order.

As discussed in previous chapters, increases in real benefits and extension of their coverage were a major cause of the explosive growth of social security expenditure. While the general relief and redistributional objectives of this policy enjoyed wide support in the countries concerned, it appears that the extent of generosity of particular schemes in some instances went beyond original intentions. One reason lies in overoptimistic assumptions about future growth rates of the economy that tended to be based on projections of trends experienced in the more prosperous 1950s and 1960s when many of the schemes were founded or improved. A second reason may derive from insufficient attention to demographic developments such as the aging structure of the population, larger female participation rates, and changes in migration patterns. A third reason may be that the legal provisions frequently did not entail immediate costs at the time of enactment, so that the financial implications were not fully perceived. However, even when it was subsequently realized that the cost implications of social security schemes could not be reconciled with growth prospects of the economies—that is, financed by economic growth—once entitlement programs were established or their generosity increased, a failure to stabilize, let alone reverse, growth trends was one of the major problems facing fiscal policy.

INCOMES POLICIES

This section deals with the interaction of fiscal and incomes policies in the smaller industrial countries over the period covered. Beginning with a brief overview of the objectives of incomes policy and the main approaches followed, the section goes on to review fiscal incomes policy measures introduced in individual countries and ends by considering the effectiveness of such measures and their wider implications.

Incomes policies generally served the immediate purpose of combating inflation and alleviating the unemployment problem. However, in countries like Denmark and New Zealand these policies were an integral part of strategies to bring about external adjustment; in other countries such as the Netherlands and Norway, redistribution of income in favor of lower income groups was a declared objective pursued within the framework of incomes policy. Persistent inflation and unemployment persuaded authorities in many countries that the imbalances could not be eliminated through demand-management policies alone, and attention was progressively directed to the cost side. Almost all countries in the group adopted some form of incomes policy in this context, although approaches varied widely with respect to their permanency, the extent and formalization of government involvement in the wage bargaining process, and the comprehensiveness of the macroeconomic base on which incomes policies were founded. Thus, in Austria and Norway, incomes policies were based on a broad social contract, or "social partnership", and these countries managed to maintain such policies over an extended period; most other countries, however, owing to insufficient social consensus and unfavorable institutional conditions, had to contend with temporary incomes policies and associated phasing-out problems. Also, formal government involvement was intense in countries like Finland, Iceland, the Netherlands, and Norway; whereas in Belgium, and in Sweden until 1978, for example, formal government involvement was minimal. Austria, Norway, and the Netherlands represent cases where tripartite agreements were well coordinated with macroeconomic policy; this also holds true for Sweden, where an economic model developed jointly by the central federations of labor and management has had a considerable influence on collective bargaining. This link was weaker in most other countries.

Although incomes policies date back to the early post-World War II period, it was not until the 1970s that fiscal incomes policy measures came to play a prominent role. This increased role reflects growing awareness of "tax-push" inflation and explains the widespread use of income tax reductions in endeavors to ensure moderate wage settlements. Otherwise, the form of fiscal and other official measures to influence wage developments varied considerably among individual countries. The most direct intervention consisted of mandatory controls in the form of temporary wage or price freezes, or a combination of the two. In New Zealand, for example, wages and other private incomes were effectively controlled during 1974–77. In 1976 Spain introduced tax reductions to make the continuation of wage controls more acceptable, and from autumn 1978 until the end of 1979, Norway implemented a complete wage and price freeze. Belgium and the Netherlands also imposed temporary wage controls over the period. Other countries have intervened by stipulating maximum wage increases at certain intervals within a fixed period either by legislation or as guidelines, most recently, Denmark and Iceland. However, the strictness with which such policies have been implemented has varied.

As indicated, tax reductions are probably the most widely used fiscal contribution to incomes policy. In order to ensure moderate wage settlements, a large majority of countries in the group implemented a series of reductions in the personal income tax over the period in the form of rate reductions, increases in exemptions, and indexation of tax scales and deductions. In addition, employers' social security contributions, which tended to distort the cost of labor against other factor costs, were reduced explicitly in an incomes policy context in countries like Belgium, Norway, Spain, and in Finland where employees' contributions were also reduced. Furthermore, temporary reductions in indirect taxes to slow down the rate of inflation were carried out in Denmark, Finland, Ireland, and Sweden.

On the expenditure side, increases in social security benefits, including pensions, child and maternity allowances, and unemployment benefits, were incorporated in the government's incomes policy strategy in a number of countries, notably Finland, Iceland, and Norway. The same countries, with the addition of New Zealand and Spain, resorted to increases in consumer subsidies to counteract inflation, frequently within an incomes policy framework. In many countries a contribution to incomes policy on the part of the government consisted of commitments to secure a high level of employment. This approach was usually expressed in general terms as a major objective of overall economic policy, whereas in certain instances such commitments appear to have played a more specific role in wage settlements, for example in Austria, as have employment guarantees in the Netherlands and Ireland. Also, in a 1981 tripartite agreement in Spain, the Government committed itself to promoting the creation of a certain number of jobs against wage restraint. Finally, a unique approach adopted by Denmark is the payment by the central government of a portion of indexation compensations due to workers into blocked individual accounts with the labor market pension fund.

Assessing the effectiveness of incomes policy is fraught with problems. The success or failure of the policy depends on a variety of social, political, institutional, and economic factors that are likely to differ among countries and change over time within individual countries. The sociopolitical factors have an important bearing on the extent to which a social consensus is achievable. Institutional factors influence the degree of centralization of collective wage agreements, but decentralized agreements reached at different times are liable to undermine the effectiveness of incomes policy through wage emulation and catch-ups. Economic factors relate to the openness of the economy and the impact of external impulses on the price level, the extent to which incomes policy is formulated in a macroeconomic context, the role assigned to complementary fiscal and monetary policies, and the exchange rate policy pursued. Austria's favorable experience with incomes policy, for example, may be explained by an advantageous constellation of these factors; to a certain extent this is also true of a relatively effective incomes policy in Norway and in Finland after 1977. Other countries in the group have had mixed results. Thus, Denmark and Iceland have encountered persistent difficulties in establishing a sufficiently strong social consensus despite government involvement in income formation and a substantial use of fiscal incomes policy measures.[15]

In view of the openness of the economies under consideration, it is relevant to note the potentially favorable interaction of incomes and exchange rate policies. Under a relatively stable exchange rate regime, incomes policy may assume an enhanced role in keeping wage increases to a rate that preserves profitability in the exposed sector of the economy. Austria provides a vivid manifestation of such a role assumed

---

[15] For an overview of incomes policies in six of the smaller industrial countries, see John T. Addison, "Incomes Policy: The Recent European Experience," in J.L. Fallick and R.F. Elliott, eds., *Incomes Policies, Inflation and Relative Pay* (London: George Allen and Unwin, 1981), pp. 187–245.

by incomes policy. In a setting of strong social consensus, exchange rate considerations figure prominently in deliberations of the social partnership. The labor market partners have appreciated the hard-currency policy pursued by the authorities, which has enhanced the effectiveness of incomes policy. However, as is the case with other aspects of incomes policy, Austria's experience is unusual among the smaller industrial countries.

While fiscal measures in certain respects effectively moderated wage settlements, especially in countries where the social consensus was strong and institutional and economic factors were favorable, these measures had wider and usually detrimental implications in other areas. As mentioned, fiscal incomes policy measures, whether on the revenue or expenditure side, generally weakened the budgetary position and thus compromised demand management; moderation in wage claims was in varying degrees offset by increased demand pressures. In this complex issue it is not possible to determine the net impact of such measures on price developments in the longer run. Econometric examinations of the effectiveness of incomes policies, including the impact of fiscal incomes policy measures, have not produced any conclusive results, one reason being disagreement among model builders about the determinants of the inflation process. An additional difficulty relates to the modeling of price expectations, which usually figures prominently in discussions of wage equations, because inflationary expectations are not observable.[16]

Apart from the demand pressure emanating from fiscal incomes policy measures, an intensive application of indirect tax reductions and increases in subsidies is liable to distort the allocation of resources. Moreover, incomes policies have a tendency to reduce wage differentials more than intended or more than is sustainable, and this may cause a destabilizing reaction that gives added impetus to wage drift.[17] Finally, ill-conceived strategies, such as premature announcement of fiscal incomes policy measures, including commitments to maintain a high level of employment and to reduce taxes, can compromise the bargaining position of governments and complicate the achievement of moderate wage settlements.

---

[16] For further discussion of these issues, see, for example, Palle Schelde Andersen and Philip Turner, "Incomes Policy in Theory and Practice," OECD Occasional Studies (Paris) (July 1980), pp. 33–50.

[17] Andersen and Turner, pp. 43–44.

6

Summary and Conclusions

The two oil crises and persistent global recessionary conditions had far-reaching repercussions on budgets and in many ways shaped fiscal policy in the smaller industrial countries over the period covered. Although policy priorities differed among these countries, there was one overriding similarity in fiscal policy response to these external impulses, namely, a defensive stance intended to cushion their adverse impact on the national economy, especially on employment and economic activity and on living standards in general. The intensity of policy responses varied from one country to another for various reasons. Thus, the action required differed according to the size of the external sector, or openness of the economies, and also because domestic energy production varied substantially among the countries. Also, political ideologies with regard to the proper role of the state and the reliance on the market mechanism differed among these countries and sometimes changed within individual countries with changes of government. Moreover, the likely duration of the recession following the first oil crisis was perceived differently and, consequently, so was the appropriate degree of fiscal stimulus.

The policy response to the first oil crisis and the ensuing world recession was generally to shift the stance of fiscal policy in a highly expansionary direction. Although initially intended to be temporary, the persistence of recessionary conditions caused a prolongation of this posture, which entailed, with a few exceptions, sharp increases in government expenditure in relation to total output, mounting tax burdens, and widening fiscal deficits. During the latter half of the period, policy was increasingly directed at the containment or reduction of these imbalances, as the large-scale absorption of resources by the public sector was widely seen as having an adverse long-term impact on economic performance. However, the problem of achieving the needed adjustment was exacerbated by rigidities in the fiscal systems that had grown over the period and severely limited the scope for fiscal action. In countries experiencing the largest deterioration in the fiscal position, the public finances had assumed imbalances of a structural character. Deficits and debt accumulation threatened to become self-perpetuating, and fiscal adjustment became an objective per se.

Despite growing efforts, limited success has been achieved in reducing fiscal imbalances. Obstacles to fiscal improvement are diverse and include elements of both an economic and a political nature. The period thus witnessed a strengthening of automatic fiscal stabilizers that tended simultaneously to trigger increased spending, notably in the social security area, and retard revenue growth. Demographic developments produced increasing claims on budgetary resources. The scope for fiscal action was narrowed by a growing tendency for future expenditure commitments to be determined by specific legislation whose budgetary burden was frequently aggravated by indexation mechanisms. Persistent fiscal deficits implied debt accumulation whose servicing requirement increasingly pre-empted budget resources. All these elements introduced growing rigidities into fiscal systems. Furthermore, there are indications that overoptimistic assumptions about the growth potential of the economy led to the setting of overambitious goals of fiscal policy, with adverse implications for the fiscal position. Lastly, the smaller industrial countries all have a system of political democracy which is often characterized by frequent changes of government. This political environment has not proved conducive to the formulation and pursuit of consistent long-term policies with clearly defined objectives, and the stance of policy tended to change frequently. There is ample evidence of inconsistent policy actions over the period that caused the impact of restrictive fiscal measures to be outweighed by subsequent measures of stimulus to promote employment and social welfare objectives. Such changes run the risk of impairing confidence in the firmness of the policy stance, with adverse repercussions on economic performance. The political element in fiscal policy thus contributed to difficulties in achieving targeted fiscal adjustment.

While the foregoing comments are fairly representative of the general situation, fiscal performance nonetheless varied markedly among individual countries. This variety applies to the expansion of the government sector, as measured by the ratio of government expenditure to GDP, and of tax burdens as well as the size of fiscal deficits and the debt accumulation they generated. While all countries experienced tendencies toward a rapid expansion of the government sector after the first oil crisis, some reacted quickly and were successful in curbing expenditure growth, for example, Australia, Finland, Iceland, and Norway. Consequently, these countries had less need to raise revenue, and the tax burden was not a cause for particular concern by the end of the period. Other countries, including Belgium, Ireland, the Netherlands, and Sweden experienced an explosive expansion of the government sector, and tax burdens also rose steeply in these countries, especially in Belgium and Ireland. However, revenue growth did not match that of expenditure, except in Norway, which implied growing fiscal deficits elsewhere. Over the whole period, the largest government deficits were incurred by Ireland, Belgium, New Zealand, and Sweden; Luxembourg had the distinction of maintaining a surplus for the major part of the period. Ireland and Belgium had the highest government debt/GDP ratios and mounting debt-servicing burden by the end of the period; this ratio was lowest in Luxembourg and Finland.

These fiscal developments and policies had far-reaching economic implications. Analyzing their impact on the economy in any precise manner is a complicated task, however; a major problem is the issue of causation, as factors outside the realm of public finance influence economic performance and their impact is not separable from that of fiscal factors. But in many instances the direction of the impact is fairly clear. On the expenditure side, while analysis at the aggregate level does not lead to conclusive findings, there is strong evidence that separate expenditure schemes in many instances increased to an extent that exerted a harmful impact on economic performance. Thus, it was a fairly general experience that employment-creating schemes contributed to a slowdown of labor mobility and thus retarded structural adjustment and efficient resource use. Various forms of industrial support designed to protect the exposed sector of the economy against adverse external impulses and to preserve regional balance had a similar effect. An explosive growth of social security expenditure was a major cause of fiscal imbalances. The generosity of pension and unemployment compensation schemes, in particular, in some instances reached a level that caused concern over the adverse repercussions on work incentives. Also, while incomes policy in a few countries, including Austria and Finland, contributed to economic stabilization, this was not the general experience, and the fiscal contribution to incomes policy invariably entailed a substantial deterioration in fiscal positions and added to demand pressures.

While revenue in most countries increased at a slower pace than expenditure, some experienced a substantial increase in the tax burden. Personal income taxes and their progressivity affected work effort and initiative adversely in countries where this tax was highest, such as Belgium, New Zealand, Norway, and Sweden. In some of these countries, the high personal income taxes encouraged tax avoidance and evasion, contributed to wage-push pressures, and discouraged savings. Social security contributions, a significant revenue source in countries like the Netherlands, Spain, and Sweden, increased rapidly over the period and added significantly to labor costs. This led to a distortion of factor costs against labor and aggravated the cost position in a depressed enterprise sector.

Finally, the large and persistent fiscal deficits implied debt accumulation whose servicing constituted increasing claims on present and future budgetary resources. There is evidence also that in countries like Australia, Belgium, the Netherlands, and Sweden, where financial markets are well developed, fiscal deficits exerted upward pressure on interest rates, with an adverse impact on business investment and economic growth. Such financial crowding-out effects were doubtless experienced in varying degrees in other countries in the group, although the imperfection of financial markets and external influences on interest rate determination make analysis of the crowding-out effects of fiscal deficits in these cases inconclusive.

One lesson that emerges from the different experiences in the fiscal field is that the degree of expenditure restraint would appear to be a significant determinant of overall fiscal performance (see Table 6.1). The rate of expansion of the government sector thus tended to be positively correlated with the rate at which deficits widened, debt ratios expanded, and debt-servicing burdens increased. Also, with a few exceptions, notably Norway and Spain, countries with the smallest government sector at the beginning of the period tended to experience the smallest expansion of that sector over the period in terms of percentage points of GDP. On the other hand, the relation between government sector expansion and growth of the tax burden exhibited, to some extent implicitly, a highly irregular pattern.

The scope for exercising expenditure restraint depends on a variety of factors and the most important ones are probably not economic in nature. Among countries that were most successful in restraining expenditure growth, it appears that certain attitudes, which had evolved through long and complicated historical processes, had an important

Table 6.1. Smaller Industrial Countries: Selected Fiscal Indicators

(Central Government, Percentages of GDP)

	Government Sector Expansion 1972–82 (Percentage Points)	Deficit in 1982	Annual Average Deficit 1972–82	Interest Payments 1982	Debt Ratio 1982	Government Sector Size 1982	Tax Burden 1982
Norway	2.4	0.8	-2.8	2.4	26.5	41.8	42.6
Australia	3.7	-0.3	-2.2	1.9	22.7	28.3	28.0
Luxembourg	3.7	0.5	1.1	0.7	4.7	35.8	34.7
Finland	5.1	-2.1	-0.8	0.9	12.3	30.6	28.6
Iceland	5.4	-2.9	-3.0	2.4	31.4	35.9	32.9
Austria	9.8	-4.4	-3.1	2.2	30.0	39.9	35.5
New Zealand	11.2	-7.4	-5.9	4.6	58.2	42.2	34.8
Spain	11.8[1]	-7.1[2]	-2.4[1]	0.6[2]	19.4[2]	32.3[2]	25.3[2]
Netherlands	12.8[3]	-7.6	-3.5[3]	3.2	39.4	58.8	51.3
Denmark	13.2	-8.3	-1.4	4.6	59.2	45.2	36.9
Sweden	13.5	-9.8	-4.7	4.6	45.4	48.9	39.0
Belgium	17.1	-12.2	-6.6	7.7	73.9	56.9	44.7
Ireland	21.1	-15.2	-11.2	9.1	108.7	57.8	42.6

[1] 1972–81.
[2] 1981.
[3] 1973–82.

bearing on the pursuit of fiscal policy. In some instances, these attitudes generated national cohesion that ensured sufficient acceptance of short-term material sacrifices against longer-term gains, and in other instances, fiscal prudence was equated with national security. There is also evidence that ideological persuasion concerning the proper role of the state caused a reversal of an ongoing process of increased government sector absorption of resources. While the nature and strength of such attitudes varied among the countries concerned, they generated in each case the required fiscal discipline to keep government sector size to more manageable proportions.

Finally, it should be reiterated that the main objective of this study has been to provide information and analysis that could enhance knowledge and understanding of public finances and the conduct of fiscal policy in this group of countries. For this reason, the scope of issues addressed has been fairly broad. It is hoped, however, that the study will provoke thought and will direct attention to separate issues that deserve more thorough research and analysis.

PART II

DEVELOPMENTS IN INDIVIDUAL COUNTRIES

Introduction

This part of the study serves as a background to the comparative analysis in Part I. It traces some of the prominent features of fiscal developments in the 1970s and early 1980s in 13 of the smaller industrial countries.[1]

In the analysis of fiscal developments and policy issues in these countries, a uniform approach is taken as far as individual conditions permit. Each country study is divided into five similar sections. The first accounts for overall economic developments over the period in broad terms, in order to indicate the general background against which fiscal policy was conducted. The next three sections analyze changes in expenditure, revenue, and the fiscal balance, both in regard to the size of these fiscal aggregates in relation to gross domestic product (GDP) and to changes in the composition of individual expenditure and revenue categories and of sources of deficit financing. The main causes of these developments are considered. The section on fiscal balance also indicates the size of government debt relative to GDP and of the external component of the debt.

The final and main section deals with fiscal policy issues. Because only the central government is covered, the extent of its role in the pursuit of overall fiscal policy is outlined by a description of its relative size within the general government sector, its relationship with local governments in regard to policy formulation and implementation, and its command over other public entities in pursuing policy objectives. Some technical aspects of budgeting in terms of forecasting techniques and assessment of the fiscal impact and, in some cases, their actual policy relevance are also considered. The section cites major aims of fiscal policy as announced by the authorities, how these may have altered with changing economic and political conditions, and what principal measures were taken to attain the stated objectives. The

---

[1] Switzerland, a nonmember of the Fund, is the fourteenth country in this group and is not discussed in the study.

89

section concludes with a brief overview of developments over the period, and considers some major implications of past fiscal policies and the policy issues that are likely to confront the authorities in the near future.

1

Australia

Compared with most of the smaller industrial economies, Australia has a small external trade sector—foreign trade amounts to approximately 15 percent of GDP. Although this and abundant energy resources have acted as a buffer to external shocks, the authorities have nevertheless been faced with the task of reducing fundamental imbalances in the economy that had developed in the first half of the 1970s. Somewhat paradoxically, these developments can be traced in part to the discovery of vast mineral resources in the late 1960s and the improved prospects for exports, which implied an exchange rate that restrained activity in the manufacturing industry. Also, and more important, a wage explosion in the 1973–75 period resulted in declining profit shares, and in subsequent years the authorities pursued a restrictive economic policy to restore balance.

These developments, together with weak foreign demand, contributed to a low growth rate of GDP throughout the period, averaging less than 3 percent a year. At the same time, the rate of unemployment rose steadily from 2½ percent to 7 percent from 1972 to 1982. The discovery of mineral resources induced capital inflows that triggered an inflationary spiral, the breaking of which has been a challenge to economic policy since the mid-1970s. Inflation rates exceeded 15 percent in both 1974 and 1975, as a result of the wage explosion and the direct external oil price impact. Since 1977 annual inflation rates ranged between 8 percent and 11 percent. After recording surpluses in 1972 and 1973, the external current account swung into deficit in the following year when domestic demand soared. Subsequently, the current account was in deficit every year, reaching a high of just over 5 percent of GDP in 1982. Despite the Australian authorities' seemingly successful containment of public expenditure growth, a fiscal deficit has been recorded in every year of the period, ranging from 0.3 percent to 5 percent of GDP.

EXPENDITURE

Commonwealth government expenditure rose sharply as a proportion of GDP in 1975, or by 5 percentage points to 29½ percent. This was the result of a deliberate policy to stimulate the economy and to enlarge public sector provision of various social services and participation in transportation. In 1976 a new government reversed the expansionary stance, with the result that the proportion declined until 1980. Between 1972 and 1982 the ratio of commonwealth government expenditure to GDP rose from 24½ percent to 28½ percent, which is among the smallest increases in this group of countries over the same period.

The composition of expenditure in terms of economic categories has changed considerably. Expenditure on goods and services, which accounted for 25 percent of total commonwealth government expenditure in 1972, had declined to less than 22 percent by 1982, while subsidies and other current transfers increased their share in the total from 47½ percent to 63 percent during the same period. This change in emphasis was in part brought about by the "New Federalism" policy pursued since the mid-1970s. The policy aimed at increasing the Commonwealth Government's financial contribution to the states in the form of general purpose grants. Such transfers amounted to 27 percent of total expenditure in 1982, having risen from 19 percent in 1972.

Interest payments on government debt declined as a proportion of total expenditure from 6½ percent to 4½ percent from 1972 to 1976; they have since been on the rise, and between 1980 and 1982 amounted to just under 7 percent of the total. Capital expenditures showed a declining trend in the latter half of the period. These accounted for some 6 percent of the total in 1982, compared with 10 percent in 1972. Net lending, which amounted to 10 percent to 14 percent of total expenditure up to 1975, has since declined sharply and in 1982 was 2½ percent of the total. This development represents a shift in financing of capital expenditures by authorities outside the budget. Until the mid-1970s, such capital outlays were largely financed through advances from the budget, whereas subsequently the entities concerned have increasingly financed their capital programs by own borrowing.

REVENUE

Between 1972 and 1982, total revenue of the Commonwealth Government expressed as a proportion of GDP grew moderately from 24 percent to 28 percent. This is a lower ratio than in most of the smaller industrial countries and may be explained in part by the absence, for

Australia: Selected Economic Indicators, 1972–82

	1972	1973	1974	1975	1976	1977	1978	1979	1980	1981	1982
Real GDP, percentage changes	3.6	6.2	1.4	2.2	3.5	0.9	3.6	3.3	2.0	3.9	0.7
Rate of unemployment	2.6	2.3	2.6	4.8	4.7	5.6	6.2	6.2	6.0	5.7	7.1
Consumer prices, percentage changes	5.8	9.5	15.1	15.1	13.5	12.3	7.9	9.1	10.2	9.6	11.1
External current account balance as percentage of GDP	1.4	1.3	−3.0	−0.6	−1.3	−2.6	−3.5	−1.5	−2.3	−4.8	−5.2

Source: Organization for Economic Cooperation and Development, *Economic Outlook*, December 1984.

Australia: Consolidated Central Government Finances, 1972–82

(Year ended June 30)

	1972	1973	1974	1975	1976	1977	1978	1979	1980	1981	1982
Total Revenue											
(as a percentage of GDP)	24.3	22.6	24.0	25.4	25.7	26.3	26.7	25.6	26.3	27.3	28.0
Percentages of total revenue	100.0	100.0	100.0	100.0	100.0	100.0	100.0	100.0	100.0	100.0	100.0
Income taxes	57.9	58.6	61.1	64.5	63.1	63.6	63.6	60.6	60.8	62.0	63.5
Social security contributions	—	—	—	—	—	—	—	—	—	—	—
Payroll (manpower) taxes	1.2	0.2	0.2	0.2	0.3	0.3	0.2	0.1	0.1	0.1	0.1
Property taxes	0.9	0.9	0.7	0.6	0.6	0.5	0.5	0.4	0.2	0.1	0.1
Taxes on goods and services	21.7	21.9	21.5	19.1	20.5	19.5	19.5	22.3	23.4	23.0	22.0
Taxes on international trade	5.1	5.3	5.1	5.7	5.7	5.9	5.1	5.6	5.4	5.2	5.2
Other taxes	—	—	—	—	—	—	—	—	—	—	—
Nontax revenue and grants	13.1	13.0	11.4	9.9	9.8	10.2	11.2	10.9	10.0	9.5	9.2
Total Expenditure											
(as a percentage of GDP)	24.6	24.3	24.5	29.4	30.7	29.6	30.4	28.9	28.1	28.1	28.3
Percentages of total expenditure	100.0	100.0	100.0	100.0	100.0	100.0	100.0	100.0	100.0	100.0	100.0
Expenditure on goods and services	25.1	24.1	23.4	20.6	19.5	20.1	20.1	20.0	20.4	21.0	21.7
Of which:											
Wages and salaries	…	…	…	…	…	…	…	…	…	…	…
Interest payments	6.6	6.4	5.6	4.9	4.3	5.7	6.0	6.7	6.8	6.9	6.8

Subsidies and other current transfers	47.6	49.8	50.2	49.1	56.2	58.7	61.0	62.8	63.4	63.2	63.2
Of which: Social security funds	⋯	⋯	⋯	⋯	⋯	⋯	⋯	⋯	⋯	⋯	⋯
Capital expenditure	9.8	9.8	10.2	11.2	10.3	8.8	7.6	6.6	6.4	6.2	5.9
Lending minus repayments	10.8	9.9	10.6	14.2	9.6	6.6	5.3	4.0	2.9	2.6	2.4
Surplus/Deficit (as a percentage of GDP)	−0.3	−1.7	−0.5	−4.0	−5.0	−3.3	−3.7	−3.3	−1.8	−0.8	−0.3
Financing:											
Abroad	−0.1	−0.2	−0.3	—	0.2	0.4	1.8	1.3	0.2	−0.1	0.3
Domestic	0.5	1.8	0.8	4.0	4.8	2.8	1.9	2.0	1.6	0.9	0.1
Monetary authorities	−2.6	−0.2	0.7	0.8	2.4	1.6	0.3	0.5	0.7	−0.6	0.1
Deposit money banks	1.0	1.2	−0.2	2.2	0.3	−0.1	—	0.5	0.3	0.5	0.2
Other[1]	2.1	0.8	0.3	1.1	2.2	1.3	1.6	1.1	0.6	0.9	−0.2
Memorandum Items:											
General government expenditure and net lending/GDP	32.3	31.7	32.2	38.2	38.9	38.8	39.2	37.9	36.9	37.2	37.6
Central government debt outstanding/GDP[2]	⋯	34.8	29.8	28.8	27.9	28.0	29.8	30.4	28.6	24.9	22.7

Source: International Monetary Fund, *Government Finance Statistics Yearbook*, 1983 and 1984.
[1] Includes adjustments.
[2] Source for debt data: Commonwealth Government, 1983–84 Budget Paper No. 8 (includes Commonwealth and State Governments).

most of the period, of social security taxes, as a number of social security schemes are funded outside the public sector. A specific levy of 2.5 percent of taxable income was imposed in late 1976, but this health insurance tax was abolished in 1978, as was the compulsory health insurance scheme that had been introduced in mid-1975.

The financing of social benefits with general revenue has in turn resulted in heavy reliance on income taxes whose share in total revenue rose from 58 percent in 1972 to almost 63½ percent in 1982. The rise is accounted for entirely by the personal income tax, as the corporate tax declined in relative importance from 29 percent of combined income taxes in 1972 to 20 percent in 1982. The rise in personal income taxes occurred despite a series of ameliorating measures during the period, such as indexation of the tax in 1976 aimed at moderation of wage claims and rate changes to reduce fiscal drag.

The second largest revenue category consists of taxes on goods and services, with a share in total revenue of around 22 percent at the beginning and end of the period. The most dynamic element in this category is a levy on domestic crude oil imposed in 1977, which is to be progressively increased until full import parity pricing is reached. In 1982 this levy, together with other—and declining—excise duties, accounted for 15 percent of total revenue, whereas total excise duties amounted to 13½ percent of the total in 1972. Nontax revenue and grants, mainly property income, declined from 13 percent to 9 percent of total revenue between 1972 and 1982. Other taxes are less significant and have not changed much over the period.

THE FISCAL BALANCE AND ITS FINANCING

Commonwealth government finances recorded deficits throughout the period 1972 to 1982. These grew substantially to 4 and 5 percent of GDP in 1975 and 1976, respectively, partly as a result of the official policy of the Labor Government to achieve a fundamental social reform and keep employment up through increased public spending. Subsequently, a stricter policy stance was adopted at the commonwealth level, mainly through expenditure restraint, as a result of which the deficit declined to the equivalent of 0.8 percent of GDP in 1981 and 0.3 percent in 1982. It should be noted, however, that in the past few years of the period covered, the deficit of state and local authorities increased as a result of restrictions on federal funding of outlays by these authorities.

While commonwealth government deficits were small in the early years of the period, they were financed in large measure by the sale of government securities to the private sector. In 1972–73 the aim of fiscal policy was to support monetary policy in reducing liquidity, and more was borrowed from the nonbank private sector than was needed to finance the deficit. Throughout the period, the nonbank private sector covered a significant portion of the Commonwealth Government's financing requirement. Foreign financing was resorted to in the period but not to a significant degree, except in 1978 and 1979 when external borrowing covered, respectively, one half and over one third of a large deficit. Since the mid-1970s, combined financing by the monetary authorities and the deposit money banks has often amounted to one half of the commonwealth government deficit. Government debt, expressed as a ratio to GDP, declined from 35 percent in 1973 to 23 percent in 1982 according to official sources, while the share of the external component in total debt rose from 8½ percent to 16 percent over the same period.

FISCAL POLICY

The framework. While Australia's constitutional system of government is characterized by large subnational units, the commonwealth budget is nonetheless the dominant instrument in formulating fiscal policy, owing both to the national character of the Commonwealth Government's role in managing the economy and the sheer size of its activities. In 1982 total general government expenditure was equivalent to 37½ percent of GDP, of which the commonwealth sector accounted for three fourths. More than one fourth of commonwealth government expenditure takes the form of transfers to state and local governments, amounting to almost one half of their total revenue and grants. The power of the states to impose taxes is strictly limited and the Commonwealth Government commands the most productive and elastic sources of revenue. Moreover, although the Commonwealth Government has limited direct control over outlays of other public entities, its indirect influence through controlling revenue sharing and through the Loan Council is substantial. The Loan Council, dominated by the Commonwealth Government, aims at coordinating all public sector borrowing, including borrowing for public works and housing programs at the state and local government level. The amount of commonwealth financial assistance to the states is based on agreements that are negotiated every five years. Despite the formal arrangements favoring commonwealth government dominance within the public sector, experience in the past few years suggests that the states nevertheless enjoy a fair amount of autonomy in expenditure matters. Thus, during the period of expenditure restraint since the mid-1970s, they were able to sustain increasing expenditure levels in real terms by drawing on their own resources and securing financing of growing deficits.

In 1971 a system of three-year forward estimates of expenditure, which had been initiated in 1965, was further elaborated to include new as well as existing programs that, unlike the previous system, required ministerial endorsement. The forward estimates procedure was integrated with the annual budget cycle and constituted, in effect, a rolling planning system. Later, the forward estimates again excluded new programs and are now more fully integrated with the annual budget cycle. While the implications of forward estimates submitted by the departments to the Department of Finance form part of the context in which the broad fiscal strategy is determined, the three-year estimates as such are not seen as policy documents. Rather, they are internal documents viewed as an aid to decision making and do not constitute a multiyear expenditure commitment on the part of the Government.[1]

Aims and measures. Prolonged success in economic performance during the 1960s provided a favorable basis for the Labor Government that took office toward the end of 1972 to promote its social policy objectives. In conformity with its policy objectives, the Government set out to increase the share of resources taken up by the public sector and to change the distribution of income over a short period of time. Measures to this end included increased rates of pension, unemployment, and sickness benefits retroactive to December 1972; also, the budget for fiscal year 1973–74 contained major increases in expenditure for social services. Increases in old age and invalid pension rates were met by raising indirect taxes rather than social security contributions (which, as already noted, were absent in Australian taxation for most of the period). In 1975 a compulsory health insurance scheme was introduced for the first time.

Fiscal policy reaction to deepening recession and rising unemployment was to strengthen the already expansionary stance through reductions in income and company taxes. Employment-oriented advances to state and local governments were maintained at a high level, and special measures were taken to safeguard employment in the motor

---

[1]James Cutt, "The Evolution of Expenditure Budgeting in Australia," *Public Budgeting and Finance*, Vol. 3 (Summer 1983), p. 18.

vehicle industry. The Government, faced with rising rates of inflation and a deteriorating external position, refrained from taking traditional demand management measures, which were seen as likely to cause still higher rates of unemployment. Instead, preference was expressed for action that directly attacked the wage-price spiral. The fiscal component of this strategy took the form of income tax reductions, introduced in late 1974, designed to reduce pressures for wage increases, which would, in turn, reduce inflation.

The upsurge in prices between 1972 and 1975 generated mounting concern about the detrimental impact on output and employment and on the external position. The new government that assumed office toward the end of 1975 regarded inflation and the sharply enlarged role and relative size of the public sector as major causes of depressed private sector activity and loss of business confidence. Revival of the private sector was seen as a precondition for sustained economic growth, but whether fiscal policy could stimulate employment amid the pessimism generated by pronounced inflation was doubted. The stage was thus set for a reversal of the previous expansionary stance of fiscal policy. Bringing inflation under control and reducing the rate of expansion of public sector absorption of resources were declared major aims of policy. In 1976, as part of the effort to slow inflation, indexation of the personal income tax was introduced. This measure had a dual purpose: moderating wage claims and thereby restoring profitability in the business sector, and containing the size of the public sector in the long run. Restrictive expenditure policy, however, was a more direct approach to containing the public sector and the Commonwealth Government followed it until almost the end of the period. Apart from general restraint in budget formulation and execution, special measures taken for this purpose included reductions in advances to state and local governments, staff ceilings for the civil service, direct expenditure cuts in specified areas, and the abolition in 1978 of the compulsory health insurance scheme (Medibank).[2]

Toward the end of the period, substantial slippages occurred in the restrictive stance, even if the consequences are only partially reflected in the statistics for 1982. Owing to increased expenditures to support employment and social security services, the share of total expenditure

---

[2] The operation of insurance schemes outside the public sector is encouraged through tax incentives for the insured.

in GDP started to rise in 1982 after five years of stability or decline. The deficit, while declining in 1982, has since widened sharply.

Overview and implications for future policy. The period covered thus witnessed a fundamental reversal in fiscal policy stance in Australia. From 1972 to 1975 the Government sought to reap the fruits of the successful economic performance in the 1960s by embarking on a course of expansion of social welfare services and an enlarged role for the public sector. The sharp increases in government expenditure resulting from this policy, together with expansionary development in other areas, led to growing imbalances in the economy. After a change of government at the end of 1975, policy was redirected to curtailing the role of the public sector and restoring overall economic balance. An important objective related to fiscal balance was to bring inflation under control, using tax policy as a significant factor of the strategy. The restrictive fiscal stance relied largely on expenditure restraint, and substantial success was achieved in containing the government sector. Actually, expressed as a ratio to GDP, the size of the commonwealth government sector was reduced by 2 percentage points between 1976 and 1982. In view of the experience in other countries in the group, the absence of compulsory social security schemes may have contributed significantly to this result. More recent developments, however, point to a renewed upsurge in expenditure growth, and a public health insurance scheme has been reintroduced.

Success in containing expenditure growth accompanied a reduction in the fiscal deficit between 1976 and 1982, although revenue increase was limited by, inter alia, tax concessions to stimulate private sector activity and to moderate wage demands. The reduced deficits at the central level were consistent with the Government's anti-inflation policy, which was seen as a precondition for achieving sustainable economic growth in the medium term and higher employment. It should be noted, however, that although the deficit was substantially reduced at the commonwealth government level in the 1980–82 period, the improvement was partly offset by the deteriorating financial position of the state and local sector.

The overall public sector deficit thus remains high and is cause for concern because of its inflationary impact, through both the monetary implications of deficit financing and the inflationary expectations it generates. As already indicated, only limited progress has been made in reducing inflation, which has remained one of Australia's main economic problems, and the achievement of better balance in the public finances is likely to remain a major task of future policy. The effort needed is accentuated by recent slippages in the pursuit of fiscal policy toward this end.[3]

---

[3] As a result of successive expansionary budgets since 1983, the budget deficit has risen sharply. Deficits in the state and local sectors have also widened. While the rate of inflation has abated in recent years, it still remains high compared with the experience in main trading partner countries. These developments have accentuated the need for fiscal adjustment to support efforts to establish sustained noninflationary growth and reduce the high rate of unemployment.

2

Austria

The openness of the Austrian economy, in which foreign trade amounts to approximately one fourth of GDP, makes it vulnerable to external disturbances; consequently, a major aim of fiscal policy has been to smooth out economic fluctuations to secure full employment. Despite variances in growth rates from year to year, the economy had an impressive growth performance over the period 1972–82, about 3 percent a year on average, although the last two years witnessed unusual slack in economic activity. The great importance assigned to the maintenance of full employment resulted in lower unemployment rates than experienced in most other industrial countries. It was not until 1981 that unemployment rose appreciably above 2 percent, and in the following year it rose to 3½ percent.

Despite strong inflationary pressures caused by the oil price crises, average annual price increases were kept at about 6½ percent during the period, which is well below the average for industrial countries. A strong social consensus among labor market partners and the Government, the so-called social partnership, coupled with a hard currency exchange rate policy, were significant contributors to this achievement.

The external current account did not show large deficits in individual years, but they were persistent. In 1982, for the first time in a decade, the current external account turned into a surplus, equivalent to a little over 1 percent of GDP. Although caused in part by sharply higher oil prices, the current account deficits also reflected the impact of fiscal deficits that were experienced in every year during the period under review. The fiscal and external deficits have become a cause for growing

Austria: Selected Economic Indicators, 1972–82

	1972	1973	1974	1975	1976	1977	1978	1979	1980	1981	1982
Real GDP, percentage changes	6.2	4.9	3.9	−0.4	4.6	4.4	0.5	4.7	3.0	−0.1	1.0
Rate of unemployment	1.2	1.1	1.4	1.7	1.8	1.6	2.1	2.1	1.9	2.5	3.5
Consumer prices, percentage changes	6.3	7.6	9.5	8.4	7.3	5.5	3.6	3.7	6.4	6.8	5.4
External current account balance as percentage of GDP	0.1	−0.3	−1.0	−0.1	−2.3	−3.6	−0.7	−1.0	−2.7	−2.0	1.1

Source: Organization for Economic Cooperation and Development, *Economic Outlook*, December 1984.

Austria: Consolidated Central Government Finances, 1972–82

(Year ended December 31)

	1972	1973	1974	1975	1976	1977	1978	1979	1980	1981	1982
Total Revenue (as a percentage of GDP)	29.9	30.3	30.8	31.5	31.5	32.2	34.7	35.0	35.3	36.8	35.5
Percentages of total revenue	100.0	100.0	100.0	100.0	100.0	100.0	100.0	100.0	100.0	100.0	100.0
Income taxes	20.4	19.8	21.4	20.4	19.6	19.8	21.2	20.7	20.6	20.5	20.0
Social security contributions	29.9	30.4	30.9	32.7	33.0	33.7	35.1	34.8	35.2	35.0	35.4
Payroll (manpower) taxes	7.2	7.6	7.6	7.8	7.9	7.9	6.8	6.6	6.5	5.8	5.8
Property taxes	2.2	1.9	1.8	1.9	1.9	1.8	1.9	1.8	1.7	1.7	1.6
Taxes on goods and services	27.9	29.5	28.1	27.0	27.7	26.9	25.6	25.7	25.0	24.8	25.0
Taxes on international trade	5.3	4.7	4.2	3.2	2.7	2.3	1.5	1.5	1.5	1.4	1.3
Other taxes	0.6	0.4	0.4	0.4	0.5	1.2	0.8	0.8	0.8	1.0	1.1
Nontax revenue and grants	6.6	5.7	5.6	6.5	6.7	6.4	7.1	8.2	8.7	9.8	9.8
Total Expenditure (as a percentage of GDP)	30.1	31.9	32.3	35.5	36.1	35.9	38.8	38.7	38.6	39.7	39.9
Percentages of total expenditure	100.0	100.0	100.0	100.0	100.0	100.0	100.0	100.0	100.0	100.0	100.0
Expenditure on goods and services	30.4	25.8	26.2	27.1	27.1	27.0	26.0	25.8	25.6	25.7	25.9
Of which:											
Wages and salaries	14.6	10.8	10.6	11.0	11.2	11.0	10.6	10.4	10.3	10.3	10.2
Interest payments	2.1	1.9	1.9	2.2	3.1	3.6	4.1	4.3	4.6	4.9	5.6

Subsidies and other current transfers	55.7	56.2	58.0	58.6	58.6	59.6	60.0	59.7	59.1	58.7	58.9
Of which:											
Social security funds	...	25.1	25.6	26.5	27.1	27.4	26.3	26.5	26.8	26.7	26.2
Capital expenditure	9.8	13.7	10.6	10.6	9.1	8.3	7.7	8.0	8.5	8.9	8.1
Lending minus repayments	2.0	2.4	3.2	1.5	2.1	1.5	2.2	2.3	2.1	1.7	1.5
Surplus/Deficit											
(as a percentage of GDP)	−0.2	−1.6	−1.5	−4.0	−4.6	−3.7	−4.0	−3.7	−3.2	−2.9	−4.4
Financing:											
Abroad	−0.3	−0.1	0.8	2.8	0.5	1.7	1.4	0.6	0.9	1.6	1.4
Domestic	0.5	1.7	0.7	1.2	4.1	2.0	2.6	3.1	2.4	1.4	3.0
Monetary authorities	—	0.1	0.1	—	—	—	—	—	—	−0.1	—
Deposit money banks	0.1	—	—	0.3	0.7	0.4	0.4	0.8	0.1	0.5	0.9
Other[1]	0.4	1.7	0.7	0.9	3.4	1.7	2.2	2.3	2.4	0.9	2.1
Memorandum Items:											
General government expenditure and net lending/GDP	41.3	43.1	44.6	48.2	49.1	48.3	51.7	51.0	51.0	52.8	52.2
Central government debt outstanding/GDP	10.5	10.4	10.0	15.3	18.5	20.8	23.6	25.2	26.3	28.0	30.0

Source: International Monetary Fund, *Government Finance Statistics Yearbook*, 1983 and 1984.
[1]Includes adjustments.

concern as have certain structural problems partly related to the emphasis in fiscal policy on employment.

EXPENDITURE

From 1972 to 1982 the ratio of government expenditure to GDP rose from 30 percent to 40 percent. Expansionary fiscal policies designed to sustain activity and employment in the wake of the first oil price shock, as well as a fall in real GDP, largely explain the 3 percentage point rise in the share of government expenditure in 1975. Following two years at this level, the share rose by a further 3 percentage points in 1978, again the result of near-stagnant growth and measures to stimulate investment and secure employment. The ratio of government expenditure to GDP remained between 38½ percent and 40 percent until 1982. Expenditure on goods and services, including wages and salaries, shared in this relative increase, with its share in total expenditure remaining fairly constant at about 26 percent throughout most of the period. Subsidies and other current transfers increased faster than total expenditure, from 55½ percent to almost 59 percent of the total, reflecting increasing transfers to public and private enterprises and, in a lesser degree, social security funds. Interest payments on government debt took up a steadily growing share of total expenditure, from 2 percent in 1972 to 5½ percent in 1982, while the share of direct capital expenditure in the total declined from 10 percent to 8 percent. Net lending averaged about 2 percent of total expenditure with small deviations during the period.

REVENUE

Although the ratio of total revenue to GDP rose in most years from 1972 to 1982, it remained below that of expenditure throughout the period and rose less, from 30 percent to 35½ percent. Income taxes shared in this increase and remained around 20 percent of total revenue. The elasticity of this tax with respect to GDP was reduced by successive discretionary actions aimed at lessening the tax burden of low- and middle-income earners, stimulating business investment and employment, and reducing fiscal drag. Social security contributions paid by employers and employees grew faster than total revenue, with their share increasing from 30 percent to 35½ percent of total revenue during the period, reflecting, inter alia, higher rates.

Taxes on goods and services, of which the value-added tax (VAT) accounts for almost two thirds, declined as a percentage of total revenue, or from 28 percent in 1972 to 25 percent in 1982. Despite increased rates, the VAT grew at about the same rate as GDP, while excises, the other main tax in this category, declined in relation to GDP, as many of these taxes are specific rather than ad valorem. The share of payroll taxes not earmarked for social security expenditure declined slightly from 7 percent to 8 percent in 1972–77 to 6 percent in 1982, while the share of property taxes remained roughly constant at slightly under 2 percent. Taxes on international trade have become less important as a result of the phased abolition of duties on imports from the European Communities (EC) during the period 1973–77. Nontax revenue, because of higher property income, increased in relative significance, and by the end of the period accounted for almost 10 percent of total revenue, compared with 6½ percent in 1972.

THE FISCAL BALANCE AND ITS FINANCING

In each year of the period the central government finances recorded deficits, which amounted to 4 percent of GDP in the recessionary year of 1975 and reached a peak of over 4½ percent of GDP in the following year. These deficits are indicative of a deliberate expansionary fiscal policy stance that was aimed at neutralizing the effect of the first oil price crisis on activity and employment. Since then, high fiscal deficits have caused growing concern, but efforts to reduce them have been hampered by the policy objective of maintaining a high level of employment through tax concessions and employment-supporting expenditures. From 1977 to 1982, the fiscal deficits ranged between 3 percent and 4½ percent of GDP.

The Austrian Postal Savings Bank makes recommendations for deficit financing. Recourse to the central bank is confined to short-term discounting of treasury bills up to 5 percent of the past published tax receipts of the central government. The financing requirement is met largely by long-term borrowing in the private domestic market or abroad, the share of external borrowing being determined with a view to the domestic liquidity situation. Except in 1975, when external financing covered 70 percent of the deficit, and in 1981 and 1982, when similar ratios were 55 percent and 68 percent, respectively, most of the financing requirement has been met by domestic sources. The persistent fiscal deficits entailed growing government debt which, expressed as a ratio to GDP, rose from 10½ percent to 30 percent between 1972 and 1982. Over the same period the share of foreign debt in total debt rose from 20 percent to 32 percent.

FISCAL POLICY

The framework. The Central Government accounts for about three fourths of total general government expenditure, which in 1982 was almost equivalent to 52 percent of GDP. This expenditure includes transfers to other levels of government that amount to approximately one third of their total revenue and grants. Local government budget deficits have been fairly constant over time (at less than 1 percent of GDP) and thus do not play an active role in countercyclical policy. In the early years of the period, however, when inflation was a major preoccupation of economic policy, local governments pursued a restrictive expenditure policy; they refrained from increasing various fees and charges, and their share in federal taxes was temporarily frozen as special deposits in the central bank. Outside the budget proper, the Central Government has relied on the national industries and, in recent years, on special government organizations to realize the fiscal objectives of sustaining a high level of employment and supporting the business sector, especially the export industry.

The budget of the Central Government is prepared on an annual basis; long-term budgeting is not practiced. Since 1972, the ordinary budget has been supplemented by a contingency budget that can be activated in case of unexpected weakening of demand. In an effort to make fiscal policy more flexible, special provisions were introduced in the 1976 budget law that allow for the contingency budget to be implemented without further parliamentary approval if certain conditions are met. Also, revenue shortfalls, up to 5 percent of the year's estimate, could be offset by borrowing without further authorization by Parliament. The contingency budget is made up of two tranches: a stabilization tranche that can be activated to alleviate problems in certain industries or regions, and a reflationary tranche that can be used to stimulate economic activity in general. The contingency budget was activated in the 1974–76 period and again in 1983.

Aims and measures. As indicated earlier, full employment was a major aim of fiscal policy throughout the period, although the emphasis naturally varied according to overall conditions in individual years. The Government's contribution to the social partnership consisted largely in commitments to secure a high level of employment. Against a background of unstable external conditions, the authorities have relied on the federal budget as their chief anticylical instrument through the exercise of a flexible fiscal policy.

Having pursued a strict fiscal policy in the first years of the period in response to growing inflationary pressures, the Government shifted its policy priorities toward sustaining employment in mid-1974 to counteract the impact of sharply higher oil prices. In the following two years, the vigorous pursuit of this new objective, through both sides of the budget, led to a sharp widening of the fiscal deficit. Among measures on the expenditure side were the activation of contingency budgets during the period 1974–76 for road construction and other public investments, as well as for subsidies to agriculture, mining, and exports, release of frozen funds of local governments, and subsidization of investment credit to the business sector. Revenue measures that aimed directly at the stimulation of employment and private sector activity included special depreciation allowances for certain types of investment and a suspension of the investment tax that had been imposed in 1973 to make up for revenue loss (repayment of taxes on inventories) caused by the adoption of a value-added tax in that year.

The expansionary fiscal policies caused considerable concern, not only because of the rising public debt, but also because of the structural character of the fiscal deficit that was gradually becoming evident, with adverse implications for the future flexibility of fiscal policy. The elasticity of the revenue system had declined owing to tax changes, especially in direct taxes, embodied in an income tax reform initiated in 1973 that was intended to reduce the tax burden of low- and middle-income earners. Company taxation was also reduced to stimulate investment. At the same time, certain expenditure categories expanded rapidly, especially subsidies to public enterprises. Transfers to the social security system also escalated, in particular for pension insurance, which, unlike the health and accident insurance, is not financed by private contributions, but by substantial transfers from the budget. The increase in pension expenditure also reflected a steady rise in the ratio of pension receivers to the work force that contributes. The sharply deteriorating current account position of the balance of payments in 1976 and 1977 was another cause for concern, as was the rising unemployment in the years following, which, at around 2 percent, represented historically high rates for Austria.

The policy response to these developments was a so-called "dual strategy," which tried to deal simultaneously with the fiscal and external deficits and the depressed state of economic activity. In the budget for 1978, the authorities announced their aim of reducing the fiscal deficit in the medium term; a target was set at about 2½ percent of GDP in that year and in the following year at about 2 percent. To restrain domestic demand and reduce the fiscal deficit, various tax measures were introduced, such as an increase in the VAT rate from 16 percent to 18 percent in 1976 and a third VAT rate of 30 percent on luxury goods in 1978.[1] Subsequent revenue-raising measures have mainly included indirect taxes, such as energy taxes, but further income tax reductions have been continued, largely to compensate for fiscal drag.

Despite the increased emphasis on reducing fiscal and external deficits since 1977, preserving a high level of employment has continued to be a major aim of fiscal policy. To fulfill this part of the dual strategy, investment promotion programs were initiated in 1978 and employment programs were introduced in 1982. Apart from direct budgetary investment outlays, these programs have included interest rate subsidies and tax credits for certain types of investment. The nationalized sector has also played a significant role in the high employment policy by traditionally maintaining employment during recessions. However, this practice has added to the financial difficulties of the sector, which, in turn, have placed a further burden on future budgets, as the Government has in recent years assumed debt repayment obligations for the nationalized industries, in addition to paying direct subsidies. Private sector activity has also received similar support from the Treasury, which has assumed obligations relating to export guarantees as a means of promoting exports.

Overview and implications for future policy. A striking feature of fiscal policy over the past decade has been its success in maintaining full employment. The wider implications of this success, however, are less satisfactory. The declining growth performance of the economy toward the end of the period is in part attributable to insufficient structural adjustment, which was presumably delayed by the high employment policy that tended to slow down labor mobility. Policymakers now face a difficult choice between the social and economic aspects of policy. Also, the growing practice of supporting selected industries by granting credit guarantees and assuming debt-servicing payments has not only entailed a future budgetary burden but might also reduce incentives for efficiency and retard the adjustment process.

An additional implication of past fiscal policy stems from the persistence of fiscal deficits. It is arguable that the impact of increased fiscal deficits on interest rates may be limited, as interest rates in Austria

---

[1] These rates were raised further by 2 percentage points in 1983.

are determined by external rather than domestic factors. While such factors may in part explain why the deficits did not appear to be crowding out private investment, the depressed state of activity and the slack in private sector demand for credit in the last years of the period may be a better explanation for the absence of crowding out. However, there is a probability that protracted deficits could affect expectations and exert an upward pressure on interest rates, and economic recovery might soon create crowding-out problems. Also, failure to reduce the deficit would increasingly restrict the flexibility of fiscal policy, which has in the past contributed significantly to successful management of the economy.

The authorities reacted to the deteriorating fiscal position by announcing in 1978 their intention to reduce the fiscal deficit in the medium term and setting specific targets in that regard. After some initial success, these aims were negated by the working of automatic stabilizers and discretionary measures to support employment. Although economic recovery abroad would ease the task of improving the fiscal balance, a change in policy priorities with greater emphasis on expenditure restraint is nevertheless necessary. An important step in that direction could be the reform of the social security system, particularly the pension system, that the authorities are contemplating.

3

Belgium

Following several years of strong growth, real GDP declined by almost 2 percent in 1975; after a sharp recovery in 1976, when over 5 percent real growth was registered, economic activity again turned sluggish. The rate of unemployment rose from 3 percent in 1972 to over 13 percent in 1982. Inflation was also rising; after recording a relatively moderate rise in the latter half of the 1960s, consumer price increases reached a peak of almost 13 percent in both 1974 and 1975. Although the rate abated to a moderate 4½ percent in 1978 and 1979, reflecting in part stringent wage and price policies, it began rising again in 1980, and was close to 9 percent in 1982. The external current account position steadily deteriorated throughout the period—from a surplus equivalent to 3½ percent of GDP in 1972 to a deficit of 4½ percent in both 1980 and 1981. A combination of structural adjustment difficulties in the domestic economy, notably in the important steel industry, expansionary fiscal policies, and adverse external factors contributed to this development. The impact of external factors is particularly strong in the highly open Belgian economy, where foreign trade amounts to over 50 percent of GDP. However, as a result of broad-based measures in 1982 to reduce domestic and external imbalances, the current account deficit dropped to 3½ percent of GDP in that year. Large and persistent fiscal deficits were experienced over the period; their harmful impact on the external current account was substantially mitigated, however, especially in the early part of the period, by an unusually high ratio of private household savings that made noninflationary financing of the fiscal deficit possible.

EXPENDITURE

Probably the most striking feature of fiscal developments in Belgium during the period under review is the explosive growth of central

Belgium: Selected Economic Indicators, 1972–82

	1972	1973	1974	1975	1976	1977	1978	1979	1980	1981	1982
Real GDP, percentage changes	5.3	6.2	4.5	−1.9	5.2	0.4	3.0	2.0	3.5	−1.3	1.1
Rate of unemployment	2.7	2.8	3.1	5.1	6.6	7.5	8.1	8.4	9.0	11.1	13.1
Consumer prices, percentage changes	5.5	7.0	12.7	12.8	9.2	7.1	4.5	4.5	6.6	7.6	8.7
External current account balance as percentage of GDP	3.6	2.0	0.4	−0.1	0.1	−1.3	−1.4	−2.7	−4.5	−4.5	−3.5

Source: Organization for Economic Cooperation and Development, *Economic Outlook*, December 1984.

Belgium: Consolidated Central Government Finances, 1972–82

(Year ended December 31)

	1972	1973	1974	1975	1976	1977	1978	1979	1980	1981	1982
Total Revenue (as a percentage of GDP)	35.4	36.5	37.4	40.1	40.4	41.7	42.7	42.9	43.6	43.9	44.7
Percentages of total revenue	100.0	100.0	100.0	100.0	100.0	100.0	100.0	100.0	100.0	100.0	100.0
Income taxes	31.2	33.0	34.6	36.8	35.8	37.3	38.8	39.6	38.2	37.6	39.4
Social security contributions	32.2	32.1	31.8	32.3	32.2	31.5	30.6	30.6	30.4	30.7	29.9
Payroll (manpower) taxes	—	—	—	—	—	—	—	—	—	—	...
Property taxes	3.0	3.1	2.8	2.5	2.7	2.8	2.9	3.0	2.4	2.0	1.8
Taxes on goods and services	28.7	27.5	26.5	24.4	25.4	24.6	24.5	23.2	24.5	24.4	23.9
Taxes on international trade	1.0	0.5	0.4	—	—	—	—	—	—	—	...
Other taxes	0.3	0.3	0.3	0.3	0.1	0.1	0.1	0.1	0.2	0.1	0.1
Nontax revenue and grants	3.6	3.6	3.7	3.7	3.8	3.7	3.2	3.6	4.4	5.3	5.0
Total Expenditure (as a percentage of GDP)	39.8	39.9	39.6	44.8	46.0	47.7	49.5	50.5	51.3	56.2	56.9
Percentages of total expenditure	100.0	100.0	100.0	100.0	100.0	100.0	100.0	100.0	100.0	100.0	100.0
Expenditure on goods and services	24.9	24.6	24.8	24.7	24.0	23.4	23.2	22.6	22.2	21.4	20.5
Of which:											
Wages and salaries	17.6	17.7	18.0	17.5	17.2	16.8	16.3	15.9	15.7	15.2	14.7
Interest payments	6.6	6.6	6.9	6.1	6.2	6.7	7.2	8.1	9.8	11.9	13.5

Subsidies and other current transfers	56.0	58.0	57.9	59.9	60.1	60.5	59.7	60.1	57.7	56.7	55.6
Of which: Social security funds	33.3	34.2	35.3	37.2	38.3	38.2	37.7	38.3	37.5	36.8	36.5
Capital expenditure	12.0	10.2	9.4	8.3	8.5	8.5	8.1	8.0	8.3	8.6	8.8
Lending minus repayments	0.6	0.7	1.0	1.1	1.1	0.9	1.8	1.2	1.9	1.4	1.6
Surplus/Deficit (as a percentage of GDP)	−4.3	−3.5	−2.2	−4.7	−5.6	−5.9	−6.9	−7.6	−7.7	−12.3	−12.2
Financing:											
Abroad	−1.0	−0.2	−0.1	—	—	—	0.4	1.3	2.4	5.9	5.3
Domestic	5.3	3.7	2.3	4.7	5.6	5.9	6.4	6.3	5.3	6.4	6.9
Monetary authorities	−0.2	0.1	0.1	—	0.6	0.6	—	—	—	—	—
Deposit money banks	—	—	—	—	—	—	—	—	—	—	—
Other[1]	5.5	3.5	2.2	4.7	5.0	5.4	6.4	6.3	5.3	6.4	6.9
Memorandum Items:											
General government expenditure and net lending/GDP	45.0	⋯	⋯	40.0	⋯	⋯	53.6	55.3	54.6	61.5	61.9
Central government debt outstanding/GDP	42.5	39.0	40.0	40.3	43.2	46.2	49.7	54.8	65.2	73.9	

Source: International Monetary Fund, Government Finance Statistics Yearbook, 1983 and 1984.
[1] Includes adjustments.

government expenditure; its ratio to GDP expanded by 17 percentage points, from 40 percent in 1972 to 57 percent in 1982. This increase was concentrated in two particular years, namely, 1975, when expansionary fiscal policy coincided with a decline in real GDP and the share recorded an upward shift of over 5 percentage points; and again in 1981, when similar events contributed to an almost 5 percentage-point rise in this ratio. Well over half the total relative increase thus occurred in these two years.

The major part of the expansion was accounted for by subsidies and other current transfers, especially to social security funds. This category roughly maintained its share in total expenditure at 56 percent over the period. Apart from deliberate policy action to improve real benefits, the growth of social security expenditures is also the result of demographic factors reflecting the aging structure of the population. Furthermore, depressed economic activity has triggered built-in fiscal stabilizers and caused an especially rapid growth of unemployment compensations. This last factor, in addition to generating increased outlays on direct unemployment benefits, has resulted in declining social security contributions from both employers and employees, thus necessitating increased central government grants.

Interest payments on government debt were the second most dynamic element underlying the expansion of the government sector. Their share in total expenditure rose from 6½ percent to 13½ percent over the period as a result of high and rapidly widening fiscal deficits and rising interest rates. While the share of expenditure on goods and services in total expenditure declined, it more than kept pace with GDP growth. Over 70 percent of this category is accounted for by wages and salaries, the growth of which is due, in part, to rising public employment brought about by the Government's unemployment relief policy. Similarly, while the share of capital expenditure in total government expenditure declined somewhat over the period, it grew in line with GDP. Net lending averaged just over 1 percent of total expenditure over the period.

REVENUE

From 1972 to 1982 the ratio of central government revenue to GDP rose by 9½ percentage points to 44½ percent in 1982, among the highest such ratio of the countries in the group. However, in the years preceding the period covered, the tax burden was lower than in many other industrial countries. The high elasticity of the tax system with respect to GDP stems largely from progressive income taxes, which for most of the period were only partially adjusted for inflation. Social security contributions also rose faster than national income. Together, these two sources of revenue accounted for 69½ percent of total revenue in 1982, their share having risen from 63½ percent in 1972. A regime of value-added taxes was introduced in 1971 and accounts for about two thirds of taxes on goods and services, which declined as a proportion of total revenue from almost 29 percent in 1972 to 24 percent in 1982. However, the ratio of this type of tax to GDP has remained almost constant. Other taxes taken together became less significant revenue sources over the period, while nontax revenue increased its share in the total from 3½ percent to 5 percent.

THE FISCAL BALANCE AND ITS FINANCING

In the years 1972–74, revenue increased faster than expenditure and the fiscal deficit declined. Since 1974 the respective growth rates were reversed, with the deficit steadily widening as a proportion of GDP, or from 2 percent in 1974 to 12 percent in 1982. The high private savings ratio that had formerly mitigated the monetary impact of the large and growing deficits became less effective, not only because the deficits were growing, but also because the households' savings ratio was declining— from 17.3 percent on average in 1972–76 to 15.9 percent during 1977–80. These contrary movements entailed a change in the pattern of deficit financing. Until 1978 the deficit had been financed entirely by domestic sources, mostly in the form of bond sales in the capital market. In that year, for the first time in a decade, the authorities turned to foreign borrowing despite their stated reluctance. Since then, an increasing portion of the deficit has been financed abroad—almost one half in 1982—with only slight recourse to domestic monetary financing, and none since 1977. As a consequence of the mounting fiscal deficits, government debt rose sharply over the period—from 45 percent of GDP in 1972 to 74 percent in 1982. This ratio has since risen further and is one of the highest among industrial countries.

FISCAL POLICY

The framework. In 1982 the ratio of general government expenditure to GDP was almost 62 percent. Including transfers to local governments, over 90 percent of total public sector spending was accounted for by the Central Government. Despite the limited size of local governments, their fast growing expenditure resulted in deficits whose financing requirement amounted to 10 percent to 15 percent of the public sector borrowing requirement (PSBR) in the 1980–82 period. In light of this rise, the Government decided toward the end of 1982 to avail itself of special powers and adopted a decree that imposed balanced budgets on the local authorities from 1988. Consequently, local governments were granted greater revenue-raising possibilities by the abolition of the previous limit on the local surtax on personal income tax.

The broad lines of the Government's economic policy are set forth in an overall plan, the National Plan, which covers five-year periods. According to the provisions of a law enacted in 1970, the plan is to be reflected annually in the budget. In practice, coordination of the budget and the plan pertains especially to public investment, while the plan in general is regarded as indicative. The plan, which is debated and passed by Parliament, sets targets for public investment that may be adjusted over the course of the period in line with short-term policy aims without upsetting the aggregate target.

The Belgian budget is made up of two main accounts: the ordinary budget, containing mainly current expenditure and revenue as well as amortization of debt; and the extraordinary budget, which includes investment expenditure. In the early 1970s, and for several preceding years, the ordinary budget remained in approximate balance; investment expenditure in the extraordinary budget was relied on to provide flexibility in fiscal policy. The flexibility initially derived from a certain part of the Government's investment program—the so-called *tranche conditionelle*—which was set aside to be used only when cyclical conditions in the economy warranted; the size of the investment program itself was determined with regard to the economic outlook. Later, the *tranche conditionelle* was replaced by a supplementary program in addition to the base program for capital expenditures. This innovation, while closely resembling the previous technique, was intended to increase flexibility in adapting expenditure levels to changes in the economic outlook. The supplementary program was first introduced in the 1975 budget and accounted for 0.4 percent of GDP. Widening fiscal deficits have severely restricted the scope for applying these techniques effectively, and vastly increased transfer payments have in particular pre-empted any large-scale use of capital expenditure to stimulate activity and employment. Fiscal multipliers are relatively small in the highly open Belgian economy, and especially so in the case of transfers.

Aims and measures. Until the mid-1970s fiscal policy was largely concerned with inflation. The main emphasis was placed on curbing capital expenditures, but the pursuit of a restrictive expenditure policy was hampered by previous and ongoing commitments in social security programs. Inflation itself was also found to be an obstacle to expenditure restraint, not only on account of salary indexation and transfers, but also because the responsive tax system made it easier to finance new expenditures. Changes of government further weakened effective resistance to pressures for increased public spending. By mid-1975, the prospects for employment and output had severely worsened and policy priorities changed; unemployment became the major concern. Special measures were announced to stimulate the economy and to prevent a further increase in unemployment without adding to inflationary pressures.

In subsequent years, fiscal policy became defensive, seeking to mitigate the impact of the depressed state of economic activity experienced in the remainder of the period. Automatic fiscal stabilizers triggered ever-increasing social security outlays and reduced revenue growth. Discretionary measures included several programs to stimulate employment in the private sector, including providing credit to finance additional hiring to firms that had agreed to cut working hours. Ailing industries also received extensive support. To counteract rising unemployment, public sector employment was increased and early retirement schemes were introduced.

The most dynamic force underlying expenditure growth, however, is the social security system. In addition to demographic and cyclical factors, the system's rising cost is the result of indexation of benefits to wages or prices and the policy, pursued by successive governments, of improving benefits in real terms and expanding their coverage. The system is quite extensive, and the various schemes are administered by separate commissions—an arrangement that tends to complicate consistent decision making and weakens effective control over expenditure. The result is that social benefits, notably unemployment compensations, have become more generous in Belgium than in most other countries. It is estimated that over 80 percent of Belgian households receive support from the system in one form or another, and that one fourth of all households are entirely dependent on it financially. In response to the deterioration in the financial position of the social security system, the authorities have taken measures to limit the increase in benefits. A comprehensive review of fundamental aspects of the system is under consideration, with the goals of improving efficiency in income redistribution and work effort and eliminating deficiencies in other areas. A change in the method of financing the system is also under consideration: employers' contributions would be based on the value added by firms rather than on the number of employees or the wage bill. This method would not distort the relative cost of labor as the present system does.

For most of the period, fiscal policy has relied on expenditure rather than tax measures. The observed significant increase in direct taxes was mostly generated automatically by the progressivity of the income tax system. Only toward the end of the period was a more active tax policy applied: certain investment incentives were introduced in 1979, and full indexing of income tax scales for lower income groups, in 1980. Moreover, in 1981 part of employers' social security contributions, which had become a heavy burden in the depressed economic conditions, was substituted by an increase in value-added and excise taxes. These measures were taken to some extent in the context of incomes policy, but with the exception of a temporary wage freeze, government intervention in income formation has been limited.

A special feature of fiscal policy in Belgium in the early 1970s was the conduct of large-scale open market operations in support of monetary policy. By borrowing domestically in excess of the financing requirement, this debt management policy aimed at sterilizing the liquidity impact of inflows of foreign funds and reducing foreign debt. Also, short-term domestic debt was converted through the sale of long-term bonds in the domestic market. As indicated earlier, fiscal policy subsequently played a reverse role in this respect.

Overview and implications for future policy. For most of the period, fiscal policy in Belgium was conducted against an unfavorable economic background. Also, the political environment was less than conducive to the formulation of consistent long-term policies. The high priority assigned to various social policies contributed to the continued growth in fiscal deficits in the wake of the 1974–75 recession, unlike in most countries in the group where the deficits tended to stabilize or decline. The large and growing deficits implied a sharp rise in the central government debt, which, as a percent of GDP, had become among the highest in industrial countries. A falling private savings ratio entailed increasing monetary financing of the deficits. Nonmonetary deficit financing, mostly by the sale of bonds, exerted upward pressure on long-term interest rates, which remained relatively high in Belgium. The high interest rates were detrimental to the economically depressed private sector, which was also burdened by rapidly growing direct taxes.

Concern has been growing over these and other implications of past fiscal policies, such as the constrictive impact of employment-stimulating measures on structural adjustment and the erosion of work incentives by generous unemployment benefits. Despite delays caused by political controversies, the authorities have in recent years been able to make some headway in implementing a financial reform of the social security system. Moreover, specific medium-term fiscal targets were announced in the 1982 budget which aimed at reducing the total public sector deficit from 14½ percent in 1981 to 7 percent in 1985, largely through expenditure restraint. A slower than expected recovery of domestic and external demand and other subsequent developments, however, obliged the authorities to revise their timetable for reducing the deficit. The task of establishing a fiscal balance that would be consistent with medium-term investment and savings volumes in other sectors of the economy and a sustainable balance on external current account is therefore likely to remain a major preoccupation of fiscal policy for a number of years. The mounting debt-servicing burden will require an especially determined effort, even if external conditions were to improve appreciably.

4

Denmark

The relatively open Danish economy, where foreign trade amounts to 25 to 30 percent of GDP, was severely affected by the two oil crises and the ensuing global recession. Denmark's heavy dependence on imported energy made it especially vulnerable; in 1973 oil imports accounted for 90 percent of its basic energy supplies.

A sudden drop in GDP growth occurred in 1974 and 1975, when GDP actually fell by about 1 percent in each year. Growth rebounded to 6½ percent in 1976, in response to a sharply expansionary policy, but in subsequent years it was sluggish and uneven. The poor growth performance during the past several years reflects not only the effect of external impulses, but also restrictive economic policies that were imposed to alleviate the persistent balance of payments problem.

Unemployment rose drastically over the period, with the rate of registered unemployed rising from less than 1 percent in 1973 to 10 percent in 1982. Although the slowdown of economic growth may have accounted for much of the rise in unemployment, increasingly generous unemployment compensations may also have contributed by undermining work incentives.

Inflation averaged more than 10 percent a year over the period, which is above the average for industrial countries. It reached high points in 1974 and 1980, 15½ percent and 12½ percent, respectively, owing largely to the oil price increases and accommodating financial policies, but the high rates have been sustained by the reliance on higher indirect taxation to curb private demand and by wage indexation mechanisms.

The external current account position was in deficit throughout the period. The deficit widened from 0.4 percent to over 3 percent of GDP between 1972 and 1974, but was halved in the following year when the

Denmark: Selected Economic Indicators, 1972–82

	1972	1973	1974	1975	1976	1977	1978	1979	1980	1981	1982
Real GDP, percentage changes	5.4	3.8	−0.7	−1.0	6.5	2.3	1.8	3.7	−0.4	−0.9	3.4
Rate of unemployment	1.4	0.9	2.1	5.1	5.3	6.4	7.3	6.1	7.0	9.2	10.0
Consumer prices, percentage changes	6.6	9.3	15.3	9.6	9.0	11.1	10.0	9.6	12.3	11.7	10.1
External current account balance as a percentage of GDP	−0.4	−1.7	−3.1	−1.5	−4.9	−4.0	−2.7	−4.7	−3.7	−3.0	−4.1

Sources: Organization for Economic Cooperation and Development, *Economic Outlook*, December 1984; for unemployment data: Danmarks Statistik, Statistisk Tiårsoversigt 1983.

Denmark: Consolidated Central Government Finances, 1972–82

(Year beginning April 1st through 1975, and Year ended December 31 after 1975)

	1972	1973	1974	1975	1976	1977	1978	1979	1980	1981	1982
Total Revenue											
(as a percentage of GDP)	34.6	34.5	35.0	33.0	34.9	34.7	36.7	37.4	37.8	37.5	36.9
Percentages of total revenue	100.0	100.0	100.0	100.0	100.0	100.0	100.0	100.0	100.0	100.0	100.0
Income taxes	39.3	41.6	45.4	40.6	37.2	35.2	34.6	33.4	33.5	33.7	33.8
Social security contributions	5.0	1.6	1.6	1.7	1.6	1.7	1.6	1.8	2.2	2.6	3.4
Payroll (manpower) taxes	—	—	—	—	—	—	—	—	—	—	—
Property taxes	2.7	3.3	2.4	2.3	2.3	3.2	3.3	3.2	3.0	2.6	2.2
Taxes on goods and services	41.4	41.5	38.2	40.0	41.1	44.2	44.3	45.4	44.2	44.3	43.6
Taxes on international trade	3.0	1.4	1.2	1.3	1.3	1.2	0.8	0.8	0.8	0.7	0.7
Other taxes	—	—	—	—	—	—	—	—	—	—	—
Nontax revenue and grants	8.3	10.4	11.2	14.0	16.5	14.6	15.5	15.6	16.3	16.1	16.3
Total Expenditure											
(as a percentage of GDP)	32.0	31.0	34.4	35.0	35.2	36.0	37.0	38.1	40.6	43.7	45.2
Percentages of total expenditure	100.0	100.0	100.0	100.0	100.0	100.0	100.0	100.0	100.0	100.0	100.0
Expenditure on goods and services	32.5	28.8	28.1	28.1	25.7	24.4	23.3	22.2	21.3	20.7	20.0
Of which:											
Wages and salaries	19.4	19.2	18.6	18.8	17.1	16.3	15.4	14.8	13.4	12.9	12.4
Interest payments	1.3	1.5	1.4	1.5	1.9	3.1	3.4	6.1	6.6	8.6	10.1

Subsidies and other current transfers	58.3	62.2	63.1	62.9	64.2	66.3	67.3	66.7	66.7	64.9	64.0
Of which:											
Social security funds	4.3	1.6	4.3	6.7	6.6	7.9	8.9	9.2	10.3	11.9	11.8
Capital expenditure	6.5	6.1	5.8	6.3	6.9	5.3	4.8	4.4	4.2	4.5	4.7
Lending minus repayments	1.4	1.5	1.5	1.3	1.2	1.0	1.2	0.7	1.1	1.2	1.2
Surplus/Deficit (as a percentage of GDP)	2.6	3.5	0.7	−1.9	−0.4	−1.3	−0.3	−0.7	−2.7	−6.2	−8.3
Memorandum Items:											
General government expenditure and net lending/GDP	...	...	...	...	...	50.3	52.2	53.8	56.6	59.8	...
Central government debt outstanding/GDP	−1.6	−3.6	−1.7	4.5	8.4	13.2	18.2	24.7	33.7	45.9	59.2

Sources: International Monetary Fund, *Government Finance Statistics Yearbook*, 1983 and 1984; for government debt data: national sources.

domestic recession deepened and a marked fall in imports resulted. With subsequent temporary stimulus measures, the external position deteriorated sharply in 1976 when the current deficit reached 5 percent of GDP. In the remainder of the period, the current account deficit ranged between 3 percent and 5 percent of GDP. The persistent balance of payments problem has been a constant cause for concern to the authorities and has significantly shaped economic policy during the period under review.

EXPENDITURE

Between 1972 and 1982 central government expenditure rose as a percentage of GDP from 32 percent to 45 percent, which represents a continuation of the rapid expansion of the government sector that began in the 1960s. Expenditure on goods and services declined sharply as a proportion of total expenditure from 32½ percent to 20 percent, and within this category the share of wages and salaries in the total declined steadily from 19½ percent to 12½ percent. Measures to alleviate the unemployment problem by increasing public employment mostly affected the local government sector. Both wages and salaries and other expenditure on goods and services grew more slowly than GDP. By contrast, subsidies and other current transfers increased their share in the total from 58½ percent to 64 percent between 1972 and 1982, owing in part to increased unemployment compensations and measures to reduce costs and improve the competitiveness of enterprises.

With widening fiscal deficits in the period following the first oil crisis, interest payments on the government debt rose from 1½ percent of total expenditure in 1972 to 10 percent in 1982; there are signs that debt servicing will impose a sharply increasing burden on the budget in future years. Capital expenditure declined as a proportion of total expenditure from 6½ percent to 4½ percent between 1972 and 1982 and was a reflection of the increased reliance on cuts in investment expenditure as part of efforts to curb overall expenditure growth in the latter half of the period. Net lending has not been significant at the central level and ranged between 1 percent and 1½ percent of total expenditure over the period.

REVENUE

Central government revenue expressed as a ratio to GDP increased moderately from 34½ percent in 1972 to 37 percent in 1982 after having dropped to 33 percent in 1975. The share of income taxes, over 90 percent of which are personal income taxes, in total revenue rose from 39½ percent in 1972 to 45½ percent in 1974 due in part to a pay-as-you-earn (PAYE) system of income tax collection that had been introduced in 1970. The share has since dropped sharply and was less than 34 percent in 1982. The drop reflects the depressed state of economic activity and a series of tax concessions designed to stimulate private sector demand and support incomes policy.

Taxes on goods and services, on the other hand, rose as a share of total revenue from 41½ percent in 1972 to 43½ percent in 1982. Increases in indirect taxes were the major fiscal instrument used to curb private sector demand—mainly through increases in the value-added tax, which was introduced in 1967 and in 1982 accounted for 60 percent of revenue in this category. A temporary reduction in the value-added tax partly explains the drop in the ratio of total revenue to GDP in 1975–77. Other taxes in this category include various excises and motor vehicle taxes, some of which are specific and have not kept pace with nominal GDP growth. Other tax revenue taken together, that is, social security contributions, property taxes, and taxes on international trade, declined as a share in total revenue from 10½ percent in 1972 to 6½ percent in 1982, reflecting in part the elimination of customs duties on products from EC member countries during a transitional period that ended at the beginning of 1978. Nontax revenue and grants, on the other hand, increased their share in the total from 8½ percent to 16½ percent over the period. The most important revenue items in this category are property income, administrative fees and charges, and grants from the EC.

THE FISCAL BALANCE AND ITS FINANCING

In most years from 1960 to 1974, central government finances were in surplus. But in the mid-1970s, automatic expenditure increases and revenue shortfalls brought about by recessionary conditions led to a sharp fiscal deterioration. In 1975 a number of discretionary measures were introduced to counteract the effects of the recession, and the fiscal position shifted to a deficit amounting to 2 percent of GDP. In the following four years the deficit contracted to about or less than 1 percent—owing to fiscal restraint in view of the worsening balance of payments position and high inflation rates. However, in 1979 it widened sharply and in 1982 reached the equivalent of more than 8 percent of GDP. The renewed upsurge in oil prices, a mounting debt-servicing burden, and expansionary measures taken in 1981 were largely responsible for the widening deficit. No data on deficit financing are given in *Government Finance Statistics (GFS)*, the basic source. There is evidence, however, that the deficit has been financed mostly by domestic sources and the external current account deficits have been financed mainly by external borrowing by the Government. The domestic financing require-ment has been met by bond issues and the sale of securities to both the banking and nonbanking sectors; the latter have in recent years covered about three fifths of the gross borrowing requirement. At times, recourse has been made to the central bank. While these debt data should be interpreted cautiously, as government borrowing is also for balance of payments purposes, International Monetary Fund staff estimates indicate that total net central government debt, expressed as a proportion of GDP, rose from minus 1½ percent to 59 percent between 1972 and 1982.

FISCAL POLICY

The framework. The size of the local government sector is relatively larger in Denmark than in all the other countries in the group except Sweden and Norway. Of the almost 60 percent general government expenditure/GDP ratio in 1981, central government expenditure inclu-sive of transfers to other levels of government accounted for 44 percent. Although local governments derive approximately one half of their total revenue as transfers from the Central Government, their financial autonomy is substantial, as local councils have the right to determine the level of local income and property tax rates. As a result of a local government reform in 1970, responsibility for certain current and capital functions was transferred to the local level, while the Central Govern-ment took over a number of social security-oriented transfers.

Because of the significance of local government activity in the economy, fiscal policy issues have had to be coordinated at both levels, and a procedural framework has been developed which places emphasis on improving control over public expenditure in the medium term. Since the mid-1960s, multiyear budgeting has been gradually introduced into the budgetary process, and rolling budgets covering a three-year period beyond the next fiscal year are prepared annually and presented to Parliament with the annual central government budget.[1] Later, multiyear budgeting was adopted at the local level, and the first public sector budget was published in 1979. Although the public sector budgets

---

[1] *The Danish Budgetary System*, pp. 4–5.

are not formally binding on the Government, they form a basis for the establishment of overall ceilings on expenditure. Negotiations take place between the Central Government and the association of local governments about overall ceilings on real expenditure growth. The outcome of the negotiations takes the form of recommendations from the Central Government.

While the multiyear public sector budget has a sound technical and informational basis, the effectiveness of the system of centrally fixed ceilings is limited, as it relates only to expenditure that is not fixed by specific legislation. Major expenditure categories, chiefly transfers to persons and to local governments, are based on law, and, at the central level, account for some 60 percent of total expenditure. This proportion has been growing over the period. Another factor that tends to complicate long-term public decision making and to upset a steady policy course is Denmark's political system, which is characterized by coalitions or minority governments.

Aims and measures. Over the period, the persistent balance of payments problem had significant implications for the pursuit of fiscal policy. While external adjustment efforts relied on incomes policy and, toward the end of the period, on exchange rate adjustments, fiscal policy sought to contribute through restraining private sector demand, supporting incomes policy, and providing incentives for the transfer of resources to the export sector. Other major objectives of fiscal policy were to cushion the impact of the international recession on employment and activity and to improve social security benefits in real terms. Stabilization also became the province of fiscal policy, as monetary policy was mainly preoccupied with preserving the foreign reserve position, which entailed high interest rates to induce the capital inflows needed to finance the external deficit.

After general restraint in the early years of the period—achieved largely through a ban on new public investment projects—fiscal policy shifted in a highly expansionary direction in the wake of the first oil crisis; a number of discretionary measures to stimulate the economy were introduced in 1975. This action was prompted by rising unemployment and an easing of the balance of payments position. The improvement in the external balance proved to be short-lived, however, and with a sharply widening current external deficit in the following year, fiscal policy resumed a restrictive stance. In subsequent years, with a persistently high external deficit, fiscal restraint focused largely on increases in indirect taxes. The effectiveness of this approach, however, was severely limited by measures on the expenditure side to contain rising unemployment and by tax concessions to stimulate demand. Fiscal restraint was further stymied by actions taken as part of incomes policy to curb inflation and to support the balance of payments adjustment process, as well as other actions, at times associated with changes of government, to improve social security benefits.

The resulting deterioration in the budgetary position was aggravated by cyclical factors that automatically caused social security payments to increase and revenue growth to slow down. Also, the inflationary conditions further weakened the fiscal position. Experience suggests that expenditure was more affected by inflation than was revenue, owing to indexation of significant expenditure components, the existence of specific excise and other taxes, and indexation of tax scales and deductions.

In contrast to the policy response to the first oil crisis, the fiscal stance remained tight in the first year after the second oil shock as far as discretionary action is concerned. However, as a result of the working of automatic stabilizers and a shift of fiscal policy in an expansionary direction in 1981, the fiscal position deteriorated markedly after 1978. With a new government in 1982, fiscal policy again assumed a restrictive stance.

The pursuit of fiscal policy toward the several goals discussed above involved a variety of measures. Measures on the expenditure side to stimulate demand and employment introduced before and during the mid-1970s included public building programs, subsidization of interest costs on loans for residential construction, and relaxation of ceilings on local government investment. Among measures to support employment in these and subsequent years was a program to increase public sector employment, financed partly by the Central Government, for retraining the long-term unemployed in the local government and private sectors. Youth employment programs were also introduced. Other measures have included subsidies for energy-conserving investment in the enterprise sector and for energy-saving repair and maintenance work in residential housing. The export industry has received grants and subsidies, as well as tax concessions.

In the social security field, in addition to full indexation of pensions, benefits have been raised in real terms and their coverage extended. In 1979 an early retirement scheme was introduced to encourage wage earners in the 60–66 age group to withdraw from the labor force. A generous system of unemployment compensations has been developed to serve the high-priority social objective of relieving distress. A rapidly growing labor force in recent years, owing mainly to a rising female participation rate, has constituted growing claims on budgetary resources.

Stimulatory measures on the revenue side included a substantial reduction in the personal income tax at the beginning of 1975. This reduction followed intense controversy over the prevailing high marginal tax rates—on average, one half of each increment to money wages was being absorbed by direct taxes—which were thought to have significantly contributed to the speed of cost-inflation. The issue had important political implications; a new party placing the abolition of income tax at the top of its platform won 15 percent of the seats in Parliament in the 1973 general elections. The income tax reduction was at the same time intended to moderate wage settlements, and similarly motivated cuts were made in subsequent years. The personal income tax scales have been indexed since 1970. One stimulatory measure taken in 1975 was a reduction in the value-added tax from 15 percent to 9¼ percent, which was maintained until 1977. Company tax reductions have taken the form of increased depreciation allowances, such as a countercyclical special depreciation allowance on investment in plant and machinery. Toward the end of the period, depreciation allowances were indexed. Measures specifically designed to support incomes policy and to contribute to the balance of payments adjustment process include the already cited cuts in the personal income tax and payment by the central government of a portion of indexation compensations due to workers into blocked individual accounts with the Supplementary Labor Market Pension Fund.

As already mentioned, the restrictive stance of fiscal policy relied on increases in indirect taxation, especially the value-added tax, which after the temporary reduction during 1975–77, was raised in stages from 9¼ percent in 1977 to 22 percent in 1980. Taxes on energy use were also raised largely for conservation, and a number of specific excise duties were increased, although these hardly kept pace with GDP growth, as indicated earlier. Rapidly expanding public sector activity has long been a cause for concern to the Danish authorities, and restraint on the expenditure side has been part of the fiscal strategy since 1976. Successive governments set targets to contain public expenditure growth, but successful realization of these targets has been limited, especially at the central level. Although local governments assumed a fair amount of the burden of containing unemployment through employment-creating schemes, their expenditure has grown less than central government expenditure over the past several years, mainly because the Central Government, in connection with the local government reform in 1970, assumed responsibility for the rapidly growing social security expenditures.

Overview and implications for future policy. Owing to the openness of the economy and in particular its high dependence on imported energy sources, the impact of the two oil crises and recessionary external developments was especially strong in Denmark. These events exacerbated the country's longstanding balance of payments problem and posed a difficult dilemma for fiscal policy, which was a major instrument of stabilization throughout the period under review. Attaining the objectives of cushioning the impact of recessionary trends and improving social security benefits in real terms without imparting undue pressure on the balance of payments has proved elusive and has been complicated by changes in policy priorities.

Official goals to contain public sector spending have not materialized, despite long-term planning that was intended to enhance public awareness of the consequences of continuing past trends for private sector activity and overall performance of the economy. Instead, the period witnessed an explosive growth of central government expenditure whose ratio to GDP expanded from 32 percent to 45 percent from 1972 to 1982, with the public expenditure/GDP ratio reaching almost 60 percent by 1981, implying a sharply widening fiscal deficit and a heavy accumulation of government debt.

The major contributor to this deterioration in the fiscal position is the generous social security system whose foundations were largely laid in more prosperous times when prospects for the economy were brighter. Unemployment benefits have been the fastest-growing element, and although they may have relieved distress, they may at the same time have generated disincentives to work. The long-term consequences of high social security expenditure are likely to inhibit the growth of the economy and employment; adjustment to the real growth prospects would seem a prime objective of future fiscal policy.

Reversing these trends was indeed a major objective of one new government. In 1982 it introduced measures to substantially reduce automaticity in expenditure determination by suspending wage and salary indexation and the indexation of certain transfers until 1985, and by limiting increases in public sector wage and salary rates during the same period. While these measures soon led to improvements in certain areas, serious external and internal imbalances remained. Despite prospects for domestic energy production and more favorable external conditions, past experience strongly suggests the need for a resolute course of fiscal policy over an extended period with a clear order of priorities, if lasting improvements are to be achieved. The effort needed is all the greater because of increasing rigidities in the fiscal system owing to indexation mechanisms, a tendency to fix expenditures by specific legislation, and a growing future debt burden.[2]

---

[2] A substantial fiscal adjustment has taken place since 1982 owing to both revenue-raising measures and expenditure restraint. Discretionary actions include the introduction of a tax on pension funds, raising of user charges, containment of certain social security transfers in nominal terms, and a reduction in transfers to local governments. The impact of the temporary suspension of indexation mechanisms is also significant in this respect. Government expenditure other than interest payments declined as a proportion of GDP by several percentage points between 1982 and 1984. The Government has announced its intention to reduce the budget deficit annually until a balance is established by the end of this decade.

5

Finland

A large external sector with imports and exports amounting to almost 30 percent of GDP makes the Finnish economy vulnerable to external influences; this vulnerability is accentuated by the country's reliance for exports on raw materials and semimanufactures, which are subject to sharp swings in demand. Such influences explain in large measure the fluctuations in economic growth over the period.

After real GDP had increased by 7½ percent and 6½ percent in 1972 and 1973, respectively, growth rates declined sharply during the world recession in 1974 and remained at 0.6 percent or less in each of the following three years. With international recovery, GDP growth picked up in 1978 and reached the pre-1974 rates in 1979 and 1980, after which a renewed stagnation set in. The rate of unemployment was kept below 2½ percent up to 1976 but increased in that and the following years, reaching a high of over 7 percent in 1978. Since 1980, however, unemployment has, at 5 percent to 6 percent, been below the average for industrial countries. The rate of inflation accelerated from 7 percent to 18 percent between 1972 and 1975 and remained high during the next two years. A stabilization program in 1977 succeeded in bringing the rise in consumer prices to between 7 percent and 8 percent in 1978 and 1979, but subsequently, inflation accelerated again. In most years from 1972 to 1982, the current external balance was in deficit. The largest deficits, ranging from 4 percent to 8 percent of GDP, were recorded in the 1974–76 period, but they have since declined substantially. The fiscal position changed from annual surpluses in the early years of the period to deficits since the mid-1970s, reflecting, inter alia, the promotion of social services, a more intensive application of fiscal policy in support of the economy, and measures to contain the tax burden.

134

Finland: Selected Economic Indicators, 1972–82

	1972	1973	1974	1975	1976	1977	1978	1979	1980	1981	1982
Real GDP, percentage changes	7.5	6.5	3.2	0.6	0.3	0.4	2.3	7.6	6.0	1.5	2.5
Rate of unemployment	2.5	2.3	1.7	2.2	3.8	5.8	7.2	5.9	4.6	5.1	5.8
Consumer prices, percentage changes	7.1	10.7	16.9	17.9	14.4	12.2	7.8	7.5	11.6	12.0	9.6
External current account balance as percentage of GDP	−1.0	−2.1	−5.3	−7.8	−3.9	−0.5	1.9	−0.4	−2.7	−0.6	−2.0

Source: Organization for Economic Cooperation and Development, *Economic Outlook*, December 1984.

Finland: Consolidated Central Government Finances, 1972–82

(Year ended December 31)

	1972	1973	1974	1975	1976	1977	1978	1979	1980	1981	1982
Total Revenue											
(as a percentage of GDP)	26.7	27.3	26.3	27.9	31.0	30.5	28.6	27.4	27.5	28.6	28.6
Percentages of total revenue	100.0	100.0	100.0	100.0	100.0	100.0	100.0	100.0	100.0	100.0	100.0
Income taxes	29.4	30.9	33.4	32.7	35.4	32.1	27.0	25.5	28.0	30.0	28.5
Social security contributions	7.7	8.7	8.5	9.4	9.6	9.4	8.9	9.8	9.6	9.5	9.6
Payroll (manpower) taxes	2.9	2.7	2.9	3.1	3.4	3.2	3.0	1.1	0.2	0.1	—
Property taxes	2.6	2.8	2.9	2.6	4.0	2.9	2.8	2.7	2.5	2.5	2.6
Taxes on goods and services	46.8	44.4	42.3	40.8	38.3	42.1	46.7	48.9	48.2	47.2	47.6
Taxes on international trade	3.1	2.9	2.8	3.1	1.8	1.9	1.6	1.5	2.0	1.5	1.5
Other taxes	0.2	0.2	0.2	0.2	0.3	0.3	0.3	0.4	0.2	0.3	0.3
Nontax revenue and grants	7.3	7.4	7.0	8.0	7.2	8.1	9.6	10.1	9.4	9.0	9.9
Total Expenditure											
(as a percentage of GDP)	25.5	24.5	25.5	30.1	31.1	32.0	30.5	30.0	29.5	29.6	30.6
Percentages of total expenditure	100.0	100.0	100.0	100.0	100.0	100.0	100.0	100.0	100.0	100.0	100.0
Expenditure on goods and services	22.7	22.4	21.2	20.2	19.7	18.9	19.9	19.7	20.5	20.2	20.4
Of which:											
Wages and salaries	12.7	12.4	11.8	11.0	11.1	10.5	10.8	10.6	10.6	10.8	10.8
Interest payments	1.9	1.7	1.1	0.8	0.8	1.1	1.4	1.9	2.1	2.4	2.9

Subsidies and other current transfers	54.6	55.1	57.8	57.7	59.3	59.5	62.2	63.5	61.5	63.1	63.8
Of which: Social security funds	17.9	18.2	18.6	16.4	16.8	16.5	17.1	15.9	15.3	16.1	17.4
Capital expenditure	15.1	13.9	13.4	13.4	11.3	11.2	10.7	10.2	10.0	9.9	9.7
Lending minus repayments	5.7	6.9	6.5	7.9	9.0	9.4	5.8	4.6	6.0	4.3	3.3
Surplus/Deficit (as a percentage of GDP)	1.2	2.9	0.8	−2.2	—	−1.5	−1.9	−2.6	−2.0	−1.0	−2.0
Financing:											
Abroad	−0.1	−0.2	−0.2	0.4	0.5	0.6	2.1	1.4	0.8	1.1	1.1
Domestic	−1.2	−2.6	−0.6	1.8	−0.5	0.9	−0.2	1.2	1.2	−0.1	0.9
Monetary authorities	—	−0.9	−0.3	1.0	0.3	0.2	−0.4	−0.4	—	0.1	—
Deposit money banks	−0.7	−1.1	−0.4	1.2	−0.9	0.1	−1.0	0.8	0.2	−0.5	0.3
Other[1]	−0.5	−0.7	—	−0.3	0.2	0.7	1.2	0.7	1.0	0.4	0.7
Memorandum Items:											
General government expenditure and net lending/GDP	34.5	33.7	34.8	40.3	41.4	42.9	40.8	40.1	39.9	40.4	41.9
Central government debt outstanding/GDP	6.6	4.5	3.0	3.5	3.9	5.2	8.5	9.1	9.3	10.1	12.3

Source: International Monetary Fund, *Government Finance Statistics Yearbook*, 1983 and 1984.
[1]Includes adjustments.

EXPENDITURE

Total expenditure as a percentage of GDP rose from 25½ percent in 1972 to 32 percent in 1977. In that year, a medium-term economic program was introduced which, inter alia, aimed at reducing the relative size of the government sector; since then, the share declined and was 30½ percent in 1982. The relative expansion of the central government sector over the period as a whole is among the smallest for this group of countries. Expenditure on goods and services, one half of which is wages and salaries, declined as a share in total expenditure from 22½ percent to 20½ percent, but kept pace with GDP growth. Interest payments on the public debt declined as a proportion of total expenditure in the first half of the period but rose subsequently and were 3 percent of the total in 1982, compared with 2 percent in 1972. Subsidies and current transfers, by far the largest economic category, increased their share in total expenditure from 54½ percent in 1972 to 64 percent in 1982. The increase largely reflects extensive reforms of pension schemes, increased transfers to local governments for various purposes, growing unemployment compensation payments, and other forms of labor market support. The proportion of capital expenditure to central government expenditure declined over the period, from 15 percent in 1972 to 9½ percent in 1982; it also declined somewhat as a proportion of GDP. Net lending rose steadily from 5½ percent of total expenditure in 1972 to 9½ percent in 1977, but subsequently fell sharply to 3½ percent in 1982. This category, which includes housing loans, inter alia, thus accounts for a major part of the decline in the share of total expenditure in GDP since 1977.

REVENUE

Between 1972 and 1982 the ratio of central government revenue to GDP rose from 26½ percent to 28½ percent. This 2 percentage point rise is the smallest relative increase experienced in any of the smaller industrial countries during this period. The figure conceals a much faster expansion up to 1976 when the ratio was 31 percent, but measures under the economic program initiated in the following year reversed the trend. As is reflected in the figures for 1972–82, income taxes, social security contributions, and payroll taxes were the principal objects of the official policy to reduce the tax burden; they also played a considerable role in the interaction between tax and incomes policies, as is discussed below. Income taxes, which accounted for 29½ percent of total revenue in 1972, rose to 35½ percent in 1976, and subsequently declined to 28½ percent in 1982. Similarly, social security contributions and payroll taxes combined, which rose from 10½ percent of total revenue in 1972 to 13 percent in 1976, fell to 9½ percent in 1982. Taxes on goods and services, the most important tax category in terms of revenue yield, followed a reverse pattern. Their share in total revenue fell from almost 47 percent in 1972 to just over 38 percent in 1976, and then rose steadily to 47½ percent in 1982. The most important of the taxes on goods and services is a general sales tax, which yields about half the revenue in this category; the other half is accounted for largely by a range of excise taxes and levies. Property taxes and taxes on international trade accounted for 2½ percent and 1½ percent, respectively, of total revenue in 1982, and nontax revenue and grants increased their share in the total from 7½ percent to 10 percent over the period. This category includes property income from nonfinancial public enterprises and various administrative fees and charges.

THE FISCAL BALANCE AND ITS FINANCING

After registering surpluses during 1972–74, government finances swung into a deficit in 1975 that amounted to 2 percent of GDP. Since then, with the exception of 1976 when approximate balance was achieved, yearly deficits ranged from 1 percent to 2½ percent of GDP. Sharp increases in various transfer payments for social welfare and in support of certain export industries were a significant contributory factor to the deteriorating fiscal position, as were measures to reduce the tax burden during the latter half of the period. The fiscal surpluses of 1972–74, which had accumulated both in a countercyclical fund and as other deposits held with the Bank of Finland and the Post Office Bank, were drawn down sharply to finance part of the 1975 deficit, entailing a large liquidity expansion that created problems for monetary policy. About one fifth of the 1975 deficit was financed from external sources. From then on, borrowing abroad assumed an enhanced role, frequently covering one half or more of deficit financing. The Government has no automatic access to central bank credit, and domestic borrowing is mainly in the form of bond sales to the public and direct borrowing from private financial institutions. Despite fiscal deficits in the past several years, central government debt as a proportion of GDP rose only slightly over the period and was 12½ percent in 1982—the second lowest ratio among the smaller industrial countries after Luxembourg.

FISCAL POLICY

The framework. In 1982, total general government expenditure was equivalent to 42 percent of GDP, of which the Central Government accounted for 30½ percent when transfers to other levels of government are included. The size of this share implies a relatively large local government sector compared with other countries in the group. Although the municipalities formally enjoy a high degree of autonomy, the Central Government exerts substantial influence on their financial decisions in two ways: first, through transfers from the central government budget that are regulated by law, and, to some extent, by budget instructions and sectoral plans relating to such areas as health and welfare services, which are financed on a cost-sharing basis (these transfers amount to approximately one third of total revenue of local governments); second, through the practice of negotiating limits on expenditure growth for a few years ahead with the central organizations of municipalities. A series of such agreements was negotiated over the period and have proved quite successful; growth targets have been generally observed, although local government current expenditure has posed problems. The budgets of local authorities are balanced as a rule by a flexible application of the proportional local income tax whose rate is set so as to cover all financing needs not met by other revenue sources.

The central government budget is thus the major tool of fiscal policy. It tends to focus on medium-term objectives in the framework of multiyear budgeting, which has been practiced in Finland since the late 1960s. The forecasts cover four- or five-year periods and serve as informal guidelines in the preparation of the annual budget without constituting future expenditure or revenue commitments on the part of the Government. From time to time the medium-term forecasts are incorporated in a government report on economic and fiscal policy that is presented to Parliament for discussion but not for decision. The nonbinding nature of the multiyear planning has preserved a measure of flexibility in fiscal policy, which is largely exercised through a frequent use of supplementary budgets. These budgets usually provide for adjustment of spending and borrowing levels in line with actual revenue and other developments within the fiscal year in an effort to maintain the appropriate medium-term course.

The annual and multiyear budgeting process is supplemented with the use of econometric models as tools of fiscal analysis. Two analytical approaches are used. One, the high employment budget balance, abstracts from the cyclical position of the economy and the workings of automatic stabilizers to estimate the impact of policy changes on aggregate activity. The other approach, the weighted budget balance, provides an alternative measure of the different budgetary impact, allowing explicitly for different impacts of separate expenditure and tax measures on the growth of real GDP.

A special feature of fiscal practices in Finland is the involvement of the Cabinet in advance expenditure control. A committee of key ministers deals with all major expenditure decisions within the year, including decrees, budgetary instructions, bills entailing expenditure, and other matters of financial significance. This is an informal procedure that ensures the provision of information on key issues and provides a basis for efficient financial control at the highest level.

Special countercyclical devices not strictly within the realm of fiscal policy have been applied over the period. Mention has already been made of the government countercyclical fund, introduced in 1970. This policy instrument has been used infrequently since the mid-1970s, however, and is considered fairly inflexible, as each transaction requires parliamentary approval. Countercyclical deposit schemes in various forms have been used more effectively. One is an investment reserve scheme, under which firms can transfer a certain proportion of their profits free of tax as interest-bearing investment reserves with the central bank. Release of the reserves is at the discretion of the Government within a specified maximum period. Similar schemes of a compulsory nature and applicable generally or to specified types of business income have also been adopted. The terms and conditions of voluntary and compulsory schemes have varied over the period.

Aims and measures. An overriding aim of fiscal policy throughout the period was full employment. In the early 1970s, the rundown of countercyclical funds, accumulated in periods of fiscal surpluses, largely served this purpose, the relevant expenditure measures, such as public works projects, frequently being introduced in supplementary budgets. Special emphasis was placed on alleviating regional unemployment by supporting construction in the northern and eastern parts of the country. Fiscal policy also concentrated on the fight against inflation, which was largely pursued in the context of incomes policy; fiscal measures were applied on both sides of the budget in an endeavor to moderate wage settlements and thus reduce inflation through the cost side.

Another high-priority aim of fiscal policy was to help restore external balance through selective export-promotion measures as well as a general tightening of the fiscal stance when conditions so required. Stimulatory fiscal policy pursued until the mid-1970s, in anticipation of an early world recovery, was associated with growing external deficits and accelerating inflation. To counteract these trends, fiscal policy assumed a restrictive stance in 1976, which resulted in a marked strengthening of the external position but, at the same time, contributed to domestic recession and rising unemployment. These adverse developments prompted the authorities to introduce a medium-term stabilization program in mid-1977, the main objectives of which were to simultaneously stimulate employment and the output of the enterprise sector and restrain the share of taxes and public expenditure in the economy. In other words, recovery was to be based on expansion of the enterprise sector and restraint in the growth of the public sector. A special fiscal ingredient of the medium-term strategy was the setting of maximum targets for public expenditure growth in real terms, reinforced by agreements with local authorities, with a view to arresting expansion of the public sector's share in GDP. Also, a target was adopted for revenue growth based on keeping the tax ratio to GDP at its 1977 level. This policy, which was generally successful, was maintained for the remainder of the period.

Apart from the general measures mentioned above, several specific fiscal measures were taken at different times over the period. Among those to stimulate business activity and employment were cost guarantee compensation payments to shipbuilding and other engineering industries to cover them against the risks of loss on exports owing to rises in the domestic cost level; grants to firms hiring persons on the unemployment register on a permanent basis; a series of reductions in employers' social security contributions; liberalization of investment reserves in the central bank; labor training and support to firms in depressed areas; and granting of loans on employment policy grounds.

The fiscal measures associated with the implementation of incomes policy included, on the revenue side, a series of selective income tax reductions followed by a general indexation of income taxation in 1977 and reductions in employees' social security contributions. Expenditure measures in this context included improvements in pensions, child and maternity allowances, increases in unemployment benefits, and consumer subsidies. Apart from these, the policy of increasing and extending social security benefits, which had received strong impetus from the expansionary fiscal policy stance of 1975, was pursued in its own right throughout the period.

Overview and implications for future policy. Despite an unstable economic environment, fiscal policy in Finland is formulated in a medium-term context through nonbinding multiyear planning. However, within this framework fiscal policy tends to react to actual developments as they occur within the fiscal year through a frequent use of supplementary budgets. While ensuring a measure of flexibility in the pursuit of fiscal policy, this strategy is liable to accentuate the problem of reconciling short-term and medium-term objectives and to bring an element of inconsistency to policy implementation. Such a situation has emerged from time to time when, for example, the impact of restrictive measures to counteract rising prices and widening deficits on the external current account has been subsequently reduced by measures to promote full employment.

Among the outstanding features of fiscal developments is the containment of the public sector, a policy that was pursued successfully in the latter half of the period under review. The environment for private sector activity, although heavily influenced by exchange rate and incomes policies, was undoubtedly helped by the containment of the tax burden. Ambitious social reform policies were pursued throughout the period, generating sharp increases in government expenditure. Commitments already made to continue reforms of the school system and pension schemes will, together with the aging structure of the population, exert an upward pressure on expenditure in future years.[1]

Another feature of fiscal developments over the period was the close interaction of fiscal and incomes policies. Whatever the beneficial impact on cost developments, the tax reductions and the increased social spending this policy mix entailed contributed significantly to the deterioration in the fiscal position. This deterioration, a cause for growing concern, was accentuated by the large monetary financing of the deficits. Servicing of the government debt, although moderate by international standards, is an additional factor that will impose a growing burden on the budget in the medium term.[2] However, the foundation laid in previous years should place Finland in a relatively good position to deal with these fiscal problems.

_____

[1] Finland, Ministry of Finance, "A Survey of the Prospects for the Finnish Economy and State Finances to 1986" (Helsinki, 1982), pp. 36, 47.

[2] "A Survey of the Prospects for the Finnish Economy and State Finances to 1986," p. 33.

6

Iceland

Iceland's growth performance depends largely on unstable fish catches and world market prices for fish products, which are subject to sharp fluctuations. Despite substantial diversification of export production over the last decade and a half, fish products still account for 75 percent of total exports, which, in turn, amounts to one third of GDP. The impact of the two oil crises on the highly open economy was mitigated by the country's rich hydro and geothermal energy sources, which were developed rapidly over the period. Real GDP growth, albeit uneven, averaged almost 4 percent a year during 1972–82, although it actually fell in two of those years, owing to reduced fish catches. Due to the instability of export prices and the impact of oil price increases on the country's terms of trade, national income has undergone substantially greater fluctuations than GDP.

Full employment was an overriding aim of economic policy during the period. As a result of a high level of investment and accommodating exchange rate and financial policies, the rate of unemployment was kept at or below 0.5 percent in all years except 1982 when it reached a peak of 0.7 percent. This is the second lowest level of unemployment achieved in the smaller industrial countries—only Luxembourg had a lower rate.

By contrast, Iceland suffered the highest inflation rate of any industrial country over the period, with rates ranging in most years between 30 percent and nearly 60 percent. Sharp increases in fishermen's incomes in individual years, the working of a demonstration effect throughout the rest of the economy, and widespread indexation mechanisms constituted a vicious circle that sustained these high rates of inflation, which at times were further fueled by external price shocks. In all years except 1978, the external current account was in deficit, peaking at 11 percent of GDP in 1974 and 1975. After a marked

144

Iceland: Selected Economic Indicators, 1972–82

	1972	1973	1974	1975	1976	1977	1978	1979	1980	1981	1982
Real GDP, percentage changes	6.5	7.9	4.0	−0.5	3.5	5.8	3.9	4.1	4.1	2.2	−1.3
Rate of unemployment	0.5	0.4	0.4	0.5	0.5	0.3	0.3	0.3	0.3	0.4	0.7
Consumer prices, percentage changes	9.7	20.6	42.9	49.1	33.0	29.9	44.9	44.1	57.5	51.6	49.1
External current account balance as percentage of GDP	−2.6	−2.8	−10.9	−10.9	−1.7	−2.5	1.3	−0.8	−2.3	−4.9	−9.6

Sources: Organization for Economic Cooperation and Development, *Economic Outlook*, December 1984; for rates of unemployment: Central Bank of Iceland, *Economic Statistics Quarterly*, November 1983.

Iceland: Consolidated Central Government Finances, 1972–82

(Year ended December 31)

	1972	1973	1974	1975	1976	1977	1978	1979	1980	1981	1982
Total Revenue (as a percentage of GDP)	27.9	29.2	29.2	29.7	28.3	27.4	29.0	30.2	29.6	31.1	32.9
Percentages of total revenue	100.0	100.0	100.0	100.0	100.0	100.0	100.0	100.0	100.0	100.0	100.0
Income taxes	17.3	17.2	12.2	8.8	9.3	8.0	9.8	12.3	10.7	10.6	11.1
Social security contributions	4.8	3.5	3.5	4.0	3.0	3.8	4.3	4.5	4.2	2.7	2.3
Payroll (manpower) taxes	-3.8	3.5	3.9	4.6	4.8	4.8	4.7	4.6	4.4	4.5	4.5
Property taxes	2.9	2.8	2.4	2.3	2.8	2.8	2.9	3.9	3.9	4.1	3.9
Taxes on goods and services	34.3	32.0	40.3	46.4	48.1	47.9	44.8	43.2	46.9	47.5	47.1
Taxes on international trade	28.9	27.7	27.4	21.9	20.6	21.6	21.6	19.7	18.2	19.1	17.6
Other taxes	0.1	0.1	—	—	—	—	—	—	—	0.1	0.2
Nontax revenue and grants	7.9	13.2	10.3	11.8	11.4	11.1	12.0	11.8	11.7	11.4	13.3
Total Expenditure (as a percentage of GDP)	30.5	32.3	33.8	35.9	30.8	31.9	31.6	32.4	30.9	31.9	35.9
Percentages of total expenditure	100.0	100.0	100.0	100.0	100.0	100.0	100.0	100.0	100.0	100.0	100.0
Expenditure on goods and services	30.7	29.3	30.2	28.3	32.4	32.0	34.8	34.1	36.3	35.8	33.4
Of which:											
Wages and salaries	20.2	19.8	20.3	18.6	20.5	21.4	23.6	23.0	24.0	23.5	21.9
Interest payments	2.6	3.1	3.2	5.6	5.0	5.2	6.9	7.4	5.7	6.2	6.6

Subsidies and other current transfers	39.7	34.6	37.7	36.1	33.2	32.1	34.8	37.9	37.1	36.6	36.9
Of which:											
Social security funds	24.0	22.0	21.2	20.3	19.9	20.4	22.9	22.7	23.6	24.5	22.9
Capital expenditure	16.3	23.7	22.2	19.9	17.4	17.9	15.2	14.2	14.6	15.3	12.2
Lending minus repayments	10.6	9.3	6.7	10.1	11.9	12.8	8.3	6.4	6.3	6.1	10.9
Surplus/Deficit (as a percentage of GDP)	−2.6	−3.1	−4.6	−6.2	−2.5	−4.4	−2.6	−2.2	−1.4	−0.8	−2.9
Financing:											
Abroad	2.8	1.6	1.2	1.9	2.0	3.1	0.7	1.7	0.8	0.9	3.1
Domestic	−0.3	1.5	3.4	4.2	0.5	1.3	1.9	0.5	0.5	−0.1	−0.2
Monetary authorities	−0.9	1.0	2.9	3.0	—	0.4	0.9	−0.7	−0.3	−0.8	−0.7
Deposit money banks	0.1	0.1			0.1	−0.1	0.2	0.2	0.1	−0.1	0.1
Other[1]	0.6	0.5	0.5	1.2	0.5	1.1	0.8	1.0	0.8	0.9	0.4
Memorandum Items:											
General government expenditure and net lending/GDP	37.4	38.5	40.6	44.0	37.7	38.8	...	...	...	...	...
Central government debt outstanding/GDP	15.8	12.5	13.4	18.1	18.9	20.7	22.4	23.9	26.4	23.6	31.4

Source: International Monetary Fund, *Government Finance Statistics Yearbook*, 1983 and 1984.
[1] Includes adjustments.

improvement in 1978 and a satisfactory outcome in the following year, the deficit widened sharply and by 1982 amounted to 9½ percent of GDP.

EXPENDITURE

Between 1972 and 1982 the ratio of government expenditure to GDP rose by 5½ percentage points to 36 percent. An especially sharp expansion occurred in 1982 when lending operations soared and real GDP fell. This expansion of the government sector is nonetheless one of the smallest recorded in this group of countries. The growth pattern was highly irregular; during 1972–75, for example, the ratio to GDP increased from 30½ percent to 36 percent, reflecting outlays in connection with a natural disaster (volcanic eruption) in 1973 and a transfer of functions from local to central government in 1974. A more relaxed attitude to government spending by a government that took office in 1971 contributed further to this rise in government expenditure. Following two years of large current external deficits, measures were taken in 1975 and 1976 to reduce the fiscal imbalance; as a result, the expenditure/GDP ratio shrank by 5 percentage points in 1976 to 31 percent. The measures taken included substantial expenditure cuts that were legislated in 1975 and incorporated in the 1976 budget, and a special 2 percent additional sales tax earmarked for a special fund that financed natural disaster expenditure and later became a permanent part of the general sales tax. General expenditure restraint was subsequently exercised and the ratio was kept relatively stable through 1981.

The share of expenditure on goods and services in total expenditure rose from 30½ percent to 33½ percent during the period, and within this category wages and salaries rose from 20 percent to 22 percent of the total. While some of the increase stems from the transfer of functions from local government, it also reflects growing public sector employment and higher wages and salaries in that sector; a further contributor to this increase was a change in the definition of outlays for the operation of state hospitals, which had previously been treated as transfers, but were increasingly being incorporated in the budget as final expenditure. Interest payments increased from 2½ percent of total expenditure in 1972 to 6½ percent in 1982, despite a rapid erosion of the nonindexed component of domestic debt, which is mostly with the central bank. Subsidies and other current transfers declined as a proportion of total expenditure from almost 39½ percent to 36½ percent over the period. Although the change in definition mentioned above explains some of this unusual decline, the main reason is negligible expenditure on unemployment benefits. Capital expenditure was kept at a relatively high, if unstable, level throughout the period, ranging from 12 percent to 24 percent of total expenditure. Net lending, which ranged between 6 percent and 13 percent of the total, represents in large measure relending by the Central Government for investment in domestic energy sources.

REVENUE

Total revenue of the Central Government expressed as a ratio to GDP rose by 5 percentage points between 1972 and 1982 to 33 percent. The importance of income taxes relative to other revenue sources declined sharply over the period from over 17½ percent of total revenue in 1972 to 11 percent in 1982. This decline reflects annual adjustments in tax scales to reduce or eliminate fiscal drag and periodic cuts in rates in an effort to moderate wage settlements. Income taxes in Iceland are substantially lower than in other industrial countries. The major revenue source of the Central Government is domestic taxes on goods and services, mainly a general sales tax at the retail stage and profits of the liquor and tobacco monopoly. Taxes in this category rose as a proportion of total revenue from 34½ percent to 47 percent between 1972 and 1982. Taxes on international trade, on the other hand, dropped from 29 percent in 1972 to 17½ percent in 1982, partly as a result of tariff reductions under the European Free Trade Association (EFTA) and EC agreements.

Social security contributions ranged between 2½ percent and 5 percent of total revenue during the period. These are borne entirely by employers and the self-employed, since contributions by employees, levied on a per capita basis, were abolished in 1971. Other tax revenue comprises payroll taxes earmarked to the State Housing Fund and property taxes, which, taken together, increased slightly from 7 percent to 8½ percent of total revenue over the period. Nontax revenue, which is mostly interest income and administrative fees and charges, accounted in most years for 10½ percent to 12 percent of total revenue.

THE FISCAL BALANCE AND ITS FINANCING

According to *GFS* data,[1] a fiscal deficit occurred every year of the period. As a percentage of GDP, the deficit widened from 2½ percent in

---

[1]Owing to different treatment of relending operations of the Central Government, data on the fiscal balance differ substantially from national sources. The latter treat

1972 until it peaked at over 6 percent in 1975, as a result of tax concessions and increases in consumer subsidies to facilitate wage negotiations, a sharp increase in loan-financed energy investment, and some relaxation in fiscal discipline. In subsequent years, general expenditure restraint and increases in indirect taxes reduced the deficit substantially. The lowest deficit of the period, less than 1 percent of GDP, occurred in 1981. Attitudes of policymakers to deficit financing have differed according to whether the Treasury proper or the investment and credit budget (see below) was involved. For the ordinary central government operations that exclude relending to autonomous public enterprises, recourse has been had to the central bank in the form of overdrafts on the treasury main account. Also, the sale of government savings certificates, which are price-indexed and carry tax privileges, has financed certain ordinary investments. But the largest financing requirement has arisen in connection with projects included in the investment and credit budget, chiefly investments for exploiting the country's rich hydro and geothermal energy sources. Foreign borrowing, with the Treasury acting as an intermediary, has been used entirely to finance these and other investments by public enterprises that are expected to service the debt out of own revenue. Financing of these projects has also been in the form of sale of government savings certificates to the general public and to financial institutions. Between 1972 and 1982, total debt of the Central Government expressed as a ratio to GDP rose from 16 percent to 31½ percent, and the foreign component of the debt rose from 10½ percent to 20½ percent of GDP.

FISCAL POLICY

The framework. The Central Government dominates public sector activity in Iceland. A fiscal reform in 1972 centralized public revenue and expenditure to a considerable degree, and in recent years, about four fifths of total public expenditure and revenue is accounted for at the central level. Thus, based on 1977 data, the size of general and central government expenditure relative to GDP was 39 percent and 32 percent, respectively. The main source of revenue of local governments is a flat-

---

borrowing and relending as offsetting items that do not affect the balance, whereas in GFS relending is entered on the expenditure side (lending minus repayments), and borrowing in this context is treated as a financing item. As a result, the data presented here (GFS) exhibit a deficit for each year, which in most instances is, as a ratio to GDP, 2 to 3 percentage points larger than data from national sources indicate. Thus, according to the national sources, there were surpluses in 1972, 1981, and 1982.

rate income tax; local governments are free to vary the rate of the tax within a range of zero to 10 percent, and may also raise it to 11 percent with the consent of the Central Government. Owing to cost-sharing arrangements and restricted borrowing authority, local government investment is in large measure determined in the central government budget and in the public investment and credit budget.

Annual budgeting is based on a forecast of the national economy for the upcoming fiscal year. In recent years, the national economic forecasts have been presented to Parliament along with the central government budget, but as a separate document in which the Government states its economic policy. Owing to inherently unstable economic conditions, measures that may significantly affect the budget plan are frequently introduced in the course of the fiscal year. Despite recent legislation that provides for multiyear budgeting as a means of facilitating fiscal decision making, such exercises have not been performed so far. However, four-year plans for the communications sector have been prepared for a number of years. From the mid-1970s, public investment and credit budgets were prepared annually and presented to Parliament, first separately, and then, after the budget was passed; in later years, emphasis was placed on finalizing the two together to facilitate coordinated decision making in the relevant areas. The investment and credit budgets, which cover one year, include total public investment and its financing, as well as forecasts of available public funds for certain private investment, such as housing. The purpose is to coordinate investment and credit policies in the framework of specified price and balance of payments objectives, and generally to ensure consistency between the financial and real sides of the economy.

While inflation automatically influenced revenue more than expenditure in the early part of the period, due to a responsive tax system that relied heavily on ad valorem indirect taxes, this stabilizing property of the fiscal system has eroded in recent years. The reason is a proliferation of indexation mechanisms on the expenditure side and a growing tendency to enact legislation that provides for present and future spending commitments. It is estimated that about 70 percent of total expenditure is "uncontrollable," in the sense that this portion of expenditure at the central level cannot be affected except by amending laws and contracts. Flexibility in fiscal policy is further restricted by the link between the cost of living index, which reflects increases in indirect taxes, and wages and salaries and social security benefits, and also by the practice of earmarking certain tax proceeds.

Aims and measures. Traditional fiscal policy attitudes in Iceland are characterized by a strong urge to balance the budget.[2] Present-day concerns over the persistent inflation have added support to the traditional view that fiscal policy should be defensive, geared toward preventing fiscal deficits, rather than restrictive, in pursuit of substantial surpluses. A manifestation of this attitude is the positive balance[3] that budgets, as approved by Parliament, invariably show, although the intended balance often turns into a deficit during the fiscal year. The fiscal objective of price stabilization tends to be pursued by selective measures designed to affect the outcome of general wage negotiations.

The balanced budget approach, although not successful in preventing deficits in actual outturns, contributed significantly to expenditure restraint. For most of the period, this restraint took account of the expenditure/GDP ratio, although the Government did not announce a specific target until 1979, namely, to prevent the ratio from exceeding 30 percent in 1979 and 1980; this target was reached if relending operations are not counted on the expenditure side. Within the constraints imposed by efforts to prevent the budget from imparting undue stimulus to demand and adding to inflationary pressures, fiscal policy has aimed at improving social security benefits and redistributing income in favor of low- and middle-income earners.

Measures toward the above objectives have affected both sides of the budget. Reductions in the personal income tax have typically been introduced to ensure moderation in wage settlements. In 1974 a particularly sharp reduction caused the share of income taxes in total revenue to fall by 5 percentage points. To partially compensate for the revenue loss, the general sales tax was raised by 4 percentage points. A series of reductions in the personal income tax and increases in indirect taxes was implemented in subsequent years.

Consumer subsidies were also typically used to facilitate wage negotiations or generally constrain price increases. In the short run, these subsidies dampened the rise in the cost of living index to which wages and salaries and social security benefits were linked, as did increases in family allowances in the years when these allowances were incorporated in the index base. While social security benefits are indexed, additional measures to extend their coverage and increase

---

[2] Blöndal, pp. 56–58.
[3] According to the operational concept as distinct from the *GFS* definition (see footnote, pp. 144–45).

benefits in real terms were frequently taken over the period, sometimes in the context of incomes policy and sometimes separately. One such measure, which particularly burdened the budget, was the introduction in the mid-1970s of guaranteed and indexed minimum income limits for old-age and disabled pensioners.

Implementation of the measures noted above was not a continuous process, however. In 1976, for example, a mounting current external deficit induced the authorities to reduce the expansionary impact of the budget and both consumer subsidies and social security benefits were curtailed. Apart from frequent increases in indirect taxes to counteract deterioration in the fiscal position, legal authorizations to cut expenditure in the existing budget were granted occasionally, although the full extent of the authorized cuts was generally not realized. To reinforce the general effort at expenditure restraint, a month-to-month fiscal reporting and expenditure control system was introduced in the mid-1970s and was further developed in subsequent years.

Overview and implications for future policy. The overall impression that emerges from the events during 1972–82 is that the application of fiscal policy for stabilization purposes was quite limited. The balanced budget approach was narrowly applied and did not prevent deficits, which, according to the *GFS* definition, were substantial in some years. This fiscal practice nonetheless made a major contribution to the general expenditure restraint that was exercised for most of the period under review. Within the constraints implicit in the general political preference for balanced budgets, selective measures to combat inflation and reduce external imbalances were taken, largely in the context of incomes policy through reductions in direct taxes and increases in consumer subsidies and social security expenditure. The effectiveness of this approach was diluted by the weakening of the fiscal position that resulted from these measures, as accompanying increases in indirect taxes usually were only partially compensating. A widespread indexation of significant expenditure categories and de facto indexation of income tax scales greatly eroded the automatic stabilization properties of the fiscal system. Moreover, increased reliance on indirect taxes that are included in the price index used for compensation purposes implied growing rigidities and narrowed the scope for fiscal policy action.

Despite the limited use of fiscal instruments for demand management, progress was nonetheless made in the pursuit of other fiscal objectives. In a situation of full employment, a virtual absence of unemployment benefits and a general expenditure restraint that was reinforced by the balanced budget attitude prevented the expenditure/ GDP ratio from rising appreciably and kept down the tax burden. Investment policy that emphasized exploitation of domestic energy sources greatly reduced the country's dependence on imported oil. However, much of the fiscal deficit as defined here stems from this policy, and the liquidity impact of foreign borrowing attached to energy projects aggravated the problem of monetary management.

If future fiscal policy is to be more instrumental in combating inflation, which is Iceland's main economic problem, a reversal of past tendencies toward indexation and rigidities in the fiscal system would seem to be required. An attempt in this direction was made in 1983 when a new government, facing a sharp acceleration of inflation and mounting external imbalance, suspended indexation of wages and salaries and social security benefits and imposed a statutory wage ceiling for two years. Further measures in this direction, such as the exclusion of indirect taxes from the price compensation index, could substantially enhance the effectiveness of fiscal policy in this regard. Decisions on such rearrangements are essentially political in nature, however, and would require a steadfast, long-run course of policy—unfortunately a rarity in a country subject to unstable economic conditions and frequent changes of government. A departure from the balanced budget approach in order to relate fiscal policy more closely to the cyclical position of the economy, although attractive from a theoretical viewpoint, would entail a substantial risk. The increased flexibility such a reorientation might permit would have to be weighed against an eventual loss of fiscal discipline that appears to have been instrumental in stabilizing the relative size of the government sector in the economy.

7

Ireland

Ireland recorded positive growth rates in every year from 1972 to 1982. The growth path was irregular, however, ranging between 2 percent and 8 percent a year, reflecting the vulnerability of the highly open economy to external influences. Foreign trade is equivalent to approximately one half of GDP. Although economic development was assigned the highest priority and fiscal policy was instrumental in stimulating economic activity, unemployment remained very high by international standards throughout the period. Registered unemployment rose from 6½ percent of the estimated total labor force at the beginning of the period to 8 percent in 1980, and even more steeply to over 12 percent in 1982, partly as a result of a switch toward restrictive economic policies to counteract growing imbalances in the economy. Over the period, the task of containing unemployment was rendered more difficult by a rapidly growing labor force.

Inflation has remained high, and the impact of the first oil price explosion was especially marked. Consumer prices rose from 8½ percent in 1972 to 21 percent in 1975. The inflation rate abated to 7½ percent in 1978, but in subsequent years, consumer prices surged upward, increasing by over 20 percent in 1981 and 17 percent in 1982. Factors contributing to the persistent price rises include the second oil price shock in 1978, depreciation of the currency against the pound sterling, increase in indirect taxation, and large increases in wage rates, especially in 1980. The external current account was in deficit throughout the period, ranging between 1½ percent and 15 percent of GDP; the largest deficits were registered during the three-year period to 1981. The policy response to adverse external influences on the economy and intensive fiscal measures to foster economic development resulted in large and continuous fiscal deficits over the period covered.

EXPENDITURE

Ireland's central government sector expanded more sharply over the period than in any of the smaller industrial countries. As a ratio of GDP, total expenditure rose from 36½ percent to almost 58 percent between 1972 and 1982. This rise accelerated in the 1972–75 period but stabilized during the following two years when the policy stance shifted in a less expansionary direction to phase out the current deficit. From 1977, when a new government resumed an expansionary policy to improve the employment situation, the expenditure/GDP ratio was on the rise, especially in 1980 when it grew by 5 percentage points. All expenditure categories, as classified by economic type, rose at a faster pace than GDP, but the relative significance of each category in total expenditure changed somewhat. Expenditure on goods and services declined from 20 percent to 16½ percent of the total, and wages and salaries, which account for more than two thirds of expenditure in this category, underwent a similar decline. However, growing public employment, stemming in part from the unemployment relief policy, led to an appreciable rise in the share of wages and salaries in GDP over the period. Interest payments on government debt rose as a share of total expenditure from 9½ percent to 15½ percent between 1972 and 1982. However, inflation had reduced the budgetary burden by eroding the stock of outstanding government debt in real terms.

Over one half of total expenditure is in the form of subsidies and other current transfers; their share in the total rose from 51 percent to 53 percent over the period, after having exceeded 54 percent in 1975. Although this increase is less dramatic than in many other countries, it nonetheless represents a substantial rise in relation to GDP. Demographic factors, including a reversal of a traditional net emigration pattern, unemployment and other social security benefits, as well as industrial support, contributed to the increase. Capital expenditure averaged almost 9 percent of total expenditure over the period, with small deviations in individual years. Net lending rose from 9 percent to 16 percent of the total between 1972 and 1974 and has since ranged between 7 percent and 9½ percent. The last two categories reflect in large measure the development effort, and, taken together, their share in GDP rose over the period.

REVENUE

Between 1972 and 1982, total revenue rose as a proportion of GDP from 31 percent to 42½ percent, which is substantially less than

Ireland: Selected Economic Indicators, 1972–82

	1972	1973	1974	1975	1976	1977	1978	1979	1980	1981	1982
Real GDP, percentage changes	6.4	4.7	4.3	3.7	1.4	8.2	7.2	2.8	3.3	2.9	1.9
Rate of unemployment	6.4	5.9	5.9	7.8	9.3	9.1	8.3	7.4	8.2	10.1	12.2
Consumer prices, percentage changes	8.7	11.4	17.0	20.9	18.0	13.6	7.6	13.3	18.2	20.4	17.1
External current account balance as percentage of GDP	−2.2	−3.5	−9.9	−1.5	−5.3	−5.5	−6.9	−13.6	−12.0	−15.1	−10.9

Sources: Organization of Economic Cooperation and Development, *Economic Outlook*, December 1984; for rate of unemployment: Department of Finance, *Economic Review and Outlook*, various issues; and *Current Economic Trends*, various issues.

Ireland: Consolidated Central Government Finances, 1972–82

(Year beginning April 1st through 1973 and Year ended December 31 after 1973)

	1972	1973	1974	1975	1976	1977	1978	1979	1980	1981	1982
Total Revenue											
(as a percentage of GDP)	31.1	31.1	32.0	31.9	35.3	34.3	33.8	35.0	38.6	40.0	42.6
Percentages of total revenue	100.0	100.0	100.0	100.0	100.0	100.0	100.0	100.0	100.0	100.0	100.0
Income taxes	28.1	29.0	29.1	29.7	30.1	31.1	31.6	32.1	32.8	32.9	31.0
Social security contributions	8.9	9.6	11.5	13.6	13.2	13.2	12.9	12.9	12.8	12.7	13.3
Payroll (manpower) taxes	—	—	—	—	—	—	—	—	0.2	0.1	0.7
Property taxes	3.2	3.0	2.8	2.4	1.9	2.0	2.0	2.0	1.6	1.6	1.5
Taxes on goods and services	32.5	33.0	31.1	29.9	30.1	30.0	29.8	26.6	24.8	23.9	25.6
Taxes on international trade	16.5	15.9	15.3	13.8	14.2	12.0	11.4	11.4	12.8	14.9	13.2
Other taxes	—	0.1	—	—	—	—	—	—	—	—	—
Nontax revenue and grants	10.8	9.4	10.3	10.5	10.4	11.6	12.2	15.0	15.0	13.9	14.6
Total Expenditure											
(as a percentage of GDP)	36.7	37.9	43.9	44.3	45.4	43.7	45.2	47.1	52.0	55.0	57.8
Percentages of total expenditure	100.0	100.0	100.0	100.0	100.0	100.0	100.0	100.0	100.0	100.0	100.0
Expenditure on goods and services	20.1	19.5	18.2	19.6	18.7	18.2	17.5	17.8	17.3	17.5	16.6
Of which:											
Wages and salaries	14.0	13.6	12.4	13.9	13.2	12.6	12.1	12.4	12.0	12.4	11.4
Interest payments	9.5	9.4	8.5	9.7	11.0	12.0	12.6	12.9	12.6	13.6	15.7

Subsidies and other current transfers	51.2	50.1	48.4	54.3	53.7	53.5	53.6	53.2	52.8	51.8	52.9
Of which: Social security funds	10.1	9.9	9.7	11.6	11.7	11.3	10.6	9.9	10.5	11.1	12.0
Capital expenditure	10.4	9.5	8.9	8.0	7.1	7.7	8.5	9.0	9.5	8.7	7.9
Lending minus repayments	8.8	11.5	15.9	8.4	9.5	8.6	7.8	7.1	7.8	8.5	6.8
Surplus/Deficit (as a percentage of GDP)	−5.6	−6.8	−11.9	−12.4	−10.2	−9.5	−11.5	−12.1	−13.3	−15.0	−15.2
Memorandum Items:											
General government expenditure and net lending/GDP	39.8	41.9	49.7	50.5	51.2	49.3	49.5	50.8	56.2	59.2	61.7
Central government debt outstanding/GDP	52.3	59.7	65.0	73.4	79.2	77.9	82.1	89.5	91.4	99.3	108.7

Sources: International Monetary Fund, *Government Finance Statistics Yearbook*, 1983 and 1984; for government debt data: national sources.

expenditure growth. The share of income taxes in total revenue increased steadily from 28 percent to 31 percent. Despite partial adjustments for inflation and successive tax relief measures to stimulate private investment, the impact of the progressive rate structure of the personal income tax more than outweighed the revenue loss. A special feature of the income tax system is the heavy concentration of the tax burden on wage and salary earners and the much lighter burden on farmers. The share of social security contributions rose from 9 percent to 13½ percent, which broadly matches the financing needs of the relevant social insurance schemes that are intended to be self-financing.

Domestic taxes on goods and services declined as a proportion of total revenue from 32½ percent in 1972 to 25½ percent in 1982 and did not keep pace with nominal GDP growth. Over half the revenue in this category is derived from a value-added tax (VAT) that was introduced in 1973 with Ireland's membership in the EC. Excise taxes, which account for most of the other revenue in this category, explain the slow overall growth and reflect the authorities' reluctance to raise the mostly specific rates in view of the resulting inflationary impact. Substantial increases in excises were implemented, however, toward the end of the period and in the VAT in 1982. Taxes on international trade declined from 16½ percent to 13 percent of total revenue over the period as customs duties were lowered in accordance with EC membership. Other tax revenue, mainly property taxes, accounted for 2 percent to 3 percent of total revenue. Nontax revenue, on the other hand, rose from just under 11 percent of total revenue and grants in 1972 to 14½ percent in 1982, reflecting mainly increased property income.

THE FISCAL BALANCE AND ITS FINANCING

As noted earlier, the central government finances were in deficit throughout the period. The deficit widened rapidly from 5½ percent to 12½ percent of GDP in the 1972–75 period when a strongly expansionary fiscal policy attempted to moderate the effects of the international recession on the economy. In response to mounting concern over rapidly growing expenditure and the monetary implications of the large deficits, the policy stance was shifted in 1976 to a less expansionary direction and the deficit was reduced to about 10 percent of GDP in that and the following year. A new government that took office in 1977 resumed an expansionary stance, however, in view of the deteriorating employment situation, and the deficit widened to 11½ percent in 1978. It continued to rise for the rest of the period and reached over 15 percent of

GDP in 1982. Information on deficit financing is not available from the basic statistical source (*GFS*), but there is evidence that in the early years of the period, domestic financing—the banking system and the nonbank private sector—covered four fifths of the borrowing requirement; the rest was financed abroad. The domestic capital market is small in relation to the size of the deficit, however, and in subsequent years over half the financing requirement was met by external borrowing. In 1981 and 1982, for example, three fourths and three fifths, respectively, of the exchequer borrowing requirement was met by external financing. The large and persistent fiscal deficits have implied mounting government debt. Expressed as a percentage of GDP, this debt expanded from 52½ percent to 108½ percent between 1972 and 1982, and a sharp expansion is foreseen in the near future as well as in the servicing of the debt. In 1982 the foreign component was 42 percent of total debt, having risen from 9 percent in 1972.

FISCAL POLICY

The framework. The central government budget is the dominant instrument of fiscal policy in Ireland. In 1982 the ratio of public expenditure to GDP was almost 62 percent, of which the Central Government accounted for over nine tenths, if transfers to other levels of government are included. Such transfers in turn amounted to almost three fourths of total local government revenue and grants in that year. This ratio has since risen, making local governments increasingly dependent on the Central Government for their revenue.

In the central government budget a clear distinction is made between current and capital expenditure and revenue; traditionally, the basic operational rule of fiscal policy was to balance current revenue and expenditure in each fiscal year. When deficits on current account threatened to emerge, the authorities took swift corrective action—often by introducing supplementary budgets. This approach was motivated by the need to avoid pre-empting resources to finance public investment as well as to contain inflation and limit the external current account deficit. Later events of both domestic and external origin caused the authorities to depart from the principle of balancing the current budget, and since 1972, substantial current budget deficits have emerged.

In 1969, in an effort to better control the growth of public expenditure and improve resource allocation, a system of program budgeting was introduced. The system was to be gradually extended to all government departments by fiscal year 1975/76. However, by that time, experience with this innovation, including difficulties with conceptual aspects, systematic ranking of priorities, and the size of the administrative machinery required,[1] had led the authorities to abandon the idea, and no budget documents in this form were published. A new approach to budgeting was introduced in 1978. This involved an annual planning process by which expenditure priorities and policy options were set out in the context of medium-term growth potential and economic and social policy issues. This form of national economic planning was to provide a comprehensive framework for the allocation of funds in the annual budget. The underlying idea was to achieve a sustained reduction in unemployment, and for that purpose an ambitious 7 percent annual GNP growth target was set. In the event, the second oil crisis grossly upset basic assumptions of the plan, and it has not been worked out in this particular form since 1979.

Aims and measures. Promotion of economic growth through industrial development and reduction of unemployment has been the overriding goal of fiscal policy throughout the period. Another policy objective was to preserve living standards and redistribute income in favor of lower income groups by tax reductions and ambitious social welfare programs. Toward the end of the period, faced with growing internal and external imbalances, the Government, in an attempt to contain domestic cost increases, adopted an incomes policy approach to prevent excessive wage settlements; however, this approach met with little success and was subsequently abandoned.

Other prominent measures aimed at promoting industrial development and sustaining employment included direct capital outlays and investment loans. In the early 1970s, the public capital program accounted for approximately one half of gross domestic fixed capital formation, and by 1982 this ratio had risen to 60 percent. Among other measures introduced for this purpose were various tax allowances to stimulate private investment. In particular, as part of the authorities' industrial policy, liberal tax advantages were offered for export-oriented investments in the manufacturing sector. Thus, in 1981 the standard rate of corporate tax for manufacturing firms was fixed at 10 percent for the period to 2000. Also, the Central Government has provided funds for employment-creation schemes and encouraged capital expenditure by semipublic bodies to sustain employment. In addition, temporary

---

[1] Maurice F. Doyle, "Management of the Public Finances in Ireland Since 1961," *Public Budgeting and Finance*, Vol. 3 (Summer 1983), p. 75.

employment premiums were offered to employers recruiting from the unemployed. Capital expenditure has at times been used as a counter-cyclical instrument; however, its effectiveness has been limited by the employment situation and the emphasis on economic development, and expenditure control has taken the form of changes in the rate of growth of capital outlays in accordance with cyclical conditions, rather than of direct reductions.

The policy reaction to the first oil price crisis and the ensuing world recession was to preserve living standards and maintain employment. The public capital program continued to operate at a high level, and various social benefits were increased in real terms and extended, including reductions in the qualifying age for pensions and extensions of pay-related unemployment and sickness benefits. Personal income and company tax concessions were also granted and items were exempted from the value-added tax. The expansionary fiscal policy continued as the recession deepened. However, by 1976 concern was growing over the rapid expansion of government expenditure and the monetary impact of the widening fiscal deficit. The Government announced in that year that it intended to phase out the current budget deficit over a three-year period; to that end, it introduced several measures, including a sharp increase in indirect taxation. Similar announcements were repeated in subsequent years, but without material success, especially after 1977 when the new government that came into office in that year adopted a highly expansionary fiscal policy stance within the framework of the national economic plan referred to above. The fiscal stimulus generated by this plan was intended to be temporary, on the assumption that the private sector would react to achieve self-sustaining growth. The Government stated that containment of domestic cost increases in the context of national pay agreements was preferable to deflationary fiscal and monetary policies. This approach found expression in an agreement reached with the social partners in 1979 of a "national understanding for economic and social development." The agreement marked a departure from the traditional wage bargaining process in Ireland, in that it involved the social partners in the formulation of economic and social policy. The agreement included new tax concessions, increased social welfare payments, and higher wage increases for public employees. Not only did this approach further weaken the fiscal position, but it did not achieve its main objective of containing domestic wage costs. It was abandoned in 1981.

Since mid-1981, the stance of fiscal policy has tightened, as a widening fiscal deficit, associated with a sharp increase in the current external deficit, won growing public and political acceptance of the need to reduce public borrowing. The brunt of the fiscal adjustment effort has so far fallen on taxation rather than expenditure. The authorities have reiterated their intention of continuing their efforts on the fiscal front, with a view to eliminating the current budget deficit over a five-year period.

Overview and implications for future policy. During the 1972–80 period, expansionary fiscal policies characterized financial developments in Ireland. The justification for these policies is, in part, the perceived need for public sector initiative to stimulate overall economic growth and employment. Economic progress and the working of an international demonstration effect have at the same time generated increased demands for improved social security. In the wake of the first oil crisis, the official policy was to stimulate consumption; by that time the principle of current budget balancing had been dropped. Both policy decisions tended to weaken effective financial constraint on the growth of social expenditure, and entitlement programs were initiated that added to the inflexibility in public expenditure and constituted a severe drain on the budget. Unstable external influences have undermined attempts to set growth targets that, inter alia, would serve as a framework within which demands for public services could be met. Similarly, the setting of consistent policy objectives has been complicated by the different political priorities of governments. These factors exerted strong upward pressure on government expenditure, while revenue growth was hampered by a narrow income tax base, specific rather than ad valorem excise duties, and a depressed economy. On the whole, while fiscal policy has been countercyclical in recessions, it has tended to be procyclical during periods of expansion.[2] As a result, fiscal deficits have been experienced on a rising scale, with wide economic implications, not least for the external position and monetary policy whose stance was for the major part of the period largely determined by fiscal developments. Debt accumulation proceeded at a fast pace, and the size of government debt in relation to GDP is the largest among industrial countries.

---

[2] Peter Bacon, et.al., *The Irish Economy: Policy and Performance, 1972–1981* (Dublin: Economic and Social Research Institute, 1982), p. 58.

While the medium-term objective of eliminating the current budget deficit poses a dilemma for fiscal policy because of the unemployment problem, the growing structural element in the fiscal deficit and the long-run implications for the development of the economy make this medium-term action highly desirable. In particular, debt servicing will constitute an increasing claim on budgetary resources in coming years and threatens to make the deficit and further debt accumulation self-perpetuating. Recent tax increases have narrowed the scope for further action on that front, so that the announced fiscal adjustment will have to concentrate on the expenditure side. The past record strongly suggests, however, that a satisfactory result would have to be associated with a major change in policy priorities and political attitudes to public spending.[3]

---

[3] Since mid-1981, fiscal policy has remained less expansionary and the exchequer borrowing requirement has been reduced. This restrictive posture was maintained despite three changes of government over a period of 18 months. The announced government objective of eliminating the current budget deficit by 1987 has been superseded by events. In early 1984, the authorities indicated their intention to reduce the current budget deficit and the exchequer borrowing requirement over the next three years in order to slow down the growth of public debt with a view to stabilizing the ratio of interest payments to both GNP and tax revenue.

8

Luxembourg

External influences predominate in the exceptionally open Luxembourg economy where foreign trade amounts to 85 percent of GDP, if services are included. The steel industry is the major contributor to exports and, although it has been declining over the period, it still accounts for about half of Luxembourg's exports. The shrinking of the steel sector called for substantial structural adjustment, which has been smoothly carried out by the rapid development of the financial sector, whose value added represents some 30 percent of GDP, and by a series of fiscal incentives.

After a strong growth performance from the late 1960s, the country experienced a deep recession in 1975 caused largely by a decline in world trade, especially in steel. Real GDP declined by 6 percent in that year. In subsequent years, real output growth fluctuated with world market conditions for steel, which again deteriorated in 1981 when real GDP fell by almost 2 percent. The rate of unemployment remained lower than in any other country in the group throughout the period; although some slackening in the employment situation occurred, unemployment did not reach 1 percent until 1981. To a certain extent, the successful employment policy was facilitated by a large foreign component in the labor force.

Annual inflation rates rose sharply to 10 percent to 11 percent during the 1974–76 period, on account of higher import prices and wage costs, reflecting, inter alia, a large upward adjustment in the minimum guaranteed wage in 1975. Price rises abated in the next two years, owing to more stable import prices and moderate wage settlements, but accelerated in 1979 and subsequent years, on account of a renewed

166

Luxembourg: Selected Economic Indicators, 1972–82

	1972	1973	1974	1975	1976	1977	1978	1979	1980	1981	1982
Real GDP, percentage changes	6.2	10.8	3.6	-6.1	1.9	0.6	4.5	4.0	1.7	-1.8	-1.1
Rates of unemployment	—	—	0.1	0.2	0.3	0.5	0.7	0.7	0.7	1.0	1.3
Consumer prices, percentage changes	5.2	6.1	9.5	10.7	9.8	6.7	3.1	4.5	6.3	8.1	9.4
External current account balance as percentage of GDP	11.2	21.6	31.6	21.6	24.5	25.2	23.3	28.3	22.6	20.8	18.4

Sources: Organization for Economic Cooperation and Development, *Economic Outlook*, December 1984; for unemployment data: Organization for Economic Cooperation and Development, *Economic Surveys: Belgium-Luxembourg*, various issues.

Luxembourg: Consolidated Central Government Finances, 1972–82

(Year ended December 31)

	1972	1973	1974	1975	1976	1977	1978	1979	1980	1981	1982
Total Revenue											
(as a percentage of GDP)	33.5	32.3	32.9	37.7	37.1	39.9	40.6	38.0	40.0	37.6	34.7
Percentages of total revenue	100.0	100.0	100.0	100.0	100.0	100.0	100.0	100.0	100.0	100.0	100.0
Income taxes	33.9	36.7	40.8	37.2	36.6	39.5	41.1	38.5	35.7	34.9	34.9
Social security contributions	27.7	26.6	26.8	29.0	30.3	29.2	27.5	28.0	26.0	25.8	25.2
Payroll (manpower) taxes	—	—	—	—	—	—	—	—	—	—	—
Property taxes	5.6	5.8	4.9	4.2	4.4	4.4	4.4	4.9	4.6	4.7	4.9
Taxes on goods and services	21.0	20.4	17.5	19.8	18.6	17.3	17.1	17.2	18.9	19.5	20.3
Taxes on international trade	0.4	—	—	—	—	—	—	—	—	—	0.1
Other taxes	0.5	0.4	0.4	0.4	0.4	0.1	0.1	0.1	0.1	0.1	0.1
Nontax revenue and grants	10.9	9.8	9.5	9.5	9.6	9.5	9.9	11.3	14.8	14.9	14.3
Total Expenditure											
(as a percentage of GDP)	32.1	29.8	29.0	36.7	36.8	39.4	37.8	38.2	39.3	37.9	35.8
Percentages of total expenditure	100.0	100.0	100.0	100.0	100.0	100.0	100.0	100.0	100.0	100.0	100.0
Expenditure on goods and services	22.7	23.1	23.7	22.7	21.7	21.1	21.8	21.7	22.1	19.6	22.6
Of which:											
Wages and salaries	17.9	18.9	19.4	18.2	17.8	17.7	18.0	17.9	18.1	15.6	18.7
Interest payments	3.1	2.8	2.4	1.9	1.8	1.9	2.1	2.0	1.9	1.9	2.0

Subsidies and other current transfers	58.9	57.5	57.6	61.4	61.9	63.1	63.0	62.4	62.8	64.8	63.7
Of which:											
Social security funds	40.7	39.5	38.0	40.3	41.2	40.8	41.6	40.3	40.9	40.5	39.5
Capital expenditure	13.5	15.3	13.6	11.8	11.5	10.2	10.7	11.1	14.4	12.6	11.9
Lending minus repayments	1.8	1.2	2.8	2.1	3.0	3.7	2.5	2.8	0.5	2.5	0.8
Surplus/Deficit (as a percentage of GDP)	1.4	2.5	3.9	1.0	0.3	0.6	2.7	− 0.2	1.0	− 1.6	0.5
Memorandum Items:											
General government expenditure and net lending/GDP	35.2	32.5	32.4	41.0	40.5	43.1	41.4	41.7	44.4	43.1	...
Central government debt outstanding/GDP	...	...	...	...	...	...	...	...	...	...	...

Source: International Monetary Fund, *Government Finance Statistics Yearbook*, 1983 and 1984.
Note: Due to a statistical adjustment to expenditure totals, figures do not add up during the period 1980–84; for the same reason surplus/deficit does not equal the difference between revenue and expenditure.

upsurge in oil prices, and reached 9½ percent in 1982. Large and continuous surpluses on external current account are a special feature of economic developments in Luxembourg. In most years since 1973, these surpluses amounted to the equivalent of 20 percent to 30 percent of GDP. Reduced export earnings of the steel industry and the increased oil bill were offset by a strengthening of the services balance, due to net investment earnings and earnings from banking, airlines, and Luxembourg Radio and Television.

The public finances were in surplus for most of the period, although the world recession and active fiscal policy to improve social services and facilitate the structural adjustment process contributed to the emergence of deficits in 1979 and 1981.

EXPENDITURE

From 1972 to 1982, consolidated central government expenditure expressed as a proportion of GDP rose from 32 percent to 36 percent. A sharp expansion, almost 5 percentage points from the base year, took place in 1975 as a result of a large increase in revenue (in large measure, revenue determines expenditure levels) and a new government's policy of increasing the public sector's role in the economy. Also, GDP declined sharply in this year, and despite resumption of positive growth rates in subsequent years, the share of expenditure in GDP continued to rise until 1977. It remained relatively stable thereafter. A large part of total expenditure is price indexed. Expenditure on goods and services, mainly wages and salaries, shared in this general expenditure growth in relation to GDP and remained a roughly constant ratio to total government expenditure at around 22 percent throughout the period. Subsidies and other current transfers increased their share in total expenditure from 59 percent to 63 percent during the 1972–77 period and stabilized around that level thereafter in response to a tighter fiscal stance. The abrupt increase in the total share of this category in 1975 is to a large extent reflected in social security outlays and subsidies to support employment and activity. The share of capital expenditure in the total fluctuated in the 10–15 percent range, while the share of interest payments on the public debt declined from 3 percent in 1972 to just under 2 percent in 1977 and has since remained at that level. The share of net lending fluctuated somewhat over the period and averaged just over 2 percent of the total.

REVENUE

The ratio of total revenue to GDP rose by 6½ percentage points from 1972 to 1980, but declined sharply in 1981 and 1982 to 34½ percent—only 1 percentage point higher than in 1972. Income taxes rose at a slightly faster pace, and their share in total revenue increased from 34 percent to 35 percent. Individual and corporate taxes shared equally in this relative growth, despite the linkage of individual taxes with the consumer price index since 1970. Corporate taxes, however, grew at a considerably faster pace between 1972 and 1978 and increased their share in total revenue from 10½ percent to 15 percent (12 percent to 16½ percent in tax revenue); they subsequently declined, as economic conditions deteriorated and tax incentives were granted to stimulate investment. Taxes on goods and services, almost entirely a value-added tax, declined as a proportion of total revenue from 21 percent to just over 20 percent, but more than kept pace with nominal GDP growth.

Social security contributions declined as a proportion of total revenue, accounting for 25 percent in 1982. The portions borne by employers and employees, 55 percent and 45 percent, respectively, remained roughly constant.

Nontax revenue accounted for 9½ percent to 15 percent of total revenue; the largest subcategory was property income in the form of interest on deposit funds, mainly social security funds. Property taxes remained around 5 percent of total revenue over the period. Other revenue sources are of lesser significance.

THE FISCAL BALANCE AND ITS FINANCING

From 1972 to 1978 central government finances were in surplus in every year. Expressed as a proportion of GDP, the fiscal surpluses ranged from a low of less than ½ of 1 percent in 1976 to a high of 4 percent in 1974. Since then, deficits were recorded in 1979 and 1981 only. This impressive fiscal record, achieved while expenditure was undergoing considerable growth, may be attributed in large measure to the budgeting practice of limiting that growth to the projected medium-term growth of revenue. The surpluses were used to build up reserves and to reduce the public debt. The emerging fiscal deficits toward the end of the period were financed by borrowing and by drawing on accumulated reserves. Borrowing on the domestic capital market was not considered likely to crowd out private domestic borrowers, as foreign participants dominate the Luxembourg capital market.

FISCAL POLICY

The framework. Luxembourg, like all other countries in the group, relies on the Central Government for the conduct of fiscal policy. The relative size of central and general government expenditure was 37½ percent and 43 percent of GDP, respectively, in 1981. About one half of local government expenditure was covered for most of the period by transfers from the Central Government. The scope for applying fiscal policy for countercyclical purposes is limited by the exceptionally large foreign trade sector, which, in the case of expenditure, implies low values of the domestic mulipliers. The authorities have nonetheless tried to mitigate the effects of cyclical variations through the use of multiyear financial programs that link the growth of government expenditure to the estimated trend growth of nominal GDP or to that of receipts. For the period 1970–75, for example, the financial program set a norm for the growth of expenditure, based on the trend growth of money GNP, which was to be kept unchanged throughout the cycle, implying that cyclical variations in the fiscal balance would be caused mainly by changes in receipts. During upswings, reserves accumulated in special investment funds and were drawn upon in times of recession to maintain the growth of expenditure according to the norm. In 1974, in a redirection of policy toward an enlarged role of the public sector in the economy, the medium-term strategy was changed. The new orientation linked expenditure to the expected medium-term growth of receipts rather than to the growth of nominal GNP, which implied a faster growth of expenditure. The countercyclical objective of fiscal policy was nonetheless maintained. In 1980, the medium-term strategy reverted to the linking of expenditure growth to that of nominal GNP. By that time, the enlarged role of the financial sector had entailed substantial net factor income from abroad (equivalent to 24 percent of GDP in 1977), and in the financial program special account was taken of the medium-term relationship between GDP and GNP. Of the 7½ percent norm for expenditure growth in the 1980 budget, for example, 1 percentage point was attributed to an adjustment factor for the GNP/GDP relationship.

Aims and measures. As implied by the financial programs, a major objective of fiscal policy was to exert a neutral impact on the economy over the medium term. Within this framework, the containment of prices, stimulaton of economic activity combined with promotion of industrial diversification, and improvement of public welfare constituted major policy objectives, and throughout the period the maintenance of full employment was given high priority.

In the early part of the period, tax reductions, both personal income taxes and the value-added tax, were implemented to mitigate price rises; in the 1975 budget, for example, further reductions in these taxes were designed to stimulate the private sector, although the authorities generally accepted that stimulation of ecomomic activity through demand-management policies was not likely to be very effective in the highly open Luxembourg economy. By 1974 reduction of the public debt and accumulation of budget reserves were considered sufficient to justify an increase in the rate of growth of public expenditure relative to GNP growth. This change in approach enhanced the role of expenditure measures in the pursuit of fiscal policy. In the following recession years, various measures were introduced to keep up employment, including special public works projects, aid to the railways, which had experienced a sharp fall in their goods traffic as steel production fell, and subsidies to firms to compensate employees put on short-term work. Expenditure also increased sharply on account of transfers to the Unemployment Fund and a reform of the health insurance system.

Since 1977, efforts to restructure industry have been stepped up by means of fiscal incentives to investment and exports and by improving infrastructure, and measures have been taken to mitigate the effect of structural change on the employment situation, particularly in the declining steel industry. These include subsidization of about 20 percent of wage costs. Also, to counteract the adverse impact of these measures on labor mobility, a series of measures was introduced, such as a bonus for workers who voluntarily transfer to new industries, retraining aids, and early retirement schemes.

Facing a further decline in steel production, the authorities embarked on a major plan to restructure and modernize the steel industry, and a special law to this effect was enacted on July 1, 1983. This involved substantial increases in budgetary outlays in the form of capital endowments, assumption of interest payments on outstanding debt of the industry, purchase of bonds, and social transfers mainly on account of early retirement schemes. The rise in expenditure was to be financed from two sources: 40 percent each from increases in direct and indirect taxes and from remaining budgetary reserves, and 20 percent from exceptional borrowing.

Overview and implications for future policy. During a decade of unstable external conditions, economic management in Luxembourg was remarkably successful, considering the strong external influences on the economy that necessitated large-scale structural adjustment. Fiscal policy played a significant role in this achievement, without incurring fiscal deficits for the larger part of the period. At the same time, however, the government sector expanded substantially, and the growing tax burden became a cause for concern to the authorities.

Toward the end of the period under review, fiscal deficits emerged as a result of the recession, which both slowed down revenue growth and caused increased budgetary support to the economy. Although financing of the deficit has not been a problem so far, the authorities are concerned, as the budget reserves have been progressively run down in recent years.

Despite the substantial budgetary burden emanating from the more recent restructuring plan of the steel industry, the authorities remain committed to a cautious stance of fiscal policy. This commitment is evidenced by their decision to finance a substantial part of the extraordinary outlays by increasing the already high tax burden. In the medium term, the fiscal position ought to return to equilibrium, given the present stance of policy.

9

Netherlands

During 1972–76, with the exception of 1975 when real GDP declined by 1 percent, economic growth was fairly strong in the Netherlands, averaging 4½ percent a year. Since 1977, however, growth rates have been sluggish and were in fact negative in 1981 and 1982, reflecting depressed domestic demand, with both private consumption and business investment in particular declining sharply in real terms. Also, a strong guilder caused problems for the manufacturing export industry, and depressed external conditions contributed to a recessionary climate in the open Dutch economy where foreign trade amounts to 45 percent to 50 percent of GDP.

The rate of unemployment was below 3 percent from 1972 to 1974 and rose moderately to 5 percent to 5½ percent in the following five years; however from 1980, unemployment soared, reaching 11½ percent in 1982. In addition to deteriorating economic conditions, a rapidly increasing labor force was responsible for this rise.

From 1972 to 1975, annual inflation rates rose from 8 percent to 10 percent. From 1976, however, the price performance was better than in most other industrial countries. The rate of inflation abated to just over 4 percent in 1978 and 1979, but subsequently rose somewhat in response to the oil price pressures. To a large extent, the good price performance in the latter half of the period is due to moderate wage settlements and the strong position of the guilder through its impact on import prices, reducing the wage-price spiral in a system of widespread indexation.

For most of the period, surpluses were recorded on the external current account. The strong energy sector in part explains this performance and, in particular, the sharp increase in the price of exported natural gas. During the last two years of the period, however, the improvement in the external current balance was also the result of a drop in imports owing to depressed domestic demand. From approximate balance in 1973 and 1974, fiscal deficits grew year by year and in 1982 reached the equivalent of 7½ percent of GDP. For the last several years of the period, the Dutch experience thus represents the somewhat unusual case of growing fiscal deficits going hand in hand with rising external current account surpluses.

EXPENDITURE

Between 1973 and 1982 consolidated central government expenditure expressed as a proportion of GDP expanded from 46 percent to 59 percent, which is one of the highest rates of expansion among the smaller industrial countries over the same period. While individual expenditure categories did not share equally in this growth, they all increased at a faster pace than GDP, with the exception of net lending, which was unusually large in the initial year. The share in total expenditure of subsidies and other current transfers, mainly social security transfers—by far the largest economic category—increased from 66 percent to 70 percent from 1973 to 1982; this growth reflected the combined effect of demographic factors, such as aging population, extension of benefits—especially disability benefits—growing unemployment compensation, and indexation of benefits. In the recent past disability schemes that relate benefits to the degree of disability and previous income have been made more generous by an upgrading of degrees of disability, so that minor disablement qualifies for high benefits. Also in this expenditure category are subsidies to ailing firms, which increased substantially in the second half of the period.

Expenditure on goods and services declined as a proportion of total expenditure from 17½ percent in 1973 to 14½ percent in 1982, although within this category wages and salaries declined considerably less.

Interest payments on the public debt showed a continuous relative increase from 3 percent of total expenditure to 5½ percent over the period; a steadily widening fiscal deficit, as well as rising interest rates, accounted for this rise.

Capital expenditure as a proportion of total expenditure fluctuated in the 6–8½ percent range, and net lending amounted to 2 percent to 4 percent of the total, except in 1973 when it was 6 percent of total expenditure.

Netherlands: Selected Economic Indicators, 1972–82

	1972	1973	1974	1975	1976	1977	1978	1979	1980	1981	1982
Real GDP, percentage changes	3.4	5.7	3.5	−1.0	5.3	2.4	2.5	2.4	0.9	−0.7	−1.7
Rate of unemployment	2.2	2.2	2.7	5.2	5.5	5.3	5.3	5.4	6.0	8.6	11.4
Consumer prices, percentage changes	7.8	8.0	9.6	10.2	8.8	6.4	4.1	4.2	6.5	6.7	6.0
External current account balance as percentage of GDP	2.8	3.8	3.0	2.3	3.0	0.7	−0.8	−1.1	−1.5	1.3	2.8

Source: Organization for Economic Cooperation and Development, *Economic Outlook*, December 1984.

Netherlands: Consolidated Central Government Finances, 1973–82

(Year ended December 31)

	1973	1974	1975	1976	1977	1978	1979	1980	1981	1982
Total Revenue (as a percentage of GDP)	46.0	47.3	49.6	49.8	48.4	48.4	48.6	49.9	50.5	51.3
Percentages of total revenue	100.0	100.0	100.0	100.0	100.0	100.0	100.0	100.0	100.0	100.0
Income taxes	32.3	32.3	32.1	31.1	31.0	30.3	30.3	29.7	28.2	27.4
Social security contributions	36.5	37.8	37.1	36.0	35.2	35.8	36.7	36.4	37.3	38.7
Payroll (manpower) taxes	—	—	—	—	—	—	—	—	—	—
Property taxes	2.0	2.0	1.7	1.8	2.1	2.3	2.4	2.2	1.9	1.6
Taxes on goods and services	22.2	20.4	20.1	20.4	21.3	21.5	20.5	20.1	19.0	18.3
Taxes on international trade	0.5	0.2	0.1	—	—	—	—	—	—	—
Other taxes	1.3	0.5	0.5	0.5	0.4	0.4	0.4	0.5	0.5	0.5
Nontax revenue and grants	5.1	6.9	8.4	10.2	10.1	9.8	9.8	11.1	13.2	13.6
Total Expenditure (as a percentage of GDP)	46.0	47.3	52.4	52.1	50.3	51.3	52.6	54.3	56.7	58.8
Percentages of total expenditure	100.0	100.0	100.0	100.0	100.0	100.0	100.0	100.0	100.0	100.0
Expenditure on goods and services	17.4	16.9	16.7	16.3	16.4	15.9	15.9	15.4	14.9	14.5
Of which:										
Wages and salaries	10.6	11.9	11.3	11.2	10.9	10.9	10.7	10.4	9.8	9.4
Interest payments	2.8	2.7	2.5	2.8	2.9	3.1	3.2	3.7	4.4	5.4

Subsidies and other current transfers	66.1	69.5	69.5	70.9	71.7	72.9	72.0	70.4	69.1	69.9
Of which: Social security funds	35.9	37.1	36.4	36.8	37.6	38.5	38.9	38.8	37.8	37.4
Capital expenditure	7.7	7.2	8.4	7.1	6.4	6.1	7.0	8.3	8.6	7.9
Lending minus repayments	6.0	3.6	2.9	2.9	2.5	2.1	1.9	2.2	3.1	2.3
Surplus/Deficit (as a percentage of GDP)	—	—	−3.0	−2.6	−3.0	−3.1	−4.6	−4.6	−6.5	−7.6
Financing:										
Abroad	—	−0.2	—	—	—	0.1	—	—	—	—
Domestic	—	0.2	3.0	2.6	3.0	3.0	4.6	4.6	6.5	7.6
Monetary authorities	−0.8	−0.7	0.7	—	0.1	0.2	0.8	−0.3	0.1	0.2
Deposit money banks	−0.4	0.2	0.9	0.9	0.5	0.3	0.9	0.8	1.3	1.5
Other[1]	1.2	0.7	1.4	1.6	2.5	2.5	2.8	4.1	5.2	5.9
Memorandum Items:										
General government expenditure and net lending/GDP	...	...	...	...	...	...	...	...	...	...
Central government debt outstanding/GDP	22.1	21.0	22.1	22.4	22.5	23.8	25.7	29.1	33.5	39.4

Source: International Monetary Fund, *Government Finance Statistics Yearbook*, 1984.
Note: Due to overall adjustment to cash basis and statistical adjustment surplus/deficit deviates in many years from the difference between revenue and expenditure.
[1]Includes adjustments.

REVENUE

Total revenue of the Central Government increased as a proportion of GDP from 46 percent to 51½ percent during 1973–82. This ratio is substantially lower than the expenditure ratio, but is nonetheless the highest among the smaller industrial countries. Over the period, income taxes declined as a share in total revenue from 32½ percent to 27½ percent, and they also declined slightly as a proportion of GDP. The decline is in part explained by periodic adjustments for inflation to reduce fiscal drag and by a series of tax rate cuts to reduce the tax burden.

Social security contributions are the most significant single revenue source at the central government level. Slightly less than one half of the contributions is borne by employers and the rest by employees. These contributions respond to requirements of the social security system, which is self-financing, and show some year-to-year fluctuations over the period; they were as high as 38½ percent of total revenue in 1982, having risen from 36½ percent in 1973.

Taxes on goods and services, the most important of which is a value-added tax, declined from just over 22 percent of total revenue in 1973 to 18½ percent in 1982, and the proportion of these taxes to GDP also declined over the period.

The most dynamic revenue element is included in the category "nontax revenue and grants," whose share in total revenue increased from 5 percent to 13½ percent; this category also rose as a proportion of GDP from 2½ percent to 7 percent during 1973–82. This growth is largely accounted for by revenue from the sale of natural gas whose price soared over the period. Other revenue items, namely, property taxes, taxes on international trade, and other taxes, all declined as a proportion of total revenue. Taken together, the share of these revenue sources in the total was 4 percent in 1973, compared with 2 percent in 1982.

THE FISCAL BALANCE AND ITS FINANCING

As already observed, the central government finances incurred a deficit in 1975 after having remained in approximate balance in the two preceding years. The deficit remained the equivalent of roughly 3 percent of GDP for the subsequent three years but started to widen in 1979 and reached 7½ percent of GDP in 1982. These deficits reflect in part the budgetary impact of stimulatory measures in late 1974 to contain the rise in unemployment, which were followed later by various fiscal incentives to stimulate private sector activity, while the depressed state of the economy in the past few years of the period limited revenue growth. That the authorities for most of the period pursued fiscal policy on the conceptual basis of a so-called structural budget deficit is relevant and is discussed in the next section.

The Government has had almost no recourse to direct external borrowing to finance the fiscal deficit, although in some years a substantial part of the government debt was taken up by nonresidents. At the beginning of the period, debt management policy was actively pursued to counteract the impact of capital inflows on domestic liquidity. The Government borrowed heavily on the capital market and repaid domestic short-term debt to the monetary authorities and deposit money banks. Domestic nonbank financing continued to be significant throughout the period, but from the mid-1970s, the banking system and the monetary authorities began assuming a role in financing; the importance of these sources fluctuated from year to year in the range of 10 to 50 percent of the central government borrowing requirement. In the last years of the period, the continuing recourse to monetary financing led the authorities to center on the actual budget deficit in the formulation of fiscal policy, rather than the structural budget deficit. Total debt of the Central Government increased substantially over the period. Expressed as a ratio to GDP, the debt expanded from 22 percent to 39½ percent between 1973 and 1982. As noted above, foreign borrowing was negligible.

FISCAL POLICY

The framework. While the activities of local governments are significant, from an economic viewpoint their financial autonomy is limited and the Central Government dominates fiscal policy formulation and implementation. In 1980 the ratio of general government expenditure to GDP was 62½ percent, and the Central Government accounted for almost 90 percent of this total, if transfers to other levels of government are included. Most current expenditure by local authorities is covered by appropriations from the Central Government. These revenue sources together with own sources generate, as a rule, surpluses on current account that finance part of the investments at the local level. These investments account for about three fourths of total public sector investment. Local authorities are also dependent on the Central Government for investment grants and loans, but in principle are responsible for arranging their own financing of investments not covered in the above manner. Such financing takes place through borrowing in the domestic capital market directly or through the Bank for Municipalities. In practice, long-term borrowing is nonetheless subject to central government control.

Each year since 1969, the central government budget has been accompanied by four-year expenditure estimates. The multiyear estimates are intended as projections of existing expenditure policies without any commitment on the part of the Government. Experience suggests, however, that spending departments and various pressure groups do indeed interpret the projections as commitments; the multiyear estimates have thus constituted an upward pressure on spending, as well as an element of inflexibility in public expenditure.[1] The political structure and government decision-making procedure in budgetary matters may also put upward pressure on government spending. Coalition governments are the rule; cabinet members may not become or remain members of Parliament; and the cabinet votes on items in the budget, with the votes of all ministers ordinarily having equal weight.[2]

Macroeconomic forecasting in budget preparation has probably had more policy relevance in the Netherlands than in any other country in the group. Since 1961, fiscal policy formulation has rested on the conceptual basis of a so-called structural budget deficit. The growth of government expenditure and revenue is related to the medium-term trends in the economy, on the assumption that there is a steady trend growth of potential output and a stable structural pattern of savings and investment, as well as a stable trend in the external current account balance.

In essence, a "correct" balance was to be maintained between the budget position of the Central Government and the volume of investment and saving in other sectors of the economy that was consistent with a desired balance on external current account. Starting from a year considered to represent optimal balance, the size of the deficit in this base year was taken as a norm from which deviations were acceptable for cyclical reasons only.

---

[1]L.J.C.M. LeBlanc and Th. A.J. Meys, "Flexibility and Adjustment in Public Budgeting: The Netherlands Experience," *Public Budgeting and Finance*, Vol. 2 (Autumn 1982), p. 60.

[2]Meys, "Spending More and Getting Less: Recent Experiences with the Allocation and Control of Public Expenditure in the Netherlands," in *The Grants Economy and Collective Consumption*, ed. by R.C.O. Matthews and G.B. Stafford (New York: St. Martin's Press, 1982), pp. 245–46.

The growth in tax receipts forecast on the basis of the trend growth of real national income and the progressivity of the tax system, as well as the increase in nontax revenue, provided the scope for expenditure increases or tax reductions, the so-called structural budget margin, with the budget deficit constant in absolute size (until 1973). In the calculation of this margin, allowance was made for price increases and expenditure components were treated differently according to their immediate impact on demand. However, general increases in wages and salaries were excluded from the budget margin calculation on the assumption that they would, in the long run, be covered by inflation-induced revenue increases. Forecasts of the trend growth of real national income were thus a significant determinant of the level of expenditure each year, as was the method of calculating the structural budget margin, which underwent a series of modifications over the period.

Amendments made in 1974 and 1975 with respect to norms for the structural budget deficit and the calculation method allowed a larger increase in expenditure, and subsequently amendments to achieve opposite results were formulated. The structural approach to fiscal policy gradually weakened, however, as growing imbalances in the economy obscured the distinction between cyclical and structural factors, and uncertainties in the external environment complicated the task of projecting medium-term trends in the economy. In 1980 the structural budget policy approach was abandoned for a more factual approach to the budget deficit, as mentioned above.

Aims and measures. The objectives of fiscal policy were closely connected with the emerging imbalances in the economy, which had assumed disconcerting proportions toward the end of the period. Ambitious social security schemes were promoted around the mid-1970s, but otherwise fiscal action centered on the problems of unemployment, depressed business activity, and inflation, although the emphasis differed from one time to another. Partly as a result of the policy pursued, fiscal developments themselves urgently needed structural adjustment.

Concern over high and rising taxation induced the authorities to announce the containment of the tax burden as a specific policy objective. Thus, in the 1972 budget the Government announced the policy of limiting the rise in the share of taxes in national income to 0.5 percentage point a year during 1973–77. Subsequently, this target was revised upward to 1 percentage point a year for 1976 and subsequent years, but in 1978 the norm was again changed and the target was set to stabilize the collective burden (tax and nontax revenue as proportion of national income) at the 1978 level.

Over the period, various forms of tax reductions were implemented to achieve these targets. The type of tax affected usually reflected separate policy objectives. The measures included cuts in business tax rates, tax relief for business investment, and accelerated depreciation of industrial buildings outside the most densely populated areas. Some of these were temporary measures and all aimed directly or indirectly at stimulating investment and activity in the enterprise sector. Personal income taxes, apart from being periodically adjusted for inflation, similarly underwent a series of rate cuts to reduce their disincentive impact, and also to moderate wage settlements and thereby contribute to the containment of inflation.

The interaction of fiscal and incomes policies is a distinct feature of Dutch economic policy. To partly offset the resulting revenue loss, indirect taxes have been increased from time to time, such as the value-added tax in 1976 (from 16 percent to 18 percent), taxes on energy and tobacco; and as already noted, nontax revenue, mainly from the sale of natural gas, increased rapidly over the period. Natural gas export contracts are almost fully indexed to Rotterdam fuel oil prices, with up to a six-month indexation lag.

Specific targets have also been set for the medium-term structural and actual budget deficit. In 1976, for example, this target was set at 5½ percent of national income, of which 3 percent was attributed to the Central Government, and again in 1982, when a new government announced its aim of reducing the deficit by 1 percentage point a year over the 1983–86 period.

The policy of limiting the tax burden and reducing the deficit placed the brunt of the fiscal adjustment effort on the expenditure side. However, several obstacles have been encountered on this front. Efforts to contain social security transfers, the fastest growing category, were complicated by political controversies and protective sentiments that tended to intensify in economically adverse years, such as in 1980 when the maintenance of purchasing power of social security beneficiaries was announced as a special aim of fiscal policy. The general social security system includes a guaranteed minimum income equivalent to approximately US$760 a month. Also, containment of expenditure in this category was at one time complicated by a separation of revenue authority and expenditure responsibility. Moreover, major policy objectives were concerned with the reduction of unemployment and resumption of economic growth by stimulating private sector activity, and the pursuit of these policies entailed vastly increased public spending. Measures to stimulate employment include special building projects, appropriations for local government investment, aid to social housing construction, subsidies to enterprises employing teenagers and to the clothing industry provided employment was kept at a specified minimum level, and wage-cost subsidy schemes for employing persons registered as unemployed for a specified minimum period of time.

Apart from tax incentives and wage-cost subsidies, the private enterprise sector receives various forms of selective and general government support. The oil crisis gave rise to the introduction in 1974 of special credit facilities for enterprises encountering liquidity difficulties on account of rising oil prices, and grants were made in the same year to small- and medium-sized enterprises in agriculture and horticulture to partly compensate for the adverse impact of the guilder appreciation on their incomes. Government support of a more general kind has taken the form of investment subsidies[3] operated since 1978 under the WIR (investment account) scheme, which is designed to affect the direction of investment by attaching different premiums to different types of investment and its location. Capital grants under the WIR scheme, and similar investment facilities in operation prior to 1978, increased sharply under deteriorating business conditions and rising unemployment in the second half of the period.

There is evidence that in addition to the factors mentioned above, certain other features of the budgetary process may have exerted an upward pressure on spending. First, as already mentioned, the multi-year expenditure estimates, contrary to intentions, are widely interpreted as minimum commitments on the part of the Government. Second, the structural budget approach has tended to assume unrealistically high growth rates for the economy, which form the basis for determining each year's expenditure levels in the budget. Attempts in recent years to cut expenditure were linked to these projected increases, which exceeded actual output and revenue trends, and thus had less than the intended effect on actual expenditure levels. A third, less tangible, factor is the impact of the political structure and decision-making procedures in budgetary matters as noted in the preceding section.

---

[3]Government assistance is also offered in the form of loans and participation through semipublic institutions and commercial banks.

Overview and implications for future policy. Fiscal policy during the period was aimed at counteracting emerging imbalances in the economy and promoting generous social entitlement programs. The pursuit of both aims resulted in an explosive growth of government expenditure. Although the self-financing nature of the social security system pushed up contributions and added to a tax burden that is among the highest in industrial countries, attempts were made to reduce the tax burden, and revenue growth experienced a cyclical weakness in the past few years. As a result, the fiscal deficit widened—quite abruptly in the last years of the period. Imbalances in the economy increasingly assumed a structural character, which, according to prevailing views, could not be dealt with adequately by conventional demand management measures.

The vast diversion of resources to the public sector is widely seen as having harmed business profits and investment and overall economic growth and employment. The growing public sector borrowing requirement, which in 1982 absorbed 70 percent of the total supply of funds, contributed to the maintenance of high long-term interest rates, which also affected business investment adversely. The generous unemployment and other social security benefits are perceived as disincentives to work effort. Thus, taking account of the hidden unemployment element in these schemes, it has been estimated that the proportion of the potentially active population that is not working is as high as 20 percent.

These and other implications of past fiscal developments have engendered growing awareness of the need to reverse the trends by a substantial restructuring of the public finances. Although the authorities have long recognized this need and have repeatedly announced targets for limiting the tax burden and reducing the deficit, progress has been hampered by political controversies and also perhaps by technical forecasting factors regarding implementation of expenditure reductions, which lie at the heart of the adjustment effort. Regaining control over public expenditure, especially social security expenditure, is therefore likely to remain a major medium-term preoccupation of fiscal policy.

10

New Zealand

Unstable and increasingly difficult export market conditions for New Zealand's agricultural products, which account for 70 percent of total exports, and the two oil crises occasioned considerable instability in the terms of trade, with repercussions on growth performance and price developments over the period covered. The impact was also reflected in sharp shifts in the stance of economic policy. After GDP had grown at over 6 percent on the average during 1972–74, a relative stagnation set in and lasted until 1980, reaching a low point in 1977 when real GDP declined by 5 percent. Growth resumed in 1980 and 1981, but declined by over 1 percent in 1982.

From 1972 to 1976, the rate of unemployment remained exceptionally low by international standards and never reached 0.5 percent of the labor force. Subsequently, and associated with the poor growth performance, unemployment began to rise and reached 5½ percent in 1982. Contributing factors were a growing incentive to register as unemployed to take advantage of unemployment benefits and an increase in the female participation rate that accounted for the entire increase in employment between 1976 and 1981.

The rate of inflation accelerated in the 1973–76 period, after which it varied from year to year between 12 percent and 17 percent, substantially above the average for industrial countries. This inflation reflects the impact of rising import prices, expansionary economic policies, and escalating wage costs outside periods of wage and price freezes.

Current external deficits were experienced every year since 1974. The position worsened sharply in 1974 when the deficit widened to 13 percent of GDP; it subsequently varied from year to year, from just under 2 percent of GDP to 8 percent. These deficits often caused concern to the authorities and were frequently a major determinant of shifts in overall economic policy. The current external deficits and inflation were associated with high and sustained fiscal deficits resulting in large measure from an active fiscal policy to stimulate employment and economic activity.

EXPENDITURE

As a result of expansionary fiscal policy to counteract the recessionary impact of the first oil price shock, the ratio of government expenditure to GDP rose sharply from 31 percent to 40 percent between 1972 and 1975. The authorities grew concerned about the adverse impact of this policy on prices and the external current account position and shifted to a restrictive policy stance in the following year. As a result, the share of expenditure in GDP dropped by 5½ percentage points in that year. This share was unstable in subsequent years, but did not exceed the 1975 ratio appreciably until 1982 when it was 42 percent of GDP. The share of expenditure on goods and services in total expenditure declined from almost 31 percent in 1972 to just under 26 percent in 1982; within this category, wages and salaries, which had been at about 20 percent at the beginning of the period, declined to 17½ percent by 1982.

Interest payments on government debt declined from 7½ percent to 5½ percent of the total between 1972 and 1975, but rose thereafter and reached 11 percent in 1982. While this high level constitutes a heavy debt-servicing burden, the impact of large deficits and rising interest rates was substantially reduced by inflation, which eroded the domestic component of the debt.

Subsidies and other current transfers are by far the largest expenditure category. It rose from 43 percent to 53 percent of total expenditure over the period and was thus largely accountable for the rise in the relative size of the central government sector in the economy. Within this category, the largest items are social welfare expenditure, mainly pensions, and grants and subsidies to the manufacturing and agricultural (including forestry and fishing) sectors under various support schemes.

Capital expenditure declined as a proportion of total expenditure from 10 percent in 1972 to 5 percent in 1982; this category was often a major object of expenditure cuts in attempts to constrain overall spending, especially in the latter years of the period. Net lending grew sharply from just under 9 percent of total expenditure in 1972 to 17½ percent in 1975, but subsequently declined steadily to 5½ percent in

New Zealand: Selected Economic Indicators, 1972–82

	1972	1973	1974	1975	1976	1977	1978	1979	1980	1981	1982
Real GDP, percentage changes	4.0	8.0	6.7	−1.1	2.9	−5.0	−0.6	0.7	2.0	4.0	−1.2
Rate of unemployment	0.2	0.2	0.2	0.4	0.3	1.6	1.8	2.2	3.6	3.5	5.4
Consumer prices, percentage changes	6.9	8.2	11.1	14.7	16.9	14.3	11.9	13.8	17.1	15.4	16.1
External current account balance as a percentage of GDP	2.9	0.2	−13.0	−8.0	−4.4	−3.8	−1.8	−3.6	−3.0	−5.1	−5.8

Sources: Organization for Economic Cooperation and Development, *Economic Outlook*, December 1984. Data on unemployment rates are derived from national sources. These, unlike other data in the table, have not been corrected for calendar variations (e.g., 1982 unemployment data refer to unemployment at the end of March 1983, i.e., the end of the fiscal year).

New Zealand: Consolidated Central Government Finances, 1972–82
(Year beginning April 1st)

	1972	1973	1974	1975	1976	1977	1978	1979	1980	1981	1982
Total Revenue (as a percentage of GDP)	27.2	28.8	30.9	30.0	30.4	33.4	32.3	32.4	32.2	33.3	34.8
Percentages of total revenue	100.0	100.0	100.0	100.0	100.0	100.0	100.0	100.0	100.0	100.0	100.0
Income taxes	61.2	64.5	68.4	65.6	66.0	67.6	64.7	65.4	67.3	66.8	66.5
Social security contributions	—	—	—	—	—	—	—	—	—	—	—
Payroll (manpower) taxes	2.2	1.3	—	—	—	—	—	—	—	—	—
Property taxes	2.3	2.4	2.1	2.3	2.1	1.6	1.6	1.3	1.1	1.3	1.1
Taxes on goods and services	19.9	18.2	16.6	19.5	18.1	17.4	18.8	18.1	18.0	18.5	19.2
Taxes on international trade	4.1	4.6	4.6	3.6	3.5	3.2	3.4	3.5	3.2	3.7	3.4
Other taxes	0.1	0.1	0.1	0.1	0.1	0.1	0.1	0.1	0.1	0.1	0.1
Nontax revenue and grants	—	—	8.2	9.0	10.1	10.1	11.5	11.6	10.3	9.6	10.7
Total Expenditure (as a percentage of GDP)	31.0	31.3	35.0	40.2	34.7	38.5	40.8	37.7	38.5	40.5	42.2
Percentages of total expenditure	100.0	100.0	100.0	100.0	100.0	100.0	100.0	100.0	100.0	100.0	100.0
Expenditure on goods and services	30.8	29.8	26.2	23.3	25.5	24.5	24.2	25.2	27.1	26.5	25.8
Of which:											
Wages and salaries	19.8	20.0	19.2	17.2	18.0	17.0	17.6	18.7	19.9	18.8	17.6
Interest payments	7.6	7.0	6.2	5.7	7.5	7.8	8.3	9.5	9.5	10.1	10.9

Subsidies and other current transfers	43.2	45.3	44.2	44.9	46.0	48.1	50.3	51.5	51.0	51.3	52.9
Of which: Social security funds	...	...	...	...	...	...	...	...	...	...	...
Capital expenditure	9.8	9.4	11.2	8.5	8.3	7.7	6.8	6.0	5.9	5.4	5.2
Lending minus repayments	8.7	8.5	12.2	17.5	12.7	11.9	10.5	7.7	6.5	6.6	5.3
Surplus/Deficit (as a percentage of GDP)	−3.8	−2.5	−4.1	−10.2	−4.4	−5.1	−8.6	−5.3	−6.3	−7.2	−7.4
Financing:											
Abroad	−1.5	−0.3	2.9	3.5	1.6	2.3	2.9	1.9	3.4	2.3	2.7
Domestic	5.3	2.8	1.2	6.7	2.7	2.8	5.7	3.4	2.9	4.9	4.7
Monetary authorities	−0.1	0.5	2.3	2.3	2.3	−4.5	0.6	−0.2	—	2.1	−3.4
Deposit money banks	2.8	1.6	−0.2	3.6	−0.6	5.6	2.3	1.4	0.9	0.2	4.8
Other[1]	2.5	0.8	−0.9	0.8	1.1	1.7	2.8	2.2	2.0	2.7	3.3
Memorandum Items:											
General government expenditure and net lending/GDP	...	...	...	...	...	...	...	...	...	...	...
Central government debt outstanding/GDP	44.6	41.2	41.8	47.8	44.7	48.7	50.5	49.2	47.6	49.2	58.2

Source: International Monetary Fund, *Government Finance Statistics Yearbook*, 1983 and 1984.
[1]Includes adjustments.

1982. The category includes such financial operations as the provision of budgetary funds for dwelling construction in line with the Government's policy of increasing the availability of housing for low-income families.

REVENUE

Total revenue of the Central Government rose as a proportion of GDP from 27 percent to 35 percent between 1972 and 1982. A striking feature of the tax structure is the significance of the personal income tax, which wholly accounted for this rise. During the period, its share in total revenue increased from 46½ percent to 58½ percent, which implies a 7½ percentage-point rise in its ratio to GDP. The rise was the result of the high rate of progressivity in personal income tax rates, which, in the inflationary environment, produced sharply increased yields despite measures to reduce fiscal drag and to supplement disposable incomes through reductions in tax rates and tax concessions in the form of increased exemptions. The share of the corporate income tax, on the other hand, declined from 14 percent to 6 percent of total revenue as a result of tax concessions and the recessionary conditions. The share of total income taxes in total revenue increased from 61 percent to 66½ percent over the period.

Another feature of the tax structure is the narrowness of the indirect tax base. Taxes on goods and services, mostly sales tax at the wholesale stage and excises, accounted for 20 percent of total revenue in 1972, but by 1981 this ratio had declined to 19 percent, which implies a growth rate somewhat higher than that of GDP. Within this category, however, sales tax revenue increased its share in total revenue from 8 percent to 11 percent, mostly on account of higher energy taxation. Property taxes are relatively insignificant at the central level and declined from 2½ percent to 1 percent of total revenue over the period. A payroll tax payable by employers on most remunerations was abolished in 1973 as part of a package to stimulate activity and reduce inflationary pressures. In 1972 and 1973 this tax yielded just over 2 percent and 1 percent, respectively, of total revenue. Taxes on international trade declined as a share of total revenue from 4 percent to 3½ percent between 1972 and 1982. Nontax revenue is mainly in the form of property income, income from nonfinancial public enterprises, and administrative fees and charges. Taken together, revenue from nontax sources averaged approximately 10 percent of total revenue over the period, with slight deviations in individual years.

THE FISCAL BALANCE AND ITS FINANCING

The central government finances were in continuous deficit throughout the period. During 1972–74 the annual deficit ranged between 2½ percent and 4 percent of GDP, but in 1975 it widened sharply to the equivalent of 10 percent of GDP as a result of a shift in the stance of fiscal policy. The stimulative impulse needed to offset the contractionary effects of the world recession and the deterioration in the country's terms of trade implied larger fiscal deficits than anticipated, however; as concern over the external position grew and inflation accelerated, the authorities shifted the fiscal policy stance to a less expansionary direction, and the deficit narrowed to 4½ percent of GDP in 1976. In subsequent years, the size of the deficit varied from year to year from 5 percent to 8½ percent of GDP, reflecting changes in both economic conditions and policy priorities.

Foreign borrowing was resorted to in every year since 1974 to finance the deficit; in most years, this borrowing covered between one third and one half of the financing requirement. Recourse to central bank financing was substantial during 1974–76, and again in 1981. Financing by deposit money banks varied greatly from year to year; from 1977 to 1981, it covered a declining portion of the deficit, but soared again in 1982. Nonbank financing, on the other hand, was a significant source of finance throughout. In the initial years of the period, nonbank financing took the form of sale of government debt to financial institutions under captive arrangements. Another method was the sale of bond certificates to the general public with associated tax incentives. Since 1977, nonbank financing has frequently covered one third of the financing requirement. Between 1972 and 1982, total debt of the Central Government rose as a proportion of GDP from 44½ percent to 58 percent, and the foreign component of the debt rose from 16 percent to 41½ percent.

FISCAL POLICY

The framework. As in other countries in the group, in New Zealand the Central Government plays a dominant role in the formulation of fiscal policy. The local governments have very limited autonomy, and their income and expenditure are closely controlled by the Central Government. Local government borrowing is also limited, requiring sanction of the Local Authorities Loans Board, which also determines interest rates on local government loans, subject to approval of the maximum rate by the Minister of Finance. From time to time, action has been taken to restrict local government borrowing in these ways.

The scope of the Central Government for influencing public sector activity is also implicit in the relative size of its expenditure, which accounts for 85 percent to 90 percent of combined central and local government spending after consolidation. Moreover, in recent years, local governments derived almost one fifth of their revenue and grants in the form of transfers from the other levels of government, largely the Central Government.

The annual central government budget has on occasion been supplemented by minibudgets during the fiscal year to accommodate changed economic conditions since the budget was prepared and changes in policy priorities. As indicated earlier, this policy contributed to a fairly unstable pattern of expenditure growth over the period. Nonetheless, endeavors have been made to take a longer-term view in expenditure decisions, as manifested in the collection by the Treasury of three-year forecasts of real expenditure from the departments. These forecasts served the purpose of containing the overall growth of the public sector, as well as increasing flexibility in fiscal policy. The actual policy relevance of the three-year forecasts was limited, however, in that no direct link existed between annual budgeting and the forecasts. However, recent procedures imply that a closer link has developed between these two functions. A committee of officials on public expenditure is now responsible for ascertaining that the departmental forecasts represent a realistic assessment of existing government policy and for preparing a survey of government expenditure requirements over a three-year period. These surveys, along with estimates of the cost implications of proposals for the adoption of new policies, are treated separately by a cabinet committee. The three-year forecasts have in this way come to serve as a basis for determining future expenditure levels, although decisions are generally limited to the first year of the forecasts. To further improve existing budgetary techniques, a new approach is being considered, whereby expenditure levels would be determined primarily in a macroeconomic context.

Aims and measures. In the early 1970s, fiscal policy was relied on as the main instrument of stabilization policy. Full employment was a high priority objective, and in 1974 and 1975, achievement of this goal involved a highly expansionary policy stance that sought to counteract the impact of recessionary external trends on the economy through employment and demand-stimulating measures. The New Zealand

authorities took the view commonly held at the time that an expansionary policy was the proper response to the recession, as growth would
soon pick up globally and a more normal policy stance could then be
resumed. Indeed, around the mid-1970s, the Government announced
that it did not accept deflationary policies as a solution to the weakening
balance of payments position and declared its preference for measures
designed to direct more resources to the export sector in the longer term,
while meeting short-term and medium-term balance of payments needs
by external borrowing. However, as it became increasingly clear that the
world recession was more intractable than had been commonly anticipated, concerns mounted over the impact of the large fiscal deficits on
the external position and on inflation.

Following a change of government in late 1975, greater emphasis
was placed on promoting adjustment in the external sector and
combating inflation. These objectives involved the pursuit of an incomes
policy that at times took the form of a wage-price freeze, and fiscal
measures, largely tax concessions and subsidies, were applied to
promote exports. Also, to contribute to the balance of payments
adjustment process, emphasis was placed on curbing expenditure
growth, as the personal income tax was already very high and steeply
progressive, and the scope for increasing indirect taxes was perceived as
being restricted, owing to the impact on prices. After the abrupt upward
shift in expenditure in 1974 and 1975, policies to curb expenditure
growth succeeded in preventing the expenditure/GDP ratio from rising
above that level for the remainder of the period covered, although the
ratio fluctuated considerably from year to year. Within this policy
restraint, however, the objective of maintaining a high level of employment continued to be given high priority, and additional measures were
taken to improve social welfare benefits, the growth of which had
assumed an automatic character through implicit indexation arrangements. Again in 1982 the authorities explicitly rejected stringent
financial policies as a main instrument for restoring balance in the
economy—on this occasion with emphasis on reducing inflation—as the
likely costs in terms of unemployment and business failures were not
acceptable.

Measures taken to stimulate demand and economic activity have
taken various forms. Tax reductions are among the most prominent. A
series of reductions in the personal income tax was implemented over
the period for this purpose and also in support of incomes policy. These
include reductions in rates, adjustments in tax scales to reduce fiscal

drag, and increased exemptions of various kinds. Measures affecting company taxation include abolition of the payroll tax, replacement of the progressive company tax structure by a flat rate tax, and increased tax-free investment allowances. Moreover, tax measures specifically aimed at directing resources into the export sector include special allowances for investment in plant and machinery to promote export production and other tax incentives for exports. Subsidies are also applied for this purpose. Other types of stimulative measures include government work programs, job creation and skill-promoting programs, and special measures to support the maintenance of farm production, inter alia, fertilizer subsidies and incentives for increases in livestock by tax deductions and concessionary loans. Measures directed at income redistribution in favor of lower income groups, but simultaneously serving the objective of stimulating demand and economic activity, include the provision of increased funds available for dwelling construction, and higher rates of social security benefits, in particular the introduction in 1977 of a national superannuation scheme.

Efforts to curb expenditure growth have relied on general restraint in budget preparation, a freeze on the number of staff in public employment, and general across-the-board cuts in expenditure. This last approach has had limited success, however, and it is widely felt that to be effective, such a measure would have to concentrate on more fundamental reductions in specific programs.

Overview and implications for future policy. Unstable economic conditions have been reflected in fairly frequent changes in the stance of fiscal policy and have generated an uneven growth path of fiscal aggregates, especially expenditure. Changes in policy priorities associated with changes of government may have contributed to this development. Although difficult to assess, since other factors, including external impulses, are involved, such changes entail the risk of impairing confidence in the firmness of the policy stance, with adverse repercussions on economic development. The move toward longer-term and macroeconomic orientation in fiscal policy formulation could contribute to a steadier course for the economy.

While the revenue/GDP ratio is one of the lowest among the smaller industrial countries, an unusually large share of total revenue is derived from the personal income tax, which is characterized by its steeply progressive structure. Despite a series of reductions over the period, the progressive rates ensured a continuous increase in the relative significance of this tax, owing to inflationary conditions. It is a widely held view that the steep progressivity of the personal income tax rates has been detrimental to work effort and initiative, has encouraged incentives for tax avoidance and evasion, and has contributed to wage-push pressures and distortions in resource allocation. A corollary of the heavy reliance on the personal income tax is the fairly narrow base of indirect taxes.

In 1982 the Government initiated a tax reform aimed at eliminating these anomalies in the tax system by reducing progressivity in the personal income tax. Further broadening of the indirect tax base or increases in indirect tax rates and service charges were not considered advisable because of the associated inflationary reverberations. However, extension of the sales tax or the introduction of a value-added tax is under consideration. Continued efforts to reform the tax system along these lines would appear to remain a major objective of future fiscal policy.

As a result of persistently large fiscal deficits, total central government debt as a proportion of GDP was in the neighborhood of 50 percent in the past several years, rising to 59 percent in 1982, which is one of the highest ratios among the smaller industrial countries. The deficits have complicated the task of overall monetary management through their liquidity impact. Also, debt servicing imposes a substantial claim on budgetary resources and may be expected to rise in future years—one cause being that the foreign component of total debt, which is not subject to erosion by domestic inflation, has increased in relative significance over the period. Given the restraints on the revenue side, a satisfactory fiscal adjustment would have to rely heavily on discretionary cuts in expenditure components that are not affected by cyclical factors and whose unrestrained growth would perpetuate the fiscal deficit.[1]

---

[1]The stance of fiscal policy was tightened by measures included in the 1984/85 budget. These included steep increases in service charges and indirect taxes, large reductions in tax expenditures, and a new tax on fringe benefits. The budget further provided for a comprehensive tax reform to be implemented over the next 18 months, which would involve a review of personal and corporate taxation and the introduction of a goods and services tax (VAT) in April 1986. It should also be noted that the significance of nonbank financing of the fiscal deficit has been increasing since 1980.

11

Norway

Economic growth was higher in Norway in the 1970s than in most other industrial countries. From 1972 to 1979, GDP growth rates averaged almost 5 percent a year in reaction to rising oil activity and expansionary economic policies; these policies were designed to counteract recessionary external impulses that weigh heavily on Norway's economy, where foreign trade amounts to 30 percent of GDP. In 1981 and 1982, however, the world recession, slower growth of oil and gas production, and more restrictive domestic policies designed to reduce inflation and improve the external position kept growth rates substantially lower and more in line with the global experience.

Throughout the period under review, unemployment remained one of the lowest among the smaller industrial countries, with rates kept below 2 percent in most years. In 1981 and 1982, the stagnation of economic growth was associated with some increase in unemployment, however, although, at 2 percent to 2½ percent, it remained quite low by international standards.

Inflation was a persistent problem, despite intensive government involvement in wage negotiations and heavy reliance on fiscal measures to secure moderate settlements in the context of incomes policy. At times, this effort was supported by a temporary wage-price freeze. In the 1972–78 period, inflation rates ranged from 7 percent to 12 percent. Inflation abated to less than 5 percent in 1979 when a general price and incomes freeze was in effect, but accelerated in the following year, and in the three years to 1982, rates ranged from 11 percent to 13½ percent annually. Expansionary economic policy based on the prospect of substantial future oil export revenues led to steadily widening current external deficits, from near balance in 1972 to 14 percent of GDP in 1977.

Norway: Selected Economic Indicators, 1972–82

	1972	1973	1974	1975	1976	1977	1978	1979	1980	1981	1982
Real GDP, percentage changes	5.2	4.1	5.2	4.2	6.8	3.6	4.5	5.1	4.3	0.9	1.0
Rate of unemployment	1.7	1.5	1.5	2.3	1.8	1.5	1.8	2.0	1.7	2.0	2.6
Consumer prices, percentage changes	7.2	7.5	9.4	11.7	9.1	9.1	8.1	4.8	10.9	13.6	11.3
External current account balance as percentage of GDP	−0.2	−1.8	−4.8	−8.5	−11.9	−14.0	−5.2	−2.1	2.0	3.8	1.2

Source: Organization for Economic Cooperation and Development, *Economic Outlook*, December 1984.

Norway: Consolidated Central Government Finances, 1972–82

(Year ended December 31)

	1972	1973	1974	1975	1976	1977	1978	1979	1980	1981	1982
Total Revenue (as a percentage of GDP)	37.9	38.4	37.8	37.5	38.7	38.6	38.8	38.9	41.3	43.1	42.6
Percentages of total revenue	100.0	100.0	100.0	100.0	100.0	100.0	100.0	100.0	100.0	100.0	100.0
Income taxes	21.7	16.0	17.2	16.5	17.3	17.6	18.0	20.6	27.2	28.5	27.1
Social security contributions	19.8	27.2	26.9	27.2	25.5	25.6	25.7	25.5	22.1	21.8	22.3
Payroll (manpower) taxes	—	—	—	—	—	—	—	—	—	—	—
Property taxes	0.9	1.0	1.6	1.4	1.1	1.1	1.0	1.1	1.0	1.0	0.9
Taxes on goods and services	46.1	43.8	42.1	43.5	44.2	46.1	44.3	41.9	39.3	37.9	37.7
Taxes on international trade	1.5	1.5	1.4	1.3	1.0	1.1	0.9	0.7	0.6	0.7	0.6
Other taxes	—	0.3	0.5	0.2	0.2	0.2	0.2	0.2	0.1	0.1	0.2
Nontax revenue and grants	9.9	10.2	10.4	10.0	10.6	8.3	9.9	10.1	9.7	10.1	11.2
Total Expenditure (as a percentage of GDP)	39.4	39.3	39.1	40.7	44.6	45.4	45.6	45.2	43.1	41.0	41.8
Percentages of total expenditure	100.0	100.0	100.0	100.0	100.0	100.0	100.0	100.0	100.0	100.0	100.0
Expenditure on goods and services	19.2	18.8	18.8	18.7	17.3	16.8	16.5	16.0	16.0	18.0	17.6
Of which:											
Wages and salaries	10.9	10.7	10.1	10.1	9.8	9.3	9.1	8.6	8.4	8.9	8.9
Interest payments	2.5	2.5	2.8	2.3	3.6	4.1	4.8	5.7	6.4	6.3	5.8

Subsidies and other current transfers	61.9	62.2	62.2	61.4	59.6	59.8	62.4	61.9	60.4	62.4	63.4
Of which:											
Social security funds	33.5	34.4	33.6	33.1	31.3	29.3	30.7	32.2	32.8	34.8	35.5
Capital expenditure	4.4	3.9	4.0	3.8	3.5	3.6	3.6	2.9	5.3	5.0	4.7
Lending minus repayments	12.1	12.6	12.3	13.8	16.0	15.7	12.7	13.5	12.0	8.3	8.4
Surplus/Deficit (as a percentage of GDP)	−1.5	−0.9	−1.4	−3.2	−5.9	−6.9	−6.8	−6.3	−1.8	2.1	0.8
Financing:											
Abroad	−0.1	−0.3	−0.1	3.0	2.4	3.6	5.3	2.0	−0.8	−1.6	−2.1
Domestic	1.5	1.2	1.4	0.2	3.4	3.2	1.5	4.3	2.5	−0.5	1.3
Monetary authorities	−1.1	−0.5	—	0.7	1.2	0.5	0.3	—	−2.0	−1.0	−0.1
Deposit money banks	1.9	1.0	0.6	−0.6	1.5	1.9	1.5	3.2	4.3	1.2	−0.3
Other[1]	0.7	0.7	0.8	0.1	0.6	0.8	−0.3	1.1	0.3	−0.7	1.7
Memorandum Items:											
General government expenditure and net lending/GDP	56.2	56.2	55.9	58.8	60.7	63.0	64.4	63.2	55.8	52.2	52.8
Central government debt outstanding/GDP	28.1	26.8	24.8	25.7	27.8	33.1	38.4	42.1	37.0	32.1	26.5

Source: International Monetary Fund, *Government Finance Statistics Yearbook*, 1983 and 1984.
[1] Includes adjustments.

A deficit of this magnitude was regarded as unsustainable, however, and after a redirection of economic policy toward a more restrictive stance in 1978 and a continued rise in oil exports, the current external position improved sharply from a deficit equivalent to 5 percent of GDP in 1978 to a surplus of 4 percent in 1981 and over 1 percent in 1982. The central government finances registered deficits throughout the period, except in 1981 and 1982.

EXPENDITURE

The expenditure of the Central Government expressed as a ratio of GDP expanded from 39½ percent to 42 percent between 1972 and 1982, which is the smallest expansion of the central government sector among this group of countries over the period. However, during 1976–79, the share was larger, 44½ percent to 45½ percent; the relative decline since then was reflected, in part, in net lending. Considerable changes took place in the size of individual expenditure categories. The share of expenditure on goods and services, which was more than 19 percent of total expenditure in 1972, had dropped to 16 percent by 1980, but increased to 17½ percent in 1982. Within this category wages and salaries also declined from 11 percent of the total to just under 9 percent. Both expenditure items also declined as a proportion of GDP. Interest payments on the government debt, on the other hand, rose sharply from 2½ percent of total expenditure in 1972 to 6 percent in 1982.

The share of subsidies and other current transfers in the total rose slightly over the period, reaching 63½ percent in 1982. The fastest growing elements were transfers to households and subsidies to support traditional industries, especially those exposed to foreign competition, and also to cushion the impact of structural change resulting from the rapid development of the oil and gas sector.

Capital expenditure, at 4½ percent in 1982, had risen slightly over the period. Net lending, on the other hand, declined as a proportion of total expenditure from 12 percent to 8½ percent between 1972 and 1982. However, this decline conceals the rapid growth of this category during the first half of the period; in 1976 its share was as high as 16 percent, reflecting the importance of central government loans to state banks, especially for housing, as part of the countercyclical fiscal policy.

REVENUE

Central government revenue rose from the equivalent of 38 percent of GDP in 1972 to 42½ percent in 1982, which, after the Netherlands and

Belgium, is the third highest ratio among the smaller industrial countries. This rise is accounted for largely by income taxes whose share in total revenue rose from 21½ percent in 1972 to 27 percent in 1982. The rise in revenue from income taxes derives largely from the corporate tax whose share in income taxes soared from 7 percent to 63 percent as a result of the rapid development of the oil sector. In fact, excluding the corporate income tax, revenue from the remaining sources taken together grew at a slower pace than GDP. The personal income tax declined as a proportion of total revenue from 20 percent to 10 percent over the period. Social security contributions increased sharply from 20 percent to 27 percent of the total in the 1972–75 period, but have since been on the decline and were 22½ percent in 1982. The decline reflects successive reductions in the rates of these taxes, usually associated with the implementation of incomes policy.

The share of taxes on goods and services in the total declined from 46 percent to 37½ percent over the period, which implies a slower growth rate than that of GDP. More than half the revenue in this category is derived from a value-added tax, the remainder comprising various excise taxes and duties. Nontax revenue and grants account for about 10 percent of total revenue and remained a relatively stable proportion during the period. The most significant items are property income and administrative fees and charges. Other revenue sources, that is, property taxes, taxes on international trade, and other taxes ranged between 2 percent and 3 percent of total revenue in most years.

THE FISCAL BALANCE AND ITS FINANCING

As already noted, the consolidated central government finances registered deficits in every year of the period, except 1981 and 1982, despite substantial surpluses of the social security system, especially in the early part of the period. The deficits widened to 6 percent to 7 percent of GDP in the 1976–79 period when an expansionary fiscal policy was pursued to counteract the impact of external impulses on employment and living standards. In 1980 the deficit dropped sharply to 2 percent of GDP, largely as a result of rapidly rising oil tax revenues, and surpluses of 2 percent and 1 percent were registered in 1981 and 1982, respectively. Data on the consolidated central government represent the overall cash deficit, but for a country like Norway where revenue from exported oil and other external transactions is significant, the domestic budget balance concept is important, especially for estimating the monetary impact of government operations. Estimates of the domestic budget balance are not available, but approximations that have been made by excluding oil tax revenue indicate that the domestic deficit is substantially larger than the unadjusted deficit and was probably 6 percent to 7 percent of mainland GDP in the last years of the period.

Sources of financing the fiscal deficit varied substantially over the period. From 1972–74 no recourse was had to external borrowing, but for the next five years, such financing frequently covered a large proportion of the financing requirement; in 1980 a policy decision was taken to cease foreign borrowing for this purpose. Financing by the monetary authorities took place in the 1975–78 period, especially in the first two years when about 20 percent of the deficit was financed in this way. Other domestic financing has fallen largely on deposit money banks, but also on the general public through bond sales. Central government debt, expressed as a percentage of GDP, rose from 28 percent to 42 percent from 1972 to 1979, but dropped to 26½ percent in 1982. The external component of the debt was 22½ percent of total debt in 1982, compared with 6 percent in 1972.

FISCAL POLICY

The framework. Norway has a relatively large local government sector. In 1982 when central government expenditure was equivalent to 42 percent of GDP, the ratio of general government expenditure was 53 percent. However, the budget of the Central Government plays a dominant role in public sector activity and, in addition, the Central Government has at its disposal certain powerful instruments to promote fiscal policy objectives. One is through its influence on local government activity. Thus, about one fourth of total local government revenue and grants, based on 1979 data, is derived from central government transfers; and the significance of these transfers has risen even further since then. Also, the Central Government is empowered to establish a maximum rate for the local income tax, which accounts for over 40 percent of total local government revenue and grants. Moreover, the Central Government, in principle, supervises borrowing by local authorities whose finances in the past several years of the period registered deficits equivalent to about 1 percent of GDP annually. Also relevant is the importance of state banks in furthering certain fiscal objectives. A major part of their operation is the financing of projects, such as housing investment, which is specifically conceived as an instrument of employment support. Lending by state banks is in part financed by direct government loans.

Fiscal policy is formulated on the basis of a comprehensive forecast of the economy for the upcoming year—the national budget—which was initiated as early as 1947. This document states the major objectives of economic policy and is presented to Parliament annually, where it is discussed along with the ordinary budget. A revised national budget is customarily presented in the course of the fiscal year and may lead to adjustments in the government budget. Longer-term considerations have been a significant determinant of fiscal policy and economic policy in general.

Long-term programs covering four-year periods were once presented to Parliament. These programs, which date back to 1948, set forth prospects for major national expenditure and production components and served as a basis for discussing medium-term resource allocation problems and stabilization policy issues. They did not, however, constitute expenditure commitments on the part of the Government. The link between annual budgeting and the long-term programs appears to have weakened over time, and recently, the long-term programming exercises were discontinued.

Lastly, although more in the realm of monetary policy, the annual credit budgets also have fiscal policy implications, as they incorporate the significant financial operations of the Central Government that are channeled chiefly through the state banks. The credit budgets, which were initiated in 1965, seek to secure consistency between the financial and real sides of the economy and attempt, more particularly, to quantify the volume and allocation of credit that would be consistent with macroeconomic objectives.

Aims and measures. The maintenance of full employment was an overriding aim of fiscal policy throughout the period. Another priority objective was the continued improvement of social benefits that had been developed at a rapid pace during the 1960s. Fiscal measures were also applied intensely to moderate cost and price pressures in the framework of tripartite incomes settlements. The fiscal content in this incomes policy approach also served the separate policy aim of redistributing income in favor of lower income groups. An additional role assigned to fiscal policy was to cushion the impact of structural change caused by the world recession and the rapid development of the oil sector by way of granting support to the sectors hardest hit.

All these objectives implied a highly expansionary fiscal policy, which to a certain extent was perceived as justified by the prospect of large future oil revenue. As a result, the fiscal deficit widened sharply between 1973 and 1978. This widening was associated with high inflation rates and increasing current external deficits, and there was growing recognition that a shift to a less expansionary direction was needed to counteract the growing imbalances in the economy. The scope for an appropriate redirection of fiscal policy was limited, however, as the maintenance of full employment continued to enjoy a high priority as did the interaction of fiscal and incomes policies, which entailed high budgetary costs. Toward the end of the period, the effects of efforts to tighten fiscal policy as set out in the original budget tended to be reduced subsequently by employment-supporting measures, improvements in social benefits, and by tax reductions granted in the context of incomes policy.

In the mid-1970s, as it became apparent that the adverse impact of the oil crisis would extend to real growth and employment in addition to prices, the fiscal policy reaction was to stimulate demand. As investment demand was already high, the main emphasis was placed on giving a boost to private consumption. Measures introduced for this purpose included income tax reductions favoring lower income groups, increases in family allowances, consumer subsidies, pensions, and other social benefits, in particular the introduction in 1978 of a sick-pay scheme.

Similar measures were repeated in subsequent years, along with other measures that specifically aimed at sustaining employment, including public construction programs, lending at concessional terms for housing through the state banks, a stock-financing scheme whereby firms received subsidies to cover a certain proportion of the increase in stocks on the condition that employment was not reduced, wage cost subsidies in the textile industry, and retraining facilities. Also, as a means of sustaining employment in separate parts of the country, employers' social security contributions were differentiated by regions.

As indicated earlier, incomes policy is a prominent aspect of overall economic policy in Norway and fiscal policy has been closely connected with it. The general demand-stimulating measures noted above, that is, income tax reductions, increased social benefits, and consumer subsidies, are typical fiscal measures incorporated in successive incomes settlements; other measures of this type include increased agricultural subsidies resulting from the raising of farm incomes, reductions in employers' social security contributions, and increased tax deductibility for trade union membership fees.

Government support to industry has increased over the period and is closely related to the full employment objective. The main recipients of industrial subsidies are state-owned companies and the shipping industry. The specific forms these subsidies take include direct grants for specific purposes, reduced fees for the use of energy, direct wage subsidies, and various financial support schemes and loan guarantees. As indicated earlier, industrial subsidies are to a large extent selective and are designed to cushion the impact of structural change on the exposed sector and to promote regional policy.

Specific measures to implement a medium-term tax reform have been under preparation since such a reform was announced in 1977, and some were initiated toward the end of the period under review. The main objective is to reduce the adverse impact of high taxation on income distribution, savings, and work effort. As already noted, Norway has one of the highest tax ratios among industrial countries, and the income tax progression is quite steep. Marginal taxes range between 30 percent and 70 percent, with about one third of the taxpayers facing a marginal tax of 50 percent or more. The proposed measures include reduced progression of personal income taxes at the lower income steps, simplified deduction rules, increased taxation of higher incomes, and an increased share of indirect taxes. The Government that took office in 1981 announced in a medium-term policy strategy its intention to reduce the tax burden on both households and enterprises. To prevent the domestic budget deficit from widening, determined efforts were to be made to reduce public expenditure growth.

Overview and implications for future policy. Since the onset of the first oil crisis, fiscal policy in Norway has contributed significantly to the fair amount of success that has been achieved in dampening the adverse impact of external recessionary trends on economic activity and employment. However, this achievement has implied a persistent expansionary stance, whose sustainability was based on the prospect of large future oil revenues. While the expansionary policy kept up employment in a general way, the full employment policy also incorporated selective measures favoring industries exposed to foreign competition, other than oil. In an environment of a vast structural change, the selective employment-supporting policy, which was also highly motivated by socio-regional considerations, evidently retarded an adjustment that would have otherwise taken fuller advantage of the country's production potential. More specifically, the extent of support under this policy obstructed labor mobility and limited the scope for structural adjustment. This problem is likely to remain a major consideration in the formulation of future fiscal and other economic policies.

The extensive application of fiscal measures to moderate wage settlements and reduce inflation appears to have enjoyed more limited success, although it is, of course, difficult to separate out the fiscal impact in this complex issue. In any case, the incomes policy-oriented fiscal measures contributed to the fiscal deficit, while the rate of inflation remained high. On the other hand, within the incomes policy approach, substantial progress was achieved in the stated policy aim of redistributing income in favor of middle- and lower-income groups.

At times in the past, the expansionary fiscal policy created problems for monetary policy, the scope of which is restricted by the government-dominated lending operations of the state banks, which, together with the domestic budget deficits, were a major cause of money supply growth. As a result, difficulties were encountered in covering the Central Government's borrowing requirement by noninflationary means. Reducing the domestic budget deficit is likely to become an important element in the strategy to bring inflation under better control. Insofar as the prospective tax reform entails a net loss of revenue, the announced efforts to limit expenditure growth will assume enhanced significance in this context.

12

Spain

From the 1960s until the mid-1970s, the Spanish economy experienced faster economic growth than most industrial countries. In the 1972–74 period, average annual GDP growth exceeded 7 percent, but economic stagnation subsequently set in, with annual GDP growth rates averaging about 1½ percent. Spain's external sector is, along with Australia's, the smallest of the smaller industrial countries, with exports and imports, excluding services, equivalent to 12 percent and 18 percent of GDP, respectively, in 1982. Despite the smallness of the external sector, the impact of the first oil crisis was nevertheless substantial, as domestic energy production was quite limited. The ensuing slowdown in world tourism also harmed the economy. The stagnation of the economy was also the result of domestic developments such as excessive increases in real wages and a heavy burden on the enterprise sector imposed by high social security contributions, both of which contributed significantly to a marked deterioration of the environment for business activity. Other contributors included marked rigidities in production processes and the financial system and a failure to adjust energy prices to international levels.

The economic slowdown was accompanied by a substantial increase in the rate of unemployment which, after having ranged between 2½ percent and 3 percent of the labor force in 1972–74, rose steadily from 3½ percent in 1975 to 16 percent in 1982. The unemployment problem was accentuated by a reversal of migratory flows owing to poor labor market conditions in host countries, and also by migration of labor from agriculture. The rate of inflation remained high throughout the period, rising from over 8½ percent in 1972 to 24½ percent in 1977; it abated thereafter, partly as a result of improved industrial relations, falling to 14½ percent in 1982.

The external current account position fluctuated over the period and caused growing concern in the post-1979 period when deficits between 2 percent to 2½ percent of GDP were experienced. Fiscal deficits, which were experienced in every year of the period, widened in the last years of the period, reaching 4½ percent of GDP in 1980. The deterioration in the fiscal position, while partly resulting from depressed cyclical conditions, was accentuated by an active policy to improve the social security system.

EXPENDITURE

Expressed as a ratio to GDP, central government expenditure rose from 20½ percent to 32½ percent between 1972 and 1981. Most of this expansion took place after 1976, reflecting the official policy to improve and extend the social security system and, to a lesser extent, increased employment costs in government service and increased net lending. The share of expenditure on goods and services in total expenditure declined from 43½ percent to 36 percent over the period, although wages and salaries, which account for about two thirds of expenditure in this category, kept pace with total expenditure growth in most years.

Subsidies and other current transfers increased their share in the total from 35½ percent to 42 percent, which accounted for more than half the increase in the ratio of total expenditure to GDP. Apart from social security expenditure, including unemployment compensations, measures to support employment and private sector activity and to cover losses by public enterprises entailed substantial expenditure increases. Interest payments on government debt remained around 2 percent of total expenditure throughout the period.

Capital expenditure was 14½ percent of the total in 1972 and played a significant role in endeavors to sustain employment. By 1981 its share in total expenditure had declined to 10½ percent, which nonetheless implies an almost constant share in GDP. Rapid growth of current expenditure pre-empted further use of this instrument for stimulating activity and employment, as measures to restrain the deficit frequently involved postponement of capital expenditure. Net lending, on the other hand, rose as a share of total expenditure from 3½ percent to 11½ percent during 1972–81. This rise reflected measures to support invest-ment and economic activity through financial intermediation by the

Spain: Selected Economic Indicators, 1972–82

	1972	1973	1974	1975	1976	1977	1978	1979	1980	1981	1982
Real GDP, percentage changes	8.1	7.9	5.7	1.1	3.0	3.3	1.8	0.2	1.5	0.4	0.9
Rate of unemployment	3.1	2.5	2.6	3.7	4.7	5.2	6.9	8.5	11.2	14.0	15.9
Consumer prices, percentage changes	8.3	11.4	15.7	16.9	17.7	24.5	19.8	15.7	15.5	14.6	14.4
External current account balance as percentage of GDP	1.2	0.6	−3.5	−3.0	−3.5	−1.8	0.9	0.3	−2.4	−2.4	−2.3

Source: Organization for Economic Cooperation and Development, *Economic Outlook*, December 1984.

Spain: Consolidated Central Government Finances, 1972–81

(Year ended December 31)

	1972	1973	1974	1975	1976	1977	1978	1979	1980	1981
Total Revenue										
(as a percentage of GDP)	20.0	20.2	19.9	21.0	20.7	22.7	23.7	24.3	24.7	25.3
Percentages of total revenue	100.0	100.0	100.0	100.0	100.0	100.0	100.0	100.0	100.0	100.0
Income taxes	15.8	16.4	17.3	18.1	20.1	18.8	20.8	21.9	23.9	20.5
Social security contributions	38.8	39.7	41.2	44.5	43.0	47.4	47.9	48.2	47.0	47.2
Payroll (manpower) taxes	—	—	—	—	—	—	—	—	—	—
Property taxes	5.5	5.8	6.1	5.6	5.3	4.8	4.7	4.2	4.3	3.5
Taxes on goods and services	23.3	23.5	19.3	17.8	15.8	13.3	13.8	13.4	16.7	18.1
Taxes on international trade	9.9	10.3	9.6	9.0	10.9	11.0	8.5	8.7	6.0	5.8
Other taxes	0.4	0.4	0.4	0.3	0.4	0.3	0.3	0.4	0.4	0.6
Nontax revenue and grants	11.5	9.2	11.4	9.7	9.3	9.7	8.1	8.1	7.2	8.7
Total Expenditure										
(as a percentage of GDP)	20.5	20.4	21.1	22.7	21.6	24.9	26.0	27.8	29.0	32.3
Percentages of total expenditure	100.0	100.0	100.0	100.0	100.0	100.0	100.0	100.0	100.0	100.0
Expenditure on goods and services	43.3	44.8	43.0	42.0	45.6	42.1	42.8	37.2	42.1	35.9
Of which:										
Wages and salaries	28.0	28.1	27.3	26.6	30.1	28.8	28.8	28.8	29.4	25.7
Interest payments	2.3	2.7	2.0	1.7	1.6	1.6	1.7	1.8	1.9	1.7

Subsidies and other current transfers	35.3	36.3	36.3	36.4	37.0	37.6	42.9	47.8	42.6	41.9
Of which:										
Social security funds	24.6	25.9	25.5	25.9	26.7	27.7	30.8	35.2	32.8	34.0
Capital expenditure	14.7	13.1	12.7	12.5	12.2	13.2	10.8	9.3	9.9	10.7
Lending minus repayments	3.7	3.5	6.1	8.5	3.5	8.0	5.9	6.4	6.6	11.3
Surplus/Deficit (as a percentage of GDP)	−0.5	−0.3	−1.2	−1.8	−0.9	−2.2	−2.4	−3.5	−4.3	−7.1
Financing:										
Abroad	—	—	0.1	—	0.4	0.9	−0.4	—	−0.1	0.3
Domestic	0.6	0.2	1.1	1.8	0.5	1.2	2.8	3.6	4.4	6.8
Monetary authorities	−0.4	0.1	0.8	0.9	−0.4	0.2	1.0	1.1	2.3	2.6
Deposit money banks	...	...	...	...	...	...	...	...	...	...
Other[1]	...	...	...	...	...	...	...	...	...	...
Memorandum Items:										
General government expenditure and net lending/GDP	21.6	21.6	22.3	24.2	23.6	26.9	28.0	29.4	31.1	35.2
Central government debt outstanding/GDP	15.6	13.2	11.8	12.1	13.0	15.3	14.3	15.4	17.2	19.4

Source: International Monetary Fund, Government Finance Statistics Yearbook, 1983 and 1984.
Note: Adjustments to total revenue and expenditure cause the totals to exceed 100 percent in most years.
[1]Includes adjustments.

Government, which directs finance to official credit institutions and state-controlled agencies through the budget.

REVENUE

Total central government revenue increased as a proportion of GDP from 20 percent to 25½ percent during the 1972–81 period, which is substantially less than the growth of expenditure. Two types of tax, social security contributions and income taxes, accounted entirely for this rise, while the share of all other tax categories in total revenue declined. The increase in revenue from the most significant indirect taxes and from nontax sources did not keep pace with GDP growth. Social security contributions are by far the largest revenue source. Their share in total revenue rose from 39 percent in 1972 to 47 percent in 1981, after having exceeded 48 percent two years before. The ratio is the highest of any of the smaller industrial countries, although not when measured as a proportion of GDP, since Spain's central government sector is the second smallest among these countries. About 80 percent of social security contributions are borne by employers.

Income taxes increased their share in total revenue from 16 percent to 20½ percent over the period, despite a series of reductions designed to redistribute income in favor of the lower income groups and to dampen wage claims. Taken together, income taxes and social security contributions accounted for almost 68 percent of total central government revenue in 1981. Domestic taxes on goods and services, largely excises, turnover tax, and profits of fiscal monopolies, declined in relative importance from 23½ percent of total revenue in 1972 to 18 percent in 1981. Taxes on international trade likewise underwent a relative decline from 10 percent to 6 percent between 1972 and 1981, as did nontax revenue whose share in the total declined from 11½ percent to 8½ percent. This revenue category consists mainly of property income and administrative fees and charges. The share of property taxes shrank from 5½ percent to 3½ percent, and other taxes remained a steady ½ of 1 percent of the total over the period.

THE FISCAL BALANCE AND ITS FINANCING

The central government finances recorded deficits in every year of the period covered. Until 1977, these ranged from ½ of 1 percent to just under 2 percent of GDP, but subsequently they widened every year and reached 7 percent of GDP in 1981. Major factors contributing to this development were increases in social security benefits and extension of their coverage, growth of unemployment compensations, and subsidies to the enterprise sector resulting from depressed cyclical conditions that also retarded revenue growth. In the early years of the period, borrowing from the domestic nonbank sector exceeded the requirement for financing the central government deficit, as fiscal policy was pursued to support monetary policy in reducing overall liquidity in the economy. The role of the Treasury in this respect was reversed later in the period and recourse was had to the central bank in most years after 1974; from 1978 such monetary financing covered one third to one half of the deficit. The Central Government's recourse to short-term credit from the central bank is restricted to 12 percent of budgetary expenditures and those of autonomous agencies. In 1976 and 1977 the financing requirement was partly met by external borrowing, which was also resorted to in 1974. Domestic financing through the deposit money banks and the general public varied considerably during the period, but usually these sources financed a substantial portion of the central government deficit, especially commercial bank financing. Because of the series of surpluses experienced in the 1960s, associated in part with the buildup of social security funds, total central government debt, expressed as a proportion of GDP, was a moderate 19½ percent in 1981, having risen only slightly from 15½ percent since 1972 as a result of inflation. External debt was about 5 percent of total debt in 1981, compared with 5½ percent in 1972.

FISCAL POLICY

The framework. The central government sector dominates public sector activity in Spain. Total expenditure of the Central Government is about 32 percent of GDP according to 1981 data; general government expenditure was 35 percent in that year. These ratios imply a smaller local government sector than in any other country in the group. Apart from own taxes, local governments rely on central government transfers under a revenue-sharing arrangement. At present, however, a movement toward regional decentralization is in progress, which has caused a deterioration in local government finances, because their revenue-raising capability has not kept pace with expenditure growth. Borrowing by local governments is subject to approval of a council composed of central and local government representatives.

A special feature of the budgetary process is the authority vested in the executive branch to implement expenditure beyond budgetary limits in the course of the fiscal year. While the budget is generally subject to ordinary legislative procedures, the Ministry of Finance may authorize excess expenditure up to 2 percent of appropriations in the budget, and the Council of Ministers may authorize up to 5 percent of budgetary expenditures for autonomous agencies and 10 percent for public enterprises. This authority provides for a substantial measure of flexibility in fiscal policy. Moreover, beginning in 1974 and continuing for a few years, budgetary appropriations were made to a short-term intervention fund that was activated in response to cyclical conditions.

Four-year development plans were initiated in 1964, and four such plans covering the period to 1980 were prepared. However, on account of political uncertainties, the 1976–80 plan was never debated in Parliament. The plans were not comprehensive and their ties to the budget were only partial; they were more or less confined to the public investment program. A new government prepared a more comprehensive economic program in 1977, as well as another medium-term program in 1979 stating its policy in general and incorporating specific economic targets. Program budgeting was promoted in an effort to link expenditure more explicitly to specific policy objectives, and zero-based budgeting is reported to have been applied to half the expenditure in the 1980 budget.

The role of the Central Government as a financial intermediary has been growing over the period. Funds obtained from the banking sector through captive arrangements are channeled through the budget to official credit institutions, which in turn provide concessional financing of medium- and long-term investment in priority sectors in line with official policy.

Aims and measures. In the early years of the period, fiscal policy was pursued flexibly for general demand management purposes. The initial response to the energy crisis was to redirect fiscal policy to an expansionary stance, and in early 1974 substantial stimulative measures were introduced. In the following year, a worsening balance of payments position and rising inflation rates led the authorities to revert to a more restrictive stance. During 1976 fiscal policy was relatively inactive, as was economic policy in general, as the authorities gave priority to the task of ensuring a smooth political and organizational transition.

The government that assumed office in 1977 announced late in that year a comprehensive economic program based on a wide political consensus. The program aimed at reducing the imbalances in the economy that had developed in the preceding period of slack economic management. The role assigned to fiscal policy was to provide stimulus to employment and activity through selective measures, while containing the fiscal deficit so as not to jeopardize the aims of reducing the current external deficit and inflation, which were to be achieved mainly through a restrictive monetary policy stance. The stage was also set for a comprehensive tax reform, with a view to making the system more efficient and equitable. A reform of the social security system was also announced. A basic aim underlying these reforms was to redistribute income in favor of lower income groups.

Measures to promote income redistribution in line with government policy were far-reaching. The income tax reform involved a replacement of the previous proportional schedular system with a general progressive personal income tax and a corporate tax. A wealth tax was also introduced. Moreover, minimum taxable income was raised in line with inflation, along with reductions of taxes on basic foodstuffs and the introduction of special taxes on luxury goods. Reform of the social security system was another major aspect of income redistribution policy concerns.

The 1977 policy announcement followed several years of substantial increases in social benefits and extensions of their coverage, especially pensions and unemployment compensation. In 1971 the system had been extended to farm workers and self-employed in agriculture, and in the following year contributions were linked to actual earnings instead of the legal minimum wage, a change that favored low-income earners. Basic reforms of the system have been slow to materialize, however. Some of the tax reductions noted above also served the purpose of dampening price increases and, as was the case in 1976, of making the continuation of wage controls more acceptable. Increases in price subsidies of consumer goods served similar purposes.

The policy of stimulating employment and economic activity largely relied on increases in public investment, both directly and through financial intermediation. While the former approach lost some of its relative significance over the period, as already noted, redirecting finance from the banking sector to official credit institutions to foster priority investments assumed an enhanced role in the budget. Other measures to promote this policy objective include tax incentives for exports and for investment in depressed regions, a commitment in a 1981 tripartite agreement to promote the creation of a certain number of jobs against wage restraint, and a commitment to reverse the trend of the constantly increasing burden of social security contributions on labor costs.

Overview and implications for future policy. For most of the 1970s, fiscal policy in Spain was directed at two basic aims: redistribution of income in favor of low-income earners, and stimulation of employment and activity. This policy was constrained by the need to contain the fiscal deficit in order to avoid undue pressure from central government transactions on prices and the external current account. Action in these areas was in large measure assigned to other economic policies, and in the latter half of the period, to monetary policy in particular.

Following the economic program in 1977, progress was made in reforming the income tax system, and indirect taxes were changed to pave the way for a value-added tax. Social security contributions grew sharply with a concomitant increase in wage costs. Thus, from 1973 to 1980, these contributions rose from 16 percent to 25 percent of the total wage bill. This development is likely to have distorted factor costs against labor, which is especially detrimental in a country faced with a serious unemployment problem. The equitable properties of the social security system have not evolved in line with the sharp increase in benefits. In particular, there is a lack of standardization of benefits and contributions, as well as an element of sectoral, age, and sex discrimination.

These shortcomings of the social security system and its negative impact on labor costs pose one of the major problems facing fiscal policy at present. The authorities recognized the need for improvement in the 1977 economic program, but progress has been slow. However, concrete proposals for a basic reform of the system are being considered for implementation with the introduction of a value-added tax, currently envisaged for 1986, that is expected to yield the required additional revenue to contain the financial deterioration of the system.

Despite persistent fiscal deficits, they were relatively low; also, as a result of inflation, total debt of the Central Government was moderate at the end of the period. Monetary financing of the deficits, on the other hand, was high and imposed a strain on monetary policy, which is the major instrument of short-term demand management. An undue restriction of domestic credit to the private sector might result from a continuation of such financing.[1]

---

[1] Since 1981 fiscal developments have changed in many respects. Most notably, the relative significance of income taxes and social security contributions has been reduced, while reliance on indirect taxes and government transfers to finance social security expenditure has increased. Moreover, government borrowing at market rates has increased substantially, and a market for treasury bills has been introduced.

13

Sweden

The growth performance of the Swedish economy was moderate over the period covered. In 1974 and 1975 the policy response to the oil price increases was to strengthen the expansionary fiscal stance in order to preserve a high level of employment, which traditionally is assigned the highest priority in Swedish economic policy. Real GDP grew by 3 percent and 2½ percent, respectively, in 1974 and 1975; these are among the highest growth rates attained by any country in the group in these years. Subsequently, except in 1979 when real GDP rose by almost 4 percent, economic growth was sluggish or negative, despite continued expansionary fiscal policy. Apart from unfavorable external conditions, this experience has been attributed, in part, to fiscal measures designed to attain various social objectives, but which have at the same time squeezed industrial profits, reduced labor mobility, and retarded structural adjustment.

The rate of unemployment remained low by international standards throughout the period as a result of extensive fiscal measures affecting the labor market; however, it rose to 2½ percent and 3 percent, respectively, in 1981 and 1982—historically high rates for Sweden.

Inflation ranged from 6 percent to 13½ percent during the period and in most years since the 1974 oil price explosion was around 10 percent, which is in the upper range among industrial countries. During the last two years of the period, the rate of inflation abated, however, and was 8½ percent in 1982.

The external current account, which had traditionally been in balance over a full business cycle, went into deficit in 1974 and remained so for the rest of the period, reaching a high of 3½ percent of GDP in 1982. Inflation and external current account deficits were associated with large and growing fiscal deficits at the central level; in 1978, the overall public sector balance swung into deficit, which grew each year, reaching over 7 percent of GDP in 1982.

EXPENDITURE

From 1972 to 1982, central government expenditure as a proportion of GDP expanded by almost 14 percentage points to 49 percent, one of the largest increases experienced among the smaller industrial countries during this period. Besides the automatic reaction of the budget to slower economic growth, two main factors contributed to this expansion, which took place mostly from 1976. First, subsidies and other current transfers, notably vastly increased social security outlays in various forms, steadily increased their share in total expenditure from 50 to 66 percent. These increases largely reflect deliberate policies to extend social security and to improve real benefits, such as pensions, which increased particularly rapidly because of automatic adjustments for inflation, reduction of the general retirement age in 1976, and the introduction of a flexible retirement option, also in 1976. Also, transfers to other levels of government have been growing as has aid to ailing industries. Second, interest payments on government debt rose as a share of total expenditure from just under 3 percent in 1972 to 9½ percent in 1982, as a result of fiscal deficits that were registered in every year of the period. The share of other expenditure categories in total expenditure declined, although not necessarily their share in GDP. Thus, expenditure on goods and services, while declining as a proportion of total expenditure from 21 percent to 14 percent, slightly increased as a proportion of GDP at around 7 percent. Capital expenditure and net lending, on the other hand, declined as a proportion of GDP, especially in the latter half of the period. Both types of expenditure were nevertheless relied on to keep up employment, both as direct capital outlays on relief work and related activities, and as concessional lending for house construction and to ailing industries.

REVENUE

Revenue as a proportion of GDP rose by 5 percentage points to 39 percent in 1982. This expansion all took place from 1976 onward, and particularly in 1976 when the share underwent an upward shift of more than 4 percentage points from the base year. Characteristic of revenue developments during the period was the rapid increase in social security contributions, which were borne increasingly by employers. As a

Sweden: Selected Economic Indicators, 1972–82

	1972	1973	1974	1975	1976	1977	1978	1979	1980	1981	1982
Real GDP, percentage changes	2.3	4.0	3.2	2.6	1.1	−1.6	1.8	3.8	1.7	−0.5	0.4
Rate of unemployment	2.7	2.5	2.0	1.6	1.6	1.8	2.2	2.1	2.0	2.5	3.1
Consumer prices, percentage changes	6.0	6.7	9.9	9.8	10.3	11.4	10.0	7.2	13.7	12.1	8.6
External current account balance as percentage of GDP	1.3	2.8	−1.0	−0.5	−2.1	−2.6	0.0	−2.2	−3.6	−2.5	−3.6

Source: Organization for Economic Cooperation and Development, *Economic Outlook*, December 1984.

Sweden: Consolidated Central Government Finances, 1972–82

(Year ended June 30)

	1972	1973	1974	1975	1976	1977	1978	1979	1980	1981	1982
Total Revenue											
(as a percentage of GDP)	34.1	32.8	32.8	33.7	38.3	39.6	39.5	38.1	37.8	38.9	39.0
Percentages of total revenue	100.0	100.0	100.0	100.0	100.0	100.0	100.0	100.0	100.0	100.0	100.0
Income taxes	26.8	22.7	21.6	21.4	25.1	23.5	18.7	18.3	18.1	15.9	15.5
Social security contributions	21.5	22.1	23.6	26.7	26.6	27.8	30.9	32.3	32.8	34.7	33.7
Payroll (manpower) taxes	3.0	4.4	5.9	5.9	5.9	6.4	6.2	3.3	3.1	3.8	3.3
Property taxes	1.6	1.6	1.5	1.3	1.3	1.2	1.1	1.1	1.2	1.1	1.2
Taxes on goods and services	33.8	34.5	32.8	29.9	27.5	27.5	28.8	29.8	29.0	29.6	29.4
Taxes on international trade	1.4	1.4	1.3	1.9	1.5	1.5	1.1	1.1	1.1	1.2	0.6
Other taxes	0.1	0.1	0.1	0.1	—	—	0.1	0.1	0.1	—	0.1
Nontax revenue and grants	11.8	13.2	13.2	12.8	12.0	12.1	13.1	14.1	14.5	13.7	16.3
Total Expenditure											
(as a percentage of GDP)	35.4	34.2	36.1	36.4	38.7	41.3	44.8	45.7	46.5	48.3	48.9
Percentages of total expenditure	100.0	100.0	100.0	100.0	100.0	100.0	100.0	100.0	100.0	100.0	100.0
Expenditure on goods and services	20.8	21.2	20.1	19.8	18.2	17.2	16.3	16.2	15.8	14.9	14.0
Of which:											
Wages and salaries	10.5	10.3	9.5	9.1	8.7	8.2	8.0	7.6	7.3	6.7	6.4
Interest payments	2.9	3.1	3.1	3.7	3.3	3.7	4.0	4.4	6.3	9.0	9.5

Subsidies and other current transfers	50.2	53.2	55.6	57.5	60.1	62.4	63.7	65.8	64.5	64.6	66.0
Of which: Social security funds	3.6	4.3	4.8	5.1	5.4	6.4	7.1	7.8	8.3	8.8	9.7
Capital expenditure	8.7	8.5	7.0	6.5	6.1	6.4	5.4	5.1	4.2	4.0	3.6
Lending minus repayments	17.4	14.0	14.2	12.5	12.3	10.3	10.7	8.5	9.1	7.5	6.9
Surplus/Deficit (as a percentage of GDP)	−1.3	−1.5	−3.3	−2.7	−0.4	−1.7	−5.2	−7.6	−8.7	−9.4	−9.9
Financing:											
Abroad	—	—	—	—	—	1.4	1.6	0.8	3.5	2.7	2.6
Domestic	1.3	1.5	3.3	2.7	0.3	0.3	3.7	6.8	5.2	6.7	7.2
Monetary authorities	1.1	−1.0	1.0	2.5	−2.7	−0.3	0.6	0.9	2.2	1.9	3.5
Deposit money banks	0.9	1.3	0.8	−0.2	1.5	−0.8	1.9	3.6	0.7	3.0	2.2
Other[1]	−0.7	1.2	1.5	0.3	1.4	1.5	1.2	2.2	2.4	1.8	1.5
Memorandum Items:											
General government expenditure and net lending/GDP	51.7	49.5	51.6	52.2	54.2	58.1	62.2	62.7	64.5	66.2	71.2
Central government debt outstanding/GDP	16.6	16.7	18.3	18.9	17.0	18.3	21.3	25.7	32.3	38.8	45.4

Source: International Monetary Fund, *Government Finance Statistics Yearbook*, 1983 and 1984.
[1]Includes adjustments.

proportion of total revenue, these contributions increased from 21½ percent to 33½ percent between 1972 and 1982. A substantial relative decline in the share of income taxes took place over the period, from 27 percent in 1972 to 15½ percent in 1982; the decline reflected a policy to reduce the detrimental impact of extremely high marginal rates on work effort, the indexation since the beginning of 1979 of income tax scales and the basic deduction, and an effort to moderate contractual wage increases through income tax reductions. The personal income tax rates, however, are still among the most progressive in industrial countries. The highest marginal rate was 85 percent at the end of the period.

Taxes on goods and services declined as a share of total revenue from 34 percent in 1972 to 29½ percent in 1982, while their ratio to GDP remained constant. More than half the revenue in this category is derived from a value-added tax whose share rose over the period, whereas the remaining taxes on goods and services, mostly excises, declined in relative importance. The share of nontax revenue in the total ranged from 12 percent to 16½ percent over the period. This revenue is mostly in the form of property income from nonfinancial public enterprises and capital funds. Other revenue sources were less significant and changed little over the period.

THE FISCAL BALANCE AND ITS FINANCING

Fiscal deficits were experienced every year since 1972, and since 1976 these grew rapidly, amounting to 10 percent of GDP in 1982. As indicated earlier, this development is the result of a variety of factors, including the Government's commitment to full employment, improvement and extension of social benefits, incomes policy measures by way of tax reductions, an environment of poor growth performance in the latter half of the period with adverse repercussions on both sides of the budget, and the ensuing increase in interest payments on government debt. It should be noted in this context that the financial balance of the public sector as a whole is substantially better than the central government balance. Mainly on account of a buildup of the National Pension Fund, the public sector showed a surplus until 1978 but experienced growing deficits thereafter, due to the sharp deterioration in the central government's financial position. The local government finances remained in approximate balance. The overall public sector deficit exceeded 7 percent of GDP in 1982, compared with a central government deficit of 10 percent in that year.

From 1972 to 1976 the fiscal deficit was financed entirely by domestic resources, that is, borrowing on the capital market and from the banking system, while borrowing from the monetary authorities in one year tended to be repaid in the following year. From 1977 recourse was had to external borrowing and domestic monetary financing, while domestic nonbank sources covered a declining portion of the central government deficits, posing problems for monetary policy, as explained in the following section. The mounting fiscal deficits entailed a sharp rise in government debt, which, as a proportion of GDP, increased from 16½ percent to 45½ percent between 1972 and 1982. The share of foreign debt in total central government debt rose from zero to 23 percent over the same period.

FISCAL POLICY

The framework. While the central government budget is the major instrument of fiscal policy in Sweden, other public entities are involved, which, especially in the earlier part of the period, were instrumental in the pursuit of countercyclical policy. In principle, local government budgets are required to be balanced and as such are not relied on for stabilization purposes. Of total general government expenditure, which was equivalent to 71 percent of GDP in 1982, the Central Government accounted for 49 percent, if transfers to other levels of government are included. These figures imply a large local government sector—indeed, the largest among the smaller industrial countries—reflecting the marked expansion of local government activity in the 1960s.

Although local governments enjoy a high degree of independence in their financial decisions, they can be influenced by the Central Government as far as certain types of taxation, expenditure, and borrowing decisions are concerned. Moreover, the Central Government makes agreements with local governments from time to time to coordinate actions for certain policy objectives, such as the maintenance of a high level of employment and the containment of taxation to limit the public sector's claims on resources and crowding out of the private sector. A special manifestation of such coordination in the early 1970s was the expansion in slack periods of subsidized housing investments, largely in apartments under municipal ownership or participation, in order to maintain high and stable employment. This policy instrument was not very effective in later years, however, as residential construction needs were gradually saturated.

Although the financing of the social security system is normally determined on a medium-term basis and thus does not play an active role in stabilization policy, the contribution rates are nonetheless subject to revisions when the Central Government's overall financial policy is formulated. As indicated earlier, financial surpluses of the social security system more than outweighed the central government deficits until 1978, but they have since shrunk, largely on account of an upsurge in benefits payments that were not matched by increases in contributions and transfers from the budget.

The operation of investment deposit funds is closely related to fiscal policy. Investment deposit funds are profits that enterprises may deposit free of corporate income tax with the central bank on non-interest-bearing investment deposit accounts. Such deposits, which may amount to 40 percent of the firm's annual profits, can be used for fixed investments whenever their release is permitted for certain cyclical or regional policy objectives. Otherwise, if they are used within a given period, the profits become subject to tax. A stockbuilding scheme with employment conditions attached to it also constituted a flexible instrument of fiscal policy, as noted below.

The annual budget documents contain an economic policy statement by the Government and a survey of the national economy. Multiyear budget estimates are also presented to Parliament. These estimates point out the implications of existing commitments and proposals for the various budget aggregates for the next five-year period and serve as a basis for ensuring consistency of sectoral resource allocation with political goals.[1] No formal decisions on the multiyear budget are taken by Parliament.

Since 1969, an estimate of the impact of certain budget components, as well as changes in the balances of investment deposit funds on the economy, has been published in the national budget. This attempt at measuring the fiscal impact on total demand and domestic production was made more elaborate in the 1974 budget with the adoption of a more disaggregated model that tried to take into account the different impact on the economy of different expenditure and revenue items. While likely to elucidate the relationship between the budget and the rest of the economy, the real impact of the model on fiscal decision making is uncertain, as is often the case with similar exercises.

---

[1] Eriksson, p. 68.

Aims and measures. Broadly expressed, the major objectives of fiscal policy over the period were the maintenance of full employment and the preservation of high living standards in the face of adverse external impulses on the economy. Special support was also given, especially in the latter half of the period, to traditional industries facing difficult structural adjustment problems. Moreover, tax policy was to some extent directed at moderating general wage settlements. The pursuit of fiscal policy toward these objectives was constrained, however, by persistent external current account deficits and high inflation rates.

Expecting the world recession following the sharp oil price increases in 1973 and 1974 to be short-lived, the authorities decided to pursue a traditional high-employment policy vigorously and applied fiscal policy measures extensively. These took various forms, the most direct including special construction programs, relief work, labor market training, temporary grants to industry and the services sector for the recruitment of additional employees, and increased local government absorption of the labor force, which was partly financed by transfer payments from the Central Government. The introduction in 1975 of a temporary stock-support scheme, whereby enterprises received grants of 20 percent of the volume increase in their inventories, was conditional upon the maintenance of employment levels by the enterprises over the relevant period, namely, through 1977. The absorption of employment by the public sector was more marked in Sweden than in most other industrial countries. Thus, between 1970 and 1978, the share of the government services sector in total employment rose from 20½ percent to almost 29 percent, compared with a rise from 12 percent to 14½ percent on the average in those industrial countries for which data are available.[2]

The continuous sharp increase in the outlays of the social security system was attributable to increased real benefits and extension of their coverage. The principal social security benefits are indexed to the cost of living. Also, demographic factors contributed strongly to the increases; in particular, the aging structure of the population had an important bearing on health expenditure. The social security system is to a large extent financed by employers' contributions. As a result, the overall

---

[2] Organization for Economic Cooperation and Development, *Economic Surveys: Sweden*, p. 42.

ratio of contributions to the total payroll has been as high as 34 percent to 35 percent in recent years, having risen from 14 percent in 1970. The strain on private sector activity was intensified by substantial wage increases in the mid-1970s.

To improve the unfavorable cost position of the economy, the authorities decided, inter alia, to eliminate the 4 percent general employers' fee in 1978, which reduced the overall rate by 1 percentage point, the first such reduction in the 1970s. Payroll taxes, however, were recently raised again. A more persistent effort by the Government was to create a favorable atmosphere for moderate wage settlements through incomes policy measures without direct involvement in the bargaining process. These included income tax reductions, which were also motivated by the perceived detrimental impact on work effort of very high marginal rates. Since 1979, the income tax brackets and the basic deduction have been indexed on the basis of consumer prices, with certain items in the index base excluded. Increased food subsidies have served a similar purpose.

To cushion the impact of structural change on ailing industries and thereby keep up domestic activity and employment, budgetary appropriations for industrial subsidies rose sharply in the latter half of the period. These were in the form of direct transfers to state enterprises and private enterprises in shipbuilding, steel, mining, and forest products industries. Industrial support measures were initially aimed at protecting employment in existing industries rather than stimulating new job outlets. With continued recessionary conditions, this kind of employment tended to become permanent, and by 1979 support to ailing industries had reached the equivalent of 5 percent of GDP. This policy stance was gradually shifted to support that was conditional upon restructuring. More recently, the improved profit situation resulting from the 1982 devaluation of the krona has resulted in a substantial reduction in industrial subsidies, and further reduction is planned.

Overview and implications for future policy. The automatic effects of the slowdown of economic activity and an expansionary fiscal policy pursued throughout the period entailed a sharp expansion of the central government sector; as local government also grew substantially, the public sector in Sweden reached the equivalent of about 71 percent of GDP in 1982—among the largest in industrial countries. The expansionary fiscal policy, while successful in maintaining a high level of employment and living standards, has widespread economic implications and poses difficult problems for future policy. It is felt that some of the major measures, such as high unemployment and pension benefits, have stimulated consumption rather than industrial investment and, together with high and increasing payroll and other taxes, contributed to balance of payments difficulties and a severe retrenchment of resource availability to industry and the exposed sector. Large-scale support to ailing industries and employment schemes may have reduced labor mobility and retarded structural adjustment.

Rapid expenditure growth was accompanied by an increased tax burden, and, as Sweden's marginal tax rates are among the highest in industrial countries, this burden is likely to have affected work incentives adversely. To remedy the situation, a major reform of the personal income tax system is contemplated, according to which the highest marginal rate would be limited to 50 percent by 1985 for the majority of taxpayers. The revenue loss would be financed by an increase in payroll taxes and energy taxes, a reduction in the indexation of tax brackets, and a 50 percent ceiling on interest deductibility.

On the monetary side, the sharp rise in the Central Government's borrowing requirement exerted an upward pressure on interest rates, with an adverse impact on industrial investment, and seriously complicated the task of monetary management. To avoid crowding out industry from the capital market, the authorities endeavored to limit government borrowing outside the banks. This led to growing monetary financing of the fiscal deficit, accompanied by excessive monetary expansion. Nonetheless, private non-housing investment fell from 12 percent of GDP in the early 1970s to 8 percent in the years after 1978.

Owing to indexation and the automaticity of a growing share of expenditure due to previous spending commitments, budgetary policy has become increasingly inflexible. It is estimated that 80 percent of central government spending is determined by such automatic mechanisms and that over 50 percent of expenditure is automatically indexed.[3] Also, the authorities have been constrained in raising indirect taxes, due to the impact on prices and inflationary expectations.

A medium-term forecast of fiscal developments prepared in the early 1980s revealed that, assuming unchanged policies, the fiscal deficit was likely to remain at around 14 percent of GDP. The Swedish authorities declared this as unacceptable and adopted a policy to reverse past trends and restructure the public finances. In the light of an already high tax ratio, major emphasis would be placed on containing expendi-

---

[3] Eriksson, p. 70.

ture growth, inter alia, by reducing indexation. The 1982 devaluation created scope for a substantial reduction in industrial support through the budget, but at the time of writing other specific details of the above policy had not been worked out.[4]

---

[4]In 1983 and 1984, the expansionary stance of fiscal policy was reversed and the fiscal balance improved in both years. Among factors contributing to this development were increases in indirect taxes, limitations placed on deductions for income tax purposes, a reduced degree of indexation of tax brackets, and sharply reduced industrial subsidies and capital contributions to ailing industries.

REFERENCES

Addison, John T., "Incomes Policy: The Recent European Experience," in *Incomes Policies, Inflation, and Relative Pay*, ed. by J.L. Fallick and R.F. Elliott (London: George Allen & Unwin, 1981), pp. 187–245.

Andersen, Palle Schelde, and Philip Turner, "Incomes Policy in Theory and Practice," *OECD Occasional Studies* (Paris) (July 1980), pp. 33–50.

Australia, Commonwealth Government (1983–84), Budget Paper Number 8.

Bacon, Peter, et. al., *The Irish Economy: Policy and Performance, 1972–1981* (Dublin: Economic and Social Research Institute, 1982).

Blöndal, Gísli, "Balancing the Budget: Budgeting Practices and Fiscal Policy Issues in Iceland," *Public Budgeting and Finance* (New Brunswick, New Jersey), Vol. 3 (Summer 1983), pp. 47–63.

Clark, Colin, "Public Finance and Changes in the Value of Money," *Economic Journal* (London), Vol. 55 (December 1945), pp. 371–89.

——, "The Scope for, and Limits of, Taxation," in *The State of Taxation*, A.R. Prest, et. al. (London: Institute of Economic Affairs, 1977), pp. 19–34.

Cutt, James, "The Evolution of Expenditure Budgeting in Australia," *Public Budgeting and Finance* (New Brunswick, New Jersey), Vol. 3 (Summer 1983), pp. 7–27.

Danziger, Sheldon, Robert Haveman, and Robert Plotnick, "How Income Transfer Programs Affect Work, Savings and the Income Distribution: A Critical Review," *Journal of Economic Literature* (Nashville, Tennessee), Vol. 19 (September 1981), pp. 975–1028.

Denmark, Ministry of Economic Affairs and the Budget, *The Danish Budgetary System* (Copenhagen, 1972).

Denmark, Denmarks Statistik, *Statistisk Tiårsoversigt* (Copenhagen, 1983).

Doyle, Maurice F., "Management of the Public Finances in Ireland Since 1961," *Public Budgeting and Finance* (New Brunswick, New Jersey), Vol. 3 (Summer 1983), pp. 64–78.

Eriksson, Björn, "Sweden's Budget System in a Changing World," *Public Budgeting and Finance* (New Brunswick, New Jersey), Vol. 3 (Autumn 1983), pp. 64–80.

Finland, Ministry of Finance, *A Survey of the Prospects for the Finnish Economy and State Finances to 1986* (Helsinki, 1982).

Heald, David, *Public Expenditure: Its Defence and Reform* (Oxford: Martin Robertson, 1983).

Iceland, Central Bank of Iceland, *Economic Statistics Quarterly* (Reykjavik, November 1983).

International Monetary Fund, *Government Finance Statistics Yearbook*, Vols. VI and VII (Washington: International Monetary Fund, 1983, 1984).

——, *International Financial Statistics* Yearbook, Vol. 37 (Washington: International Monetary Fund, 1984).

Ireland, Department of Finance, *Economic Review and Outlook* (Dublin), various issues.

____, Department of Finance, *Current Economic Trends* (Dublin), various issues.

LeBlanc, L.J.C.M., and Th. A.J. Meys, "Flexibility and Adjustment in Public Budgeting: The Netherlands Experience," *Public Budgeting and Finance* (New Brunswick, New Jersey), Vol. 2 (Autumn 1982), pp. 53–64.

Lindbeck, Assar, "Stabilization Policy in Open Economies with Endogenous Politicians," *The American Economic Review* (Nashville, Tennessee), Vol. 66 (May 1976), pp. 1–19.

McKersie, Robert B., and Werner Sengenberger, *Job Losses in Major Industries: Manpower Strategy Responses*, Chapter IV (Paris: Organization for Economic Cooperation and Development, 1983).

Meys, Th. A.J., "Spending More and Getting Less: Recent Experiences with the Allocation and Control of Public Expenditure in the Netherlands," in *The Grants Economy and Collective Consumption*, ed. by R.C.O. Matthews and G.B. Stafford (New York: St. Martin's Press, 1982), pp. 242–66.

Organization for Economic Cooperation and Development, *The Challenge of Unemployment* (Paris: OECD, 1982).

____, *Economic Surveys* (Paris: OECD), various issues.

____, *OECD Economic Outlook* (Paris: OECD, December 1984).

Peacock, Alan T., and Jack Wiseman, *The Growth of Public Expenditure in the United Kingdom* (Princeton: Princeton University Press, 1961).

Price, W.R., and Jean-Claude Chouraqui, "Public Sector Deficits: Problems and Policy Implications," *OECD Occasional Studies* (Paris) (June 1983), pp. 13–44.

Robinson, E.A.G., ed., *Economic Consequences of the Size of Nations* (London: Macmillan & Co., Ltd., 1960).

Saunders, Peter, and Friedrich Klau, "The Role of the Public Sector: Causes and Consequences of the Growth of Government," *OECD Economic Studies*, (Paris) (Spring 1983), pp. 11–229.

Tanzi, Vito, *The Individual Income Tax and Economic Growth: An International Comparison* (Baltimore: The Johns Hopkins Press, 1969).

United States, Department of Health and Human Services, *Social Security Programs Throughout the World* (Washington: Government Printing Office, 1984).

LIBRARY OF DAVIDSON COLLEGE

Books on regular loan may be checked out for **two weeks**. Books must be presented at the Circulation Desk in order to be renewed.

A fine is charged after date due.

Special books are subject to special regulations at the discretion of the library staff.

APR. -4. 0

NORTH/SOUTH
TECHNOLOGY TRANSFER
THE ADJUSTMENTS AHEAD

ORGANISATION
FOR ECONOMIC CO-OPERATION
AND DEVELOPMENT
PARIS 1981

The Organisation for Economic Co-operation and Development (OECD) was set up under a Convention signed in Paris on 14th December 1960, which provides that the OECD shall promote policies designed:

— to achieve the highest sustainable economic growth and employment and a rising standard of living in Member countries, while maintaining financial stability, and thus to contribute to the development of the world economy;
— to contribute to sound economic expansion in Member as well as non-member countries in the process of economic development;
— to contribute to the expansion of world trade on a multilateral, non-discriminatory basis in accordance with international obligations.

The Members of OECD are Australia, Austria, Belgium, Canada, Denmark, Finland, France, the Federal Republic of Germany, Greece, Iceland, Ireland, Italy, Japan, Luxembourg, the Netherlands, New Zealand, Norway, Portugal, Spain, Sweden, Switzerland, Turkey, the United Kingdom and the United States.

Publié en français sous le titre :

LES ENJEUX DES TRANSFERTS
DE TECHNOLOGIE NORD/SUD

*
* *

CONTENTS

Acknowledgements 6
Preface 7
Summary 9

Chapter I

TECHNOLOGY TRANSFER TO DEVELOPING COUNTRIES: APPROACHES TO THE PROBLEM

A. Concepts and Definitions 17

  a) Technology 17
  b) Transfer of technology 18

B. The Dynamics of Transfers 19

  a) Markets for technology 19
  b) Objectives of the firm 20
  c) The policies of host countries 22
  d) Mastery of technology 22

C. The Sector Studies 25

  a) Petrochemicals 25
  b) Rubber tyres 25
  c) Consumer electronics - Television 26
  d) Pharmaceuticals 26

D. Developing Countries for Study 27

Chapter II

FLOWS OF TECHNOLOGY

A. Introduction 31

B. Industrial Production 33

  a) Sources of technology for industrial production 34
  b) Destinations of technology for industrial production 37
  c) Transfers of industrial production capabilities: Discussion of indicators 38

C. Technology Production 43

  a) Training programmes and skill development 43
  b) Location of research and development activities 45

D. Financial Flows 47

E. Summary 49

  a) Autonomous flows of technology 49
  b) Captive flows of technology 49

3

Chapter III

EFFECTS OF TECHNOLOGY TRANSFER

A. Positive and Negative Effects 51
  a) Micro-economic approach 51
  b) Macro-economic approach 51

B. Trade Effects 53
  a) Trade in manufactured products between developing countries and the OECD area 53
  b) Analysis by product group and country: industrial restructuring 54
  c) Technology transfer and changes in trade flows 62

C. Employment Effects 64
  a) Net effects 65
  b) Gross effects 67
  c) Medium-term outlook 68

Chapter IV

LONGER-TERM OUTLOOK

A. Relevant Features of Technology Transfers 69
  a) Transfers to "export platforms" 69
  b) Transfers to countries with large domestic markets 70
  c) Transfers to oil producing countries 71

B. Elements Influencing the Diffusion of Technology 72
  a) Favourable technical factors 72
  b) Economic and financial factors 73
  c) Legal factors 78

C. Intensification of Competition 79
  a) Outlook for the eighties 79
  b) Differences between OECD countries 80

Chapter V

GENERAL POLICY ISSUES

A. Controls on Technology Export 88
  a) Feedback effects and controls on exports 88
  b) Transfers and a "fair price" for technology 89

B. Adaptation Strategies 89
  a) The overall framework 90
  b) Technological renewal 90
  c) Technological differences between OECD countries 91
  d) The renewal of industrial dynamism 94
  e) Comprehensive action to stimulate innovation 97
  f) Transfers of technology: some specific aspects of policy 98

Concluding Remarks 101

Annex I

DEFINITIONS AND EXPLANATIONS

A. Nomenclature 103

B. Description of performance indices 103

Annex II

Graphic 1 105
Graphic 2 106
Graphic 3 107

Notes and References 108

5

ACKNOWLEDGEMENTS

This report, prepared by the Secretariat and published under their responsibility, is part of the work on technology transfer of the OECD Committee for Scientific and Technological Policy. An Ad hoc Group on Technology Transfer to Developing Countries, composed of government experts, gave guidance to the work of the Secretariat. The composition of some delegations changed during the course of the work; all delegates who participated are listed below.

Chairman: Mr. M. Turpin (France)

Australia

Mr. J. Lonergan
Mr. J.D. Bell
Mr. M. Cobban

Austria

Mr. E. Musyl
Mr. W. Jilly

Belgium

Mr. F. Delecluse
Mr. G. Hoyos
Mr. B. Remiche
Mr. H.M. Van Der Stichele
Mr. P. Van Speybroeck

Canada

Mr. O. Silverman

Denmark

Mr. I. Bodenhagen

France

Mr. R.F. Bizec
Mr. A. Marelle
Mr. G. Vitry
Mr. A. Weil

Germany

Mr. P.C. Von Weyhe
Mr. R. Krause
Mr. H. Bornemann

Greece

Mr. C. Gotsis

Italy

Mr. B. Caprettini
Mr. B. Grassetti

Japan

Mr. T. Bito

Netherlands

Mr. M.W. Van Den Brink
Mr. E. Kronenburg

Norway

Mr. O. Austveg

Portugal

Mrs. E.S. Ferreira
Mr. J.M. Caldas Lima

Spain

Mr. J. Suris Jorda
Mr. A. Bernad Sanz

Sweden

Mrs. G.B. Andersson
Mr. E. Von Bahr
Mr. A. Teikmans
Mr. U. Svedin

Switzerland

Mrs. M. Muller-Haegeli
Mr. O. Wyss

United Kingdom

Mr. J.R. Perrett
Mr. R. Roberts
Mr. M.J. Brebner

United States

Mr. J.F. Blackburn
Miss H.D. Grayson
Mr. F. Kinnelly
Mr. R.C. Malley

Yugoslavia

Mrs. M. Lukic
Mr. M. Mladjenovic

E.E.C.

Mr. H. Nagelmackers

Secretariat: Mr. G. Bell
Mr. G. Vickery
Miss M. Briat

PREFACE

Technology transfer between advanced industrial countries and developing countries has already been the object of an abundant literature. So why add another study to an already long list?

The reply is that the approach of this study is different. It attempts to re-examine a problem that has often been the subject of rhetoric or ideological justification.

It does not seek to study, again, the consequences of technology transfer for receiving countries or how to improve their capacity for technological absorption. Instead, it begins from the observations that technology transfer, in whatever form, represents an important part of the trade between developed and developing countries and that there has been a steady increase in OECD imports of manufactured goods from developing countries.

Until now, OECD industrialised countries have been, if not the only source, then the principal suppliers of technology. The report attempts to identify the consequences for OECD economies that may follow the increasing flow of technology towards the most rapidly advancing developing countries.

Faced with the complexity of the subject, the lack of widely accepted statistical measures, and the methodological assumptions that must be made to unravel the problem, this work has concentrated on the economic consequences that follow transfers. In particular, effects that are relayed through international trade are considered. Nevertheless, to complete the picture other specific aspects have been considered: legal questions, the terms and conditions of transfers and the effects on a number of industrial sectors. The subject is also set in its historical perspective, because the current situation is not new. Industrial Britain, in the past, faced newly industrialising countries—countries such as France, Germany and the United States.

The present work also recalls something that is often overlooked: there is no technological determinism. Technological monopolies exist, but they are temporary and everything threatens them—beginning with the false security that is given by their advances.

Backwardness can progressively be overcome, to the extent that people can be trained and processes transferred and mastered, or it can disappear suddenly with a technical advance. Moreover, we must not forget that the industrial tissue of OECD countries is made up of a wide diversity of enterprises. Even in the same sector, technologies are far from level and different enterprises are vulnerable in different ways to new competition.

Technology transfer enables developing countries to catch up and participate in the world industrial trading system that has contributed so much to our prosperity over the last 25 years. And in recent years increases in exports of capital goods to developing countries have helped some industrial countries to offset the effects of lowered domestic demand.

But though the effects of technology transfer are generally beneficial to both parties, producers as well as consumers, there are problems which it is dangerous to ignore or underestimate. Traditional industries which have widely known and easily available technology continue to feel the full thrust of new competitors. This is felt more acutely when there is slow growth in demand and in industries which are regionally concentrated and which use workers with little training and rather low mobility (for example in textiles and clothing). To a certain extent these problems justify positive transition policies in industrial countries to regulate the speed of transformation. But transition measures must be sharply distinguished from protection. Increases of technology transfers require continuing, progressive, and general trade liberalisation in manufactured products.

It is clear that there is only one realistic means of breaking out of the current dismal period when even apparently solid enterprises are suffering from winds of extreme competition—winds that do not only blow from the South. This is to take a resolute stake in continued innovation and technical change, with a heavy accent on improving skills and mobility of labour.

Governments have a role to play and policies to implement, and the important differences between OECD countries requires that policies must be adapted to each of them individually. Furthermore, the best policies will be ineffectual if neither management nor workers are persuaded that the survival of their work requires acceptance of change and the search for new markets, new products and new activities. Numerous examples show that there is no need for fatalism. Even inside the crisis-bound industries, there are prosperous firms.

M. TURPIN
Ancien Délégué chargé de la
Recherche Industrielle et de la Technologie
Ingénieur en Chef des Mines

SUMMARY

Transfer of technology is currently a topic of great interest—at both national and international level. In this report we shall enter a highly controversial field, where the basis of theory and fact is not substantial, and where speculations abound [1].

To a certain extent the situation that one meets when studying technological relations between industrialised and developing countries is similar to that between OECD countries during the second half of the 1960's when the controversy on the "technology gap" between the U.S. and Europe was at its height.

For example in the "domination" or "technological dependence" theories that have been prominent in the thinking on under-development in the seventies, the assumptions and arguments are similar to those used in the debate on the technology gap in the sixties, and very similar conclusions have been reached. Then the cry was for a "Marshall plan" for science; now the call is formulated as "free access to technology, the common heritage of mankind". These demands are variations on the same theme—it is only the style that has changed.

Now among industrialised countries there is some of the same uneasiness towards developing countries that was felt in the U.S. towards other industrialised countries shortly after the debate on technology gaps.

Some ten years after this debate European (and Japanese) industry, far from being crushed by the technological power of the United States, is now causing concern there, particularly among trade unions. At the OECD's third meeting of Ministers of Science (11-12th March, 1968), one of the main topics for discussion was the technology gap; some observers noted subsequently that only three years after this meeting exports of high technology products from the U.S. began to fall and imports began to rise. It was easy to jump to the conclusion that American competitiveness was losing its edge as a direct result of the United States' liberal policy on technology transfer; a number of observers did so without hesitation.

These changes should remind us that no situation is necessarily final. The "technology resource" which developed countries are sometimes accused of monopolising appears to be only a transient advantage. Post-war experience in European countries and Japan shows that handicaps can be overcome and that technology transfer is an effective instrument for bringing countries gradually to similar levels of technical development.

This is not to suggest that the developing countries' position is identical to that of Europe or Japan immediately after the Second World War. The nature of the situation is completely different, and different approaches and policies are required. But one group of developing countries is already well on the way towards industrialisation, and another is not far behind. These countries have to be considered separately from the extremely poor countries.

Furthermore, while OECD countries have recently experienced slower industrial growth (lower growth rates of productivity, innovative activity and

9

investment) slower economic growth, and rising raw material and energy costs, the growth rates of the more dynamic industrialising countries have exceeded what was thought possible by economists and planners in the early fifties [2]. This has largely been due to the accelerated development of industry: which has shown rates of growth unknown in developed countries, including Japan.

A whole series of consequences varying in scale and economic impact for different OECD countries are to be expected from this process of industrialisation which, if not entirely caused by technology transfers, is certainly enhanced by transfers. In particular, trade in manufactured products is likely to benefit sectors supplying capital goods and technology, and have negative effects on sectors producing standardised goods. For example, firms operating in sectors where there is intense competition from LDCs may be expected to slow recruitment, and in some cases to reduce their workforce. Price competition in standard products is likely to prove difficult when wage costs in the textile industry in some developing countries are one-tenth to a quarter of average wage costs in OECD countries [3], and in the electrical and electronic industries equal to only half of wage costs in Japan [4].

In the light of such observations a number of questions may be asked: Is the industrial fabric of OECD countries capable of adjusting to changes which may be inevitable, but which are speeded up by transfers of technology? Will the rate of adjustment adequately match the rate of industrial transformation implied by transfers? *In particular, will national capacities of technological renewal be able to compensate for the erosion of technological comparative advantages as technology is transferred?* These questions are addressed in the latter part of this report.

The general approach of the report provides an analytical background to technological aspects of the continuing North-South dialogue. As the report is specifically concerned with scientific and technological activities and their contribution to the economic health of OECD countries, these are dealt with in some detail. Indeed, the problems linked with North-South technology transfer are a sub-set of the overall set of problems of competitivity, change, and the creation and diffusion of technology. On the other hand, the social effects of modern technology in developing countries have not been considered, neither have aid policies and programs—these one adequately dealt with elsewhere.

The following summary is organised in the order of the report and covers:

i) The technology transfer process
ii) Flows of technology
iii) Effects on OECD economies
iv) The longer-term outlook
v) General policy issues.

The policy section of the report deals with long-term general problems facing OECD countries and does not attempt to prescribe short-term policies for individual countries.

A. THE TECHNOLOGY TRANSFER PROCESS

Technology may be transferred in many ways. The awarding of licences to firms abroad is only one way of utilising technological know-how. Know-how that the donor has developed or acquired in other ways can also be transferred to third parties by supplying advanced industrial goods, by planning, constructing and putting into operation complete turnkey production plants, by supervising the running of such plants and equipment (a service which often follows the delivery phase) and by giving employees in the customer country training and/or further training. Direct investment, agreements on scientific and technical cooperation, agreements between enterprises from different countries on cooperation in the production field, international contract research and development, international scientific and technological agreements, likewise contribute to transfers of technological know-how. These operations may take place singly or in combination with each other.

There are a range of possible effects on advanced industrial countries from transfers of technology. First, there is the transfer itself—involving for example the international sale of know-how, services or equipment, direct investment or other activities. Subsequently there are effects coming from the extra output or increased production efficiency of the new technology. These "feedback effects" will appear most directly in trade—either as imports into the technology-exporting country, into third countries (developed or developing), or as losses of exports to the technology–receiving country. Changes in trade may then be translated into changes in employment and prices. There are wider subsequent effects on national incomes and income distributions which will link through to changes in international investment patterns and flows of capital, technology, and other mobile production factors and to inter-regional trade. In this report we concentrate on direct trade effects and related employment effects as far as they can be isolated.

The actual effects of any one transfer are determined in part by the objectives of technology holders (usually private sector enterprises in OECD countries) and receivers and by their technological capacities, negotiating skills and strategies. They are also determined by economic demand and supply factors, including natural resource endowments, by government policies and by the economic and social conditions in the country receiving technology and the country exporting it.

B. FLOWS OF TECHNOLOGY

As no single widely accepted indicator exists, a number of different indicators have been used to describe the flows of technology to developing countries. Each indicator describes different aspects of technology transfer. For example, international payments for licences and technical and commercial services are closely related to transfers of know-how, whereas exports of machinery and equipment are more general indicators of industrial investment. Financial flows to a certain extent suggest the potential for industrial development and the economic prospects of borrowing countries, even though they may also go to finance external deficits, roll-over previous debt or build up reserves.

The following were some of the features of the period 1970-1979:

— Exports of capital goods and equipment showed the strongest growth: over 10% p.a. in real terms. The building of basic industry and infrastructure in OPEC countries helped to boost exports of capital equipment to developing countries to over 40% of total exports of these goods from OECD countries. Construction of turn-key plants showed signs of flattening off towards the end of the period with some geographical diversification away from the Mid-East OPEC members.

— Payments for licences and technical and commercial services grew moderately (about 4% p.a. in real terms) while foreign direct investment increased at a similar rate.

11

— Commercial financial flows increased strongly during the period but were somewhat reduced in 1979 (and 1980). International borrowing—now going to finance increased external deficits and refinance debt but also paying for imported technology—increased by about 10% p.a. in real terms, and the expansion of OECD export credits encouraged exports of capital goods.

— Training activities and skill development have been important in the private sector, but little quantitative data exists on the extent of scientific, technical and management training. In the public sector most training activities financed by OECD countries are not directly related to industrial development. Transfers of R&D activities have not been extensive.

The major suppliers of technology have been the U.S., Japan, Germany (the latter two growing rapidly), the U.K. and France. Between them these countries supplied about 70% of total OECD flows going to developing countries. However, when scaled by GDP, almost all OECD countries were suppliers of similar magnitudes, but with different national specialisations. Latin American and Asian countries have remained important destinations for technology exports despite the increased importance of OPEC countries.

C. EFFECTS ON OECD ECONOMIES

It is difficult to satisfactorily determine all of the effects coming from transfers. Not only are there direct trade and related employment effects, but also induced effects on income and income distribution and prices. There are also trade and employment effects in other industries as the ripples from any single transfer spread through the economy.

In this report we concentrate on trade and employment. We assume that we may attribute to technology transfer some fraction of total changes in trade and employment caused by the industrialisation of rapidly developing countries. Furthermore we examine gross effects on particular industrial activities and net effects over the whole economy.

It is argued that net return effects on Member countries have been, overall, positive in terms of trade and employment and consumer benefits. However, the gross effects have fallen rather unequally on different industrial activities and on different countries. While engineering enterprises and machinery and equipment industries have been boosted by demand for their products from developing countries during a period of low activity in OECD countries, other manufacturing industries have had their problems compounded by competition from a limited number of developing country exporters.

Traditional industries such as clothing, footwear and light manufacturing have been affected most by increased imports. Despite recent advances, these industries have not been generally noted for their technical sophistication, and their problems cannot be attributed specifically to recent transfers of modern industrial technology. Rather, the driving force for rapid increases in imports has been the dynamics of industrialisation in some developing countries based on suitably skilled low-cost labour, widely available technology and, often, retail sourcing.

However, rapidly increasing gross effects are also noticeable in the electrical and non-electrical machinery industries. Here technology is more advanced and the importance of both transnational enterprises and the policies of developing countries to move up the technological scale is much more marked.

Finally, the medium-term outlook is for increased imports, both in volume and range of industrial products. Depending on assumptions, the net results appear positive in general, but with serious gross effects localised geographically and sectorally. However, structural changes need to be distinguished from cyclical trends to enable further analysis as a basis for long-term policy formulation.

D.   LONGER-TERM OUTLOOK

It is suggested that the effects on OECD countries of technology transfer depend very much on the countries to which technology is transferred. Recipient countries may be grouped as: export-oriented, domestic-market oriented and OPEC. The return effects on OECD countries appear so far to be respectively: large, moderate and minimal with respect to the volume of technology transferred to each of these groups of countries.

Transfers are likely to continue at a significant rate because, on the supply side, there are more sources of technology (developing countries themselves are now increasingly important as relays for more standardised technology); on the demand side, people in industrialising developing countries have been rapidly mastering received technology; and rapid rates of industrial growth suggest that (apart from political factors) industrialising developing countries are attractive prospects not only for direct investment, but also as borrowers from capital markets and as recipients of export credits.

One general concern is whether the external deficits and debt burden of some developing countries can be financed in the near and medium term. It is argued that this problem has direct relevance to technology transfer because of:

— the effects of balance of payments constraints on OECD exports of machinery and equipment and supply of technical services to developing countries (until recently these rivalled oil imports in value for many developing countries);

— the pressures on developing countries to export manufactured goods to cover deficits and the resulting pressure on OECD imports and exports to third markets.

Next, some of the likely effects of changes in the national and international legal environment for technology transfer are discussed briefly.

Finally, evidence is presented that competition with developing countries is likely to increase in the period to 1990 and that this competition will, as in the past, affect different industrial branches and different Member countries very unevenly. Furthermore, the positions of Member countries in industries that are likely to confer technological control on future industrial activities is distributed unequally. The three large industrial countries (U.S., Germany, Japan) appear to be retaining a large share of these activities.

E.   GENERAL POLICY ISSUES

Policy solutions for individual OECD countries have not been proposed. Rather, particular points that are relevant to most Member countries are discussed.

Positive aspects of technology transfer have been emphasised and it is concluded that controls on North-South transfers are unrealistic if not counterproductive.

13

Transfers of technology are an important aspect of the processes of adjustment and adaptation to imbalances in OECD economies. As far as adjustment is concerned, transfers may lead to short-term trade and other return effects. Adaptation is a longer-term dynamic and continuous process. Transfers of technology are part of this dynamic process for it is innovation and change that allow transfers to take place and it is transfers that spur further innovation and change.

It is argued that an overall strategic policy for adaptation is necessary for Member countries. This should be based on a comprehensive analysis of *benefits* as well as costs of transfers and related structural changes. Strategic policy should emphasise progressive technological industrial renewal based on a more equal, complementary development of competitive technological capabilities within the OECD area. This should ideally result in an improved but *different* competitivity of all Member countries.

It is suggested that it is desirable to maintain a healthy and competitive industrial sector and that the long-term trend towards service activities may present some short and medium term problems. It is also suggested that a graduated reduction of trade and related barriers may be one certain way of stimulating innovation. This report emphasises that technology transfer is both a sign of structural transformations and a contributor to these changes. These transformations will continue and it is necessary to face them as positively and flexibly as possible—by looking to the future.

*
**

This report has relied heavily on the analytical and sector studies prepared by consultants and the OECD Secretariat. The studies and their authors are listed below and for more details the reader should refer to them.

i) *Analytical Studies*

— Prepared by Professor J.H. Dunning, University of Reading, U.K.: methodological notes, "Towards a Taxonomy of Technology Transfer and Possible Impacts on OECD Countries";

— Prepared by Professor N. Rosenberg, Stanford University, U.S.A.: "The International Transfer of Industrial Technology: Past and Present";

— Prepared by the Secretariat: "The International Flows of Technology to Developing Countries";

— Prepared by the Secretariat: "Outline of the Main Characteristics of Industrialisation in the Developing Countries";

— Prepared by Drs. L. Scholz, E. Von Pilgrim, H.G. Braun, IFO, Germany: "Developing Countries and the International Division of Industrial Labour: Identification of Sensitive Industries, Technological Trends, and Implications for Technology Policies of OECD Countries";

— Prepared by Dr. E.M. Graham, Alfred P. Sloan School of Management, M.I.T., U.S.A.: " The Terms of Transfer of Technology to the Developing Nations: A Survey of the Major Issues";

— Prepared by Mr. J. Delorme, Vice-President, European Patent Office, The Hague, and the Secretariat (Annexes): "The Changing Legal Framework for Technology Transfer: Some Implications";

— Prepared by the Secretariat: "Tentative Identification of Main Feedback Effects";

ii) *Sector Studies*

— Prepared by Professor J.-M. Chevalier, University of Paris-XIII, France: "Transfer of Technology in the World Petrochemical Industry";
— Prepared by Dr. E. Sciberras, University of Sussex, U.K.: "Transfer of Technology in the Consumer Electronics Industry—The Television Sector";
— Prepared by Mr. I. Senior, Economists Advisory Group, U.K.: "Transfer of Technology in the World Tyre Industry";
— Prepared by Dr. M.L. Burstall, University of Surrey, U.K.: "Transfer of Technology in the Pharmaceutical Industry";

iii) *Other Studies*

— Prepared by the Business and Industry Advisory Committee to OECD, Group of Experts on Technology: "Industrial Technology and Know-How".

TECHNOLOGY TRANSFER TO DEVELOPING COUNTRIES: APPROACHES TO THE PROBLEM

Feed-back or return effects on an economy are complex and difficult to quantify completely. The effects coming from transfers of technology are more than usually complicated because of the variety of actions and reactions involved. Strictly speaking we should measure flows of technologies, the transformations which they bring about in host countries, the return effects on OECD countries *and* subsequent flows of technology, goods and services that the first round of transformations have induced.

This is a difficult task. Concepts are vague, the theoretical base is inadequate. Furthermore, transfer of technology covers two separate situations: the transfer of industrial production capacities, and the transfer of capabilities to master, adapt and further develop imported technology. The two sorts of transfers do not necessarily occur at the same time, or at the same rate.

Furthermore, developing countries are a heterogeneous group and classifications by per capita income do not always help the analysis. To reduce the variables to be considered, a small number of competitive industrialising countries were chosen for study throughout most of this work.

Some of the above points will be dealt with individually to enable clarification of concepts used in the remainder of this report.

A. CONCEPTS AND DEFINITIONS

a) TECHNOLOGY

Because it is a special category of resource and is so varied in its content and in the meaning attached to it, "technology" has been defined in many different ways. These definitions have been discussed elsewhere [1]—[4] and need little further comment. Apart from very broad definitions such as technology is "the body of knowledge that is applicable to the production of goods" [5], the main feature of most definitions is that they highlight one or more special aspects of technology, such as its subject, method and type, whether it takes a material or non-material form, or else its legal or systemic characteristics.

This suggests the range of perceptions regarding the nature of technology and the difficulty of finding an all-embracing definition. A further point is that while technology is embodied in tangible products such as machinery or industrial complexes, or in legal documents such as patents, licences or know-how contracts, it may also be expressed in the form of a skill, a practice or even a "technology culture" which finally becomes so diffuse that it is no longer noticed. However, it is on such a "culture" that the proper functioning of a given technical system ultimately depends. For example, a firm wishing to transfer a particular technology for the first time ever may have to produce a vast set of written rules and descriptions defining its management and shop-floor practices [6].

This cultural aspect of technology has led some authors to say that "technology is, in fact, the use of scientific knowledge by a given society at a given moment to resolve concrete problems facing its development, drawing mainly on the means at its disposal, *in accordance with its culture and scale of values*" [7]. However, the philosophical clarity of this definition has to be set against its applicability. Furthermore, despite the risk of restricting and limiting our study, the definition used here must be confined to *commercial and industrial* aspects of technology.

During negotiations for an international code of conduct on the transfer of technology, the OECD countries proposed the following: "Technology means systematic knowledge for the manufacture of a product, for the application of a process or for the rendering of a service, including any integrally associated managerial and marketing techniques"*. This definition appears satisfactory, it covers more closely a suitable notion of technology and the areas in which it is applied. However, some problems remain as we will see when discussing the measurement of flows of technology in Chapter II. This notion will only be partly illustrated by available statistical data until there is a systematic investigation of all aspects of the nature and effects of technology transfer.

b) TRANSFER OF TECHNOLOGY

"Transfer" covers a whole range of activities and as H. Brooks has pointed out, the concept is difficult to pin down. It may be defined, however, as "the process by which science and technology are diffused throughout human activity" [8].

This very broad definition needs to be explained clearly. For example, it broadly covers any activity by which "systematic rational knowledge developed by one group or institution is embodied in a way of doing things by other institutions or groups... This can be either transfer from more basic scientific knowledge into technology, or adaptation of an existing technology to a new use. *Technology transfer differs from ordinary scientific information transfer in the fact that to be really transferred it must be embodied in an actual operation of some kind*" [8].

This highlights one of the fundamental features of transfer: it is the outcome of a deliberate, systematically organised act. Again the operation may be either vertical, i.e. from the general to the particular, or horizontal from one application to another (without the two necessarily being linked, e.g. application of a military technique to a civilian use).

With this approach we can begin to see that the transfer concept concerns the enrichment of any given field through an input from *outside*. For the purposes of our definition "outside" is relative to the "field" or "sector" and transfer consists of the operation whereby knowledge is *diffused*.

The "transfer" concept has subsequently become increasingly identified with the systematically organised exchange of information between two enterprises which may or may not be located in different countries [9]. Obviously, the enterprises may belong to different branches and may be at different levels of technical development [10]. Such an exchange may be the object of a formal co-operation agreement.

---

*   UNCTAD, TD/CODE TOT/C.1/WG1/CRP.3, 27th February, 1979.

18

i) *Commercal transactions involving transfer of technology*

Technology transfer often takes the form of commercial transactions of different kinds that may be related or independent. Several distinct operations may be distinguished [11]:

— assigning or granting of industrial rights,
— handing over technical or non-technical know-how in the form of documents, plans, diagrams,
— the communication of technical or other know-how in the form of supply of services,
— providing a combination of services with a view to commissioning an industrial complex,
— providing technical services related to the selling or leasing of machinery.

ii) *Non-commercial transfers of technology*

Alongside these purely commercial transfers, there is a whole range of other transfers. These include transfers under multilateral or bilateral co-operation agreements with the LDCs. They generally relate to infrastructure projects of all kinds—government services, urban management, scientific, educational and research services—but they also cover other activities such as agriculture.

The transfer agents involved are also different (usually national authorities) and they operate within the framework of agreements that are usually explicitly designed to further the host country's development. However, the way that the transfer is carried out is often the same; there is provision of documentary information and training courses and various services are given by expert teams.

*
**

Whatever definition is used, the breadth and content of the technology transfer concept highlights the importance of its more qualitative aspects and the difficulties involved in attempting to *quantify* transfers. This difficulty is magnified when it is necessary to distinguish between the "ability to use" and the "ability to master" a complete process from design and development to production and marketing. This second capacity characterises a more complete technological mastery.

As a consequence of technical progress, technology is a mobile factor that responds to changes in the economy. But transfers of industrial production capacity do not necessarily coincide with transfers of the mastery of technology.

B. THE DYNAMICS OF TRANSFERS

If technology is the subject of commercial transactions, production and flows of technology are not governed by fluctuations in supply and demand on a conventional market.

a) MARKETS FOR TECHNOLOGY

Technology is the subject of economic activity, but it does not have the usual characteristics of an economic good: *technology is not usually produced directly for sale* [12]. The transfer of technology is usually seen in the context of trading objectives such as the sale of products or services [13]. Moreover technology transfer does not involve irreversible transfer of the use of the technology for the "seller" [14]. Because it is not usually produced for sale, the pricing and diffusion of technology does not usually conform to "technology market laws" as there are no real technology markets as such [15].

The ability to master a technology gives the technology holder an advantage over others without this ability. It is an ability to do what others cannot do, or the ability to do it better. The possession of this technological mastery implies a substantial benefit. It should give the holder the possibility of building up a profitable, temporary monopoly with regard to a product, or if it is a process, to reduce production and distribution costs. This justifies devoting considerable resources to acquiring such abilities.

For the producer, technology is usually a costly but essential instrument in economic competition for an enterprise—particularly as price competition may be too costly for what are often modest results in terms of market shares. As an instrument of strategy, technology development is usually planned with a view to ensuring the maximum flow of income in the long run and to supply the maximum number of markets.

The transfer of technology will therefore only take place when the interests of the enterprise so demand. Transfer will then occur with maximum precaution, so that the technological monopoly is affected as little as possible [16]. It is very important that a climate of confidence is established between those transferring the technology and those receiving it. The maximum precautions and effectiveness of technology transfer are usually ensured when an enterprise deals with its own subsidiary, but dealings between related enterprises are not always possible. Transfer must then take other negotiated legal forms, but competition between rival enterprises will often lead to advantages for the recipient, such as a more comprehensive transfer or more favourable financial terms. A driving force for the dissemination of technology is thus the competition between firms seeking to use the transfer to fulfil their own objectives.

Firms transferring technology may have a number of the objectives discussed below. (Cross transfers of technology are generally not applicable to transfers to developing countries.)

b) OBJECTIVES OF THE FIRM

There are a range of objectives and the mix of objectives may change over time. They include:

— to gain or keep a market (or to have a market presence),
— to acquire factors of production at a competitive price,
— to gain access to regular supplies of raw materials,
— to maximise the use of assets which may not have profitable alternative uses.

i) *Market strategy*

After first exploring the market by exporting to it, a firm may endeavour to consolidate its position by installing local production capacity. Depending on local conditions, the firm will have a choice between setting up a wholly-owned subsidiary or some form of joint venture with a local partner. In determining this choice, the complexity of the technology concerned and the degree of control exercised by the holder will be as important, if not more important, than provisions for transfers laid down by the host country.

Explanations of incentives for transfer are similar to those in the theory of international investment and in particular, they broadly correspond to those of Vernon in explaining the "product cycle". For a whole series of transfers related to production of consumer goods and some intermediate goods, the technology-exporting OECD countries are now behaving as did the United States in the 1960s. Now it is a group of developing countries that are also receiving substantial inputs of technology, whereas in the 1960s it was mainly other OECD countries that were recipients.

Keeping the product cycle approach in mind, transfer of technology allows the enterprise to cover research costs, prolong the life cycle of products that are threatened with obsolescence on the home market, find new, growing markets, and ensure its own survival in a climate of intense international competition.

The other three objectives for technology transfer are more straightforward.

ii) *Costs of inputs*

This is most easily described in terms of the Heckscher-Ohlin theory. Technology, a mobile factor, moves towards less mobile factors. The firm holding the technology needs to organise production to minimize production costs; in a competitive situation with rising wage costs and a downward trend in prices for products, one short-term answer for a firm with a high proportion of labour costs may be to transfer segments of production to countries where labour costs are lower. This particularly applies to industries which incorporate few raw materials in production (clothing, electronics) and which can bear increased transport costs.

Transfers take many forms: including direct investment, licencing, sub-contracting, joint ventures. The holder of technology will try to obtain inputs at the lowest price for the different stages of elaboration of final products. For a subsidiary, labour and other inputs are purchased directly and the technology remains within the enterprise. In sub-contracting, transfer is externalised in the sense that factors are purchased in the form of more highly elaborated inputs: spare parts or components requiring strict quality controls (there are numerous examples in, for example, the electronics and automobile industries).

iii) *Natural resources*

In this case production is located where raw materials are found. However, the organisation of manufacturing may be complicated. The decision to set up some stages of the manufacturing process where raw materials are produced rather than where finished products are consumed depends on the size of the market, cost of transport, and the selling price and access to raw materials [17]. These are usually beyond the control of the firm and they may effectively determine the final decision.

iv) *Utilisation of assets*

In this case the assets, of for example, petrochemical engineering firms, are essentially the know-how to build production plants; this know-how may be based on processes held by what are principally production enterprises. The engineering firm may be independent, or a subsidiary of a producer enterprise. Producers may even have engineering sections to commercialise their technology.

Furthermore, a firm may account for 80 per cent of its turnover with only 20 per cent of the total range of products that it manufactures. It may be in the interest of the firm to transfer the technology for production of some of the less important products in its range. Such a policy may allow substantial savings in stocks, after sales service, advertising, and other services. It may also lead to increased profits if the transfer to a more specialised firm allows higher levels of production because of better organisation and greater economies of scale.

21

c) THE POLICIES OF HOST COUNTRIES

Besides the basic objectives underlying the decision of the firm to transfer technology there are other factors that are important. Amongst these are the policies of host countries.

Such policies can provide incentives or disincentives. Among the incentives are the well-known policies of import substitution and a whole range of taxation and financial subsidies. Import substitution policies make it more difficult to export to these markets, but the added protection provides security and profits for local producers. This is a powerful incentive for local production if the market is large enough to allow a minimum efficient production capacity to be established. Disincentives may include policies that are aimed at encouraging firms to meet the objectives of national authorities but which may run counter to important objectives of the firm [18].

The above summary suggests that transfers of technology are linked to changes in the world economy. In a world where economic conditions are constantly changing, they are one of the ways that enterprises may cope with the constraints upon them, so that they may change and survive.

Of the factors that influence firms in deciding whether to transfer technology, it is economic factors such as intensity of competition, barriers to entry to the industry, the size of markets and their development prospects which have a decisive influence. Political factors, including the investment climate and incentive policies in the host country (free zones, grants, interest subsidies), and controls and regulations on transfers of technology, play a supporting role that may be positive or negative. However, these factors may be important, particularly when it comes to setting up a subsidiary [19].

The decision to transfer technology is the result of a wide variety of influences on the strategy of the firms involved (those holding *and* those acquiring technology) and the strategy of the host country. Because these influences are constantly changing it is possible to say that there are no general cases of technology transfer, but only specific examples which make up the total known as technology flows*.

d) MASTERY OF TECHNOLOGY

It is clear that transfer of technology involves the transfer of production capacity to a different country. This may be relatively simple technology when it is only part of a production process that is transferred to another country. It may be more complex technology when a complete process producing a finished product is to be established. However, in both cases the object of the transfer is to begin production from an installed capacity in a given country, under given economic and technical conditions.

In industrialised countries, the technology transferred usually supplements existing capacity. In addition to the know-how which is directly supplied, the transfer raises the possibility for subsequent mutually beneficial co-operation [20]. Mastery of the technology will often be more rapid, either by supply of documentation or by training of personnel.

This may also be true in developing countries, but in many cases the circumstances are different. Although transfer of technology still involves installation of production capacity the technology is not necessarily mastered completely or

---

* See Chapter II.

22

quickly. Transfers from industrialised to developing countries may involve bridging a considerable "technological distance". This has not been the case for transfers between industrialised countries except perhaps concerning Japan at the very beginning of industrialisation.

In the early stages of industrialisation in what are now industrialised countries, technology was largely based on artisanal or engineering skills. A country importing technology usually possessed these skills in sufficient quantity and foreign techniques could be adopted without too much difficulty. Moreover, the technology was usually in the form of separate elements such as machinery, products, or processes [21]. Subsequently, the parallel technological development of industrialised countries made it possible for them to exchange technology without major problems as techniques became more complex. Advances in a particular field, whether they were technical or organisational, were usually matched in other countries by increasing abilities to acquire, adapt, and further develop these new techniques. The growth of the educational system has played an important part, and Japan's educational system largely explains that country's capacity to catch up with what were more advanced economies.

Today in most cases technology is no longer simple. The factory is no longer a line of machines that facilitate a simple division of labour or that allow the use of an energy form which is difficult to transport. In the final stages of standardised production the factory itself is a tool, with carefully planned, prepared and defined functions, designed to supply a specific market with a standard product made with specific materials [22].

Modern technology may no longer be readily acquired by a few individuals with some professional experience as was the case in the early stages of industrialisation. Acquirers of technology should have the necessary institutions: these include enterprises that are built around collective technical, commercial, financial and scientific know-how, and the wider network of institutions for research and for diffusion of scientific and technical change. So that the economy as a whole can gain the maximum benefit from transfers, the enterprises should be located in an industrial fabric which permits interaction with complementary technologies and which allows the further diffusion of the new techniques.

It is understandable that technology conceived in one environment may be difficult to transplant to another quite different environment. The success of the transplant will depend on such elements as the capacities of host countries to receive it, as well as on the legal and practical transplanting procedures that are adopted. The form and success of the transfer will depend on interactions between the supplying and receiving ends of the operation.

In many cases the enterprise in possession of the technology will set up a subsidiary to ensure the security of the transaction [23]. This will help to ensure that anticipated production targets and standards will be achieved.

Alternatively, and depending on the economic situation, industrial development, and political circumstances of the host country, the receiving enterprise may be a joint venture or be totally independent. In the second case the supplier of technology may contract to supply not only production capacity but also help the recipient reach the necessary levels of skills. The receiver of technology may not directly have the capabilities to:

— repair and maintain;
— modify and adapt;
— design and produce new equipment or products.

Various measures may be introduced to build these capabilities: training programmes in many cases involve temporary supply of staff who can substitute for lack of local skills. Some measures will extend beyond activities directly related to the enterprise: these include the organisation of training and research

23

Transfer may take very different forms, comprising:	One-off operations	— Sale of turnkey factories, and supply of capital goods, — Design and contracting for industrial complexes, — Training of personnel, — Sale of patents and licences, — Technical assistance (start-up, manufacture, management and marketing), — Joint ventures where local capital has a majority (controlling) share;
	Permanent links	— Maintenance of installations, — Supply of intermediate products, — Buying back of part of production, — Marketing, — Continued technical assistance.

Source: [25]. (There is considerable overlap between these forms.)

centres and supply systems, and organising access to existing marketing networks or the establishment of new ones [24]. (See Table 1.) Such measures can be taken directly by the technology supplier or by sub-contractors.

Thus the notion of transfer of technology is relatively straight-forward between industrialised countries but it is much more fluid when transfers are to developing countries.

Problems involving mastery of foreign technology do not arise in the same terms for exchanges between industrialised countries. The balance between transfer and mastery is more easily attained. The problem is more one of protection for the supplier of technology and the extent to which the supplier will gain from opening new technological outlets [26].

For developing countries, the capacity transferred is not pre-determined to the same extent. As we have seen, it can range from the mere transfer of production capacity to the mastery of a complete process—from design through to production.

These differences in the capacity to master technology can raise important political problems. People in some developing countries have considered that disappointing results of transfers come from deliberate actions by technology suppliers to maintain monopolies that they may have been losing elsewhere. These suspicions have resulted in a number of attempts to regulate what is regarded as an abuse, and such regulatory efforts have added controversy to an already complicated situation.

Furthermore, because of the technological backwardness of many developing countries, it is clear that transfers of modern technology are essential if they are to industrialise in the same way as industrialised countries. But technology transfer is more than simply the extra production capacity that is acquired. Due in part to past transfers, a number of developing countries have already established themselves as competitive suppliers of manufactured goods. While competition has so far been based on lower production costs, it is gradually extending to other areas such as marketing and design of new products. The extent of this potential competitiveness must be based on individual case studies.

The above general discussion may be illustrated with the four sector studies that were carried out for this project.

C. THE SECTOR STUDIES

a) PETROCHEMICALS

In this industry projects are underway or are being planned that will supply petrochemical products either to local markets (Brazil, Mexico, South Korea), regional markets (Singapore) or general export markets (Saudi Arabia). In the last case local processing of natural resources will enable Saudi Arabia to use some of its gigantic reserves of gas instead of burning them.

A relative slow-down in development of new products and processes has considerably weakened the capacity of chemical and oil companies to control the spread of technology. Enterprises acquiring technology may exploit competition between many alternative sources—chemical and oil companies on one hand, engineering firms on the other hand—particularly if, like in Brazil, Mexico and Korea, they possess basic technological skills. When they lack such technological capacity as in Saudi Arabia, the control of oil resources strengthens bargaining power with respect to technology holders. However, if production is geared to exports, the balance may be restored in favour of those chemical and oil firms which have established marketing networks. The state of world markets will also determine implementation of some projects.

The development of local technological abilities, combined with competition between the different holders of technology, largely explains the conditions offered by sellers when transferring technology. This applies to both the participation of local equipment suppliers, and the short- and long-term opportunities for mastery of the different levels of technology. These are set out in Table 2 for steam-cracking technology.

Table 2
Transfer Structure for Steam-cracking Technology

Transfer	Saudi Arabia	Singapore	Korea	Brazil	Mexico
Ability to operate	No	Yes	Yes	Yes	Yes
Ability to maintain	No	Yes	Yes	Yes	Yes
Ability to modify	No	No	Yes	Yes	Yes
Ability to design	No	No	Long-term	Long-term	Long-term

In Brazil and Mexico the absorption of previous transfers has increased bargaining power in these countries. This has allowed more favourable payment terms and an increasing level of transfer of know-how. The different behaviour of petrochemical-producing firms and engineering firms has been an important factor.

It is evident that when there are a number of different sources of technology and these holders adopt different strategies, then a technology receiver will have considerable room for manoeuvre. This will be more limited if the technology is tightly held as is the case downstream from basic petrochemicals. Study of the sector suggests that there has been a gradual international, intra-sectoral division of petrochemicals technology.

b) RUBBER TYRES

The evolution of the tyre industry has been entirely different to that of the petrochemical industry. Tyre technology has been relatively stable so far.

25

However, the industry is constantly making improvements in products (quality, reliability, product life) and processes, so that know-how is of great importance [27].

This situation means that technology is tightly held by the three or four firms with sufficient turnover to carry out the amount of R&D that is necessary to remain competitive. Transfer has been fairly strictly controlled by the firms possessing and developing technology, and which are firmly committed to the industry. Transfers usually go to subsidiaries that supply a local market (production is generally located near outlets). Licences are largely granted by firms whose long-term strategy is to diversify or leave the industry.

Because the leading firms tightly hold their technology, they have considerable room to manoeuvre. However, they are obliged to follow market trends and the strategy of competitors. Failure to transfer production capacity through direct investment or licencing may in the long-term mean the loss of markets.

c) CONSUMER ELECTRONICS - TELEVISION

Transfers of technology in this branch mainly go to Asian countries and export processing zones, and to some areas in Latin America—particularly the Mexican border zone. As the specific details of transfers to these areas have been extensively studied, only the dynamics will be discussed below.

The establishment of subsidiaries or the organisation of sub-contracting arrangements has enabled firms (notably American ones but to a lesser extent European ones also) faced with cost competition to decrease their labour costs. Host countries have benefited from job-creation and increases in exports.

Once again, the transfers were in response to international competition—in most cases United States-Japanese competition. Transfers to supply the local market were limited. There is also a link between the long-term strategy of firms in a branch and the sort of transfer taking place. The decision of American firms to compete on price made it necessary to lower production costs by transferring some segments of production abroad. This decision was an accounting type of response to increased competitiveness of Japanese firms whose organisation and production structures had already allowed them to automate extensively.

Complete electronics industries were not installed in host countries because of rapid technical change, the search for lower labour costs for only some segments of production and the influence of tariff and quota arrangements (for the U.S. for example). Transfers mainly concerned assembly or production of some parts of the final product. Relatively little know-how has been transferred directly. However, indirect effects have benefited such countries as Singapore that are now adopting policies to encourage the establishment of industries at higher levels of technology.

When faced with restrictions on their exports, some Japanese firms also switched their production and exports to subsidiaries in developing countries. This has now been followed by production in industrialised countries. Although the first shift was only temporarily successful, it illustrates another strategic aspect of technology transfer.

d) PHARMACEUTICALS

This last example takes us to the other end of the spectrum, where the influence of host governments is important. The study on this sector suggests that the transfer of pharmaceuticals production capacity to developing countries is not necessarily the result of an economic choice, as markets could often be readily serviced by exports. However, local authorities have often given a high political value to the establishment of a domestic industry. When combined with

26

health and marketing controls exercised by states and the large number of sources of technology for many standard drugs, the transfer of production capacity is often the only means of access to markets which are small but which have good growth prospects.

While local authorities' powers are considerable with regard to transfer of production capacity for standard products, this does not apply to more recent products. For the transfer of high level skills, considerable problems have been raised by policies adopted by some developing countries. These policies may even discourage the setting up of research centres in countries with skilled scientific manpower at their disposal, and transfers of advanced know-how may be limited [28].

*
* *

After this rapid review of the dynamics of technology transfers in general and in some industries, a number of conclusion may be drawn:

Except for some common technology, it is not possible to consider technology as a product. Thus transfers do not respond to "inducements" coming from a technology market, but usually depend on the objectives of the enterprises transferring and acquiring technology.

While it is relatively easy to identify changes brought about by transfers of production capacity that have direct and immediate effects on trade, it is rather difficult to record *all* the consequences of the gradual acquisition of know-how except in the most general way.

In attempting to assess the feed-back effects of transfers we will concentrate on some of these effects only—for example on international trade. Our discussion will not cover the "mastery" aspects in detail.

D. DEVELOPING COUNTRIES FOR STUDY

As has been emphasised, the nature and intensity of feedback effects on OECD economies will depend not only on the type of technology transferred, but also on the degree of development of industrial structures in developing countries. Their capacity to absorb and assimilate imported technology determines their ability to compete with OECD countries and comprehensive analysis of the problem requires systematic examination of this capacity. This has not been possible within the framework of this study, and we confine ourselves to making a selection on the basis of general indicators.

There is demand for modern technology from all developing countries. However, the demand varies in intensity and sophistication according to the evolution of their industrialisation. As N. Rosenberg has pointed out, and as U.N. studies have recently shown [29], industrial development roughly follows a logistic curve and the period of maximum growth and profound structural change coincides with per capita income between $ 500 and $ 1,000 (1975 values). Industrial development continues at a steady but slower rate when per capita income rises to $ 1,000-$ 2,000. The demand for technology follows the logistic curve of industrial development but it is not necessarily identical with it. As the experience of industrialised countries has shown, technology trade intensifies as per capita income increases. To this criterion linked to demand for industrial products, we may add the following (in order of importance):

—   share of industrial production in GDP,
.   —   rate of growth of industrial production, and
—   natural resources.

We then have a set of criteria to identify developing countries that may significantly participate in a widening "international division of technology".

Out of 23 countries selected on the basis of at least two of these criteria (GNP/per head above $ 500, share of industrial production equal to or above 20 per cent of GDP, possession of considerable natural resources, rate of growth of industrial production during the period 1960-1975 above the average for the LDCs), we can identify three groups (see Table 3).

—   The first fulfils all four criteria and consists of Brazil and Mexico.
—   The second fulfils the three most important criteria (GNP/per head, industrial production as a share of GDP, performance) and consists of the Asian countries of South Korea, Taiwan, Hong Kong and Singapore.

Table 3

Selection Criteria of Developing Countries with Good Industrial Prospects

Country	1 Share of industrial production in GDP over 20%	2 GNP per head over $500 $500-1,000	2 GNP per head over $500 > $1,000	3 Natural resources	4 Performance above average (7.4%)
Latin America					
Argentina	x		x		
Venezuela			x	x	
Panama			x		
Brazil	x		x	x	x
Mexico	x		x	x	x
Chile	x		x	x	
Costa Rica	≃		x		x
Arab countries					
Algeria		x		x	x
Libya			x	x	x
Saudi Arabia			x	x	x
Iraq			x	x	
Tunisia		x			x
Asia					
India					
Iran					
Indonesia			x	x	x
Thailand				x	x
South Korea	x	x			x
Taiwan	x		x		x
Malaysia		x		x	x
Hong Kong	x		x		x
Singapore	x		x		x
Philippines	x		x	x	
Africa South of Sahara					
Nigeria				x	x
Zaire				x	x
Ghana		x		x	x

Sources: U.N. and national publications. Years 1975-1977 depending on country.

28

— The third fulfils at least the criteria of GNP/per head and past performance and includes the oil-producing countries of Algeria, Libya, and Saudi Arabia, and Panama, Costa Rica, Tunisia, Iraq, Malaysia and Ghana.

The first two groups of countries are our main interest. These countries are already well on the way to industrialisation, and their economic structures are becoming similar to those of OECD countries. The remaining countries are industrial candidates. These countries possess GNP/per head and past growth performances and/or natural resources which suggest that the foundations exist for rapid industrialisation.

It is clear that this classification is only indicative and requires qualification. For example Argentina (industrial production as a share of GDP=33 per cent), and India should perhaps be classified in the first group [30]. It must be pointed out however, that the six selected industrialising countries accounted for about three-quarters of the industrial growth of developing countries between 1960-1975 [31].

These six countries are the main area of study in this exercise. While other countries have not been overlooked, we mainly refer to this group as industrialising developing countries.

In this work we have used quantitative measures as much as possible supplemented by case studies and by detailed analyses, for example of legal aspects and of changes in the terms and conditions of transfer. The discussion that follows concentrates as far as possible on the dynamic and temporal evolution of relations between OECD countries and industrialising developing countries. Since this work is concerned with technological development, it is only by taking the long view that changes taking place may be grasped and policies be planned.

Chapter II

FLOWS OF TECHNOLOGY

A. INTRODUCTION

This chapter summarises some ways of measuring flows of technology from the OECD area to developing countries. Flows from developing countries and CMEA countries are also discussed briefly. As well-developed indicators of technology flows are not available, a range of proxies has been used to build a mosaic picture with each adding different elements to the picture. Amongst these measures are payments for licences, know-how and technical services which are closely related to transfers of skills and knowledge; on the other hand financial flows not only lubricate transfers of technology, but also serve other purposes. Because it is difficult to precisely determine flows of technology and their contribution to increasing the stock of technology in developing countries, the return effects from transfers may be quantified only very approximately. Indeed, one way of estimating *effective* transfers of technology is by assuming that a measurable fraction of total increases in the industrial output and foreign trade of developing countries has been caused by transfers (see Chapter III).

The indicators have been classified into those that are: related directly to industrial production, and those that contribute to increases in capabilities to produce new technology. International financial flows (e.g. international borrowing, export credits) are not direct indicators of technology flows. However, borrowing countries may have more choice in purchasing their technology and determining domestic industrial investment projects, and the size and terms of flows suggest which countries have relatively attractive economic prospects and financial management skills (notwithstanding present problems with external deficits and debts). Financial flows have thus been included in the analysis below.

Indicators that we will examine in some detail are listed approximately in order of their clear relation to technology transfer:

For *Industrial Production* they include:
— International payments for technology taken from balance-of-payments data ("balance of technological payments"). This indicator is directly related to the international diffusion of technology.
— Trade in capital goods and equipment.
— Construction of complete industrial plants ("turn-key plants").
— Direct investment.

For *Technology Production* they include:
— Training programmes and skill development in OECD and developing countries, both private and public.
— Transfers of research and development activities.

31

Financial Flows include:

— Export credits, borrowing from international capital markets and official development assistance [1].

Balance of technological payments data are closely related to transfers of industrial capabilities. International payments cover the use of industrial property and supply of know-how and related technical services. They may also include payments for technical assistance and management fees. Payment statistics may not be directly comparable between countries because payments for different countries cover different combinations of licences, know-how and services. There are also a variety of ways of making payments—including lump-sum on transfer, royalties on production, sales or profits, non-cash payments with production, technology swap arrangements, or supply of technology in return for market access or other commercial benefits. Furthermore, payments between related enterprises are a significant proportion of total transactions, and taxation and regulations may affect both the value and method of payment of fees between related enterprises. Finally, the supply of management and organisational skills are of great importance in determining the effective use of technology. These are only partly, and rather broadly, captured in the balance of technological payments for a few countries.

Know-how may be transferred between countries with the supply of industrial goods. However, the capability to operate, maintain and repair machines is different from the capability to produce them and the two capabilities are often not transferred at the same time. Exports of industrial *capital goods* and related equipment and the construction of complete industrial plants give a measure of potential increases in industrial output in recipient countries. Net imports also give a measure of the ability of domestic machinery manufacturers and engineering suppliers to service their domestic market.

Direct investment flows give a measure of the potential of developing countries as locations for industrial production—to service local or international markets—rather than a direct measure of transfers of industrial technology. But foreign direct investment carries technical know-how, management, organisational skills, and access to marketing networks as well as creating employment in the host country. The changing pattern of international investment gives an indication of relative changes in international production structures.

The transfer of skills to produce new technology is more difficult to measure. The most important real transfer involves the effective education of technicians, engineers and scientists, through *training and educational programmes* (including infomal on-the-spot industrial experience), and through migration. The transfer of skills to operate, or duplicate, or going higher up the scale, design and produce industrial resources is the most vital part of the process of technology transfer. Training programmes are relevant to industrial production *and* to technology production, but the major part of training will be concentrated on improving industrial skills. Furthermore, the transfer through training or experience of management and organisational skills is extremely important—and difficult to quantify.

Re-location of *research and development* activities to developing countries is a measure of their potential to contribute to new knowledge. However, re-location is conditioned by such factors as the strategies of transnational firms (they tend to centralise R&D), size and characteristics of the domestic market, national policies, and the availability of a stock of R&D and technical personnel and a developed technical infrastructure.

All of these indicators of flows of technology will give an even more limited picture of technology transfer if they are interpreted statically. In reality there is a dynamic "technology cycle": Industrial technology is first developed and introduced in one country. It is then transferred with tight control (usually to affiliates or with restrictive licences) to other developed countries, and later to developing countries. It is subsequently diffused with weakening control (widespread licencing and sale of equipment) as the technology becomes standardised and available from a number of sources. Thus, what is essentially the same technology may be transferred by different methods during its cycle. The working of the cycle will depend on the sector of technology generation and on the objectives of suppliers (see Chapter I). These dynamics will also be affected by shifts between countries and, importantly for this study, the extent and way in which some developing countries are catching up to their traditional suppliers of technology and, in general, by the rate at which technology is being diffused relative to the rate at which it is being generated. Some aspects of the changing dynamics are touched on when discussing indicators in this chapter. Despite some limitations the indicators do give a useful, if incomplete, picture of technology transfer and the part that this plays in industrialisation in developing countries.

Financial flows to developing countries assist the diffusion of technology. Without international finance it would not be possible in many cases to purchase licences, technical assistance, machinery, turn-key plants or any other form of technology. *Export credits* are one of the financial mechanisms which have helped expand exports of capital goods. Borrowing from international *capital markets* have to a certain extent been devoted to industrial investment and they suggest the economic and industrial potential of countries that are able to borrow to maintain economic growth and external balance. Borrowings also indicate the extent to which countries rely on external financing to service their development. A small proportion of official *development assistance* goes to industrialisation and transfers of industrial technology. (Aid flows are thoroughly dealt with elsewhere [1].)

In the following pages we first discuss the sources and destinations of flows of technology-related items and financial flows. Then, balance of technological payments, trade in capital goods, construction of turn-key plants, and direct investment from OECD countries are examined in turn. This is followed by a discussion of activities that are more directly related to technology production —including training and skill development and location of R&D facilities. Finally, some financial flows are examined briefly.

B. INDUSTRIAL PRODUCTION

In common with industrial countries, developing countries are large importers of industrial technology. These imports have directly contributed to the high levels of growth in industrial output that have been evident in many developing economies. The ways in which technology has been imported have varied between recipient countries: however, like almost all OECD countries they will probably remain large *net* importers of technology even after they have built up their own primary technological activities.

By value, total exports of capital goods to developing countries have dominated flows of factors that can be used in productive industrial activities. (Details of flows are set out in Table 1). Export credits from OECD countries have been about 20% of the value of exports of capital goods, but they have accompanied and matched the high rates of growth of capital goods exports. Additions to foreign direct investment have remained significant although growing more slowly,

Table 1

Values and Annual Compound Growth Rates for some Broad Measures of OECD Technology Exports and Financial Flows to Developing Countries

Growth rates based on current dollar values of variable in first and last year of period

	Values (billion current U.S.$)					Growth rates (%): 1970-1979	
	1970	1976	1977	1978	1979	Current values	Constant values[5]
Receipts for technology (balance of technological payments basis)	0.68[1]	1.55[2]	1.66	2.04	2.28[e]	14.4	3.7
Exports: Capital goods[3]	16.7	69.2	78.3	94.8	102.8	22.4	12.1
Exports: Manufactured goods[3]	34.1	122.6	144.4	180.4	202.0	21.8	9.3
Foreign Direct Investment: Net[4]	3.7	7.9	9.5	11.2	13.5	15.5	4.7
Technical Assistance (Bilateral ODA)[4]	1.54	2.89	3.07	3.80	4.68	13.1	0.5
Official Development Assistance: Total bilateral+multilateral[4]	6.79	14.0	15.7	20.0	22.4	14.2	3.1
Financial Flows: Private Export Credits: Gross	5.22	15.2	18.1	21.9	21.8	17.2	6.2
Official Export Credits: Gross	1.51	3.78	4.70	5.88	5.40	15.2	4.4
International borrowing: Net[4]	3.3	16.2	18.7	25.5	19.7	22.0	10.5

1 France, Germany, Italy, Netherlands, United Kingdom, U.S.A. Data from national sources.
2 Including Japan from 1972. OECD developing European countries are excluded for Japan, included for all other countries, including estimations for the U.S.A.
3 OECD, *Trade by Commodities*. Capital goods defined by Secretariat. Manufactured goods=SITC 5+6+7+8—68. Excluding OECD developing European countries, including Yugoslavia.
4 Net disbursement basis, *Development Co-operation, op. cit.*, DAC regional definitions. International borrowing includes bank sector and bond lending.
5 Values are indicative only.
e Secretariat estimates.
Note: Gross data are given where series readily available.

and payments for technology by developing countries (for licences, know-how, technical and commercial services) have grown at a rate close to that of foreign direct investment, but values of these payments are about one-fifth of the value of foreign direct investment. The technical assistance component of official development assistance has largely been concentrated on poorer developing countries and relatively little is directly related to manufacturing activities.

a) SOURCES OF TECHNOLOGY FOR INDUSTRIAL PRODUCTION

i) *OECD countries*

OECD countries are by far the major suppliers of technology for industrial production. Turning to individual countries, the United States remains the largest individual source of technology flowing directly to developing countries. However, this relative position has tended to decline, with a clear-cut leadership now only applying to foreign direct investment flows and to the role of U.S. banks in international capital flows [2]. In an intermediate position are Germany and Japan, both with increasing direct investment activities and significant exports of machinery and equipment. These two are followed by the U.K., and France. Now that both Japan and Germany are in deficit on balance of payments current account, their rates of capital outflow may slow down, depending on the duration of payments deficits. These five countries between them supply some 70-80% of OECD exports of technology for industrial production, with the rest of OECD supplying 20-30%. Overall, the sources of technology have increased

Table 2
Exports to Developing Countries of Technology-related Items and Financial Flows per 1,000 units of GDP: 1977
Values in brackets per 1,000 units of manufacturing GDP

Country	Receipts for technology Total[1]	Receipts for technology Industrial[2]	Capital goods Total	Capital goods Industrial	Direct Investment	For reference: Total private investment and credit[3]
France	0.51	(0.47)	19.5	(47)	0.70	7.3
Germany	0.12	(0.32)	24.1	(48)	1.64	7.9
Japan	0.25	(0.81)	25.1	(48)	1.04	3.6
United Kingdom	0.53	(1.97)	28.8	(80)	5.0	23.7
United States	0.47	(0.64)	9.9	(25)	2.6	3.3
Denmark	0.13	(0.72)	13.6	(46)	0.54	2.1
Italy	0.15	(0.08)	24.4	(60)	0.83	8.1
Netherlands	1.8	(0.48)	22.8	(37)	4.6	10.6
Spain			8.1	(18)	1.04	
Total OECD	0.45		16.7		1.93	6.3

1 Using national definitions—including technical assistance and management fees.
2 Narrow definition, manufacturing industry, excluding technical assistance and management fees where details allow, or Secretariat estimates.
3 Direct investment, bilateral and multilateral portfolio investment, export credits.

in number with the ranks of major technology suppliers being swelled and the smaller more specialised exporters maintaining their relative importance. The multipolarity of international economic relations is clearly evident.

Exports of technology for industrial production have been scaled by the size of the domestic economy of exporting countries and results are given in Table 2. Most OECD countries (including the smaller countries) export similar amounts of technology per unit of GDP. The U.K., because of historical links and its relatively open economy, continues to be relatively highly involved with developing countries given the size of its domestic economy [3].

Scaled in terms of their domestic economies, synoptic Table 3 summarises information in Table 2 and illustrates the main areas of activity of OECD countries.

Table 3
Areas of Activity of OECD Technology Exporters

Country	Licencing, know-how	Technical and commercial services	Engineering services[1]	Direct investment	Other capital flows including export credits	Capital equipment, Machinery
France		x	x		x	x
Germany			x	x	x	x
Italy					x	x
Japan	x					x
United Kingdom	x	x	x	x	x	x
United States	x	x	x	x		
Netherlands	x	x	x	x	x	x

1 Design only. Construction and construction management show different patterns.

Regional affiliations are weakening. Japanese and German direct investment is vying with that from the U.S. in Latin America, particularly in Brazil. The U.K. is now one of a number of suppliers to Commonwealth countries, and Africa has changed from being the preserve of former colonial relations and is receiving technology from a wider range of suppliers. Asian countries are still the major destination for Japanese technology, but Japan is diversifying. Bilateral interstate agreements are of significance both for countries trying to maintain traditional links and for those attempting to forge new ones.

ii) Developing countries

The leading industrialising countries are becoming more important suppliers of industrial equipment and of know-how and construction and engineering skills and direct investment [4]. (Values were generally about 3-5% of OECD total values in 1977-1978.) Most activities have been within the same region as the supplying countries, and for intermediate level technologies.

India with highly protectionist policies has developed the greatest range of activities—including management and consultancy services and supply of turnkey plants [5]. The advantages of developing countries have been greatest where the pace of change is relatively slow, where detailed, often labour-intensive, engineering capabilities are required and where large R&D efforts are not necessary.

The importance of South Korean firms in the Mid-East market for construction contracts is well-known, but this now-declining market is also shared by Brazil, Yugoslavia, India and Taiwan [6]. Of the top 50 international contractors in 1979, there were 4 Korean companies (with $ 3.9 billion in foreign contracts, 8% of the total value of contracts for the top 50) and Argentinian and Filipino firms (one each)—as well as 3 Greek, one Yugoslav and one Israeli firm. All of these firms were contracting to build manufacturing and power plants, using already developed technology and processes, as well as organising the civil engineering for infrastructure projects. Moving up the scale to construction management, the ranks of firms from developing countries thin out (two Koreans in 1979, and Argentinian, Greek, Indian, Filipino, and Yugoslav firms in the top 50). Among design firms there were only firms from Lebanon and Brazil (one each) in the top 50.

Overseas contracting and engineering is a desirable activity because it not only gives a flow of fees for construction services and remittances of workers' earnings in the invisibles on balance of payments current account, but also because domestic manufacturers of industrial and construction equipment can supply overseas construction activities [7].

Asian exporting countries and Latin American countries have investments in their less-developed regional neighbours. These are most frequently in consumer goods industries and in low-technology industries that tend not to compete directly with TNEs based in OECD countries.

iii) CMEA countries

CMEA countries have been taking a declining share of technology and equipment exports (less than 10% of OECD total values in 1977-1978 excluding military). Exports were mainly concentrated on bordering countries with some geographical expansion to include North African and Mid-East states. Declines have been due to: political factors as some former client states have turned to OECD sources; the logical working out of the long-term integration plan of the CMEA economies; and a division of labour whereby the USSR in particular tends not to purchase manufactured goods from developing countries. This has led developing countries to expand their links with OECD economies where there is greater potential for two-way trade in industrial products.

A large proportion of CMEA activities have been carried out within "framework" agreements. These lead to tied equipment purchases, financed on relatively hard terms. Activities are concentrated on heavy and basic industries using relatively large contingents of technical assistants [8]. Until now, the industrial capacities installed have mainly supplied domestic markets in developing countries and, to a lesser extent, have allowed repayments under buy-back schemes. However, there has been recent growth in commercial technical and engineering activities and even some direct investment, particularly by the East Europeans. This has been largely in manufacturing and raw material-based joint ventures, but the variety of contacts has increased notably. Whether these contacts will continue and enable the non-aligned and industrialising developing countries to draw on alternative sources of industrial technology is not clear. However, the CMEA countries have shown a certain flexibility and market-oriented approach towards dealings with non-satellite developing countries.

b) DESTINATIONS OF TECHNOLOGY FOR INDUSTRIAL PRODUCTION

When scaled by GDP, imports of technology by developing countries have significantly high values. These values are usually higher than values of OECD exports of technology to developing countries scaled by GDP (compare Tables 2 and 4). In other words, imports of technology by developing countries have greater significance for them than have technology exports for OECD countries. There are also great differences between developing countries. Large, middle-level developing countries such as Brazil and Mexico (and Spain) that have pursued import substitution strategies coupled with high levels of foreign direct investment have had relatively low levels of imports of capital equipment [9] (see Table 4). Smaller, export-oriented developing countries, such as Hong Kong, Korea, Singapore and Taiwan that have more outward-looking

Table 4

Imports of Technology-related Items and Financial Flows per 1,000 units of GDP: 1976-1977

Values in brackets are per 1,000 units of manufacturing GDP

	Payments for technology[1]	Capital Goods Total	Industrial	Direct Investment[2]	For reference: Financial flows Total[3]	Export credits
Brazil	0.7	20	(52)	10.3	37	5.1
Mexico	1.4	35	(95)	7.8	63	4.4
Hong Kong	2.4	83	(190)			19
Korea	1.2	68	(160)	2.8	44	24
Singapore	4.8	261	(510)	80	105	1.3
Taiwan	1.3	86	(180)	3.3	24	9.0
Spain	1.3	24	(72)	2.3	22	0.9
All Developing	1.3	58		4.9		7.9

1 Estimates, based on payments *received* by OECD countries. Payments recorded by developing countries are often broader in scope, include miscellaneous items, and are (often much) higher in value.
2 IMF, from all sources in the reporting country.
3 IMF, Direct investment, portfolio investment n.i.e., other long-term capital n.i.e. from all sources. *Net.*
Note: Imports are from all OECD countries combined.

policies, have had relatively larger inputs of both capital goods and equipment [10] and payments for licences and related technical services. In general, export credits have also been higher. Direct investment has been relatively low in Korea and Taiwan, high in Hong Kong and Singapore. However, the role of Hong Kong and Singapore as off-shore banking centres makes origins and destinations of financial flows—particularly in the non-manufacturing sector— difficult to determine [11].

Developing countries that have restricted direct investment have used other forms of capital inflow to finance industrial development, to pay for imports of industrial equipment, and to cover balance of payments deficits.

A number of summary points can be made regarding flows of factors related to industrial production. Foreign direct investment in developing countries has risen from most OECD countries when these flows are expressed as a proportion of OECD domestic capital formation in the private sector (excluding government and housing). Developing countries as a group have also become more important destinations for capital goods exports, largely due to exports to OPEC countries. Exports to Mid-East countries have slowed down because basic infrastructure projects have been completed, and because the social and political costs of ambitious development plans are being reassessed. However, the further development of the OPEC "high-absorbers"—Venezuela, Nigeria, Indonesia—and non-OPEC oil-producers can be expected to maintain high rates of exports of plant and equipment from OECD countries. There is a rather low likelihood that there will be significant flows of industrial products from these countries to the OECD area in the short to medium term.

Imports of capital equipment by developing countries expressed as a proportion of gross fixed capital formation have:

— remained low for large Latin American countries with a developed infrastructure and some local capital goods industries (developed through direct investment);
— increased rapidly to high levels for OPEC countries and their clients;
— remained high but steady for the Far East countries.

Foreign direct investment expressed as a proportion of gross fixed capital formation has:

— declined for most Latin American countries (except Brazil);
— declined for most OPEC countries;
— declined for most other countries (Malaysia, Singapore, Thailand, Philippines are exceptions).

There has been very strong growth in domestic capital formation in developing countries. This explains the paradox that flows of direct investment to developing countries from OECD countries have generally increased relative to OECD capital formation, *but remained rather low* (between 1% and 3%) while the relative contribution to developing countries of these investment flows has generally decreased relative to their domestic capital formation.

c) TRANSFERS OF INDUSTRIAL PRODUCTION CAPABILITIES:
DISCUSSION OF INDICATORS

i) *Payments for licences and supply of know-how, technical and commercial services (from balance of technological payments)*

Payments for licences and supply of know-how, technical and commercial services are heterogenous; different combinations of transactions are used by different countries [12]. For example, management fees are included in U.S.

data, but not for other major countries. Furthermore, a large proportion of royalty and fee payments are between related enterprises and taxation and regulation may have pronounced effects on methods and values of payments.

Developing countries have on average contributed about 20% of total OECD receipts for licences, know-how and related services. For manufacturing industry taken alone, the proportion has declined to below 10% for the U.S. in recent years [13], but has remained at about 50% in manufacturing industry for Japan, increased to about 25% for the United Kingdom [14], and remained close to or above 20% for Germany. For OECD countries these international receipts have been of relatively minor importance when compared with GDP. But for developing countries *payments have often been roughly the same value as expenditures on R&D* (0.2-0.5% of GDP). These net payments may be expected to remain high until domestic industrial and economic activities begin generating substantial technologies of their own [15].

If technology being transferred to developing countries is becoming more standardised relative to that being transferred between developed countries, then licencing to unrelated enterprises in developing countries may be expected to increase. Similarly, if the innovation rate has dropped markedly in developed countries and the average age of successful innovations has increased then licencing in general and to unrelated enterprises may also increase. However, there is no evidence from data on receipts of fees and royalties to suggest that there has been a major trend towards licencing of technology to unrelated enterprises in developing countries.

— For the U.S.A., receipts of fees and royalties from unaffiliated foreign enterprises have not increased significantly as a proportion of total receipts of fees and royalties from affiliated and unaffiliated enterprises [16].
— Total sales of U.S. majority-owned foreign manufacturing affiliates have grown at a faster rate than have receipts of fees and royalties from unaffiliated firms.
— Only very aggregated data are available for the U.K., but receipts of royalties from unrelated concerns in developing countries increased by only a relatively small amount as a proportion of total receipts of royalties from related and unrelated concerns [17].

Furthermore, there seems to be no clear-cut evidence to suggest that as industrialising countries have developed they have tended to buy more licences and advanced technical services, rather than buying machinery and equipment. For seven out of eight industrialising developing countries for which data is available, the value of payments for licences and services has remained steady or declined when compared with the values of imports of machinery and equipment [18].

In Latin America, the relative decline in payments of fees and royalties requires explanation. For example, U.S. manufacturing affiliates showed a growth rate of payments of fees and royalties that was less than one-half of the growth of repatriated "interest, dividends and earnings" during the period 1970-1978 [19]. Repatriated interest, dividends and earnings kept pace with the rising stock of direct investment during the period, but royalties and fees from affiliates declined sharply compared with the stock of direct investment. The growth in receipts of royalties from affiliates of U.K. concerns in Latin America was also lower than growth in remitted earnings. Reasons which may be advanced for this decline include: the effects of Latin American technology transfer regulations in limiting recurrent payments for licences and technical services; changes in policy which have led to a re-classification of payments formerly described as royalties and fees; or a reduction in licencing in Latin American countries. Whether the impact of regulation and review boards has led to a real decrease in licencing activities rather than changes in payment size and structure remains an open question.

The relative decline in payments from Latin America has been offset by a rapid build-up in payments from Asian countries that have shown rapid growth in industrial and economic activities. In contrast, OPEC countries building basic infrastructure and industrial capacity have imported machinery and equipment rather than licencing extensively. Regular licence payments will not increase markedly, if they do so at all, until industrial output has also increased. However, payments for technical services have been high during the initial industrialisation phase to compensate for the lack of skilled manpower and technical infrastructure.

What are the sectoral trends in licencing and related technical and commercial activities between OECD and developing countries? Differences are to be expected because of differences in industrial structures between developing countries and because of the trade-offs between licencing and direct investment. In fact the patterns across countries are conflicting for the most recent years for which data is available. However, for Germany, Japan and the U.S. a few general trends emerge. Payments from Latin America have concentrated on chemicals, machinery and basic metals industries (particularly iron and steel), whereas those in Asia have concentrated on consumer goods industries: electrical engineering and "other" industries including textiles, plastics, optical and precision equipment. These trends parallel regional patterns of industrialisation and are different from trends in intra-OECD receipts.

Furthermore, there is a different distribution of payments between affiliated and unaffiliated enterprises in developed and developing countries. A *smaller* proportion of royalties and licence fees comes from affiliates in developing countries than in developed countries. This holds for all major industries except transport. This result corresponds to the notion of a technology cycle, where *affiliates* in developed countries are provided with the latest technology. As the technology becomes standardised later on in the cycle, it may be supplied under licence to unrelated enterprises in developing countries.

ii) *Capital Goods and Complete Industrial Plants*

Capital goods

Developing countries have been the destination of only about one quarter of total OECD manufactured exports in recent years, but they have been the destination of about 40% of exports of capital goods. The concentration on

Table 5
Destinations of OECD Exports of Capital Goods
% of total exports

	1968	1970	1971	1972	1973	1974	1975	1976	1977	1978	1979	1980ᵉ
Developing countries	35	34	34	34	35	38	44	43	44	40	38	38
of which: OPEC	5	5	6	6	6	8	14	16	17	16	12	13

Developing countries includes developing OECD.

Davidson College Library

capital goods in commodity trade is partly explained by the investments in infrastructure and basic industrial capacity in OPEC countries that have taken place since 1974. It is further explained by the continuing lack of broadly-based capital goods industries in most developing countries despite their build-up in India, some Latin American countries, Korea and Taiwan.

Complete industrial plants

The growth in construction of complete industrial plants has levelled off or even declined due to political problems and completion of the first round of major infrastructure and industrial projects in the Mid-East and North Africa, the major markets for these plants [20]. Competition for work has increased —particularly in basic construction—and there has been a trend towards local partnerships and joint ventures to obtain contracts in developing countries and to provide a wider range of services [21].

In the Mid-East there have been rapid increases in values of contracts won by developing countries—particularly by South Korean firms, but also by firms from Brazil, Yugoslavia, India and Taiwan (see Table 6 and B. *a*), *ii*) above). Whether this is likely to occur in other regions is not clear. Enterprises from developing countries have had the advantage of being able to organise and supply skilled and semi-skilled labour to areas lacking manpower. Although

Table 6

Contract Values Including Complete Industrial Plants in Mid-East

% of total

	1975-1978	1978-1979		1975-1978	1978-1979
Germany	17	15	France	8	6
Japan	17	12	Netherlands	8	—
Italy	8	16	United Kingdom	3	3
United States	10	2	Switzerland	2	1
South Korea	5	21	Belgium	2	—
			Total value	$ 86.3 bn	$ 21.8 bn

Source: *Engineering News-Record*, November 29th, 1979. Excluding military.

activity remains high in some Arab OPEC countries, attention is now also turning towards high-absorbing OPEC countries, non-OPEC countries that OPEC will fund, Mexico, Brazil, S.E. Asian countries, China and other resource-rich countries. In many of these the advantages of cheap manpower will probably not be so important [22]. Compared with the Mid-East many of these countries have surplus labour of their own, have been building their own engineering and contracting skills, and are increasingly insisting on joint ventures and the use of local engineering enterprises. It can be expected that the influence of technological factors in competition will become even more keen. Furthermore, countries with external deficits will continue to be interested in fostering service receipts from international engineering activities and exports of machinery and equipment to foreign construction projects and in limiting their foreign payments for construction of domestic industrial plants.

However, enterprises from OECD countries are still dominant in the management, organisation and design of projects. Joint ventures and the use of local engineering resources in developing countries can be expected to increase, but the size of OECD domestic markets (particularly the U.S.) and the accumulated experience of OECD firms has enabled them to attain and, so far, maintain the critical mass of high level skills necessary for complex design and organisational tasks despite increasing competition at home as well as abroad.

iii) *Foreign Direct Investment*

Foreign direct investment in developing countries is more important for the technology that it brings than for its direct contribution to capital inflows. For, example, additions to direct investment positions in manufacturing in developing countries were about $ 10 billion in 1978-1979, including reinvested earnings [23], and against them have to be counted outward flows of remitted profits, payments for technology, and various other service charges. But foreign direct investment brings modern technology and rapid increases in manufacturing output and exports, and through the parent enterprise links to the world economy are multiplied. The investing enterprise gains market access and an expanded asset and turnover base, while retaining financial and technical control. These benefits for the enterprise have to be weighed against exposure to political, social and economic currents in the host country.

Patterns of investment are available for four major OECD countries. Japan continues to concentrate on Asian manufacturing (42% of total manufacturing investment in 1978), with recent developments in petrochemicals in Singapore and aluminium plants in Indonesia. However, there were major diversifications in the mid-1970's with large-scale petrochemical projects in the mid-East, and the development of steel, paper pulp and aluminium plants in Brazil. Investment in the four Asian exporting countries has slowly switched away from small-scale labour-intensive light industries such as textiles, and miscellaneous goods. In the 1976-1977 period, electrical and non-electrical machinery received more than half of manufacturing investment. Upstream investment in components has been accompanied by investment deepening.

German investment has been very extensive in Latin America, particularly in Brazil for motor vehicle, electrical engineering and chemical industries, and in Spain for chemical and mechanical engineering industries. The U.K. pattern has been concentrated on former Commonwealth countries. However, there has been diversification in *manufacturing,* with increasing investment in Latin America (food and tobacco), and Africa (chemicals), and relative declines in Asia (major investments were in food, and chemicals, but electrical engineering has increased rapidly). U.S. investment has been diversifying away from Latin America to a certain extent. Manufacturing investment in developing countries has also taken a slightly larger share of total overseas investment in manufacturing industry in recent years [24]. Major investments are in Brazil in machinery, chemical, and transportation industries, in Mexico in chemicals and machinery, in Venezuela in chemicals, and investments in the four Asian exporters are increasing rapidly. For all investors there has been a preference for investing in developing countries with relatively high income levels.

Generally, foreign enterprises have deployed relatively low values of investment per worker in Asian developing countries. The values in Southern Europe and Latin America are in an intermediate position and in OPEC and African countries values of investment per worker are highest. These initially surprising trends reflect the availability of skilled labour in manufacturing (with capital substituting for skilled labour) and, to a certain extent, the age and mix of industries and technological choices when manufacturing capacity was installed— newer investment is generally more capital intensive. The patterns of output per unit of direct investment are the opposite of the above. Africa and OPEC/Mid-East give the lowest output per unit of investment, Latin America occupies an intermediate position, and Southern Europe and Asia give the highest output per unit of investment. (From German and U.S. data.)

As mentioned above, foreign direct investment is important because it brings organisational skills and technology to developing countries over and above contributions to balance of payments on capital account. Regarding capital account: for enterprises from OECD countries with a long tradition of foreign investment, reinvested earnings in manufacturing are higher in value than new additions of capital flowing to the country of investment. For new investors and investments, the reinvested earnings component is lower simply because it takes time to start up new affiliates and make them profitable.

Furthermore, total outflows of repatriated interest, dividends and payments for technology may be greater in overall value for a developing country than inflows of new investment. However, these total outflows are not generally as high in value as reinvested earnings [25]. The developing country gains organised manufacturing activities that contribute to employment, exports and domestic growth. Furthermore, domestic capital expenditures by the foreign investor may often be greater than total book additions to direct investment—due to possibilities for borrowing on local or international capital markets to finance investment plans.

Apart from direct contributions to employment and production in developing countries, foreign direct investment stimulates trade. Investment promotes a flow of capital equipment, intermediate inputs and industrial products from the home country to the developing country, and a flow of exports back from subsidiaries to the home country. In fact, exports from subsidiaries are directed to a greater extent towards the home country (as a proportion of total exports to the home country) than to third countries (as a proportion of total exports to third countries).

Both the geographical region and industry of direct investments are important in determining export activity. Investments in Latin America and Africa tend to be oriented towards supplying the domestic or regional market, whereas those in Asian countries have a larger proportion of output being exported to the home country and other developed countries. This is in part determined by the industry in which investments have been made. In Latin America investments have concentrated on heavy and basic industry aimed at import-substitution, whereas investments in Asian exporting countries were initially in textiles and light manufactures for export (particularly for Japanese investment).

C. TECHNOLOGY PRODUCTION

a) TRAINING PROGRAMMES AND SKILL DEVELOPMENT

i) *Private sector: manufacturing industry*

Training programmes and skill development in manufacturing are initiated through the activities of affiliates of enterprises based in OECD countries *and* in the framework of technical assistance, management and licencing agreements, joint ventures, sub-contracting, and as part of the building and supply of turn-key plants. Unfortunately there is rather little information on the extent of these activities or on the results coming from them.

In the early 1970s it was estimated that about 20,000 employees in foreign-controlled affiliates were receiving formal training at any one time. There were an estimated 8-9 million workers directly employed by affiliates of OECD enterprises in developing countries at the end of 1977, and unskilled and semi-skilled workers would have experienced on the job instruction, skilled workers would have had more extended instruction, and indigenous senior and managerial staff formal training. (Senior staff have often been educated through aid and development schemes from OECD countries or their own countries.)

The final results have been the subject of debate. Although there has been some criticism that people with high-level skills may move out of the local economy (the "brain-drain" problem), these people and their skills are not lost from the overall system. A balance has to be reached on the extent to which it is necessary to have managers and technicians and engineers of the nationality of the host country. How administrations in developing countries can ensure that a reasonable number of their people are employed at more highly skilled levels, and whether the situation is changing in a satisfactory way are complementary issues. Some different approaches to development of indigenous skills are illustrated with the sector studies.

In the petrochemical industry, five developing countries have adopted different strategies towards building their skills. Saudi Arabia depends largely on foreign workers and is adopting the highest technology and buying the greatest international experience that is feasibly possible. Singapore is encouraging foreign partnerships to help build up operating, repair, and management skills geared to domestic and regional production. This is part of a comprehensive strategy to develop skill-intensive activities. The South Korean experience has been somewhat more outward-looking than that of Singapore. Local operating, maintenance and management skills were initially built up through the formation of foreign operating subsidiaries of OECD-based firms, and subsequently through joint ventures with foreign operators. There followed a period of concerted efforts to build up engineering capacity through joint ventures with engineering firms. These activities have built up engineering skills which are an important element in international contracting. Brazil has developed local skills with foreign direct investment partners, and is now moving up the scale by participating in projects managed by foreign engineering firms. Mexican (Pemex) engineering and development skills were built up through joint ventures in basic petrochemicals—ammonia, ethylene and methanol. These activities were backed with a commitment to build up local R&D, and the engineering industry is now strong enough to build later generations of basic petrochemical plants without foreign assistance [26]. However, foreign participation is still vital in many down-stream activities.

The mastery of *basic* petrochemical technology has been achieved in countries that have built up the necessary engineering skills and that have an adequate technical infrastructure. Joint ventures have been important in building these skills. Downstream techniques and know-how are more tightly held by chemical producers and independent mastery of the technology is more difficult.

The situation in the T.V. industry is different. The technology is tightly controlled through licences and other restrictions. In assembly operations in developing countries, 90-95% of workers are semi-skilled, and design and production engineers are often supplied from the parent company. There has been little hiring and training of manpower at the engineering or technician level. The development of indigenous skills in South Korea and Taiwan has largely been due to local efforts.

In the tyre industry, formal training schemes are usually allotted $\frac{1}{2}$ to 1% of turnover. Technical training of local staff in subsidiaries is common in S.E. Asia. In the pharmaceutical industry, local affiliates of transnational companies still account for the bulk of production of new products. As a matter

44

of routine local personnel are trained. For standard products there are many sources of expertise and technical assistance, and sub-contracting is fairly widespread. Through these routes developing countries such as Egypt, India and S. Korea have built up substantial production capacities and skills.

Overall, the sector studies suggested that the participation of OECD enterprises in manufacturing and related activities has led to substantial increases in skills in developing countries.

Turning to another aspect of skill development: a large number of workers from developing countries (Pakistan, India, South Korea, Philippines, Turkey, Thailand, Egypt) were recruited during the boom in Mid-East construction to make up for local shortages of semi-skilled and skilled workers. Recruits are now operating many of the industrial facilities and are carrying out much of the local administration in labour-scarce Middle East countries. This new variant on the traditional "brain-drain" problem brings mixed benefits and costs to the developing countries supplying and receiving workers.

ii) *Public sector*

Students and trainees in all areas have continued to be supported by development programmes financed by OECD countries. Student numbers increased by about 3-4% p.a. during the 1970's, and there were about 110,00 in 1979. However, the numbers of technical co-operation personnel decreased somewhat over the same period [27]. Most activity has been in general education, but in recent years about 5% of total technical assistance went to support manufacturing, mainly in poorer developing countries. Manufacturing technical assistance commonly involved training activities, but feasibility and investment studies, and national technology centres were also supported. Many of the activities of multilateral organisations (IBRD, IDA, IFC, and regional development banks) have a strong technological and technical assistance content. (See [1] for a brief overview, or the annual reports of individual organisations.)

b) Location of research and development activities

Although industrial output in developing countries has increased rapidly, the efforts in R&D linked to manufacturing have not increased to the same extent. This is in spite of a great deal of effort to build up *general* R&D capabilities—often with significant support from official and private sources in OECD countries. For example in 1973 12.6% of total world R&D scientists and engineers were active in developing countries and this proportion has probably increased. However, their use in manufacturing industry is not as well developed as in OECD countries [28]. Against this background, transfers of R&D operations or technical activities which may contribute to innovative output in developing countries have received special attention.

There are a number of general factors which determine the distribution of location and type of R&D activities between affiliated enterprises. These comprise:

— the *primary purpose* of the R&D investment. Purposes include: *a*) *transfer of technology* and provision of related technical services; *b*) development of new or improved products or processes for the local market; *c*) development of new products or processes for the *world* market; (*d*) *long-term research* as part of the overall strategy of the enterprise. The industrial *sector* of operations will in part determine which purpose will dominate and hence influence the distribution of R&D and related activities [29];

45

— the degree of *control* exerted by the parent company. Highly centralized enterprises will display centralized patterns of R&D activities in comparison with enterprises with a large degree of autonomy between different divisions and more autonomy in research and innovative activities [30];

— the size of the *market* serviced by the affiliate. The larger the market, the more likely it is that the minimum economic size for R&D activities will be achieved [31];

— the national *scientific and technical infrastructure* will determine the ease with which new R&D and related activities can be organised and maintained;

— government *policies* of the host country can be an inducement provided that the other factors are favorable.

What have been the changes in R&D location in the 1970s? Unfortunately, there is very little information regarding the extent to which R&D directly related to manufacturing has been transferred to developing countries. For earlier years, U.S. data is the most comprehensive. In 1966 and 1970 8% of total R&D expenditures of U.S. multinational firms took place outside the United States. Most of this expenditure was concentrated in Canada, the U.K. and Germany. The remainder was spread very thinly, with perhaps 0.5% of the total in developing countries [32]. R&D was concentrated in a small number of industries that manufacture consumer goods requiring adaptation to local markets, or in industries whose technology requires adaptation to local conditions. Industries that performed adaptive research included those producing soaps, toiletries and food products, and agricultural and industrial machinery. Often, the adaptive activity involved alteration of what basically remained a U.S. product.

Little information on transfer of R&D activities could be gathered in the sectors studied. However, the scattered evidence suggests that the situation has changed a little. With strong government incentives a number of foreign multinationals are undertaking pharmaceutical research in India, and to a lesser extent in Argentina and Mexico. The potential for research, and government interest, is notable in Korea, Singapore and Taiwan. The tropical drugs programme of the WHO is also being carried out with the participation of several large drug companies. However, so far no product or process that is in general use has originated in a developing country.

Licencees (T.V's, pharmaceuticals, rubber tyres), and those involved in joint ventures (petrochemicals, pharmaceuticals) have incentives to perform R&D in order to ensure their long run future, and they have strengthened their technical capacities through involvement with those transferring technology.

Turning to other research, a recent survey of R&D being performed abroad by multinational firms showed that there have been some increases in applied research and development activities in industrialising countries such as Brazil, India and Mexico [33]. Applied research and development was generally performed by enterprises with local market and technology transfer goals. In such cases, products require development and adaptation to local markets or manufacturing processes may need modification to suit local conditions. The survey concluded that host government incentives were not as important as potential market growth in determining the location of R&D, but countries with attractive market prospects can ensure that firms perform some R&D locally. This R&D may initially be at a low level, but provided there is a minimum scientific and technical infrastructure, it appears that incentives can have positive results.

On the basis of the factors listed above, the following conclusion can be drawn:

— as relative market size increases (directly or through development of regional markets),

— as the requirements for product differentiation or adaptation increase, and

— as scientific and technical infrastructure improves,

there will be a progressive increase in transfers of R&D and technical activities to developing countries. (There will probably be exceptions to this trend for highly centralized enterprises with tight control over their world-wide activities.) The progression can probably only be accelerated a little by conventional government incentives.

D. FINANCIAL FLOWS

Export credits

Export credits have facilitated the growth of exports of capital goods by making the terms of sales more favourable and subsidising interest rates in many cases. Long-term credits for capital goods have mainly gone to the limited number of middle income and industrialising countries (40% of the total) and OPEC countries (50%) which have been rapidly expanding their industrial bases (see Table 7).

Table 7
Export Credits: Selected Major Recipients 1977-1978
% of total

Total going to developing countries 1977-1978 $ 23.5 billion (net disbursements)

Latin America:		OPEC:	
Brazil	3.0	Algeria	20.5
Peru	1.6	Iran	9.0
Argentina	1.3	Libya	2.2
Mexico	1.2	Saudi Arabia	2.0
		Indonesia	1.5
Asia:			
Korea	7.0	Europe:	
Philippines	2.4	Turkey	5.4
Thailand	0.6	Yugoslavia	3.5
Taiwan	0.5	Portugal	3.3
		Spain	1.2
Africa:		Greece	1.1
Egypt	3.1		
Ivory Coast	2.7	Total of countries listed	76.7
Morocco	2.1		
Kenya	1.5		

Total net official and private export credits from DAC countries to developing countries, *Development Co-operation*, 1979, 1980.

Not all export credits or capital goods go to manufacturing industry, but about 65% of both can be assigned to manufacturing. In 1978, major industrial sectors for credit commitments for complete plants were steel and metals (15%) and chemicals and fertilizers (30%), and in 1979 Italy, France, Germany, Japan and the U.S. made up more than 70% of export credit gross disbursements. Gross disbursements covered about 25% of the value of capital goods exports in 1978-1979.

47

Commercial borrowing and other financial flows

The most spectacular development during the mid-1970s was the growth of borrowing by developing countries (including OPEC) from international capital markets. Total borrowing subsequently declined in 1979 and 1980. Borrowing has been largely related to financing balance of payments deficits, refinancing existing debt, and building up reserves, but about 40% of total Euro-credit borrowing in 1976-1978 went to industrial development via financial systems in developing countries, or via government or semi-government industrial or development bodies [34]. Borrowing to service balance of payments deficits has been of major concern in the period since the most recent round of petroleum price increases. However, even financial flows going to finance balance of payments deficits allow imports of technology and other goods and services to continue. Ultimately of course, increases in external deficits and debt in relation to real or potential exports will restrict borrowing and imports. (This problem is discussed in Chapter IV.)

The flow of finance going through the international financial system to developing countries has increased rapidly. Some recent trends have been:

— *Net borrowing* by developing countries (including OPEC) from international banking markets during *1978* was $ 22.5 billion—a dramatic increase from $ 3 billion in 1970, but this declined to about $ 16.7 billion in 1979.

— *Gross* medium- and long-term international bank loans going to non-OPEC developing countries rose to $ 36 billion in *1979* [35], (half of total borrowing and a small increase in real terms over 1978), but borrowing by OPEC and OECD countries declined in real terms; total borrowing by all countries increased somewhat in 1979. During 1979 re-financing of debt on more favourable terms was common, as maturities lengthened and interest rate spreads became more favourable even though interest rates rose. During *1980* borrowing by non-OPEC developing countries and OPEC countries fell sharply as a proportion of the total (to 35% and 9%), while OECD countries increased their share of the total. Due to the sharp fall of non-OECD borrowing the total volume of loans fell by over 15% in real terms. Argentina, Brazil, Mexico, Philippines, South Korea and Yugoslavia remained major borrowers.

— Central and commercial banks, development agencies, energy utilities and industrial groups such as Pemex (as well as international development institutions) have all used *bond issues* to raise finance. However, bond issues are generally not important for developing countries, with net disbursements of $ 3.0 billion in 1978. During 1979 and 1980, new issues by both OPEC and non-OPEC developing countries declined in real terms and seem unlikely to increase while interest rates remain high. Argentina, Brazil, Mexico and Spain remained the most important issuers amongst developing countries.

— *Multilateral non-concessional lending* from the development banks totalled about $ 1.7 billion *for manufacturing* in 1978 (19% of funds lent by these banks). The same list of countries were major recipients of loans—Korea, Philippines, Argentina, Brazil, Mexico, Turkey and Yugoslavia.

Official development assistance

Very little official development assistance goes directly to manufacturing —about 4% of bilateral O.D.A. in 1978 ($ 0.8 billion) and 6% in 1979 ($ 1.4

billion)—and the major part goes to poorer developing countries. Germany, Japan and the U.S.A. were major suppliers. Similarly only a small proportion of technical assistance goes to manufacturing ($ 0.2 billion in 1978). Multilateral institutions likewise devote only a small proportion of concessional assistance to manufacturing development ($ 0.26 billion in 1978).

E. SUMMARY

Flows of technology and finance may be autonomous, with a large degree of independence of action being exerted by the receiver in choice and use of technology [36], or captive with a large degree of control being exerted by the exporter. As technical and economic expertise increases in industrialising countries, and as technology suppliers multiply at enterprise and country level, autonomous flows of capital equipment and finance and formation of joint ventures are increasing. To some extent the technology cycle is being contracted. However, captive flows, including new direct investment and licencing to affiliates, have also grown steadily during the period since 1970.

a) AUTONOMOUS FLOWS OF TECHNOLOGY

Capital equipment exports to developing countries have increased rapidly during the 1970s, and increases have been largely due to basic development in OPEC countries. Although OPEC development has been increasingly financially autonomous, technological *reliance* has been high because basic technical infrastructures have been weak. Furthermore, OPEC countries will have to seek the assistance of established industrial, commercial, and trading organisations if production targets are to be reached and if exports require access to OECD markets. However, the independent financial strength of OPEC countries and doubts regarding the desirable extent of industrialisation strengthen their positions.

International financing allows increased flows of technology (along with other goods and services) and increased investment in countries facing short-falls in capital formation or with external deficits. Lending to non-OPEC industrialising countries has increased, partly to offset balance-of-payments deficits, partly to finance development, and this may allow a measure of autonomy in domestic financing of industrial expansion.

b) CAPTIVE FLOWS OF TECHNOLOGY

Direct investment and payments for licences and know-how between related enterprises have grown at a lower rate than flows such as capital goods exports. The strategy of the firm and its hold on technology is a vital element in determining the effect of technological control on development. Market access, rates of return, potential growth, costs of factors of production and of raw materials, and intra-industry competition are all important determinants of enterprise strategy. The interplay between the strategy of enterprises and the industrial strategy of a country has an important bearing on the final form of technology transferred.

*
**

49

During the 1970s developments may be briefly summarised as follows:

i) *Industrial production*

Non-OPEC developing countries remained major destinations of exports of industrial technology from OECD countries. These transfers were partly financed by borrowing from international capital markets which, in turn, was facilitated by the relative slowdown of investment in developed OECD countries. In other words, OPEC balance-of-payments surpluses have been used to increase productive investment in non-OPEC developing countries. A large number of export activities now rely on this process, and its continuation depends on external deficits remaining manageable for industrialising countries and on their being able to increase exports to finance expansion and cover external deficits and debt.

OPEC countries are now showing relative declines as destinations for exports of industrial equipment and turn-key plants after very rapid growth in the 1970s. Whether this trend is temporary or a long-term one is unclear, but some of the more sparsely populated OPEC countries appear likely to slow their rates of development. More heavily populated OPEC countries are likely to continue industrial development but at a more moderate pace.

The increasing range of suppliers of industrial equipment and know-how suggests that the build-up of industrial capacity in developing countries is likely to continue at a relatively high rate. However, it must be recognised that the export of industrial capabilities implies return effects of increased imports of industrial products by OECD countries. Moreover, if developing countries are to continue to take up some of the slack in the world economy, and are to continue to grow rapidly, then they have to be given manoeuvering room—particularly in trade in manufactured goods.

Developing countries with an industrial base have begun exporting industrial equipment and related goods and services. Comparative advantages have been in low-cost labour and basic engineering using developed technology, combined with a facility for moving rapidly up the learning curves.

ii) *Technology production*

So far there have been few indications that the rapid increases in competitive production capacities in developing countries have been matched by similar rapid increases in capacities to create new, commercially useable technology. However, some developing countries have already moved closer along the technology cycle towards the position of OECD countries. The role of government policy in both OECD and developing countries needs to be examined closely if the transfer of abilities to create new industrial technology is to be favourably influenced.

50

Chapter III

EFFECTS OF TECHNOLOGY TRANSFER

A. POSITIVE AND NEGATIVE EFFECTS

a) MICRO-ECONOMIC APPROACH

The total effects coming from transfers of technology are difficult to isolate and measure in any comprehensive way. As pointed out in Chapter I, an enterprise transferring technology will usually try to protect its technological advantages, for example by setting up fully-owned subsidiaries or by applying limiting conditions when granting licences. Clearly enterprises are acutely aware that they are potentially undermining the advantages which protect them, and that they are running the risk of increasing direct competition if they do not apply careful control.

However, after laying the groundwork carefully the transfer should bring benefits. For example, the enterprise may improve its financial situation or gain access to new markets. In exchange the enterprise may ultimately limit the potential for some sorts of production in the home country or may cease these activities altogether. In general a decision to transfer technology implies trade-offs between short-term and long-term competitive strategies or between old and new productive activities, but overall the future balance must necessarily appear positive for the enterprise as a whole, or the transfer would not take place.

Do the positive benefits arising from technology transfer at the micro-economic, firm level mean that it is necessarily positive at macro-economic, national level? Here, the situation is not so clear.

b) MACRO-ECONOMIC APPROACH

We noted earlier* that transfers of industrial production capacity and know-how are the result of both the forces that are driving the restructuring of world industry and of the economic and industrial policies adopted by governments in industrialising countries in attempting to maximise benefits from transfers. This sometimes conflicting coincidence of events has allowed rapid growth of industrial output in developing countries in the last 25 years. Growth has been largely in Latin America where over 50 per cent of industrial production is concentrated, and in South East and East Asia where the most dynamic exporters of manufactures are located. More recently, the concentration of

---

* See Chapter I, Section B, the dynamics of transfers, and Chapter II.

finance and natural resources in the Middle East has led to many projects for resource-based industries, such as iron and steel-making, petrochemicals, and non-ferrous metals.

The emergence and increasing strength of these industrial growth centres has involved changes in existing industrial structures and equilibria. The most obvious results are the changes in trade flows between developed and developing countries, between developing countries, and the effects on flows between industrialised countries themselves.

However, these are not the only effects. It is generally assumed that when a new producer enters a market for manufactured goods there are a series of direct and indirect effects which may cause appreciable changes in the pattern of production of countries which are already industrialised, whether or not they are large exporters of technology or of manufactures. Sooner or later a new equilibrium will be achieved and according to neo-classical theory this will be beneficial. During this process, gross (or direct) effects and net (or total) effects can be distinguished.

Gross effects come directly from the establishment of new competitive industrial capacity. *Net effects* take into account new trade patterns, price and income effects, modifications to income distribution, and additional demand changes for sectors other than those directly affected by the new competition.

It is clear that the establishment of a new equilibrium and the operation of adjustment and adaptation mechanisms takes time. While some sectors will be stimulated by technology transfer others will encounter serious difficulties. The central policy issue concerns the differences between rates of industrialisation and changes in exports and imports from developing countries and the rate at which the industrial structures of OECD countries can adapt. Indeed it is often simpler to create new structures than to change old ones, and rather drastic policy measures may be necessary to facilitate changes which are difficult and painful in an unpromising economic climate. To design such policy measures, it is desirable to have a relatively comprehensive picture of the different sorts of feedback effects.

But total net effects will vary between countries and will depend on such factors as a country's cyclical, structural and social situation, and on the time scale and industrial sectors that are examined. In Table 1 are shown some of the very different effects which must be considered to determine the overall results of transfers. Furthermore, to have a complete evaluation it is necessary to consider an alternative position *excluding transfers* and compare the effects with transfers and without. However, for simplicity and brevity the alternative position is only referred to in passing as it is not a realistic proposition for detailed consideration. Neither have we attempted to list the different effects which may occur in each OECD country. Instead we draw attention to a number of significant continuing changes and suggest that these should be considered in assessing the repercussions of transfers.

It is not claimed that technology transfer is the exclusive cause of the changes we discuss below [1]. However, these changes are at least partly due to technology transfers: transfers were in many ways necessary if not sufficient conditions for their occurrence.

Taking account of the economic situation and main policy preoccupations of Member countries, the changes in trade and employment are considered in some detail. Special attention is paid to a few OECD countries where effects seem most significant.

Yet it is clear that this will only give a partial and somewhat mechanistic view. To begin with it must be remembered that the countries transferring technology are not necessarily those which receive the full following effects.

Table 1
Impacts of Technology Transfer

	Positive		Negative
Short-term	— Sales of technology: processes, engineering, know-how, assistance — Sales of equipment — Opportunities for no-risk investment by simply providing technology		— Loss of export markets — Emergence of new competition (which may be disruptive) in domestic markets and third markets — No job creation or loss of jobs in countries which have long-established competing industries

Medium and Long-term	— Opening of new markets with growing effective demand
	— Dynamic reorganisation of long-established industries in the direction of: advanced technologies, technological services, complex equipment, high-technology products
	— Faster innovation
	  - Improved processes
	  - Improved product performance
	  - New products
	— Availability of cheaper products
		job creation	— Serious crisis in countries where structural rigidities and low technological potential inhibit adaptation to new competitive conditions

Furthermore, relative changes between OECD countries should be analysed along with changes in North-South economic relations. Finally, an analysis of each sector in each country is not feasible for this report. (The alternative position, without technology transfer, is not explicitly considered. However, by concentrating on the principal exporters of technology this notion is implicitly introduced. If their situation appears satisfactory overall, it suggests that there are advantages in transfers. This is further reinforced if these countries also have the best general economic performances of OECD Members.)

B.   TRADE EFFECTS

It is mainly through trade in manufactures that impacts are first observed, but their importance depends on the industrial activities and countries that are considered.

a)   TRADE IN MANUFACTURED PRODUCTS BETWEEN DEVELOPING COUNTRIES AND THE OECD AREA

Trade in manufactures with industrialising countries has increased steadily over the last ten years or so. Imports are particularly notable from the more advanced of these countries. The result is that exports of industrial products from developing countries have taken an increasing share of their total industrial

Table 2

Export Effort and Domestic Market Share of Developing Countries
for Manufactured Products (%)

	1965	1969	1973	1976
Exports to developed countries (X1/Y1)	10.7	13.9	15.9	18.0
Exports to developing countries (X2/Y1)	4.2	4.7	6.0	8.1
Share of developing countries domestic markets M1/(Y1+M1−X1)	35.2	38.8	36.5	42.5

X1: Volume of exports of manufactures from developing countries to developed countries (1970 prices).
X2: Volume of exports of manufactures from developing countries to developing countries (1970 prices).
Y1: GDP of developing countries manufacturing industries (1970 prices).
M1: Volume of developing countries imports of manufactures from developed countries (1970 prices).
Source: [2] based on U.N. National Accounts and Foreign Trade (SITC 5 - 8).

production since the middle 1960s (see Table 2). More recently, between 1970 and 1976, OECD imports from LDCs increased at an annual rate of 28.9 per cent (in current values) and, although the rate has recently been lower, it was 19 per cent in 1977, 32 per cent in 1978, and 26 per cent in 1979, the last years for which complete statistics are available.

Meanwhile, OECD countries have increased exports to developing countries. Exports rose by 23.8 per cent per annum (current values) during the period 1970-1976, but the increase slowed down at the end of the period and fell to 17.7 per cent in 1977, 22.4 per cent in 1978 and 12 per cent in 1979. The rapid rise in exports was due to demand from the oil-producing countries and the rapidly industrialising countries, and is reflected in the sudden increase in the OECD countries' share of domestic markets in developing countries after 1973 (see Table 2). Developing countries also took a larger share of total manufactured exports from OECD countries; they went from 21.4 per cent in 1970 to 28 per cent in 1978 and 26.3 per cent in 1979.

For certain products, markets in developing countries have become even more important. For example, the slowdown in economic activity in OECD countries made developing countries, especially the oil producers, major customers for capital goods. In 1978, 1979 and 1980 (estimated) about 40% of capital goods exports went to developing countries, compared with only 34 per cent in 1970 (developing OECD are included in these figures).

Along with this increase in exports, the LDCs raised their share of OECD total imports of manufactures from 5.3 per cent to 10.1 per cent between 1970 and 1979. This good performance does not yet match OECD exports to developing countries which are still in very large surplus.

Thus globally and for almost Member countries, the trade balance with developing countries in manufactured products is positive. If we look at the small group of developing countries with the best performance, then OECD manufactured exports to them increased 2.1 times in volume in the period 1970-1979 compared with a total export volume increase of 1.8 in the same period. This clearly supports the idea that industrialisation stimulates trade.

However, within these overall figures there is a concentration on a more limited range of products which reflects the restructuring of some industrial activities.

b) ANALYSIS BY PRODUCT GROUP AND COUNTRY: INDUSTRIAL RESTRUCTURING

Only a few salient points are discussed below (for more details see Secretariat analytical study). In a few products developing countries have increased exports rapidly and have changed prior trade patterns. For example, of ten broad product groups, developing countries now hold a large share in OECD's imports of three—clothing, textiles, and footwear (see Table 3). In two other categories, "electrical machinery, apparatus and appliances" and "other manufactured products", their share is increasing rapidly to take up a significant proportion of imports. (See Graph 1 for growth in current values.)

Table 3
Share of Imports from Developing Countries in Total OECD Imports of Manufactures (%)

	1970	1976	1977	1978	1979
Chemicals	4.5	3.9	4.1	3.8	4.1
Iron and steel	2.9	4.3	4.2	4.6	5.5
Textiles	13.0	17.1	17.0	19.8	20.5
Clothing	27.4	44.0	42.8	45.5	44.7
Footwear, leather goods and furs	16.4	31.9	31.6	34.5	33.9
Non-electrical machinery	0.8	2.2	2.4	2.7	2.9
Electrical machinery and appliances	5.3	12.6	13.2	15.4	17.2
Road motor vehicles	0.2	0.6	0.6	1.1	1.1
Other transport equipment	2.0	3.9	5.3	8.2	5.5
Other manufactures	6.8	9.5	10.3	11.1	11.1
All manufactures	5.3	8.7	9.0	9.9	10.1

Source: OECD. For classification see Annex I. From 1978 data not strictly comparable with previous years.

Table 4
Shares (%) of Developing Countries in OECD Imports

	1970	1977
Textiles and clothing	31	45
Textile and clothing accessories	21	31
Unbleached cotton cloth	59	56
Bleached cotton cloth	7	14
Hosiery	27	41
Knotted carpets	83	76
Fur clothing	7	27
Leather clothing	22	46
Footwear	11	29
Travel goods and handbags	24	45
Plywood	29	30
Furniture	6	8
Plastic goods	13	13
Internal combustion engines	1	4
Electrical household appliances	1	5
Electric generators and distribution equipment	3	8
Equipment for electric circuits	0	7
Telecommunications equipment	5	13
Radio receivers	11	32
Transistors and electronic tubes	13	29
Sound recording and reproducing apparatus	0	12
Calculators and calculating machines	1	9
Motor vehicle spare parts	0	2
Watches, movements and cases	2	24
Toys and games	18	31

Source: [3].

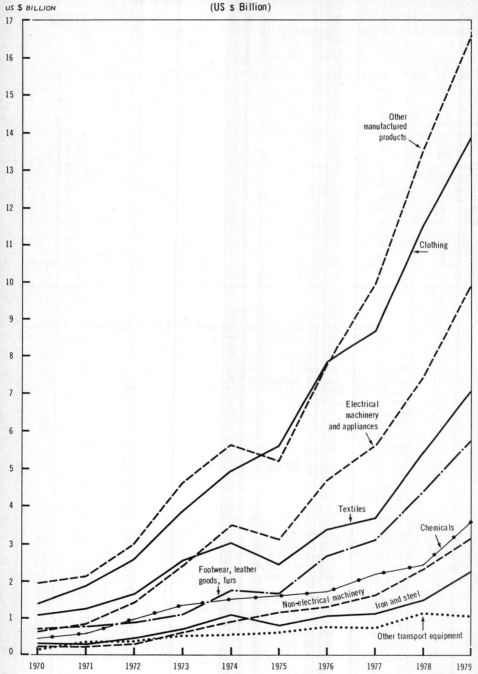

Graphic 1

OECD IMPORTS OF MANUFACTURED PRODUCTS FROM DEVELOPING
COUNTRIES : BY BROAD PRODUCT GROUPS - 1970-1979
(US $ Billion)

US $ BILLION

Other manufactured products

Clothing

Electrical machinery and appliances

Textiles

Chemicals

Footwear, leather goods, furs

Non-electrical machinery

Iron and steel

Other transport equipment

Source : OECD.

A detailed breakdown (Table 4) shows that developing countries have taken large and increasing shares in imports of a range of products in traditional industries that use rather simple, widely diffused technology and which produce textiles, made-up clothing, leather goods, and related articles. These trends are not new, even though imports have further increased in some sectors such as clothing. However, there are a number of new products in the list which require considerable technology transfer and international organisation of production. These products include electronic and telecommunications equipment, watches and clock movements, and sound recording apparatus. Moreover, the commodity composition of imports shows increasing shares of total imports taken by these new manufactures (see Table 5).

Meanwhile, OECD exports to developing countries have been increasingly composed of capital goods (Graph 2 shows the rapid increases in exports of electrical and non-electrical machinery after 1972 and again after 1976).

Analysis of trade by countries shows that most of the OECD imports come from a few countries of which Hong Kong, South Korea, and Taiwan are prominent (see Graph 3).

This concentration of sources of imports is matched by a concentration of importers in terms of volume. (Capacity to import depends on the size of domestic markets). The five major OECD markets account for three-quarters of OECD imports of manufactured products from developing countries. The United States' market is easily first, followed by Germany, the United Kingdom, Japan and then France.

The United States and then Japan have the highest proportions of their manufactured imports coming from developing countries. This also applies to imports of clothing and electrical equipment (see Annex II, Graphs 1, 2 and 3). Furthermore, if one takes the volume of exports of capital goods as a very rough overall indicator of transfers of technology to developing countries, one finds that the United States, Germany and Japan are by far the biggest exporters from the OECD area, followed by the United Kingdom and then France. These exports have been dominated by the United States whose share has been

Table 5

Commodity Composition of OECD Imports of Manufactures from Developing Countries (%)

	Share in				Annual average growth rate 1970-1976	Growth rates 1976-77 1977-78 1978-79 Current values		
	1970	1977	1978	1979		1976-77	1977-78	1978-79
Chemicals	10.1	5.9	4.7	5.4	17.4	2.7	8.2	45.2
Iron and steel	4.7	3.0	2.9	3.4	22.0	4.4	33.9	46.9
Textiles	15.6	10.0	10.7	11.0	21.4	9.4	46.8	29.0
Clothing	19.8	23.2	22.8	21.9	34.2	10.0	34.3	20.8
Footwear, leather goods and furs	6.4	8.4	8.6	8.9	35.5	15.6	40.0	29.8
Non-electrical machinery	3.0	4.3	4.7	4.8	36.3	23.6	47.2	29.8
Electrical machinery	9.4	15.0	14.5	15.4	39.2	20.0	32.0	40.0
Road motor vehicles	0.4	1.0	1.6	1.5	46.3	32.3	117.1	20.3
Other transport equipment	1.5	2.0	2.4	1.6	29.1	60.5	63.3	−18.6
Other manufactures	29.3	27.1	27.0	26.2	25.5	29.9	36.0	22.3
All manufactures	100.0	100.0	100.0	100.0				

Source: OECD.

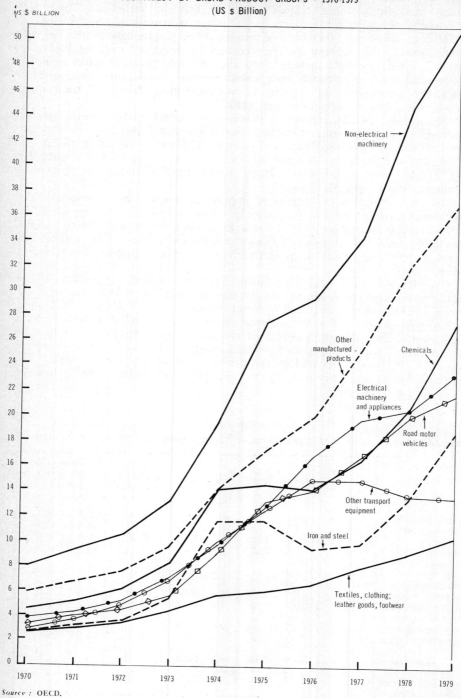

Graphic 2

OECD EXPORTS OF MANUFACTURED PRODUCTS TO DEVELOPING COUNTRIES: BY BROAD PRODUCT GROUPS - 1970-1979
(US $ Billion)

US $ BILLION

Non-electrical machinery

Other manufactured products

Chemicals

Electrical machinery and appliances

Road motor vehicles

Other transport equipment

Iron and steel

Textiles, clothing; leather goods, footwear

Source : OECD.

58

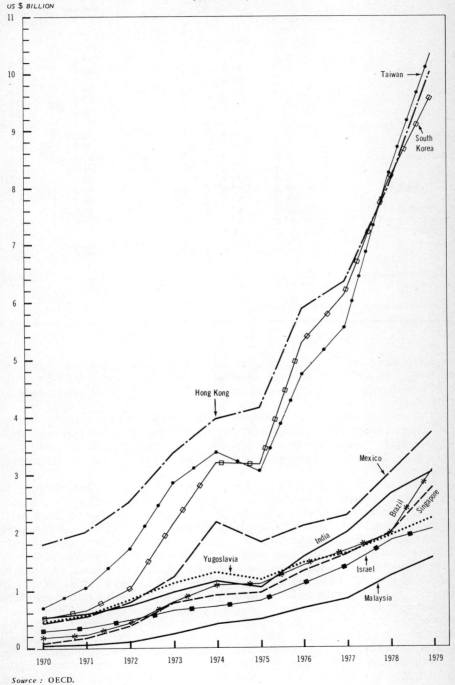

Graphic 3

OECD IMPORTS OF MANUFACTURED PRODUCTS FROM
THE PRINCIPAL DEVELOPING COUNTRY EXPORTERS 1970-1979
(US $ Billion)

Source : OECD.

Table 6
U.S. Related-Party Imports as a % of Total Imports of Selected Manufactured Products from Selected Newly Industrialising Countries: 1977

	Textiles 65	Non-electric machinery 71	Electric machinery 72	Clothing 84	Footwear 85	Scientific instruments 86	Total Manufacturing
Israel	18.9	32.8	62.9	14.0	0.0	13.0	18.2
Portugal	2.8	24.7	78.4	0.4	0.2	82.5	12.5
Greece	3.7	52.2	99.1	5.0	0.8	2.2	7.8
Ireland	36.3	78.5	77.8	8.3	42.2	91.7	59.0
Spain	1.5	36.3	32.6	3.7	10.1	7.8	24.1
Yugoslavia	0.1	14.0	2.0	2.3	2.2	3.6	4.9
Argentina	0.5	39.1	76.1	2.9	0.8	10.0	9.2
Brazil	9.2	59.9	95.3	18.0	0.5	38.4	38.4
Colombia	1.5	16.8	3.9	15.7	81.2	87.8	14.1
Mexico	9.6	87.8	95.6	68.0	60.9	93.6	71.0
Taiwan	13.1	19.3	58.1	1.2	3.1	67.1	20.5
Hong Kong	4.9	68.5	43.4	3.4	3.6	30.4	18.1
India	6.1	30.5	58.7	15.8	6.1	16.7	10.1
South Korea	5.5	64.2	67.3	7.1	1.8	12.1	19.7
Malaysia	0.2	83.2	97.0	1.9	0.0	91.9	87.9
Philippines	28.9	69.7	31.7	53.4	0.0	27.0	47.5
Singapore	4.3	90.5	97.0	0.5	0.0	85.3	83.3
Haiti	2.9	33.7	36.5	24.8	77.2	97.9	28.4
Total all developing countries	7.8	63.5	75.2	11.5	4.4	51.2	37.0

Source: [5], based on SITC classification.

decreasing since 1970, and by Japan and Germany whose shares have been increasing. In 1978, these three countries together accounted for 62 per cent of OECD exports of capital goods that can be broadly assigned to industrial activities.

The overall effect is an industrial restructuring process whereby there is a transition in some industrialised countries from labour-intensive industries which are no longer competitive towards industries in which they have comparative advantages. Technology transfer is of course both a cause and an effect of this restructuring [4].

A number of factors allow this process to take place. They include the establishment of export processing zones and labour-intensive export industries in some developing countries, the increased ease of communications and transport, and price competition in industries such as electronics. Transnational enterprises are involved in some of these industries but in others they have not played a significant role in re-locating manufacturing facilities. For example, data exists for the United States which gives an indication of the importance of "internal trade" within U.S. TNEs as a proportion of U.S. imports from developing countries. For the rapidly industrialising countries, U.S. TNEs exercise significant control over three out of six selected product groups (see Table 6). These groups comprise new products, whereas traditional exports such as clothing, footwear, and textiles are not controlled to anywhere near the same extent by U.S. TNEs. If the sectoral penetration by transnational enterprises in industrialised countries is considered along with their penetration in developing countries and exports from developing countries, it is evident that transnationals play only a limited role in traditional sectors (see Table 7 and [6]; Japanese investment was the exception).

The development of South Korea's textile industry illustrates the capacity of some countries to develop traditional industries in conjunction with TNEs, but to a certain extent outside of their direct control. On the other hand, the relatively favourable evolution of Germany's textile and clothing industries suggests that it is possible to take advantage of opportunities offered by the development of labour-intensive industries in developing countries.

These results are all part of the restructuring of industries world-wide. This does not necessarily mean that simpler and more labour-intensive products are destined to be made only in developing countries. Some such products are already produced in highly automated plants in industrialised countries [7]. However, a situation that is satisfactory for developed and developing countries is not found in all industries of Member countries. This is discussed below.

Table 7
Ranking of Industries in Developed and Developing Countries
According to Degree of TNE Penetration of the Industries and Export Performance

Degree of TNE penetration	Developed Countries	Developing Countries	Exports A	B
I High	Petroleum processing	Petroleum processing	n i	n i
	Electrical machinery	Rubber	nsa	nsa
	Transportation equipment	Electrical machinery	15.7	14.7
	Instruments	Transportation equipment	2.3	8.5
	Chemical products (pharmaceutical products and petrochemicals)	Instruments	nsa	nsa
		Chemical products (pharmaceutical products and		
	Rubber products	petrochemicals)	7.5	2.4
	Non-Electrical machinery	Non-Electrical machinery	4.0	7.8
		Food (incl. beverage and		
		tobacco)	n i	n i
			29.5	6.2
II Medium	Fabricated metal products	Primary metals	3.6	4.6
	Primary metals	Fabricated metal products	4.9	7.2
	Food (incl. beverages and	Construction materials (stone,		
	tobacco)	clay, cement, etc.)	3.2	3.2
	Paper and paper products	Printing and publishing	nsa	nsa
	Printing and publishing	Textile	13.6	3.3
	Construction materials (stone, clay, cement, etc.)	Miscellaneous manufactures	11.0	4.3
			36.3	3.6
III Low	Textile	Wearing apparel	21.8	6.4
	Wearing apparel	Wood, wood products and		
	Wood, wood products and	furniture	5.3	6.5
	furniture	Leather and leather products	6.9	5.9
			34.0	6.3

A: Share of total manufacturing exports from developing to developed countries in 1974.
B: 1974 exports divided by 1967 exports.
Developed countries: Australia, Austria, Canada, the Federal Republic of Germany, France, Japan, Sweden and the United Kingdom. *Developing countries:* Argentina, Brazil, Hong Kong, India, Mexico, Singapore and Turkey. Data from UN; Export data from Keesing. n i=not included. nsa=not separately available.
Source: [6].

61

c) Technology Transfer and Changes in Trade Flows

This brief analysis shows that industrialisation in developing countries and contributing technology transfer from OECD countries have been accompanied by an increase in bilateral trade between these countries. South-South trade has also increased and this has led to changes in traditional trade flows between OECD countries and developing countries and between OECD countries themselves. It is clear that such factors as exchange rates, trade and tariff policy, and the formation of trade pacts affect trade flows as well as technology transfer and the establishment of new production facilities. However, some trends are obvious.

First, although developing countries' sales of manufactured products to one another are relatively small (U.S.$ 26 billion in 1979, 12 per cent of their imports of manufactures), they increased at higher rates than OECD exports to them (see Table 8). The trend has been maintained for 15 years and is continuing, suggesting that exports from some OECD countries are slowly losing their positions in expanded trade with developing countries (CMEA countries have lost an even bigger share in recent years).

Table 8
Increase in Volume of Manufactured Trade of South and West
Annual growth rate % for manufactured products at 1970 prices

	1965-1969	1969-1973	1973-1976
South's exports to the South	10.8	15.3	16.0
South's exports to the West	14.5	12.4	9.4
West's exports to the South	10.6	5.5	13.1
West's exports to the West	13.4	8.8	1.8

Source: [2].

Table 9
Shares of Trade in Manufactured Goods 1973 to 1978

Exports to:	Exports from:				
	EEC	North America	Japan	Developing Countries	Centrally Planned East
United States	− − − − −	− − −	+ + + + +	+ + + +	0
EEC (9)	−	−	+	0	0
Centrally Planned East	+ +	0	+ + +	−	− − − − − −
Non-oil developing countries	0	−	+	+ +	0
Japan	0	−		+	− −
OPEC	+	0	+ +	−	− −

+ gain of one percentage point from 1973 to 1978.
− loss of one percentage point.
0 no change.
Export markets in order of decreasing market size.
Source: Secretariat calculations from U.N. *Monthly Bulletin of Statistics.*

PERCENTAGE SHARES OF US IMPORTS OF TELEVISION RECEIVERS

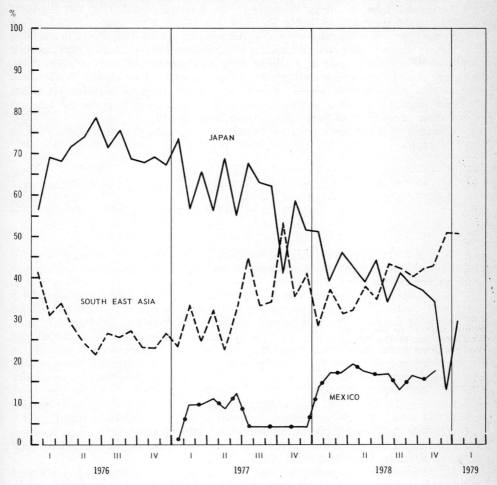

Source : Calculated from data of the US Department of Commerce.

Competition from developing countries is not confined to their own markets. It is also noticeable within the OECD area. For example in the United States, the world's largest import market, the Japanese and some developing countries are taking increasing shares of total imports and European countries have been losing their share [8]. For this market between 1973 and 1978 the proportion of total imports of manufactured products from the EEC fell from 28.8 per cent to 24.4 per cent, while the "rest of Europe's" share declined from 6.1 per cent to 5.0 per cent. During the same period developing countries' share rose from 17.7 per cent to 22.5 per cent and, of OECD countries, Japan raised its share of the market from 20.5 per cent to 25.2 per cent. The EEC's imports from outside the EEC area are comparable in value to those of the United States but changes in the origins of imports into the EEC were not as marked between 1973 and 1978. Japan's total imports of manufactured products are small. A relatively high proportion continues to be imported from developing countries and there have been no major changes in the relative positions of the suppliers of imports (see summary in Table 9).

Some transfers of technology and resultant changes in trade flows are related to market access. Factors influencing the re-location of production include unfavourable exchange rate and labour cost movements and import restrictions, including orderly marketing agreements. For example, data shown in Graph 4 suggest that o.m.a.'s with respect to United States' direct imports of television receivers from Japan were accompanied by increases in United States' imports of the same product from South East Asian countries [9].

Changes in trade flows have an impact on employment and we now turn to these impacts.

C. EMPLOYMENT EFFECTS

It is difficult to give a clear-cut satisfactory answer to the question whether transfers of technology to developing countries have favourable effects on employment or not.

Technology transfers are complex operations and the effects arising from them will continue over a prolonged period and there will be different gains and losses of employment in different industrial activities and at different times.

Gains: New jobs are directly created as a result of exports of capital and intermediate goods (and even consumer goods) and services related directly to the transfer and as a result of the greater economic activity generated in the importing country. Technology transfer will create further jobs through multiplier effects in the exporting country.

Losses: To the extent that industrial capacity and jobs are created outside the OECD area and this production capacity leads to competing exports, there will be direct negative effects on employment. Spread effects may then transmit losses to related industries and service activities (including regional activities such as public administration and retail trade).

In addition to any problems that we may have in calculating gains and losses there is also the problem that we are comparing real events with hypothetical ones. For example, the creation of production capacity in a developing country does not necessarily mean a loss of jobs for the exporting country. It does not automatically follow that if a plant had *not* been set up overseas, a similar plant would have been set up in the OECD area. In fact a large proportion of technology transfers appear to be determined by market access, import and investment policies, and growth prospects in developing countries rather than by factor costs and export possibilities.

Keeping in mind these general reservations we have summarised below the results of studies carried out by various national or international bodies to determine the employment effects directly related to the increasing competitive capacity of LDCs in exporting manufactured products.

This assumes that once technology transfer has enabled developing countries to acquire production capacity, then employment effects are transmitted through international trade [10]. From this point of view the findings of most of the studies converge. While the net effects of total trade are positive, the gross effects are not. Gross effects of import penetration on particular industries are often quite considerable. In addition it is generally concluded that the speed of change in patterns of employment is destined to increase.

a) NET EFFECTS

In general the job content of OECD exports is less than that of LDC exports. The ratio of jobs "created" per unit value of exports to LDCs to jobs "lost" per unit value of imports from them is less than one. Thus the following coefficients of jobs created to jobs lost have been calculated for individual countries: Germany 0.96, Netherlands 0.93, Belgium 0.84, the United States 0.65 (these values are not directly comparable).

For the OECD area a recent study [11] calculated the following coefficients: OECD total 0.65, United States 0.61, EEC 0.65, Japan 0.73. Because of positive manufactured trade balances between OECD and developing countries, application of these coefficients gave strongly positive employment effects through to 1976. The ratio of total job content of exports to that of imports came to 2.8 for the OECD, 3.4 for the EEC, 7.9 for Japan and 1.4 for the United States. These positive results were due to the OECD area's export surplus.

According to this study, the surplus of exports to developing countries meant a net "gain" of 150,400 jobs for the United States, and 501,600 jobs for Japan [12]. For the EEC as a whole the gain was 706,800 (see Table 10). These positive results are confirmed by the country studies available. Without attempting to directly compare all of the figures (the methods used and periods taken are different), for 1970-1976 Germany "gained" over 160,000 jobs, and France "gained" about 100,000 jobs from its export surpluses [13]. In the United Kingdom between 1970-1975 only 26,200 of a total reduction of 113,700 jobs in 24 industries exposed to competition from LDCs was attributed to imports from them (23 per cent of the total). In a larger group of industries the "losses" directly due to competition from developing countries between 1970 and 1977 should not have exceeded 2 per cent of the workforce [14].

The Netherlands Economic Institute has obtained similar results for the Netherlands. Between 1974 and 1978, 41,000 industrial jobs were lost, of which 4,000 or slightly under 10 per cent could be directly attributed to competition from developing countries.

These conclusions clearly depend as much on continuing good export performances as on import effects. Thus a recent study [15] assumed that every $ 1 million exported "created" 25 to 30 jobs and every $ 1 million imported from industrialising countries meant a "loss" of 40 jobs (a coefficient of 0.75 to 0.62). These assumptions led to the conclusion that Canada and the United States suffered net losses of employment in 1977 (see Table 11 for trade with nine industrializing countries, including Portugal, Spain and Yugoslavia) [16].

These figures may be attributed to the relatively poor export performance in manufactured goods of the United States and Canada with industrialising countries. This may reflect the low competitive power of their products compared with similar products from their OECD partners (as well as exchange rates, regional effects, export financing mechanisms, etc.).

However, even these relatively pessimistic estimates only gave maximum "losses" of 1.8 per cent of total manpower employed in manufacturing industry, which is much less than 0.5 per cent of the OECD's total working population. On the other hand, there are modest gains from trade with industrialising countries for other OECD countries, and significant gains for Japan.

Finally, all of these estimates suggest that competition with developing countries accentuates existing trends—to increase efforts to improve productivity

65

Table 10

Total Employment Effects of Trade in Manufactures between Developed and Developing Countries, 1976

Thousand jobs

	OECD			USA			EEC			JAPAN		
	Export	Import	Balance	Export	Import	Balance	Export	Import	Balance	Export	Import	Balance
1 Textile Mill Products	138.9	192.2	−53.3	15.4	62.5	−47.1	48.7	74.3	−25.6	61.7	18.8	42.9
2 Apparel and Other Textile Products	40.8	218.2	−177.4	13.0	81.5	−68.5	19.8	90.1	−70.3	3.4	13.7	−10.3
3 Lumber and Wood Products	10.4	26.3	−15.9	2.0	11.5	−9.5	5.2	8.9	−3.7	0.3	2.2	−1.9
4 Furniture and Fixtures	19.7	10.6	9.1	3.4	4.1	−0.7	12.8	3.4	9.4	1.7	1.6	0.1
5 Paper and Allied Products	33.3	2.8	30.5	8.6	1.0	7.6	6.5	1.2	5.3	3.6	0.1	3.5
6 Printing and Publishing	25.0	2.7	22.3	4.5	0.8	3.7	15.3	0.8	14.5	1.4	0.2	1.2
7 Chemical and Allied Products	163.4	23.4	140.0	37.5	10.4	27.1	73.8	6.6	67.2	28.8	2.8	26.0
8 Petroleum Products	1.1	0.0	1.1	0.0	0.0	0.0	0.7	0.0	0.7	0.0	0.0	0.0
9 Rubber and Plastic Products	32.2	63.1	−30.9	4.4	41.8	−37.4	16.0	11.5	4.5	8.1	3.2	4.9
10 Leather and Leather Products	10.1	36.2	−26.2	2.5	15.1	−12.6	3.7	13.7	−10.0	3.1	2.0	1.1
11 Stone, Clay and Glass Products	51.6	10.9	40.7	6.6	4.5	2.1	25.7	3.2	22.5	11.0	1.3	9.7
12 Primary Metal and Allied	194.2	27.7	166.5	25.7	11.9	13.8	77.4	9.8	67.6	73.1	2.8	70.3
13 Fabricated Metal Products	91.9	7.3	84.5	15.9	2.8	13.1	49.5	2.2	47.3	13.5	0.3	13.2
14 Non-electrical Machinery	527.4	18.7	508.7	142.7	6.4	136.3	261.7	6.6	255.1	71.5	1.6	69.9
15 Electrical Equipment and Supplies	417.3	122.7	294.6	106.3	77.9	28.4	187.1	29.9	157.2	88.6	10.8	77.8
16 Transportation Equipment	486.2	13.7	472.5	108.0	2.6	105.4	145.1	5.0	140.1	177.4	3.0	174.4
17 Instruments and Related Products	72.7	17.8	54.9	16.3	9.5	6.8	22.3	4.5	17.8	17.2	1.5	15.7
18 Misc. Manufactured Products	47.7	58.0	−10.3	9.1	27.2	−18.1	25.3	18.3	7.0	9.4	6.3	3.1
Total	2,363.8	852.5	1,511.3	521.9	371.5	150.4	996.7	289.9	706.8	573.8	72.3	501.6
of which sum of positive balances			1,825.4			344.3			816.3			513.8
negative balances			314.1			193.9			109.5			12.2

Source: [11].

66

Table 11

**Hypothetical Job Losses and Gains from 1977 Trade in Manufactures
with Industrialising Countries**

	Thousands			% of manufacturing employment	
	Jobs lost	Jobs created	Balance	Jobs lost	Balance
United States	532	294	−238	2.7	−1.2
Germany	184	215	31	1.9	0.3
Japan	96	352	256	0.9	2.3
France	96	99	3	1.6	0.1
United Kingdom	92	96	4	1.1	0.0
Canada	44	14	−30	2.6	−1.8
Italy	44	85	41	0.7	0.7
Others	168	182	14	2.2	0.2
All developed OECD	1,256	1,337	81	1.8	0.1

Source: [15].

in competing industries and to improve patterns of occupational skills in industry.

Changes in occupation patterns that are attributable to trade with developing countries have been roughly estimated by Balassa [11]. It was concluded that OECD countries export products that intensively use skilled labour and import products that intensively use unskilled labour. However, all Member countries except the United States continued to have a favourable export/import ratio as regards the least skilled labour.

b) GROSS EFFECTS

While net employment effects are modest, specific effects are appreciable in some sectors. These are the traditional and/or labour-intensive activities which are often regionally concentrated and in which there are often considerable problems with retraining and re-employing labour. The sector studies did not show notable gross labour displacement effects—but these industries are, in general, technologically advanced, are integrated on a global scale, or have been the object of trade limitation arrangements.

Of employment losses in the United States recorded for the period 1964-1971, almost 45 per cent were concentrated in clothing and electrical equipment and supplies. In Germany between 1970 and 1976, 43 per cent of employment losses were concentrated in the clothing industry, 18.5 per cent in the textile industry and 16.8 per cent in the electrical engineering industry. The same trend was found in the United Kingdom, where almost 80 per cent of the losses attributable to imports from developing countries were concentrated in the ready-made clothing, hosiery and textile sector. For France, 25 per cent of losses were concentrated in the textile industry and 13 per cent in the wood and furniture and miscellaneous industries.

These results confirm the impacts on a limited number of industrial branches from imports of specific product lines. These effects have often been more appreciable because they strike one-industry regions. Positive employment effects are often much more diffuse and are usually located in different areas [13].

It must be emphasised that most of the studies that are summarised above only give approximate orders of magnitude, but they all point out that the employment effects of imports from developing countries are in general less than those caused by: *i*) trade with industrialised countries, *ii*) increases in productivity (which are often inspired by increased competition), or *iii*) the slowdown in economic activity and changes in domestic demand [17].

c) MEDIUM-TERM OUTLOOK

While the effects produced by increased trade with developing countries in manufactured products in the first half of the seventies were relatively slight, they seem destined to increase as trade expands. However, it is difficult to identify the direction which these effects will take. For example a recent French study suggested that, depending on assumptions, either some 284,000 jobs might be created in the period 1980-1985, or else there might be a loss of 257,000 jobs. This is a wide margin of uncertainty.

Other calculations for the OECD area as a whole suggest that up to 1986 total employment should not be affected [11]. As usual the assumptions determine the results. However, the number of sectors that are likely to be affected is increasing. This suggests that there may be faster changes in the structure of productive activities and in employment patterns.

As we have noted above it is practically impossible to satisfactorily evaluate return effects coming from *past* technology transfers. The data concerning employment, for example, may be disturbed by cyclical effects [6]. Furthermore, changes in trade patterns cannot all be attributed to transfers. Asymmetric structural changes must also be taken into account as developed countries have concentrated on capital goods and developing countries on consumer and intermediate goods. Thus it is necessary to consider structural changes that may escape purely conjunctural considerations. Such changes are discussed in the next chapter.

Chapter IV

LONGER-TERM OUTLOOK

The analysis above of trade and employment effects is fairly positive. Scrutiny of some of the instruments on the instrument panels of Western economies indicates: trade is increasing, the capital goods sector of OECD countries has benefited from technology transfers to developing countries, trade balances have tended to improve on both sides (mainly with respect to industrialising countries) particularly as the proportion of value added in the total value of commodities exchanged is increasing on both sides, and net employment effects are positive. However, as discussed above, the gross effects may be particularly painful.

It may be assumed that these are the results so far of continuing changes that are at least partly facilitated by transfers. Can it thus be concluded that the adjustment process is proceeding satisfactorily—both at the *level* of economic activity and in terms of *structure?*

This may clearly be too optimistic; there are many factors *more important* than competition with the newly industrialising countries which may intervene. This competition may then only aggravate an already difficult situation.

Concerning structural changes, the significance of the information discussed above must be carefully weighed and it must be considered whether past experience is likely to continue. For example, the positive scenarios outlined in Chapter III, C. *c*) and elsewhere are based on fairly optimistic assumptions and projections [1]. It is necessary to ask whether the recent performance of OECD countries justifies optimism or whether there are obstacles in the way that could prevent the achievement of scenario targets.

A. RELEVANT FEATURES OF TECHNOLOGY TRANSFERS

The relative weakness of feedback effects so far is due to a range of factors which are unlikely to be repeated in the future. Some of these factors are discussed below.

One of the results of technology transfer will be changes in industrial location and trade flows. However, it is clear that there is no simple relation between transfers of technology in a given period and return effects perceived in the following period.

a) TRANSFERS TO "EXPORT PLATFORMS"

If exports of capital goods are taken as a rough index of technology transfer, then Hong Kong, South Korea, Singapore and Taiwan were only relatively small customers for technology in 1968 and the following years [2]. For example, in

1968 their imports of capital goods were only 9% of the total for developing countries. However, these four countries provided two-thirds of manufactured imports from developing countries in recent years.

It seems therefore that there is no simple relation between the volume of technology transferred and the return effects on OECD trade and employment. If it does exist then it is on initial examination a very elastic relation, particularly for traditional industries.

Furthermore, effects may be very strong on trade, but for certain sectors or industries weak on employment. Why?

First, most problems have been in traditional industries such as the textiles, clothing, leather and footwear industries, which are usually not capital-intensive (except for textiles). Second, these are long-established industries in developing countries, and it was easy to assimilate readily available technology. The only thing lacking was the connection with the OECD countries' wholesale and distribution networks, and once this was established exports to OECD countries could increase substantially.

By acting as subcontractors for retail chains or for wholesalers, or for manufacturers wishing to take advantage of low labour costs, enterprises in developing countries could compete keenly—particularly with enterprises in OECD countries that required ever-rising trade barriers to survive. Thus it became necessary to negotiate newer and stricter agreements, for example the Multi-fibre Arrangement 1978-1981, and orderly marketing arrangements.

But for new products (for example consumer electronics) the production technology transferred was elementary, and it formed a segment of a complex manufacturing scheme controlled by transnational enterprises. As a result the feedback effects that were *directly under the control* of the enterprise were included in the firm's plans and minimised at firm level. To replace those products which were left almost entirely for manufacture in developing countries (e.g. radio receivers), there was a wide range of innovations available in the electrical equipment and electronics industries to allow firms to maintain their dynamism.

Thus the competitivity which is shown in some products and the disproportion between volume of technology transferred and its effects on trade may be explained by the rapidity with which some production technology could be assimilated by the receiving country. Further, links between productive activities and world marketing and manufacturing networks and the outward-looking growth policies followed by the host country helped to maximise effects. Thus some feedback effects could only be limited by trade protection; in other industries they have been limited by the control exercised by firms owning the technology.

b) Transfers to countries with large domestic markets

Transfers to Latin American countries (Brazil, Mexico and Argentina) and India have been relatively larger; in 1968 and subsequent years total imports of capital goods were more than twice those for Asian exporting countries (but less if scaled by industrial GDP, see chapter II, Table 4). However, the pressure of exports to OECD markets a few years later has been much lower when compared with the Asian exporting countries. This is a situation where the relation between transfers and exports is lower because of the domestic or regional market orientation of industrial production.

There are further explanations for this phenomenon: transfers are of capital-intensive technologies for heavy industry and infrastructure that formed part of overall policies for import substitution rather export-led growth. They may be likened to product cycle transfers where production is oriented towards local markets [3].

70

Feedback effects are not immediate but delayed, and they tend not to appear in bilateral trade between the countries exporting and importing technology. Technology transfer does not lead immediately to more exports of manufactured products to OECD countries, but effects on patterns of trade are inevitable. Exports of finished products from the OECD are replaced by exports of capital goods and intermediate products. Moreover, the relative industrial strength of the countries concerned are changed.

Furthermore, when technology is transferred as part of the worldwide production strategies of transnational enterprises (as has often been the case in Latin America), trade and associated effects may be limited—for example in transfers of capacity for producing motor vehicles, tyres and pharmaceuticals [4]. This is certainly the case when production is primarily for the domestic or regional market. This may not be the case when there is less direct investment control over new facilities—for example in iron and steel making, and shipbuilding.

c) TRANSFERS TO OIL-PRODUCING COUNTRIES

Oil producers may be classified as densely populated (high absorbers) or sparsely populated (low absorbers). Densely populated countries such as Iraq, Algeria, Nigeria and Indonesia have a strategy which in many ways resembles that of other countries with large domestic markets. Oil resources will be used to set up industries to supply domestic markets and, possibly later, world markets.

For countries such as Saudi Arabia and Libya, transfers have been mainly to build up infrastructure and to enable a start on ambitious industrialisation projects (in petrochemicals, iron and steel, and aluminium).

In both cases massive technology transfers are too recent to have produced appreciable feedback effects.

*
**

To summarise, the industrialised countries have experienced a somewhat exceptional situation in recent years. Trade competition has come from countries that are not the biggest customers for capital goods and technology. OECD countries have so far been able to protect and even strengthen threatened industries without risk of direct retaliation as the countries importing most technology did not produce on a very large scale for export (large domestic markets, type of product, running-in time required for plant and equipment). In addition, apart from traditional and standardised technologies, enterprises possessing tightly held technologies have been able to exercise some control over technology transfers and integrate them into a world-wide production strategy.

There are no guarantees that this favourable situation will continue. As industrial development advances in countries with large domestic markets, the need for sophisticated technologies will increase and there will be increasing pressures to pay for such imports by exporting manufactured products, or further increasing international borrowing with attendant debt-servicing problems. A renewed swing towards export promotion policies is one way of financing imports of technology. For OECD countries the exact effects of this evolution will depend on whether new exports and income outweigh imports and losses of markets, and on how successfully the adjustment process works.

Furthermore it is possible that it will become more difficult to control technology as the number of sources increases and the diffusion of technology accelerates both vertically and horizontally.

B. ELEMENTS INFLUENCING THE DIFFUSION OF TECHNOLOGY

a) FAVOURABLE TECHNICAL FACTORS

Once started, the process of transferring and disseminating technology continues vertically, i.e. from simple towards more complex technologies, and horizontally, i.e. as the number of sources of technology increases [5].

i) Vertical diffusion

Vertical diffusion is best illustrated in the petrochemical industry. In this industry there is an increasingly widespread ability to participate in the more complex engineering tasks of various projects. For example, the technique of steam-cracking was owned at the beginning of the 1960s by two project engineering enterprises. This technique has gradually spread to similar enterprises, and competing technologies have appeared which increase competition and spread knowledge of the technique. In these circumstances, the bargaining power of purchasers (and their governments) must increase. This is reflected in the changes in the content of recent contracts negotiated by Petrobras and Pemex, and by progress made by such countries as Algeria, South Korea and Taiwan [6].

In spite of the theories of technological dependence, there is nothing pre-ordained about a technology gap. However, there is a long learning process for local entrepreneurs and authorities preparing to receive technology. Transnational enterprises contribute to the development of skills that will enable the host country to assimilate more complex technologies, and the learning process to receive technology is well under way in the main industrialising countries [7].

Adaptational engineering skills will also develop. These lower real costs of imported techniques and allow economies of scale that may facilitate entry to new domestic and foreign markets. Japan has used this approach, as have other Asian countries. For example, the South Korean motor vehicle industry has produced a medium-sized car at about one-third of the price of a similar European model. In ship-building, South Korean yards can produce at prices 30% lower than Japan [8]. In many respects the South Korean experience is atypical, but rapid progress has been made; for example, in Mexico in iron and steel and oil technology, and in Brazil in ship-building and hydro-electric technology.

Recent experience suggests that benefits have also flowed to the most backward countries. The transfer of technology has become a better understood phenomenon, and the specialised enterprises supplying technology are, to a certain extent, enabling recipients to avoid some of the unfortunate experiences of their predecessors [9]. Similarly, structural changes in leading industrialising countries have become models for the countries following them and this too, speeds the process of change in the countries that follow.

The collective experience accumulated in the transfer of industrial activities should lead to an acceleration in their diffusion; this is analogous to the accelerated diffusion of new processes between industrial countries [10].

ii) Horizontal diffusion

At the same time, horizontal diffusion has occurred and the more advanced industrialising countries are supplying a wide range of technologies. For example Argentina, Mexico, Brazil, India and some East Asian countries are now active suppliers of technology.

India's exports of engineering and technical services, plant and equipment in the textile, sugar refining and cement industries are well established. Recently the range has been extended to include electric power stations, telephone exchanges, pharmaceutical manufacturing plants, turn-key fertiliser plants, steel works, and machine tool plants.

Argentina exports turnkey plants for food refrigeration, fruit processing, and cotton oil extraction, while Brazil exports plants for iron and steel making, engineering products, and turbine equipment [11], Mexico for iron and steel making, and South Korea and Taiwan for making machine tools [12].

Exports of plant and equipment have been accompanied by provision of services; thus Indian, South Korean, Mexican and Brazilian project engineering is well known and dynamic in many fields (see Chapter II).

The technologies disseminated in this way are usually not new, but have already been adapted to use in developing countries and are usually highly price-competitive. It should also be noted that while the technologies mastered and transferred by suppliers from developing countries are usually mature, they also embody a high level of engineering and technical skills.

The conclusion that can be drawn is that for a growing number of techniques transfers will occur rapidly and former technological advantages are likely to be eroded (by bargaining or catching up). In many cases it is only where technology evolves rapidly that advantages will be retained [13].

This may mean losses of export markets when restructuring of industrial activities is involved; industries in OECD countries may not expect major increases in exports shares in such industries. Furthermore, there is the possibility of keener competition in OECD and third markets.

b) ECONOMIC AND FINANCIAL FACTORS

Although technical factors are important, they are not sufficient and can only operate if certain economic conditions are fulfilled.

i) *Economic factors*

Technology transfers are both the result and cause of changes in the world economy. These changes include high industrial growth rates or potentials in some developing countries, and a slowdown in growth and demand in industrialised countries.

The slowdown is shown in the index of output of manufactures for market economy countries as represented in Graph 1 [14]. A break in the trend appears around 1969. This break is concentrated on developed market-economy countries, as the trends of industrial production in developing and developed countries diverge after 1970 (see Graph 2).

The break in the growth trend *before 1973* may be attributed to demographic factors and to changes in demand for such goods as construction materials, and electrical engineering products (see Graph 3), which in turn affect production of intermediate inputs from iron and steel and metal-working industries [14]. For industries such as textiles and clothing, leather goods, chemicals and wood and paper, the break after 1973 may be attributed to effects of the economic slow-down itself.

The trend of technology transfers follows these changes quite closely. Transfers became sizeable from the late Sixties and developed further after the oil price rises in 1973. They were in response to changes in the outlook for some industries at the end of the Sixties, and later they embraced a wider range of technologies—the result being that transfers helped in the short-term to combat rising unemployment and to pay an increasingly heavy oil bill after 1973.

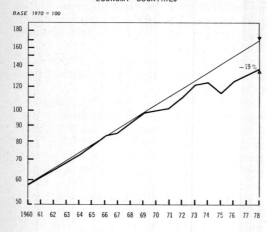

Graphic 1

VOLUME INCREASE IN TOTAL MANUFACTURING
PRODUCTION : MARKET
ECONOMY COUNTRIES

BASE 1970 = 100

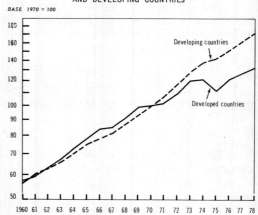

Graphic 2

VOLUME INCREASE IN TOTAL MANUFACTURING
PRODUCTION : DEVELOPED COUNTRIES
AND DEVELOPING COUNTRIES

BASE 1970 = 100

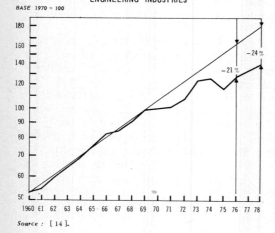

Graphic 3

VOLUME INCREASE IN DEMAND FOR PRODUCTION
FROM THE ELECTRICAL AND MECHANICAL
ENGINEERING INDUSTRIES

BASE 1970 = 100

Source : [14].

74

Transfers were one means whereby some OECD enterprises or industrial activities were able to show good performances, despite the generally poor economic situation. Studies that have attempted projections of economic performance for the next few years conclude that growth in the OECD area will probably remain low because of the continuing relative slow-down in demand for durable goods, lower birth rates, rising relative prices for raw materials and energy, and such factors as environmental protection.

On the other hand, despite the relation between possibilities for growth in developing countries and growth in the OECD area, prospects in developing countries remain good. Although their present performance is slower than in earlier periods, this performance is still good in comparison with that of OECD countries; particularly for industrial output in industrialising countries. In 1978 all developing countries combined had a GNP growth rate of 5.8 per cent, compared with 3.9 per cent for the OECD according to the World Bank [15]. All the main geographical areas except Africa south of the Sahara showed higher growth rates than the developed countries. Growth rates for 1979 were 4.6 and 3.4 per cent respectively.

Enterprises in Member countries are likely to continue to look to growing LDC markets for further openings and this should maintain or increase flows of technology to the Third World.

The existence of such openings does not necessarily ensure that they will be exploited. Financial resources must be available, either through the capacity to save in importing countries, through borrowing, or through the conditions offered to foreign investors so that they will supply capital. The external deficits of some main industrialising countries coupled with the rising cost of energy has led to some pessimism regarding the future financing of development.

ii) *The problem of external deficits*

External deficits and related international debt problems are not of central interest in this report. However, these problems are relevant to technology transfer and its effects on OECD economies and must be considered briefly. Of direct relevance are:

— the effects of balance of payments constraints on technology transfer itself, including exports to developing countries of machinery and equipment and payments for technical and commercial services;
— the effects on OECD imports of manufactured goods from developing countries.

First, the distribution of capital goods and equipment exports—with about 40% of total exports going to developing countries and a large proportion of total international engineering and construction activities in developing countries—makes OECD exporters of machinery, equipment, and engineering services very vulnerable to economic downturns induced or aggravated by balance of payments problems. This is particularly so at a time when some OPEC countries have also reduced their rapid modernisation.

Second, as balance of payments problems mount, pressures will increase for developing countries to export manufactured goods, and construction and other services, so that they can cover deficits. External deficits also makes it more difficult to use devaluation as a tool for increasing exports of goods and services [16]. The time that the developing economy spends in the pit of the J-curve should be as short as possible.

Although there is considerable strain on the external positions of non-OPEC developing countries, their combined visible trade deficits and debt-servicing as

Table 1

Developing Countries (excluding OPEC and OECD): Some Balance of Payments Series

Billion current U.S.$

	1972	1973	1974	1975	1976	1977	1978	1979	1980e
Trade[1]: Exports (f.o.b.)	45.8	66.5	95.7	96.0	113.0	134.6	152.7	196.1	243.2
Imports (c.i.f.)	57.7	78.9	129.3	139.8	143.7	160.2	191.5	237.5	310.1
Balance of trade	−11.9	−12.5	−33.6	−43.8	−30.7	−25.6	−38.8	−41.4	−66.9
As % of exports	26	19	35	46	27	19	25	21	28
Petroleum[2]: Total imports	6.1	9.2	26.2	27.8	33.4	36.6	41.3	61.3	(80)
Net imports	2.2	3.6	12.4	10.8	13.3	14.9	14.5	17.3	24.9
Exports of manufactures to OECD[3]	11.2	17.6	23.3	22.6	31.3	37.1	48.8	61.6	76.8
Capital goods imports from OECD[4]	17.1	22.8	33.2	42.1	41.9	45.7	55.1	67.2	77.7
Debt service[5]	9.3	11.8	15.1	17.8	21.9	26.6	37.2	47.1	56.3
As % of exports	20	18	16	19	19	20	24	24	23
Reserves[6]	21.2	29.0	31.2	30.0	41.4	53.0	68.0	78.7	80.3
Months of imports covered by reserves	4.4	4.4	2.9	2.6	3.5	3.9	4.2	3.9	3.1

e Estimates.
1 IMF, International Financial Statistics.
2 U.N. sources, partly estimated by Secretariat. Netherlands Antilles, Singapore, Trinidad and Tobago are included.
3 OECD, *Trade by Commodities*, SITC 5+6+7+8—68; including Yugoslavia and China.
4 OECD, *Trade by Commodities*.
5 *Development Co-operation, op. cit.*, and World Bank, *Annual Report*, 1980.
6 IMF. Gold valued at SDR 35 per ounce. Reserves at end of period. For 1980, end-October.

76

a proportion of exports were marginally better in 1978-1980 than they were during the 1973-1975 period [17] (see Table 1).

The question mark hangs over the near and medium term future. Some of the higher-income industrialising countries with few or no oil resources have the greatest external deficits, have been the major borrowers from international capital markets and have continued borrowing through 1980—although at a reduced rate. There have been suggestions that banks re-cycling the surpluses of OPEC countries may face problems in continuing this process effectively, there are moves to increase controls over international financial flows, and some OPEC countries are seeking to diversify their short-term flows in the international banking system. This means that new borrowing to finance industrial investment, to cover external deficits or to re-finance debt may become difficult for countries that have large deficits and debt burdens in comparison with export receipts.

These generalisations cover a wide range of different situations. An important factor in short term movements in external positions remains petroleum prices. But some non-OPEC developing countries are significant producers of petroleum and petroleum products: they range from being net exporters of oil (Egypt, Malaysia, Mexico), through producers but net importers (Argentina, which is nearly in balance, Brazil is a minor producer), to being totally reliant on external supplies (the four Far East industrialising countries).

Projections to 1985 and 1990 suggest that the situation for non-OPEC countries will improve somewhat, and net *quantities* imported will decline through the forecast period [18]. However, the more reliant a country is on external petroleum supplies, the greater are deficits on balance of payments current account likely to be. This is a particular problem for developing countries as they usually experienced current account deficits even before the added oil bills.

Individual developing countries: Exporters of manufactures

Turning to the exporters of manufactures, there are large differences between them. For example, Argentina and Mexico have no real or potential constraints on trade balance of payments that will magnify their borrowing or debt servicing problems.

Brazil has large commodity exports which depend on a different dynamic cycle, but the financing of external deficits and the debt problem are important constraints. However, a high proportion of the very large debt position is reasonably long-term and capital inflow to finance development has continued strongly.

The Far Eastern exporters are in different positions. Taiwan has consistently shown a surplus on visible trade (and current account) in recent years, and has not borrowed heavily on international capital markets. This offsets the early maturity of a large proportion of its debt and development borrowing should continue. Hong-Kong and Singapore are facing low debt servicing problems, but deficits on current account [19]. Their orientation of exports towards labour-intensive rather than energy-intensive production (except for petroleum refining and petrochemical projects in Singapore), and their role as off-shore banking centres with very large capital inflows, probably eases the constraints imposed by the external debt/financing/oil import problem. Korea faces problems in this regard, with large current account deficits, moderately high debt with a relatively large proportion maturing within the next few years, and a reduced economic growth rate.

OPEC

The financing problems of OPEC countries are not a major constraint, particularly following the trimming of some of the more ambitious industrialisation programmes of OPEC countries with high absorption capacities and large populations. Management of financing may be of more significance than financing itself.

Poor countries

For the poorest developing countries, the oil import, external deficit and debt problems are the most serious. They have few manufactured imports to reduce and few non-traditional goods to export. Even though aid and financial concessions come on the easiest of terms to these countries, for many of them there seem to be few alternatives and the outlook is poor. Proposals by the IMF, World Bank, OPEC, and others to increase graduated balance of payments financing and oil surplus recycling will be of assistance to the poorest countries.

*
**

To summarise, barring accidents, the more industrialised developing countries with good prospects should continue to be able to tap the commercial international capital markets. This should help to keep their economies financed without them having to resort to excessively deflationary balancing of their current accounts in the short term and, in turn, flows of technology to them should continue.

c) LEGAL FACTORS

These factors are usually secondary, but they may have side effects in directing flows of technology. A country's legislation may impose heavy obligations on a supplier of technology, and such obstacles to the creation of a viable contractual relationship may limit flows of technology.

So far, the national legislation of LDCs has in general been flexible enough in application to prevent such situations arising, and it has usually been drafted without outright prohibition of certain kinds of contract (even if they may be regarded as incompatible with national development targets). However, the situation may be different in the future because national legislation is introducing a new element. This is the arbitrary intervention by competent national authorities to decide *a priori* or *a posteriori* whether a contract is valid. It is clear that a restrictive attitude on the part of the authorities might have unfavourable effects on the flow of technology to that country, particularly if the potential and size of the country's market are not important in the view of firms exporting technology.

Consequently, enterprises providing technology will be obliged to take account of factors not expressly connected with their own commercial strategy. Moreover, technology transfer usually involves a partial loss of ownership in that the right of exploitation of protected technology is usually sold either to the licensee or to the local subsidiary. The result of these two circumstances is that only enterprises with adequate financial backing are likely to take the risk. Thus, unless the legal framework is changed, SMEs will have more difficulty in gaining access to markets in such developing countries by transferring technology.

78

C. INTENSIFICATION OF COMPETITION

The foregoing analysis suggests that in future the technological protection which many industrial activities in Member countries have enjoyed may be considerably reduced. However, it is difficult to distinguish at aggregate level between effects that may arise from the restructuring of world production that is organised by TNEs and for which negative effects may be limited (at least within the firm), and effects that may arise from the increasingly dynamic autonomous growth of enterprises in industrialising countries. Direct competition from the latter enterprises may be extensive, particularly when production comes from modern plants employing cheaper labour and where there are not the social and industrial overheads that are associated with long-established industrial activities [20].

On the other hand, it is clear that the industrialisation process brings increases in cost structures. In principle, conditions of competition will converge in the long run. Furthermore, as has already been the case in Brazil and S. Korea, rapid growth may build up opposing tensions which may take the form of inflation or other dislocations. These may lessen competitivity unless countered by successive devaluations and a variety of economic and social counter-measures. However, this equalisation process is a long-term one.

Keeping these qualifications in mind, some aspects of competition during the 1980s are outlined below.

a) OUTLOOK FOR THE EIGHTIES

It has been suggested that in a non-protectionist situation, the pressure of competition on Member countries' industries should keep increasing up to 1985. This may lead to accelerated obsolescence of the lower levels of industrial skills and to an even sharper reduction in jobs in industries that declined during the last decade. OECD countries as a group should be able to bear most of this pressure, but sharp reductions are likely in OECD's trade surplus in manufactured products. The ratio of exports to imports may fall from 4.3 in 1976 to 2.3 in 1986, a minimum level to maintain a measure of balance in employment (see Chapter III, ref. [11]).

Using a different approach, these trends have been confirmed to 1990 in analytical work prepared for this report. *All* of the 2-digit ISIC divisions will face increasing pressure from developing countries, if only because of their policies to develop domestic industries (see Table 2, column D). At a finer level of disaggregation, only the major groups of machinery manufacture will not face these pressures. For the machinery industries, both product and production characteristics provide a natural protection (see columns A and B, Table 2). But, for other industrial activities there is a risk that competitive pressures will become more significant and that these industries will require active government policy measures to help face such pressures.

In other words, the trends which emerge in the first half of the Eighties are likely to be reinforced in the second half. There are likely to be an increasing number of industrial activities in Member countries which will face the results of import substitution policies in developing countries, or which will face increased competition at home (at least in products requiring relatively less skill for production). As well as industries that have traditionally been the object of adjustment policies—textiles, clothing, leather and footwear—such industries as electrical equipment, optical, clock and watch-making, and petrochemicals, steel and aluminium are also likely to face increased competition.

Table 2
Sensitivity of Industrial Branches to Transfer of Technology to Developing Countries

Division	Industries	A	B	C	D	E	F
31	Manufacture of Food, Beverages, Tobacco	+	—	+	+	—	—
32	Textile, Wearing Apparel, Leather Industries	+	+	+	+	+	+
33	Manufacture of Wood/Wood Products, Furniture	+	+	—	Ø	—	—
34	Manufacture of Paper/Paper Products, Printing and Publishing	+	—	—	Ø	—	—
35	Manufacture of Chemicals and of Chemical, Petroleum, Coal, Rubber and Plastic Products	+	—	Ø	+	Ø	—
36	Manufacture of Non-Metallic Mineral Products	+	Ø	—	Ø	—	—
37	Basic Metal Industries	+	—	+	+	+	+
38	Manufacture of Fabricated Metal Products, Machinery, Equipment	—	—	Ø	Ø	+	Ø
39	Other Manufacturing Industries (jewellery, musical instruments, sporting goods)	+	+	+	Ø	—	—

Legend: + important   Ø significant   — unimportant.
With respect to:
A: Characteristics of product technology
B: Characteristics of production technology
C: Market characteristics
D: Industrialisation strategies of industrialising countries towards import substitution
E: Industrialisation strategies of industrialising countries towards export orientation
F: Structural effects within OECD countries

However, even this scenario for the next ten years may still be somewhat optimistic when it is applied to all OECD countries since Germany was chosen as a model to illustrate possible trends. In fact, Germany appeared to be one of the OECD countries that was best equipped to traverse the 1980s in favourable conditions [21]. Thus it is not certain that this scenario can be applied to all Member countries, particularly if there are not energetic policies to change national conditions.

However, it should be remembered that rising income levels and increasing sophistication of demand in developing countries provides opportunities for industries in OECD countries. How they adapt to new opportunities and challenges is the key to their long term prosperity.

b) DIFFERENCES BETWEEN OECD COUNTRIES

As has been discussed above, industries and countries in the OECD area do not have the same ability to adapt to the different effects of technology transfer that they will experience. First of all, only a few countries supply most of the technology and capital goods that go to industrialising countries. These include the countries that have always been major suppliers—the United States, Germany and the United Kingdom and, more recently, Japan and France.

(There is, of course, less difference between OECD countries if the size of their domestic economies are taken into account—see Chapter II, Table 2.) In countries where domestic producers have participated in exporting capital goods and related services to developing countries there are not only direct positive effects, but there may be more opportunities to switch production in favour of capital goods. Moreover, capital goods have continued to increase as a proportion of international trade (see Graph 4), and, so far, these goods have not been dramatically effected by import substitution policies.

Furthermore, all Member countries did not experience the same favourable changes in their industrial structures in the period of high growth up to 1973-1974. Thus their capacities to face new challenges are distributed unevenly. For example, as shown in Table 9, Chapter III, European countries as a group lost part of their shares of U.S. import markets to developing countries (and Japan) in the period 1973-1978. The EEC have recently published a detailed study that looks at this problem and at changes in industrial structures in Europe since 1973 [22].

The study distinguished between categories of activity according to their content of skilled labour and/or capital, and changes in trade structures were summarised in export specialisation indices and in import dependence indices*.

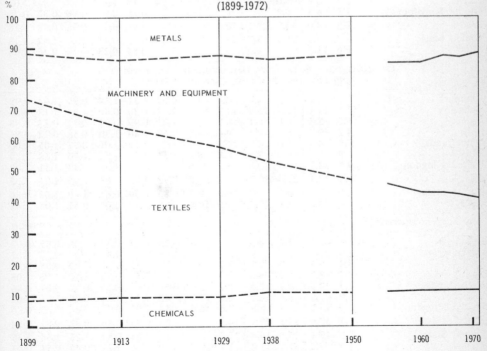

Graphic 4

STRUCTURE OF EXPORTS OF MANUFACTURED PRODUCTS
FROM MAIN INDUSTRIALIZED COUNTRIES
(1899-1972)

Source: A. Maizels until 1950; UN for subsequent years. Taken from *Economie et statistique*, February 1978.

---

* Indices are described in detail in Annex IB.

Table 3
Specialization Indices and Indices of Relative Dependence for Products Facing Keen Competition from the NICs on the Basis of their Skilled-Labour and Capital Intensities

	Market shares (%)						Export specialization indices			Indices of relative import dependence		
	1963		1970		1977							
	M	X	M	X	M	X	1963	1970	1977	1963	1970	1977
A. ACTIVITIES WITH VERY LOW SKILLED-LABOUR CONTENT												
Denmark	2.8	1.1	2.6	1.4	2.2	1.4	1.00	1.33	1.39	0.97	1.08	1.04
Germany	14.5	12.0	15.4	13.8	17.0	15.4	0.62	0.73	0.79	1.33	1.23	1.23
France	5.6	9.6	7.0	8.2	9.1	8.8	1.13	1.00	0.97	0.66	0.79	0.91
Italy	3.9	9.3	3.7	11.1	3.6	12.0	1.60	1.64	1.69	0.54	0.67	0.72
Netherlands	7.6	4.8	7.6	4.8	7.5	4.6	1.19	1.16	1.05	1.01	1.13	1.15
BLEU	6.4	6.9	5.8	7.1	7.6	7.2	1.29	1.27	1.34	1.03	1.06	1.20
United Kingdom	11.1	10.7	10.2	10.0	11.1	10.7	0.78	1.03	1.25	1.38	1.35	1.25
EEC[1]	21.5	29.8	21.1	27.0	26.1	27.4	0.86	0.92	0.92	1.15	1.22	1.35
United States	23.4	14.8	22.8	8.9	18.1	8.9	0.70	0.50	0.60	1.58	1.20	0.97
Japan	1.2	12.0	5.8	12.7	3.9	10.3	1.64	1.15	0.71	0.37	0.80	1.19
B. ACTIVITIES WITH VERY LOW CAPITAL CONTENT												
Denmark	2.5	2.1	2.4	2.4	2.0	2.2	1.92	2.19	2.10	0.87	0.97	0.94
Germany	16.0	11.5	18.1	13.1	20.5	16.9	0.59	0.69	0.87	1.47	1.46	1.48
France	6.1	13.6	6.7	10.6	8.5	11.6	1.60	1.30	1.27	0.72	0.76	0.86
Italy	2.7	18.7	2.2	22.1	1.9	23.8	3.23	3.24	3.37	0.37	0.39	0.38
Netherlands	8.9	4.3	9.4	4.4	9.2	4.0	1.05	1.06	0.92	1.19	1.40	1.41
BLEU	5.3	6.6	5.0	6.6	6.5	6.3	1.24	1.18	1.17	0.84	0.91	1.02
United Kingdom	11.3	8.3	6.2	7.3	6.7	8.0	0.61	0.75	0.93	1.40	0.82	0.75
EEC[1]	18.2	34.0	14.2	28.1	22.7	28.3	0.99	0.96	0.95	0.98	0.82	1.18
United States	23.7	9.5	26.9	5.7	21.2	6.1	0.45	0.32	0.41	1.61	1.42	1.13
Japan	0.6	11.5	1.7	9.5	3.5	3.3	1.58	0.85	0.23	0.18	0.46	1.06
C. ACTIVITIES WITH VERY LOW SKILLED-LABOUR CONTENT AND LOW OR VERY LOW CAPITAL CONTENT												
Denmark	2.7	1.1	2.5	1.4	2.1	1.4	0.97	1.31	1.34	0.93	1.04	0.99
Germany	13.5	14.1	13.9	15.9	14.7	15.6	0.72	0.84	0.80	1.24	1.12	1.06
France	6.0	8.8	6.8	8.1	8.7	8.6	1.03	0.99	0.94	0.71	0.77	0.88
Italy	4.2	9.2	4.0	9.5	4.4	9.2	1.59	1.40	1.30	0.58	0.72	0.86
Netherlands	7.3	4.7	7.0	4.9	6.6	4.6	1.15	1.19	1.06	0.97	1.05	1.00
BLEU	7.9	7.0	6.5	7.5	8.8	8.2	1.31	1.34	1.54	1.26	1.18	1.39
United Kingdom	9.1	12.7	11.4	13.8	13.2	13.6	0.92	1.31	1.58	1.13	1.51	1.49
EEC[1]	17.7	32.1	21.0	30.7	26.1	30.8	0.93	1.05	1.03	0.95	1.21	1.35
United States	20.7	17.5	20.5	8.9	16.0	9.0	0.83	0.50	0.61	1.40	1.08	0.86
Japan	1.7	13.0	3.9	16.4	4.6	14.8	1.78	1.48	1.02	0.51	1.05	1.41
D. ACTIVITIES WITH HIGH CAPITAL CONTENT AND LOW OR VERY LOW SKILLED-LABOUR CONTENT												
Denmark	3.1	0.3	2.4	0.3	2.0	0.3	0.25	0.25	0.32	1.09	0.99	0.92
Germany	11.0	20.0	12.0	18.9	12.1	19.5	1.03	1.00	1.00	1.01	0.97	0.87
France	8.4	9.7	8.3	9.1	9.3	9.9	1.14	1.12	1.08	0.99	0.94	0.93
Italy	8.2	3.7	5.9	4.6	5.3	5.5	0.65	0.67	0.77	1.13	1.06	1.05
Netherlands	6.9	2.8	5.9	2.5	5.7	2.6	0.69	0.60	0.59	0.92	0.87	0.86
BLEU	6.0	7.9	5.6	8.6	6.5	7.2	1.48	1.54	1.34	0.96	1.03	1.03
United Kingdom	7.0	15.6	5.5	8.9	7.6	6.6	1.14	0.92	0.77	0.86	0.73	0.86
EEC[1]	17.1	35.6	14.1	27.4	14.3	25.6	1.03	0.94	0.86	0.92	0.81	0.74
United States	18.9	17.1	25.5	14.4	25.3	12.2	0.81	0.81	0.81	1.28	1.34	1.35
Japan	1.5	7.2	1.9	11.2	1.4	17.6	0.99	1.01	1.21	0.45	0.51	0.43

1 Extra-Community trade (excluding Ireland).
  M: imports.
  X: exports.
Source: [22].

These indices summarise the main trends in trade (and industrial development) in the major OECD economies and show to what extent there has been specialisation in exports of high-technology products, and in imports of simpler products, particularly from industrialising countries.

In Table 3 it can be seen that EEC countries export products which are vulnerable to competition from the newly industrialising countries to a greater extent that do the United States or Japan. Although these exports are concentrated on intra-Community trade rather than on extra-Community trade, it is clear that European countries as a group seem more likely to face increased trade competition with industrialising countries. There are of course differences between Community members. For example, Germany is performing similarly to the United States and Japan, while the United Kingdom is increasingly exporting products that are labour intensive.

Several aspects of this situation require examination. First, it is difficult to imagine OECD countries sustaining or re-attaining growth without "interdependence with the LDCs". This suggests that OECD countries should retain relatively open markets for imports from industrialising countries. Furthermore, it seems essential (as high growth scenarios such as that in Interfutures have assumed [23]) that Member countries' economic structures converge in competitive abilities, or at least do not diverge more than they currently do. If divergence in general competitive abilities occurs, then some countries are likely to experience further pressure from industrialising countries in labour-intensive products and competition from other countries in specialised high-technology products. Are active technology policies one possible way of avoiding such a divergence in competitive abilities?

It has been pointed out that three countries are major suppliers of capital goods—the United States, Japan, and Germany. Furthermore, these three countries occupy leading positions in electronic developments which will play a vital part in the worldwide reorganisation and restructuring of industrial activities [24]. Because of their leads in developing technology these countries should

---

"Fundamental" Products

The new competition from developing countries will not only compel the most advanced countries to make efforts at restructuring or conversion in the most traditional sectors or industries. There will be a growing tendency for the most industrialised countries to retain the sectors of activity considered the most productive. In this new phase of competition between advanced countries, control of the sectors in the forefront of technical progress is a key factor in the strength of productive systems (cf. Table 4, A, B and C).

For this reason, the OECD foreign trade products with a more or less high-skilled labour content have been reclassified into three specialised categories:

— a "technological control" category, grouping together the activities which are undergoing the greatest changes and which are the pacesetters in technical progress: activities linked to research and development, computers, telecommunications, machine tools;
— an "intermediate-goods" category: goods used in all the major production processes and hence conditioning the functioning of the productive apparatus;
— a "principal capital goods" category: machinery, electrical equipment, and engines, but excluding transport equipment that is not directly productive.

Source: [22].

83

Table 4

Changes in Market Shares, Specialization Indices and Dependence Indices, 1963-1977

	Export market shares (%)			Export specialization indices			Indices of relative import dependence		
	1963	1970	1977	1963	1970	1977	1963	1970	1977
TOTAL FOR FUNDAMENTAL PRODUCTS (SUB-TABLES A+B+C)									
Denmark	1.2	1.1	1.1	0.62	0.73	0.77	1.34	1.34	1.31
Germany	22.0	20.6	21.3	1.46	1.30	1.26	0.85	0.98	1.06
France	8.0	8.2	9.2	0.97	1.01	1.02	1.15	1.21	1.18
Italy	4.7	6.0	6.8	0.90	0.99	1.06	1.30	1.00	0.96
Netherlands	4.0	4.3	4.6	0.78	0.79	0.74	1.42	1.20	1.13
BLEU	5.9	5.9	5.0	1.18	1.10	0.93	1.06	0.96	0.97
United Kingdom	13.3	9.2	7.9	1.13	1.04	0.96	0.54	0.76	1.02
EEC[1]	35.4	29.9	32.3	1.21	1.15	1.19	0.60	0.71	0.75
United States	22.1	18.6	15.3	0.93	0.94	0.90	0.65	0.84	0.88
Japan	7.0	12.7	15.9	1.26	1.42	1.38	0.61	0.47	0.31
A. PRODUCTS PROVIDING TECHNOLOGICAL CONTROL									
Denmark	0.9	0.9	0.8	0.45	0.61	0.55	1.12	1.09	0.97
Germany	21.6	19.7	20.2	1.43	1.24	1.19	0.62	0.91	1.01
France	6.0	7.1	7.5	0.73	0.88	0.83	1.08	1.07	0.95
Italy	4.2	6.0	4.8	0.80	0.99	0.73	1.40	0.90	0.93
Netherlands	6.7	5.3	5.1	1.32	0.97	0.81	1.98	1.27	1.15
BLEU	3.0	3.2	3.4	0.59	0.59	0.63	0.99	0.77	0.80
United Kingdom	12.3	8.5	7.3	1.05	0.96	0.89	0.61	0.72	1.06
EEC[1]	35.3	29.7	30.5	1.20	1.14	1.12	0.72	0.75	0.93
United States	27.3	18.3	16.1	1.15	0.93	0.95	0.67	1.18	1.23
Japan	8.2	18.6	23.7	1.47	2.08	2.04	0.86	0.57	0.32
B. PRINCIPAL CAPITAL GOODS									
Denmark	1.9	1.6	1.5	0.97	1.07	1.04	1.24	1.26	1.39
Germany	23.6	21.9	22.6	1.56	1.39	1.33	0.76	0.88	0.92
France	6.6	7.2	8.8	0.80	0.89	0.98	1.15	1.23	1.16
Italy	5.6	6.9	6.8	1.08	1.13	1.04	1.29	0.96	0.86
Netherlands	1.8	3.3	3.5	0.55	0.61	0.56	1.36	1.16	1.14
BLEU	2.2	2.4	2.5	0.44	0.45	0.47	1.17	1.00	0.94
United Kingdom	14.0	10.1	9.0	1.20	1.14	1.09	0.56	0.96	1.19
EEC[1]	35.3	31.1	35.7	1.20	1.20	1.32	0.64	0.76	0.79
United States	28.4	26.4	21.6	1.20	1.34	1.28	0.36	0.58	0.66
Japan	3.1	7.1	10.5	0.56	0.79	0.91	0.85	0.62	0.42
C. PRINCIPAL INTERMEDIATE GOODS									
Denmark	0.7	0.9	0.9	0.37	0.46	0.60	1.50	1.51	1.41
Germany	20.7	19.8	20.5	1.37	1.25	1.21	1.00	1.09	1.18
France	10.1	9.5	10.4	1.22	1.17	1.15	1.18	1.26	1.31
Italy	4.1	5.2	8.0	0.79	0.85	1.23	1.28	1.07	1.06
Netherlands	3.9	4.8	5.5	0.76	0.88	0.88	1.25	1.21	1.11
BLEU	10.0	10.3	8.4	2.10	1.93	1.55	1.01	1.00	1.07
United Kingdom	13.0	8.7	7.1	1.11	0.98	0.86	0.50	0.63	0.87
EEC[1]	35.5	28.8	29.8	1.21	1.11	1.10	0.53	0.64	0.67
United States	14.1	11.6	8.4	0.60	0.59	0.50	0.87	0.92	0.88
Japan	10.0	15.3	17.7	1.79	1.72	1.53	0.33	0.31	0.22

1 Extra-Community trade (excluding Ireland).
Source: [22].

84

be able to play a vital part in transferring technology and also be able to reorganise industrial activities that are affected by transfers. The situation in other Member countries seems less satisfactory, particularly if they depend on markets that are being eroded by exports or import-substitution from industrialising countries. After all, it is not necessarily the country transferring technology which will be most affected by it.

To further amplify this point, the EEC study discussed above reclassified some of the "fundamental products" in which there are high rates of technical change and heavy use of skilled labour in production into a category where "technological control" was likely to be high (see description in box). In 1977 the United States, Germany and Japan between them accounted for 60 per cent of exports of goods which confer "technological control". Countries such as France were gradually improving their position, but for others such as the United Kingdom, this was deteriorating (see Table 4). It has been stressed that technological leads are not static. However, it may be necessary for governments to intervene in the present economic situation to avoid trends that run counter to the cohesion that has been demonstrated between Member countries.

Chapter V

GENERAL POLICY ISSUES

It is clear that the assessment of feedback effects of technology transfers to developing countries is not completely straightforward. For one thing, with the information available it has not been possible to identify any effects that could purely and simply be attributed to transfers of technology as they are partly attributable to other factors. For another, the importance and growth of technology transfer are clearly not temporary phenomena related to balance-of-payments disequilibria in OECD countries. Technology transfer is the result of complex processes which must be treated as comprehensively as possible in order to devise appropriate policies. In the course of our work, it was possible to identify and explain only some aspects of these processes.

For those feedback effects of technology transfer to LDCs that have been identified, it is clear that while they do raise serious problems in some industries, the effects are usually marginal in relation to the overall macro-economic problems facing Member countries, such as unemployment, inflation, and rising energy prices. The contribution of feedback effects to macro-economic problems such as unemployment is also marginal, although locally they may considerably aggravate an already difficult situation.

The identified feedback effects do not therefore seem to require technology policy measures for the *short term*. They appear rather to call for active positive adjustment measures—including regional, employment, and trade policies [1]. In the *medium* and *long term,* however, Member countries' prospects are far more uncertain, suggesting that there is a need to introduce suitable remedial policies now. It is towards this more distant horizon, which constitutes the time frame for most technology policy, that we must turn our attention.

Although the economic crisis has drawn attention to technology transfers, they have been a continuing feature of the world economy and are signs of major changes that have been taking place in industrial structures. In other words, technology transfer to the developing countries acts as an indicator of these changes. While transfers create new situations and may raise questions regarding the ability of some industries *in some OECD countries* to meet the resulting new competition, transfers are also a response to technical, economic and social changes within OECD countries. Transfers are part of the process of adaptation to new conditions and current prospects. They are also the cause of pressures to adapt in economies that are adversely affected by transfers without having necessarily received any of the immediate benefits. Other problems such as the rising cost of energy and raw materials also suggest that we have entered a period of accelerating structural change.

We are consequently faced with an extremely complex situation. It cannot be said to be wholly satisfactory or wholly unsatisfactory, nor can it be attributed solely to changes in North-South relations. The relative positions of members of the world community are changing and those of OECD countries may also become very different. In these circumstances, national policies can only be specific to the situation of each country. At most, we can affirm that co-ordination is more than ever necessary in circumstances where all countries are so closely dependant on both the overall situation and on what each other decides.

We do not therefore intend to propose policy solutions that would be appropriate for all. Instead we shall concentrate on those points that have been identified in the course of our work and that are relevant to most Member countries.

Our comments must be placed in the context outlined at the last meeting of the OECD Council at Ministerial level: that the development of North-South trade is one of the essential means of promoting industrialising economies *and* stimulating the economies of Member countries [2]. First, however, it is important to consider what the alternative of increased protection has to offer. This alternative is attracting increased support as more and more sectors are affected by recession or by keener world competition.

A. CONTROLS ON TECHNOLOGY EXPORT

a) FEEDBACK EFFECTS AND CONTROLS ON EXPORTS

If sectoral problems continue to increase then government may face increasing pressure from all quarters to protect more endangered industries [3]. As well as trade-related pressures there have also been pressures against "social" or "ecological dumping" with the aim of restricting transfers to developing countries which do not, for example, apply laws as strictly as those commonly in force in OECD countries. However, despite the validity of some of these concerns it is doubtful whether attempts at restrictions would really help a great deal.

First, it is practically impossible to control technology transfers. As was the case for the United Kingdom in the nineteenth century, attempts in the past to maintain the technological leadership of a country through the most stringent controls have been unsuccessful. Second, technology transfer is to a certain extent governed by the strategy of the firms in possession of the technology and it is aimed at ensuring their growth or even their survival*. Thus restrictions on transfers may not only jeopardize the economic situation of the firms involved, but also the industries supplying capital goods and services that go with transfers and thus hinder part of the necessary overall adaptation process.

It would be wrong to interpret the rejection of controls as making common cause with firms in a conflict between their micro-economic objectives and macro-economic objectives of government such as full employment. As has already been pointed out, technology transfers have made a major contribution to the survival of industries producing capital goods or intermediates and have thus helped them through the difficult macro-economic situation [4]. However, while the positive effects of transfer are fairly widely felt throughout the economy, the negative effects have been centred on specific sectors and geographical areas, heightening policy problems. This concentration of problems makes it essential to forsee that additional competition in an industrial sector is one possible result of technology transfer. Otherwise, sudden crises may make it difficult for governments to resist pressures from threatened industries.

---

* See Chapter I, Section B.

Although those in favour of controlling transfers remain a minority, it is contended in other quarters that certain aspects of technology transfer to LDCs may need reviewing. This contention is based on observations concerning the costs of technology development and public aid to industrial R&D.

It has been argued by some observers that the cost of research is rising and that it is taking longer to recover these costs [5]. If this is so, the price obtained for technology transferred may be insufficient to help finance technology renewal. This is difficult to clarify in the absence of sufficient reliable data. However, this argument is the converse of that put forward by developing countries, who have argued that the price of technology is too high. Both arguments have been justified by the same sort of theoretical reasoning. However, in principle the price is neither too low or too high, it is simply the price accepted by both parties to the transfer, and in principle this must represent an acceptable compromise between the objectives of each party. If the party selling the technology does not obtain a price "high enough" to help it to finance renewal of its technology, it is because the technology can be obtained from other sources and this potential competition reduces the bargaining power of the supplier [6]. Nontheless, the renewal of technology is a serious issue which we will examine below.

Technology transfer to developing countries also raises a further financial problem: compensation of the public share in research funding. Industrial research receives a significant amount of state aid in most OECD countries, even if only through tax exemptions to stimulate research activity. If technology trade is a two-way process between countries where financial aid provisions are similar, then a degree of compensation may occur.

This obviously does not apply to one-way technological trade to developing countries. Here it can be said that there is some (modest) transfer of resources to developing countries, or to the technology-holder, or to both, depending on the balance of bargaining power. This situation is difficult to resolve in practical terms and does not readily lend itself to policy measures.

In short, given that "reactive policies" of controls on technology exports or technology prices appear to be ill-suited to the problems, there is one clear solution for OECD economies: prepare for progressively increased trade in manufactured products with developing countries in the framework of "positive" policies (of the sort approved by the OECD Council [1]) aimed at preparing enterprises and OECD economies for the future. This implies that overall adaptation strategies be devised to improve efficiency and resource allocation.

B.   ADAPTATION STRATEGIES

As we have been careful to point out several times in this report, the problems raised by technology transfers to developing countries and their medium- and long-term implications are *not self-contained*. They cannot be dissociated from other related or causal processes.

Technology transfers cannot be dealt with in isolation; they are part of major changes taking place in world industrial structures and in the related competitivity of Member countries. Similarly, North-South relations cannot be isolated; all economic links must be taken into account, including those betwen OECD countries.

Thus it is practically impossible to formulate a specific policy response for transfers in isolation. Responses to the changes causing and coming from transfers must be considered. More precisely, it is necessary to formulate government strategies aimed at extensive development of the capacities for innovation and technological renewal.

a) THE OVERALL FRAMEWORK

The need for a comprehensive framework of analysis logically follows from the above. The wider view is required to appreciate the countercyclical role played by technology transfers and related sales of capital and intermediate goods to developing countries.

In some industries feedback problems must be dealt with by flexible and positive adjustment policies, but such policies for the capital goods industries have in general not been required. Exports have been a spontaneous reaction of firms to relatively greater opportunities in developing countries during the downturn in OECD countries. But these exports may also contribute to increases in external deficits and international debt of some developing countries. Moreover, during a period when there has been a somewhat diminishing role of direct investment in total financial flows, capital goods exporters have been supported by the extension of various sorts of credit facilities to developing countries.

Industrializing countries have used these credits to help sustain high growth rates of imports of equipment and high growth rates of industrial development. But because capital goods and engineering industries in OECD countries export an appreciable share of their output to developing countries (about 20% of output in some countries and some branches) they are vulnerable to slowdowns that may be linked to balance of payments deficits for example. These external deficits can be aggravated by the application of restrictive trade policies to the manufactured exports of industrialising countries [7]. It is contradictory to encourage industrialization by supplying equipment and credit and then to create obstacles to repayment by applying trade restrictions when new competition threatens lagging industrial sectors [8]. The necessity of taking the comprehensive view is quite clear.

This is also obvious for technology transfers that are used to circumvent legislation judged to be over-restrictive (for example in environmental or social areas). Clearly, before embarking on the dead-end solution of imposing systematic controls, the reasons why firms attempt to avoid compliance need to be investigated. This can only be done with an approach which includes technological and other aspects.

In other words, adaptation strategies should take account of all explanatory factors so that policy measures may be identified early. These can then help the process of technology renewal to meet increasing pressures from new competitors.

b) TECHNOLOGICAL RENEWAL

The objective of such strategies should clearly be a sustained effort to support the renewal of industrial technology in Member countries. This clearly requires support for industrial innovation. The reasons are summed up simply and succintly by P. Krugman as follows: "Wages will be higher in (the) North, even if labor in the two countries is equally productive in comparable occupations (owing to transfers), because of North's monopoly position in new goods (which it is putting on the market)... a slowing of innovation or an acceleration of technology transfer narrows the wage differential and may even lead to an absolute decline in living standard of workers in (the) North" [9].

At first sight this seems to clash with the traditional economic theory that through direct effects (capital goods and often intermediate goods exports) and

90

induced effects (changes in prices, incomes, and income distribution) technology transfer sets off a whole set of compensatory mechanisms leading eventually to a satisfactory new equilibrium for both parties.

In fact the theories are not necessary conflicting. The first is explicitly based on the assumption that if the North is to retain its comparative advantages its' innovatory capacity must be maintained at a high level: "this monopoly (of the North for the production of new products) is continually eroded by technological borrowing (by the South) and must be maintained by constant innovation of new products. Like Alice and the Red Queen, *the developed region must keep running to stay in the same place*" [10]. The neo-classical theory presupposes that this ability is maintained provided market freedom is not impeded in any way.

In other words, if in reality we are to obtain the satisfactory results envisaged in the traditional theoretical scheme then the rate of renewal of technology held by the North must offset the acceleraion of technological obsolescence coming from transfers to the South.

However, before proposing a government adaptation strategy it is necessary to know whether the productive systems of OECD countries have a satisfactory technological capacity for renewing or replacing the combination of production factors that has become obsolete. If this is so, can economic mechanisms spontaneously mobilise the necessary capacities or is government stimulation required?

Naturally, answers are bound to vary between countries and according to the time horizon envisaged.

c) TECHNOLOGICAL DIFFERENCES BETWEEN OECD COUNTRIES

After considering technology that is already available or being developed, it is clear that the OECD area is capable of substantially renewing or replacing its productive system:

   i)   In the medium term (1980s) and *for the best placed Member countries,* the technological possibilities for meeting competition seem satisfactory. However, although both process and product innovations should be potentially competitive they may not necessarily lead to increased domestic capacity and the creation of new jobs that will help counter-act unemployment (although in the long-run, improvements in efficiency should release resources which can be used in new activities and the creation of jobs). Unemployment is a major problem which seems likely to increase in the near future, when we shall see the accumulated effects of population trends, rationalisation measures and innovations derived from advances in electronics (for example in data communications, robotics, office computer systems), and competition from newly industrialising countries—particularly in traditional industries.

   ii) *In the long term* however, there should be no grounds for pessimism. Some experts have claimed that the technology explosion is likely to be even greater in the next 30 years than in the past [11] since present resources in laboratories are probably considerably greater than in 1945 [12].

Added to this, OECD countries have never before had such a well-trained workforce at their disposal, given that new entrants to the labour market have benefited from the technical and scientific education of the last 20 years.

However, this technological potential is distributed unevenly between OECD countries and national differences in technology-based competitive capabilities may disturb the cohesiveness of the OECD grouping. But a degree of cohesiveness between OECD countries based on competitive equality and complementarity is essential if international policy objectives such as continued trade liberalization are to be achieved. In other words, differences between the scientific and technological potential of OECD countries may help increase tensions between them because of the importance of S&T resources in determining international competitiveness.

Indeed, although some OECD countries have intensified their industrial research efforts (see Graph 1), others have slackened off or have implicitly counted on efforts being made elsewhere. Thus in spite of some general upward movement in R&D expenditures due to relative increases in France, Germany, Japan and some smaller OECD countries and small relative declines in expenditures in the United States and the United Kingdom, there is still a considerable dispersion between countries and sectors in R&D intensiveness (particularly as measured by the ratio of enterprise-financed R&D expenditure to industrial GDP) [13]. In particular, the R&D effort was often not in line with shares of industrial production (see Table 1).

Table 1

Shares of R&D Financed by Business Enterprises in OECD Countries and Shares of OECD Industrial Production: 1977 (%)

Country	National R&D financed by business enterprises as share of total	Share of total industrial production	Share of total production of manufactured goods
United States	44.3	35.7	34.0
Japan	17.5	15.8	17.0
Germany	13.2	13.0	13.6
United Kingdom	4.9	5.2	4.9
France	6.2	7.7	8.1
Italy	2.0	4.9	5.0
Netherlands	2.3	1.7	1.8
Belgium	1.3	1.4	1.5
Denmark	0.5	0.7	0.8
Ireland	0.1	0.2	0.2
EEC	30.4	34.9	36.0
Sweden	2.0	1.4	1.4
Canada	1.4	3.5	3.0
Switzerland	2.4	0.8	0.9
Australia	0.5	1.9	1.6
Spain	0.3[1]	2.8	3.0
Austria	0.3[2]	1.0	1.0
Finland	0.4	0.6	0.6
Norway	0.4	0.6	0.4
New Zealand	<0.1	n.a.	n.a.
Portugal	<0.1	0.4	0.5
Greece	n.a.	0.4	0.4
Iceland	<0.1	n.a.	n.a.
Total	100	100	100

1 1974.
2 1975.
Source: Data from: OECD, STIU, using current exchange rates and estimates for 1977 calendar year where data is for a different period; OECD, *Indicators of Industrial Activity.*

92

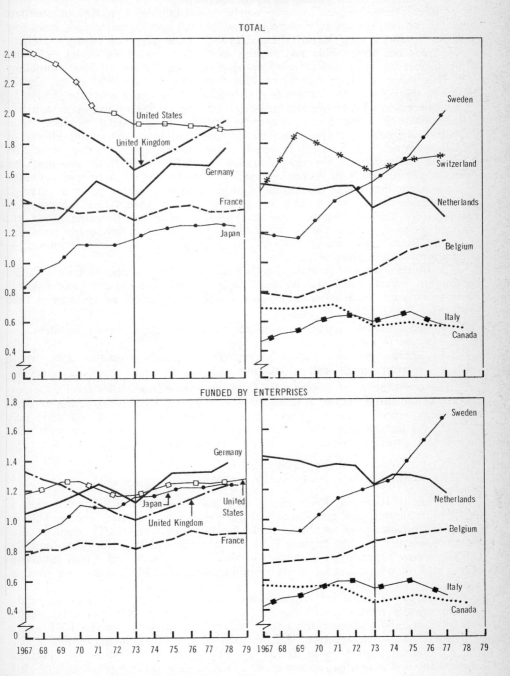

Graphic 1
INDUSTRIAL RESEARCH AND DEVELOPMENT
(as % of domestic product of industries)

TOTAL

FUNDED BY ENTERPRISES

Source : OECD, Science and Technology Indicators Unit.

93

These differences in relative R&D expenditures partly reflect differences in industrial structures but they also reflect firm strategies and self-financing capacity, and in some respects, they suggest once more the vulnerability of some industries in some countries to impending competition [14].

Direct price competition with newly industrialising countries in standard products can be expected to become increasingly difficult for enterprises in various Member countries in a world where exchange rates may not adjust rapidly to visible trade balances. This may require reconsideration of the strategy of being technological followers and catching-up by purchasing the use of new technology.

This being so, it is important that the technological level of all OECD countries should increase; or better still become more equal and complementary *without* necessarily becoming identical or all seeking to develop the same industrial activities at the same time. Otherwise imports of industrial products from industrialising countries may continue to have marginally important effects on OECD countries and be held responsible for many of the changes in relative industrial performance. Certainly there are new patterns of trade emerging that reflect changing levels of technology and a new division of industrial activities. It seems clear that under conditions of more open competition fewer enterprises in Member countries will be able to continue to meet their future technological requirements through intensive or exclusive reliance on licencing when the licenced technology may also be available to enterprises in developing countries. It will be increasingly necessary for enterprises to generate their own technology—largely through intensified R&D efforts [15].

To do this, ways of improving self-financing and investment in industry must be sought. Efforts could also be made by governments to expand basic research on improving materials substitution, and to explore technical alternatives in such areas as:

— commodities, particularly on substitutes and recycling possibilities;
— new forms of energy;
— energy and materials conservation, simplified processes and, where relevant, small scale production.

The convergence of effective R&D efforts (towards a higher level as a percentage of industrial output) is necessary if OECD countries are to retain or build their technological positions. Some observers have already noted that there may be problems for the industrial structures of the OECD area connected with what they see as diverging trends in innovative capabilities in OECD countries [15].

d) THE RENEWAL OF INDUSTRIAL DYNAMISM

Pursuit of increased R&D efforts as a policy objective is not worthwhile if another problem is not considered: whether domestic industries are capable of taking full advantage of increased R&D inputs. The two OECD countries that have consistently had the highest R&D intensity in industry (the U.K. and the U.S.) are now experiencing a decline in their relative shares of world industrial output and trade in industrial goods (some measures of R&D intensity are given in Table 2).

There are a range of explanations including industrial structural trends, relative growth rates, productivity trends, investment in the productive sector and its distribution between the home country and foreign countries [16], and a progressive long-term structural shift towards relative "de-industrialisation".

De-industrialisation as measured by the decline in the share of industrial workers in total active population is now becoming a general phenomenon after starting in the United States and the United Kingdom: the proportion of the

Table 2
Various Measures of R&D Intensity in Industry: 1975

	Expenditure		Manpower		Intensity
	BERD / DPI	Man R&D / Man DPI	BEMP / BELF	Man BEMP / Man LF	
MAJOR PERFORMERS:					
United States	1.93	6.90	1.51	..	
United Kingdom	1.75	4.56	1.09	2.13	
Germany	1.59	3.28	1.02	2.00	
France	1.37	3.40	0.81	1.97	high
Japan	1.19	3.20	0.77	2.17	
MEDIUM PERFORMERS:					
Switzerland	1.69	..	..	..	
Sweden	1.71	3.80	0.90	1.87	
Netherlands	1.47	3.92	0.94	2.37	
Belgium	1.07	2.85	0.70	1.58	
Italy	0.67	1.61	0.27	0.59	
Canada	0.60	1.83	0.38	0.96	
Australia[1]	0.76	..	0.43	0.90	
SMALL PERFORMERS:					medium
Norway	0.81	2.52	0.50	1.23	
Denmark	0.63	1.61	0.42	0.98	
Finland	0.63	1.59	0.37	0.94	
Austria	0.52	..	0.37	0.83	
Ireland	0.43	..	0.15	0.45	
Spain[2]	0.21	..	0.09	0.30	low
Portugal[3]	0.11	..	..	..	

1   1973.
2   1974.
3   1972.

Key to abbreviations:

BERD	=	Business Enterprise R&D (total intramural expenditure from all sources)
DPI	=	Domestic product of industries
Man R&D	=	R&D expenditures of Manufacturing industries
Man DPI	=	DPI of Manufacturing industries
BEMP	=	Business Enterprise R&D Manpower
BELF	=	Total Business Enterprise Labour Force
Man BEMP	=	Total R&D Manpower of Manufacturing industries
Man LF	=	Total Labour Force of Manufacturing industries

Source: [13].

labour force employed in industry in the main industrialised countries has declined steadily in recent years.

Furthermore, with the slowdown in growth and increases in unemployment, and reflecting a trend of opinion in favour of low or no growth, the "post-industrial society" of the kind announced by Colin Clark (1940) and described by J. Fourastié (1949) and D. Bell (1974) again has its proponents — but under changed circumstances: the premise is that the industrial sector tends to decline while the service sector grows. Advanced countries will achieve higher future growth in services which will also provide the exports needed to offset the progressive restructuring of some industrial activities.

Can we be sanguine about these prospects, particularly when we take into account technology transfer and the rapid industrialisation of some developing countries?

So far relative de-industrialisation has been offset by higher industrial productivity: the share of industrial value added in GDP has remained relatively unchanged at constant prices despite relative declines in industrial employment. Further, the shift to service employment has not been smooth or unidirectional. For example, during phases of intensive innovation in the United States since 1948 the decline in industrial employment has slowed, or employment has temporarily increased (Table 3 gives data for key years). Declines in industrial employment do not appear to be irreversible or as smooth as some analyses imply it depends on the vitality and drive of the industrial sector concerned. This vitality is revealed in job-creating innovations which are often linked to the creation of new industrial firms [17]. But in the U.S. and in OECD countries generally the number of new firms being created fell until the mid-1970s, with some signs of a subsequent revival but at lower levels [18]. A number of reasons have been advanced for this decline. They usually concentrate on the accumulation of difficulties faced by potential heads of firms rather than any lack of new ideas [19]. There might also be some disenchantment with industry whose prestige has declined considerably. Furthermore, new industrial activities may face greater risks, such as higher levels of foreign competition, than new service activities tailored to indigenous cultural and social elements.

Table 3
United States: Evolution of Manufacturing and Services Sectors (%)

	1948	1961	1966	1977
Share in value added at 1972 constant prices				
Manufacturing	25.0	22.8	26.0	24.3
Services	58.2	60.3	58.9	62.8
Shares in total employment				
Manufacturing	32.3	27.9	28.6	24.1
Services	54.0	60.0	60.6	65.6

Services sector includes financial and non-commercial activities.
Source: Bureau of Economic Analysis, United States Department of Commerce.

It may thus be argued that difficulties facing new industrial activities may be compensated by growth of service activities and in exports of services. However there are limits to the expansion of commercial service activities. They have grown rapidly in areas such as banking, insurance, soft-ware and data processing which often require high levels of skill and know-how and in which advanced countries still generally retain advantages. But these activities only represent a small part of services. For example, much of the rest of office employment is taken up with routine work that is likely to be increasingly affected by standardisation and automation [20]. Furthermore, there are signs that some service activities can be transferred to "export processing zones" in developing countries and that developing countries will take a larger share of their own and international commercial service industries. For example, some South-East Asian countries are already offering banking, financial and other services which are remarkable for their quality and dynamism.

Furthermore, although service activities have a higher average value added per employee, their rates of productivity increase have been lower (Table 4).

Table 4

Productivity in the United States

Percentage charges per year

	1948-1966	1966-1977
Total economy		
GDP	3.9	2.8
Numbers of wage earners	1.7	1.8
Numbers of hours worked	1.0	1.2
Productivity per hour worked	2.9	1.6
Manufacturing		
Value added	4.2	2.2
Numbers of wage earners	1.1	0.2
Numbers of hours worked	1.2	−0.2
Productivity per hour worked	2.9	2.4
Productivity per head	3.1	2.0
Services		
Value added	4.0	3.4
Numbers of wage earners	2.4	2.5
Numbers of hours worked	1.4	2.0
Productivity per hour worked	2.8	1.4

Source: Chapter III, Ref. [2].

If it continues to be easier to create employment in services than in industry then transfers of technology may be interpreted rather pessimistically. Jobs with higher average productivity growth rates in industry may be replaced by jobs with lower productivity growth rates in services and public employment [21]. In effect, it appears more difficult for industry to underpin a growing service sector if its own productivity growth continues to decline for reasons that are not clear [22] and the relative costs of R&D and change increase. Some observers such as the Industrial Research Institute of Japan have even noted an inverse relation between a country's competitive capacity and the weight of its service sector [23].

It thus appears desirable to maintain a healthy and competitive industrial sector. The solution is more than just increasing technological research and development; it requires the continuing vitality of the whole industrial fabric. The process is circular: if technological renewal of industry requires renewed innovative activity then it is essential that there be a vigorous, vital and progressive industrial climate.

e) COMPREHENSIVE ACTION TO STIMULATE INNOVATION

Technological renewal can only take place if economic conditions are favourable. But the outlook at present is not conducive to taking the risks associated with uncertain innovation. When the inflation rate runs into double figures (12.4 per cent between November 1979 and November 1980 for all OECD countries) the outlook becomes very hazy and the uncertainty and risk associated with innovation becomes even more of a deterrent [24].

Innovation also means investment; but this has been virtually stagnant since the first oil price rise (see Table 5) and the second one may make things even more difficult. What makes the situation all the more disturbing is that an increasing proportion of investment has been taken up by rationalisation,

Table 5
Private Investment Performance in Eight OECD Countries

Country	Average growth of business investment		Share of private machinery and equipment in total private investment[1] (volume)			
	1960-1973	1973-1978	1960	1968	1973	1978
United States	4.9	0.7	36.9	43.8	44.9	48.0
Japan	14.3	0	50.0[2]	51.7[2]	59.7[2]	55.6[2]
Germany	4.2	−0.2	34.7	39.1	42.9	48.6
France	7.2	0.2	43.6	46.1	50.3	52.5
United Kingdom	4.0	3.5	47.4	46.7	51.3	52.3
Italy	4.6	−1.2	38.8	37.6	46.7	48.0
Canada	6.0	2.4	34.1	37.7	40.0	41.3
Sweden	4.1	−2.8	40.6	41.9	46.3	47.2[3]

1 Data not comparable between countries. For France, the United Kingdom, Italy and Sweden, total machinery, transport and other equipment expressed as a percentage of gross fixed capital formation in industries. It is assumed that government investment is in non-equipment items.
2 Japanese figures are on a fiscal year basis.
3 The ratio reached almost 52 per cent in 1977.
Sources: OECD National Accounts: Annual Report on National Income Statistics of Japan, as presented in OECD, *Economic Outlook,* December 1979.

by adaptation to news fuels and by compliance with environmental and safety standards rather than with job-creating innovations [25]. And as can be seen from Table 6, capacity utilisation rates have been reasonably high until very recently, suggesting that it is not overcapacity that might explain the sluggishness of investment.

Obviously, improvements in the general economic outlook should have an immediate effect on firms' propensity to invest and perhaps to innovate. Mansfield is certainly right when he says that the best road to renewed innovation is the one that is founded on improved economic health [26].

But the transformations that have occurred since the beginning of the 1970s, particularly in the energy sector, suggest that even the concept of economic health may need to be redefined: it may no longer be identified with strong economic growth of the type that was experienced in the 1960s.

There is thus a great risk that firms will not innovate and take risks. They may prefer to wait until the business outlook clears. Furthermore, it is not evident that measures being taken to stimulate innovation are suited to the slow and difficult economic situation which confronts us.

Many of these measures to promote innovation were designed to encourage activities in difficult technical fields. They therefore may not have the necessary salutary effects in a situation where acute economic uncertainty is the dominant factor. Thus a comprehensive range of policy measures—economic, fiscal, commercial and industrial as well as scientific and technological—need to be considered if innovative activity is to be encouraged. Furthermore, the compatability of various policy objectives needs to be examined with care if innovation and change are not to face severe handicaps when they are most needed.

f) TRANSFERS OF TECHNOLOGY: SOME SPECIFIC ASPECTS OF POLICY

Areas which require specific mention are the possibilities for reducing technological and industrial scale, the role that small and medium enterprises may play if their participation increases, and the effects of progressive restructuring of world industry on innovation and change in OECD countries.

Table 6
Manufacturing Capacity Utilisation Rates Seasonally Adjusted (%)

	Average 1964-1973	Average 1974-1978	1976	1977	1978	1979	1979 Q3	Q4	1980 Q1	Q2	Q3
United States Federal Reserve Board	85.5	80.5	79.5	82.0	84.4	85.6	85.4	84.4	83.4	77.9	75.6
Japan MITI Index[1]	92.6	84.9	84.5	83.9	86.4	92.8	93.1	94.9	96.5	95.5	91.2
Germany IFO[2]	86.4	80.0	80.2	80.3	81.3	84.7	85.3	84.5	85.9	83.8	81.2
France INSEE[3]	84.8	82.7	82.9	83.4	83.6	81.8	82.3	81.8	82.5	83.0	82.4
United Kingdom CBI[2,4]	45	32	25	32	35	42	49	38	36	30	24
Italy ISCO[5]	78.5	73.2	74.0	72.8	73.1	76.3	75.9	77.6	77.7	76.6	70.8
Canada Statistics Canada	87.0	84.5	82.8	82.2	86.1	84.9	84.8	84.3	83.1	79.4	78.5

1 1973 average=100.
2 First month in period. From 1979 quarterly, see *Main Economic Indicators*.
3 March, June and October.
4 Percentage of firms at full capacity.
5 Last month in period; average covers 1969-1973; total industry.
Source: OECD *Economic Outlook*, December, 1979 and *Main Economic Indicators*, 1980.

i) *Technological and industrial scale*

From the point of view of a phased adaptation of industrial structures some aspects of scale and appropriateness of technology deserve re-examination.

Many authors have described how the technology exported by industrialised countries may be ill-adapted to the needs of developing countries. The main emphasis has been on differences in factor endowments and on the development of industry in enclaves.

However, Western enterprises can only transfer their own know-how or equipment, what they are sure about, and what they have been asked for. In other words, they usually transfer advanced technologies. Furthermore, with the international diffusion of advanced technology it is obvious that the standard international scale may be too large for the domestic market in a particular developing country. Hence the choice between operating inefficiently below capacity or attempting to channel surplus output on to export markets, which in depressed economic conditions may lead to potentially severe price competition [27].

Under these circumstances, it appears reasonable to encourage enterprises to investigate ways of optimising operations other than by simply increasing scale economies. There have already been some promising results in reducing optimum efficient size of plant by changing the technology in industries as different as petrochemicals and steel [28]. Furthermore, recent developments in electronics promise many possibilities for decentralisation and scale reduction [29]. This may make it possible, particularly for developing countries with large domestic markets, to increase the number of projects that are sequentially implemented; to reduce capital costs associated with very large projects; and to further increase employment opportunities for the same amount of capital invested by increasing the effective completion rate and capital efficiency of projects. Pressures exerted on some sectors in OECD countries may also increase more gradually and lengthen the time available for adaptation.

ii) *Transfers of technology and SMEs*

Small and medium sized enterprises have participated rather little in technology transfer. If they had the means they could play a more significant role in strengthening the local industrial fabric and consequently increasing income and absorptive capacity in developing countries. In view of the limited role of SMEs in international trade, transfers of their technology may also tend to have local effects on developing economies rather than large-scale trade effects on OECD economies. However, their small size and lack of resources and personnel means that SMEs obviously require assistance to enhance their participation. This may not necessarily only be financial; it may also effectively take the form of information and contacts with other enterprises operating abroad [30].

iii) *Return effects and innovation*

In the present economic climate the clear acceptance of trade-related implications of technology transfers may be a most effective tool for stimulating technological change.

As noted above, investment has been discouraged by uncertainty about the future and government incentives may not adequately counteract this uncertainty. It may also prove difficult to provide further incentives when real public revenues are decreasing and while inflation remains high. An alternative, or complementary, incentive could come from a clear continuation of trade liberalization with a continued and progressive reduction in trade restrictions with clear

100

arget dates. The presence of defined competitive risks may end some of the uncertainties paralysing firms at present and provide future survival as a clear incentive for innovation [31]. At both macro- and micro-economic levels, the transfer of technology is a powerful incentive for a transitional adaptation strategy.

CONCLUDING REMARKS

With the first increase in oil prices the underlying structural weaknesses and long-term structural transformations in Member countries became starkly apparent. In these circumstances the consequences for industrial countries of transferring technology to developing countries began to receive attention. It suddenly became clear that the survival of some enterprises and industrial activities had been due to exceptional cyclical conditions, but that for some it appeared that their economic foundations had been undermined.

Because the effects on industrial economies of technology transfers are diverse and cannot be analysed simply, they may not appear to require specific policy responses. However the continuing process of technology transfer and industrialization requires a comprehensive policy response: profound changes are working to modify the system of world economic relations and technology transfers are part of these changes.

In concluding this report, we do not claim to have answered all of the questions raised by the radical changes which industries in OECD countries have to face. Nor do we claim to have raised all of the questions; these vary with the economic and social characteristics of each country.

However, we have attempted to demonstrate that technology transfers have been one important factor in these changes and sometimes the determinant one, and that the fundamental causes of change require clear identification. These causes may lie in the developing countries, but they also lie in OECD countries.

Furthermore, although transfers may have helped to undermine some lagging industries, they have enabled other activities to develop, creating new markets and opportunities to participate in widening the technological base of developing countries.

This analysis clearly suggests that OECD countries are facing a situation which is very different from that of the past. They have the scientific and technological means to respond, but the new challenges go beyond technical research. Our societies are being affected in new ways by new pressures and these must be taken into account. The implications of some of these changes are as yet unclear: what must be borne in mind is that our common future has a greater chance of being satisfactorily attained in a climate of flexibility and concertation.

DEFINITIONS AND EXPLANATIONS

A. NOMENCLATURE

All trade values used in this study are in U.S. dollars and current value terms. Export values are f.o.b. imports values are c.i.f., except for those of Australia, Canada and the United States which are also f.o.b.

SITC definitions of the product classification are set out below. A description of the products contained in each of the SITC sections and divisions is contained in the OECD Statistics of Foreign Trade.

PRODUCT GROUP	SITC (REV. 1) SECTIONS OR DIVISIONS
Total primary and processed primary products	$0 + 1 + 2 + 3 + 4 + 68$
Chemicals	5
Iron and Steel	67
Textiles	65
Clothing	84
Footwear, leather goods and furs	$61 + 83 + 85$
Machinery and Transport equipment	7
Non-electric machinery	71
Electric machinery and appliances	72
Road motor vehicles	732
Other transport equipment	$73 - 732$
Other manufactures	$62 + 63 + 64 + 66 + 69 + 8$ $- (83, 84$ and $85)$
Total manufactures	$5 + 6 + 7 + 8 - 68$
Residual	9
Total trade	0 to 9

Note: From 1978 the SITC Revision 2 classification has been used and China is included with developing countries.

B. DESCRIPTION OF PERFORMANCE INDICES*

INDICES OF FOREIGN TRADE PERFORMANCE

Three types of index were used:

1 *An export specialization index:* which relates a sector's share in the total exports of a particular country to the same sector's share in total exports of a reference set of countries. The formula is:

$$Sjk = \frac{Xjk}{Xjt} : \frac{Xnk}{Xnt}$$

where: X = exports,
$\quad\quad j$ = the exporting country,
$\quad\quad n$ = the reference set of exporting countries (in this instance, the OECD countries),
$\quad\quad k$ = the product sector or category,
$\quad\quad t$ = all manufactures.

---

* *Source:* Ch. IV, Ref. [22].

2 *An index of relative dependence on imports:* which is calculated in the same way as the export specialization index. It is, in fact, an import specialization index. The formula is:

$$Ijk = \frac{Mjk}{Mjt} : \frac{Mnk}{Mnt}$$

where: M = imports.

3 *A market share index:* which measures a country's share in OECD exports or imports of a particular category of product. The formula is:

$$\frac{Xjk}{Xnk} \text{ for exports or } \frac{Mjk}{Mnk} \text{ for imports.}$$

MEASURING THE SKILLED LABOUR AND CAPITAL CONTENT OF FOREIGN TRADE PRODUCTS

Classification of the products in question according to the two criteria of capital intensity and skilled-labour intensity produced eight major product categories.

An initial estimation of these intensities was made on the basis of data compiled by B. Balassa ("A 'Stages Approach' to Comparative Advantage"—paper presented to the IEA symposium in Tokyo in 1976). Balassa uses two measures of capital intensity and skilled-labour intensity, but only the stock measure has been employed here since it seems better suited to the purposes of this study. The intensities are calculated for the sectors of activity in which the products are manufactured. The capital intensity P_k of sector k is the capital stock per person employed. For the purposes of combining skilled-labour intensity with capital intensity, a degree of skill (h_k) has been estimated to represent the notional stock of "human capital" per person employed, using the following formula:

$$h_k = \frac{w_k - w_k^u}{r^h}$$

where: k = the sector
w_k = average wage in sector k,
w_k^u = average wage of unskilled workers in sector k,
r^h = the notional return on "human capital", estimated here at 10 %.

Total intensity for the two variables is thus:

$$lk = P_k + h_k$$

The indicators used do not claim to give an exact measure of the stock of capital and skilled labour employed in the production process; they give an order of magnitude and make it possible, above all, to establish the relative position of one product category in terms of the others.

Using Balassa's calculations, the products were then classified according to the respective degree of capital or skilled-labour intensity. However, in view of the imperfect nature of the indicators chosen, corrections were made to this classification:

— either through comparison with other indicators used in studies employing a broadly similar nomenclature: data compiled by J. De Bandt ("Analyse comparative des structures industrielles", IREP, Documentation française, 1975), with capital per person employed being estimated on the basis of gross fixed assets related to the number of workers and skilled-labour intensity on the basis of the ratio:

$$\frac{\text{executive staff} + \text{supervisory staff}}{\text{total workforce}} \text{ for 1970 in the United States, relying on data}$$

from the Bureau of the Census in Washington;

— or in line with opinions of industry specialists on the relative position of certain activities.

With the help of these data, the products were grouped into major categories and a second classification established by combining the two criteria. Such an analysis, which is necessary for interpreting the results, is of course difficult to make and any decision to allocate a given group involves some element of arbitrariness. So as to reduce this element, a two-fold approach was adopted.

— Firstly, the distribution of the activities according to the criterion of capital intensity produced a number of groups that made it easier to determine thresholds and proved accurate by combined application of the criteria.

— Secondly, by taking into account the importance of each product for general economic activity it was possible to find the nucleus around which the different product groups could be built up and to drop the groups that were of little relevance because of their small size.

In all, eight groups were established each comprising products that have quite different production characteristics from those in the other groups and that play an important role in economic activity.

Graphic 1
THE SHARE OF DEVELOPING COUNTRIES IN
IMPORTS OF MANUFACTURED PRODUCTS

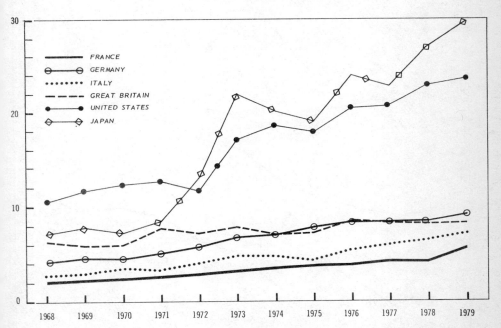

Source : Les cahiers français, supplément Nº 192, July-September 1979, modified by the Secretariat.

105

Graphic 2

THE SHARE OF DEVELOPING COUNTRIES
IN IMPORTS OF CLOTHING

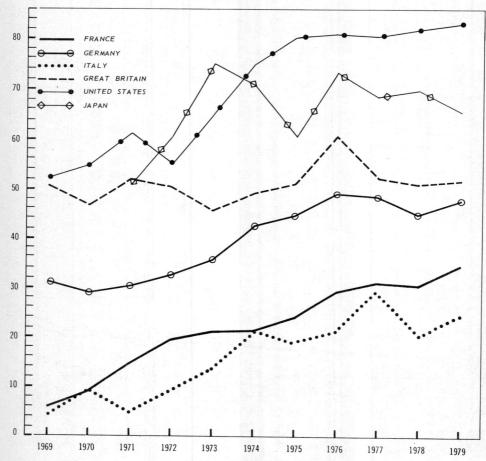

Source : Les cahiers français, supplément N° 192, July-September 1979, modified by the Secretariat.

Graphic 3
THE SHARE OF DEVELOPING COUNTRIES
IN IMPORTS OF ELECTRICAL EQUIPMENT

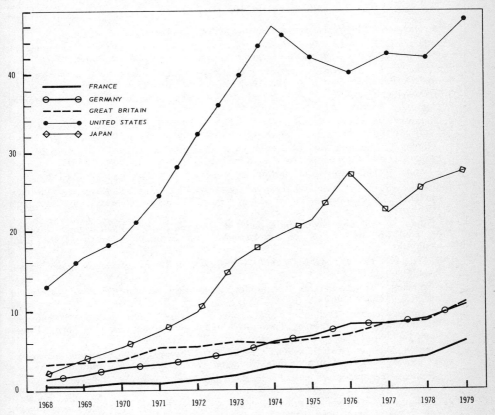

Source : Les cahiers français, supplément N° 192, July-September 1979, modified by the Secretariat.

NOTES AND REFERENCES

SUMMARY

[1] The following bibliography may be consulted for various points of view.

P. Judet and J. Perrin, "Problématique économique (of the transfer of technology)", *Transfert de technologie et développement*, Librairies Techniques, Paris, 1977.

C. Vaitsos, "La fonction des brevets dans les pays en développement", *Economie et Société*, Paris, Series T, No. 10, April 1974, pp. 389-540.

J.M. Wagret, "Vers un plan Marshall des brevets d'invention", *Revue de Marché Commun*, Brussels, April 1967.

J. Baranson, *International transfers of industrial technology by U.S. firms and their implications for the U.S. economy*, Dewit, Washington D.C., 1976.

R. Gilpin, "Technology development, technology export and American security", *Symposium on Science and the Future Navy*, Washington D.C., October 1976.

H.E. Meyer, "Those worrisome technology exports", *Fortune*, 22nd May, 1978.

National Academy of Sciences, *Technology, Trade, and the U.S. Economy*, Washington D.C., 1978, Report of a Workshop held at Woods Hole, Massachusetts, August 1976.

R. Gilpin, *Technology, economic growth and international competitiveness*, a report prepared for the use of the Sub-committee on Economic Growth of the Joint Committee, Congress of U.S., Washington D.C., July 1975.

U.S.-ITC, U.S.-DC, U.S.-DL, *Technology Transfer, A Review of the Economic Issues*, Washington D.C., 1978.

M. Boretsky, "Trends in U.S. Technology: A political economist's view", *American Scientist*, January-February, 1975.

C. Cooper, "Science, Technology and Production in the Under-developed Countries: An Introduction", in *Science, Technology and Development*, ed. C. Cooper, Frank Cass, London, 1973.

F. Stewart, *Technological Dependence in the Third World*, OECD Seminar on Science, Technology and Development in a Changing World, Paris, 1975, mimeo.

P. Streeten, "Technology Gaps between Rich and Poor Countries", *Scottish Journal of Political Economy*, November, 1972.

V.V. Bhatt, "On Technology Policy and its Institutional Frame", *World Development*, Vol. 3, No. 9, September, 1975.

UNCTAD, *Major issues arising from the transfer of technology to developing countries*, U.N., New York, 1975.

UNCTAD, *Handbook on the acquisition of technology by developing countries*, U.N., New York, 1978.

V.N. Balasubramanyam, "Transfer of technology: the UNCTAD arguments in perspective", *The World Economy*, Elsevier, Vol. I, 1977-1978.

[2] UNCTAD, *Towards the technological transformation of the developing countries*, TD/238, Manila, May, 1979.

[3] Supplement to *Les Cahiers français*, No. 192 on the French textiles and clothing industry, July-September, 1979.

[4] Kawagushi, "Roles and functions played by the Japanese firms in the manufactured exports of developing countries", *Staff Paper, World Bank*, November, 1978, mimeo.

TECHNOLOGY TRANSFER TO DEVELOPING COUNTRIES

[1] J.H. Dunning, "Towards a taxonomy of technology transfer and possible impacts on OECD countries", analytical study for this report.

[2] US-ITD, US-DC, US-DL, *Technology transfer, A review of the economic issues,* Washington D.C., 1978.

[3] W.A. Fischer, "Empirical approaches to understanding technology transfer", *R&D Management,* No. 6, 1976.

[4] UN/ECE, Proceedings of the UN/ECE Seminar on *The Management of the Transfer of Technology within Industrial Co-operation,* Geneva, February, 1976.

[5] F.R. Root, "The role of international business in the diffusion of technological innovation", *Economic and Business Bulletin,* Summer, 1968.

[6] LES-France, "L'assistance technique dans le transfert international des techniques et de la maîtrise industrielle", Record of Forum, 1st June, 1978, mimeo.

[7] OECD/Interfutures, "The Problems of Technology Transfer between Advanced and Developing Societies", *Midway Through Interfutures,* Chapter XII, Paris, February 1978, mimeo.

[8] H. Brooks, "National Science Policy and Technology Transfer", *Conference on Technology Transfer and Innovation,* NSF, 1966, mimeo.

[9] "Enterprise" is broadly defined—parties to technology transfer have tended to diversify. This is clearly reflected in the definition given in the Draft International Code of Conduct on the Transfer of Technology. UN TD/CODE TOT/25 of 6 May, 1980.

[10] The juridical notion that there are two separate groups facing each other often masks a more complex reality. As we shall see later transfers are often between related enterprises (parent-subsidiary, or between affiliates).

[11] The International Code of Conduct on the Transfer of Technology uses a similar classification in Chapter I "Definitions and Scope of Application", Art. 1.3; see TD/CODE TOT/25.

[12] This may not apply to some engineering firms. However, their know-how is not a "good" for sale. It is a service made temporarily available to an entrepreneur for the carrying out of a project. Completion of the project does not necessarily mean that the know-how has been transferred.

[13] Lowell W. Steele, Proceedings of the UN/ECE Seminar on *The Management of the Transfer of Technology within Industrial Co-operation,* held at Geneva, 14-17 July, 1975.

[14] The terminology used here is not exactly the same as that used for transfer of technology transactions which cover such activities as the sale of rights to use a patent and the granting of a licence. This is intentional, in order not to complicate the argument.

[15] This is a much-argued point. One school has deduced from the "poor working of the market for technology", that the system of private appropriation of technology leads to a social sub-optimum (within the meaning of Pareto's law). Technology is classed as "information" and it should be a free good, since only free information allows the efficient working of a market economy and the achievement of optimum welfare. See for example C. Cooper and K. Hoffman, OECD/Interfutures, "The Problems of Technology Transfer between Advanced and Developing Societies", *op. cit.,* Part II.

[16] From a legal point of view licensing agreements do not lead to a break in technological monopoly, but rather in the possibilities to exploit that monopoly. Once a process is disclosed, it also allows the sharing of knowledge and a possible reduction of technological monopoly by those prepared to make an independent R&D effort.

[17] See the sector study on Petrochemicals. Variations in the selling price of the raw material may ensure a return on petrochemical projects in oil and gas-producing regions.

[18] See national policies introduced by the LDC's that are directly concerned with the transfer of technology, in the analytical study of E.M. Graham for this report. See also: John Dunning, "The Determinants of International Production", paper presented to a conference on "The Growth of Multinational Enterprises", Rennes, France, 1972, and "Controls on international direct investments", 1978, mimeo.

[19] Kawagushi, "Roles and functions played by the Japanese firms in the manufactured exports of developing countries", *Staff Paper, World Bank,* November, 1978, mimeo.

[20] By grant-back provisions, for example.

[21] V.V. Bhatt, "On technology policy and its institutional frame", *World Development,* Vol. 3, No. 9, September, 1975.

[22] Th. Gaudin, *A l'écoute du Silence,* Coll. 10/18, Paris, 1978, points out that in 1939 only a few weeks were needed to convert Renault factories for the production of tanks and that this would not be possible today.

[23] When technological infrastructure is not highly developed the success of transfer may be ensured only by internal transfers within the firm creating the technology.

[24] S. Seurat, *Réalités du transfert de technologie,* Masson, Paris, 1976.

[25] A. Weil, *Les transferts de technologie aux pays en voie de développement par les petites et moyennes industries,* Ministry of Industry, Paris, March, 1980.

[26] The capacity to master the technology varies with the technology in question and with the enterprises concerned. As a general rule, however, on the expiry of the period of protection of the technology, a firm which has the necessary technical resources is usually in a position to dispense with the services of its technological "mentor".

[27] The Michelin Company, has built its strategy on technical superiority and preserves its lead by preventing the disclosure of any information: even the machinery used for the manufacture of tyres is made by Michelin.

[28] The author of the pharmaceutical industry sector study has also pointed out that in many developing countries the necessary infrastructure is not sufficiently developed to receive pharmaceutical research laboratories. However, for some tropical illnesses, the trends appear more promising.

[29] UNIDO, *World Industry since 1960: Progress and Prospects,* Special issue of the Industrial Development Survey for the 3rd General Conference of UNIDO, New York, 1979. See also UN/ECE: *Structure and Change in European Industry,* New York, 1977.

[30] Such figures can be misleading. In India, IP as a proportion of GNP is not an accurate indicator of the development of industry. Given its rank as the world's ninth industrial power and strength in some certain scientific fields (such as nuclear R&D), India is obviously in the first group.

[31] UNIDO, *World Industry since 1960, op. cit.* and analytical studies.

Chapter II

FLOWS OF TECHNOLOGY

[1] Aid flows are dealt with for example in OECD, *Development Co-operation, 1980 Review,* Paris, 1980.

[2] Data available from the B.I.S., OECD sources and national sources vary because of the complexity of inter-bank flows and for reasons of definitional and geographical coverage.

[3] In the U.K. capital goods industries, 360,000, or 13% of employees, were engaged in producing exports for developing countries in 1977; this was about 5% of total manufacturing employment. In industries producing mainly industrial machinery and equipment, 190,000, or about 16% of employees, were producing goods for developing countries (Secretariat estimates).

[4] For example, Brazil has consistently covered 30-50% of total payments for technical assistance, royalties, etc., with technological receipts from other developing countries. This is in part due to TNE's using Brazil as a regional entry point.

[5] See S. Lall, "Developing Countries as Exporters of Industrial Technology", *Research Policy,* 1980, pp. 24-52.

[6] *Engineering News-Record,* November 29th, December 6th, December 13th, 1979. Values were: S. Korea 21% of new contract values awarded in the Mid-East, May 1978 to June 1979, Brazil 6%, Yugoslavia 4%, India 2% and Taiwan 2%; the USSR (2%) and Eastern Europe gained 6% of new totals between them. Saudi Arabia was the biggest source of contracts ($ 39 billion June 1975-June 1979), followed by Iran ($ 28 billion), Irak, Gulf States and Libya. 1979 data: *Engineering News-Record,* July 17th, July 31st 1980.

[7]   For example, in 1978 S. Korea received $ 2.1 bn in payments for construction services world-wide and exported $ 1.0 bn of machinery, equipment and construction materials, including $ 0.2 bn of these products and $ 0.3 bn of ships to the Middle East.

[8]   Of potential OECD competitors both India and Egypt have high proportions of steel, aluminium, electricity and electrical equipment coming from Soviet-supplied plants.

[9]   However, the 1977-1986 Mexican (Pemex) energy and petrochemicals expansion plans alone called for imports of about ¾ of the projected $ 7 billion (1977 values) expenditure on machinery and equipment. *Commercio Exterior de Mexico*, Vol. 25, No. 9, September 1979.

[10] Capital goods exports to Hong Kong are overstated as re-exports take 20% of total capital goods imports. Singapore acts both as a re-exporter (20% of imports) plus a regional assembler of capital equipment (drilling rigs, transport, etc.). However, values still remain high for domestically absorbed capital goods.

[11] The formal and informal "Overseas Chinese" networks add to the flows to and from Singapore and Hong Kong.

[12] Payments cover different combinations of patents, licences, know-how, technical and management services and designs for different countries and data may also include copyrights, leasing fees and a vague "etc.". Payments may also be royalties on production—such payments continue for extended periods *after* transfer.

[13] Affiliated and unaffiliated combined, excluding management fees. Unaffiliated payments from developing countries rose to 14% of the total in manufacturing in 1978.

[14] Technological and mineral royalties only.

[15] It is assumed here that there is a uniform pricing structure between countries and enterprises for the same technology. However, Latin American countries have reduced their fee and royalty payments relative to other international payments, suggesting that the "price" for technology can be negotiated downwards. The use of payments for technology as a vehicle for transfer payments within the firm has probably been reduced. Technological expertise and reasonably strong and consistent bargaining positions are necessary to limit payments. On the other hand, the "price" for technology will have to reflect inadequacies in the technical infrastructure that have to be overcome by the supplier in order to ensure subsequent operation of the transferred technology.

[16] Unaffiliated values were 13.5% of the total in 1970, 14.5% in 1978. World-wide the trend has been the reverse with unaffiliated payments/total payments declining from 24.6% to 18.1% between 1970 and 1978. The decline also applied to Canada, Japan and Western Europe. Unfortunately there are few details of unaffiliated payments by industry and country. Data from *Survey of Current Business*, various issues.

[17] Values from unrelated concerns in developing countries increased from around 55-60% of total receipts in the early 1970s to 65% in 1978. This is largely due to increased unrelated receipts from oil exporting countries that are not Commonwealth members. Receipts of royalties from Commonwealth countries, Southern European and Latin American countries came increasingly from related concerns. World-wide the trend was also towards related concerns, unrelated concerns paying 61% of total receipts in 1970, 56% in 1978. All data cover summaries of returns received *not* estimates of total. Data from *Business Monitor MA4*, various issues.

[18] The countries are: Argentina, Brazil, Mexico, India, Hong Kong, Korea, Singapore, Taiwan. Data are based on Secretariat estimates of receipts by OECD countries and in part reflect the impact of technology transfer regulations. If broader definitions of payments by developing countries are used (IMF or central banks) then payments by Brazil and Taiwan of royalties and fees have also increased relative to imports of machinery and equipment; other countries have declined.

[19] Declines or slow growth in U.S. receipts (in current dollar terms) of fees and royalties from manufacturing industry in Latin America were noticeable in the period 1970-1978 in Argentina (decline until 1978), Brazil (decline), Colombia (decline), and Mexico (decline since 1975). For Asia, the growth in U.S. receipts of fees and royalties from affiliates was lower than the growth of repatriated earnings but the divergence was not as great. See also UNCTAD, "Legislation and Regulations on Technology Transfer: Empirical Analysis of Their Effects in Selected Countries", TD/B/C.6/55, 28 August 1980.

[20] *Trade and Industry,* 23rd November, 1979: value of work outstanding and new contracts obtained declined (in current £ terms) in 1978-1979 for British companies and subsidiaries; *Engineering News-Record,* November 29th, 1979: total new contracts declined (current $ terms) in the Mid-East in 1978-1979; *Monthly Report of the Deutsche Bundesbank,* Vol. 31, No. 12, December 1979: German foreign receipts for construction and assembly declined by one-quarter in August-October 1979 compared with the previous period.

[21] The data concern all phases of international contracting, including infrastructure and civil engineering. However, about one-half covers manufacturing, process, and power plants. German firms are leaders in turn-key plant construction, usually building plants based on their own processes. However, many large projects are handled by international consortia. For example, the contract for the Dumai (Sumatra) oil refinery was won by a Spanish-Taiwanese consortium incorporated in Hong Kong: design will come from a U.S. firm, Spanish firms will supply engineering, Taiwanese will supply management and organise the sub-contracting, and a large part of the construction will be done by an Austrian firm. Finance includes Spanish and Austrian export credits and a Eurocurrency syndicated loan led by a U.S. bank. *Far Eastern Economic Review,* 15th February, 1980.

[22] Some of the price advantages of labour from rapidly developing countries have been undermined as construction wages have risen faster than productivity improvements.

[23] For 1978 values were: Japan, $ 1.6 billion (commitments only, excluding reinvested earnings, year to end March 1979), Germany, $ 0.66 billion, U.K. $ 0.6 billion, U.S. $ 2.2 billion (1979: $ 2.3 billion).

[24] During the 1970's there was a general trend by most OECD countries towards increased investment in manufacturing in developing countries. This was largely due to increased investment in the small group of rapidly growing industrialising countries.

[25] For U.S. investment in *manufacturing,* in developing countries 1970-1979: Inflows: additions to direct investment positions $ 10.7 billion, of which equity and inter-company account $ 3.8 billion, reinvested earnings $ 7.4 billion. Outflows to the U.S.: interest dividends, earnings $ 4.9 billion, fees and royalties $ 1.8 billion. U.K. not available for manufacturing only, but patterns similar for all industry combined.

[26] Internal self-sufficiency does not apply to equipment manufacture. Although 50-100% of basic towers, process receptacles and heat exchangers will be sourced domestically for the refining and petrochemical expansions of 1977-1986, almost all pumps, compressors, instruments and valves will be imported. Overall, imports will take more than $\frac{3}{4}$ of the value of refining and petrochemical equipment. *Commercio Exterior de Mexico, op. cit.*

[27] For countries that reported consistently during the period 1970-1978, the decrease was about 2% per year. See *Development Co-operation, op. cit.*

[28] Jan Annerstedt, Worldwatch Paper 31, Washington D.C., 1979.

[29] Based on Robert C. Ronstadt, "International R&D: The Establishment and Evolution of Research and Development Abroad by Seven U.S. Multinationals", *Journal of International Business Studies,* Spring 1978.

[30] Based on William A. Fischer and Jack N. Behrman "The Coordination of Foreign R&D Activities by Transnational Corporations", *Journal of International Business Studies,* Winter 1979.

[31] See Edwin Mansfield, David Teece, and Anthony Romeo, "Overseas Research and Development by U.S.-Based Firms", *Economica,* 1979, *46,* pp. 187-196.

[32] U.S. Senate, Committee on Finance, *Implications of Multinational Firms for World Trade and Investment and for U.S. Trade and Labor,* Washington D.C., 1973, pp. 581-593.

[33] J.N. Behrman and W.A. Fischer, "Corporate and Government Policies and Practices on Science and Technology for Development", Fund for Multinational Management Education, July 1979, mimeo. In another study the same authors listed Hong Kong, Spain, Argentina, Colombia, Ecuador, Egypt, the Philippines and Taiwan as the location of foreign research and development activities of U.S. enterprises, and Argentina, Spain, Greece, Hong Kong and Singapore as the location for European enterprises. Only in Spain was there new product research. See "Overseas R&D Activities of Transnational Companies", mimeo, June 1979. See also OECD Sector Studies on the "Impact of Multinational Enterprises on National Scientific and Technological Capacities" forthcoming.

[34] U.N. Commission on Transnational Corporations, "Progress Towards the Establishment of the New International Economic Order: The Role of Transnational Corporations", New York, 1980.

[35] OECD, *Financial Statistics Monthly.*

[36] Range of choice may not result in freedom of action once the choice has been made. However, increased competition tends to lead to more limited overall control; control is "bargained away" during the competitive lead-up to final contract agreement.

Chapter III

EFFECTS OF TECHNOLOGY TRANSFER

[1] For example, exchange rates may be influential.

[2] See Centre d'études prospectives et d'information internationales (CEPII), *La concurrence industrielle à l'échelle mondiale,* La documentation française, Paris, 1979.

[3] Calculated by J. Lemperière, from OECD, *Trade by Commodities; Les Cahiers français,* Suppl. No. 192, July-September 1979.

[4] It is difficult to determine to what extent enterprises from OECD countries generally have adopted this strategy. However, it appears to be a part of the strategy of many Japanese enterprises, less common for the U.S. Observers such as Gilpin and Baranson (see references in Summary) have suggested that technology transfer exports the comparative advantages of the U.S.

[5] G.D. Helleiner, "Transnational Corporations and Trade Structure", University of Toronto, 1979. Calculations based on U.S. Department of Commerce data.

[6] See John H. Dunning, *The Consequences of International Transfer of Technology by TNC's: Some Home country Implications,* Discussion papers in International Investment and Business Studies, No. 45, November 1979, mimeo.

[7] Examples are in Ch. Stoffaes, *La grande menace industrielle,* 2nd edition, Coll. "Pluriel", Paris, 1979.

[8] Movements in exchange rates and increased intra-EEC trade may partly explain the changes in Europe's trading patterns.

[9] This has led to the establishment of import quotas for colour TV receivers from South Korea and Taiwan (*Financial Times* reports).

[10] Only approximate estimates can be obtained in this way. Export performance depends on such factors as growth of demand, exchange rates, import barriers.

[11] B. Balassa, *The Changing International Division of Labour in Manufactured Goods,* World Bank, May, 1979, mimeo.

[12] It is not strictly correct to calculate gains or losses of jobs by applying co-efficients to trade figures for one year. Such calculations can only indicate that certain trade flows represent a certain volume of jobs and that they may lead to actual gains or losses. The results are only potential changes.

[13] Commissariat au Plan, *Rapport du Groupe d'étude sur l'évolution des économies du Tiers-Monde et l'appareil productif français* ("Rapport Berthelot"), Tardy, January, 1978.

[14] U.K. Government Economic Service, *The Newly Industrialising Countries and the Adjustment Problem,* Working Paper No. 18, January, 1979.

[15] A. Edwards, *The New Industrial Countries and their Impact on Western Manufacturing,* E.I.U. Special Report No. 73, December 1979.

[16] Brazil, Mexico, Hong Kong, Singapore, Taiwan, South Korea *and* the Mediterranean Member countries of OECD: Spain, Portugal, Yugoslavia. The last three countries make no significant difference to the figures for the U.S. and Canada.

[17] See the summary by UNIDO of studies of the United States, the United Kingdom, France, Germany, and the Netherlands: UNIDO, "The Impact of trade with developing countries on employment in developed countries. Empirical evidence from recent research", UNIDO Working Papers on Structural Change, No. 3, October, 1978. See also OECD, *The Impact of the Newly Industrialising Countries on Production and Trade in Manufactures,* Paris, 1979, Annex II.

Chapter IV
LONGER-TERM OUTLOOK

[1] See OECD/Interfutures, *Facing the Future : Mastering the probable and managing the unpredictable,* Paris, 1979, Part V, p. 293 *et seq.*

[2] We have taken 1968 as the base year to allow for time lags between transfers and "feedback effects". For more details see Secretariat analytical study.

[3] The "product cycle" cannot, strictly speaking, be applied to capital goods. See N. Rosenberg, *Perspectives on Technology,* Cambridge University Press, 1976; and William B. Walker, *Industrial Innovation and International Trading Performance,* JAI Press Inc., Greenwich, Connecticut, 1979.

[4] Presumably there is a decreasing growth rate in production capacity in the source country. Restructuring can also lead to the closing of older production facilities and supply from new facilities in a growth market. See J.L. Malaussena de Perno, "Spécialisation internationale et développement économique", Economica, Paris, 1975. However, even though the effects in general have been less in industries dominated by TNE's, this does not imply that TNE's do not transfer activities from one host country to another when they judge this necessary.

[5] Assuming the established framework for protection of industrial property over a limited period. See Petrochemical Sector Study for details of the Natta catalytic polymerisation licences, and TV Sector Study for details of the PAL TV licences.

[6] In the petrochemical industry, Brazilian and Mexican firms are working up the scale of complexity of transfer of know-how. See also: Jack Baranson, *North-South Transfer of Technology: What realistic alternatives are available to the U.S.?* Dewit, Washington, December, 1977.

[7] Through training of staff, sub-contracting arrangements and by the efficiency standards that are introduced. See N. Rosenberg, historical analytical study and *Perspectives on Technology, op. cit.* pp. 156-157.

[8] P. Mayer, "Où sont les changements majeurs de l'évolution en cours ?", Colloque LES, Paris, 9-10th October, 1979.

[9] Poor past performances have been largely due to inadequate preparation.

[10] N. Rosenberg, *Perspectives on Technology, op. cit.*

[11] This includes nuclear technology and the recent contract with Iraq.

[12] *L'Expansion* No. 23, November 1979 and S. Lall, "Developing countries as exporters of industrial technology", *Research Policy,* No. 9, 1980. See also Ariyoshi Okumura, "Newly Industrialising countries in Asia and Japan's Response", *International Conference on New and Old Industrial Countries in the 1980s,* Sussex European Research Centre, 6-8th January, 1980.

[13] However access to technologically exposed sectors may be restricted by other barriers; see discussion in petrochemical sector study.

[14] G. Lafay, "La mutation de la demande mondiale", *Spécialisation et adaptation face à la crise.* Economie prospective internationale, Paris, No. 1, January 1980.

[15] World Bank, *Annual Report 1980,* Washington D.C., 1980.

[16] This has not deterred Brazil, South Korea and some other countries from devaluing recently—but these devaluations are partly due to high domestic inflation rates.

[17] During the pre-World War I period developing economies such as that of Australia had very high debt service ratios—up to 40% of exports—with strains on balance of payments, but the economy was essentially sound and usefully absorbed foreign capital. The use to which foreign capital is put is of essential importance. See Helen Hughes, "Debt and Development: The Role of Foreign Capital in Economic Growth", *World Development,* 1979, Vol. 7, pp. 95-112.

[18] From IEA forecasts, October, 1979. The forecasts do not include China which will probably become a significant exporter during the period, and if included in the non-OPEC group would bring them closer to overall balance.

[19] Reliable statistics for capital account items and current account items other than foreign trade do not exist for Hong Kong.

[20] In the petrochemical industry, low labour costs do not always guarantee profitability of operations for transferred production capacity.

[21] At least up to the beginning of the 90's, the fall in the German birth rate is likely to reduce considerably the dynamism of the German economy.

[22] Commission of the European Communities, *European Economy,* Special Issue, October, 1979.

[23] See OECD/Interfutures, *Facing the Future, op. cit.* page 289 et. seq.

[24] See OECD/Interfutures, "Industrial Electronics: Structural Trends and World Prospects", October, 1979, mimeo.

Chapter V

GENERAL POLICY ISSUES

[1] See OECD, *The Case for Positive Adjustment Policies,* Paris, May 1979, and related work.

[2] See Council Communiqué, 6th June, 1980.

[3] Of the sort that are affecting steel, shipbuilding and new automobiles.

[4] Some observers equate transfers with direct benefits to economic growth rates in recipient developing countries. See John H. Dunning, *op. cit.* Ch. III [6].

[5] See OECD, *Technical Change and Economic Policy,* Paris, 1980.

[6] The price obtained might bear no relationship to renewal costs—taking into account technological trends—but this is a different problem.

[7] As is emphasised in the report by the Economic Council of Canada: "For a common future", 1978, p. 44.

[8] Many enterprises are vulnerable to all competition in technologically stagnant sectors.

[9] P. Krugman, "A Model of Innovation, Technology Transfer, and the World Distribution of Income", *Journal of Political Economy,* 1979, Vol. 87, pp. 253-266. What is important is to *maintain* living standards in the North and not the differences between North and South. These differences would be better reduced.

[10] The model is highly simplified and based on restrictive hypotheses. However, it provides a clear illustration that changes in competition resulting from transfers make it necessary to maintain innovation in products or find new production methods. Competition between the U.S. and Japan in consumer electronics led U.S. firms to transfer production to low wage countries. The Japanese approach to this new situation was automation of production of TV receivers.

[11] A. Danzin, *Dynamisme comparé de nos principaux concurrents dans le domaine des transferts de technologie.* Colloque LES, 9-10th October, 1979.

[12] Laboratory discoveries do not necessarily lead to technological renewal.

[13] OECD, *Trends in Industrial R&D in Selected OECD Member Countries, 1967-1975,* Paris, 1979.

[14] This applies to a large number of Member countries some of the conditions specifically discussed for EEC countries (see Chapter IV).

[15] See K. Pavitt, "Technical Innovation and Industrial Development: 1. The New Causality; 2. The danger of Divergence", *Futures,* December 1979, February 1980.

[16] J. Mistral, "Compétitivité et formation du capital en longue période", *Economie et statistique,* February 1978.

[17] J. Utterback, *The Dynamics of Product and Process Innovation in Industry,* Centre for Policy Alternatives, MIT, December 1978. Industrial jobs are created during the launching phases for new product lines when product change and adaptation are high. During such periods, new firms are set up to exploit new markets or to supply raw materials, intermediates, or equipment. These dynamic periods are followed by periods of rationalisation and process innovation. During the later periods there are improvements in labour productivity, and a levelling off in recruitment by any individual enterprise that has followed the cycle through. Developments in electronics have typically followed this pattern. See also J.L. Floriot, "L'Innovation: une stratégie parmi d'autres", *Revue de l'Entreprise,* June 1977.

[18] See OECD work on The place of small and medium firms in the OECD countries and trends in their development, publication forthcoming.

[19] See *Technology, Trade, and the U.S. Economy, op. cit.,* and *New Technology-based Firms in the United Kingdom and the Federal Republic of Germany,* Arthur D. Little Ltd, 1977.

[20] See OECD work on the consequences of micro-electronics for productivity and employment. See also *Technical Change and Economic Policy, op. cit.*

[21] This is based on the idea that it is always easier to create jobs in services than in industry. There is also pressure on public authorities in the present conjunctural situation to multiply their service activities that may absorb the unemployed. See also E.F. Denison, "Explanations of Declining Productivity Growth", *Survey of Current Business,* August, 1979.

[22] Some hypotheses place emphasis on cyclical causes, and others on structural causes. See, for example, OECD, *Technical Change and Economic Policy, op. cit.,* OECD work on Productivity trends in the OECD area, and E.F. Denison, *op. cit.*

[23] IRI, *The Role of technology in the change of industrial structure,* Japan, August 1978. This is not necessarily representative of all Japanese studies. See in particular Kazuo Nukazawa, *Japan's emerging service economy and the international economic implications,* Rockefeller Foundation, January 1979.

[24] C.T. Hill, *Technological Innovation. Agent of Growth and Change,* Centre for Policy Alternatives, MIT, December, 1978.

[25] OECD, *Economic Outlook,* No. 26, 1979.

[26] E. Mansfield, *Innovation in the United States, Its State of Health,* The Fourth Franklin Conference, Innovation and the American Economy, Philadelphia, Pennsylvania, Autumn 1979.

[27] For example, total steel production capacity in developing countries is less than total consumption, but exports have been more than marginal. Furthermore, in 1960 a standard integrated steel plant produced 1 million tons p.a. while today it often exceeds 5 million tons p.a. It is possible that capacity in the 1990s will be 10 million tons p.a. Small scale steel works have also been developed with a capacity of 100-600,000 tons p.a. using electric arc furnaces with or without pre-reduction.

[28] OECD, *Steel in the 80s.* Symposium organised by the OECD, Paris, February, 1980.

[29] See OECD/Interfutures, "Industrial Electronics", *op. cit.*

[30] See A. Weil, *op. cit.,* Ch. I, ref. [25].

[31] B. Klein, *The Slowdown in Productivity Advances: A Dynamic Explanation,* Centre for Policy Alternatives, MIT, January 1979.

OECD SALES AGENTS
DÉPOSITAIRES DES PUBLICATIONS DE L'OCDE

OECD PUBLICATIONS, 2, rue André-Pascal, 75775 PARIS CEDEX 16 - No. 41795 1981
PRINTED IN FRANCE
(1200 QH 92 81 02 1) ISBN 92-64-12159-5